Cases in Congressic

During the 2008 elections, nowhere was change more anticipated than in the House and Senate. Going into Election Day, most analysts predicted a large majority of Democratic wins in both chambers. However, while many Republicans lost and Democrats came away with a clear majority, some of the most vulnerable managed to hang on and win reelection. *Cases in Congressional Campaigns* illustrates how embattled incumbents defended their turf in such a difficult year for Republican candidates, the Republican Party, and the Republican brand. It focuses on how selected congressional incumbents "played defense"—successfully or not—in an election cycle that was dominated by the theme and message of change.

Each chapter is written by political scientists on the ground and familiar with the district they are analyzing. Analysis of broader trends from the 2008 cycle bookend the volume with Adkins and Dulio's insightful framing. More than just a collection of case studies, this book offers a common framework for understanding who won, who lost, and why. In addition, the companion website at **www.routledge.com/textbooks/9780415873888** provides instructors with useful teaching tools, including sample assignments, dynamic PowerPoint slides, graphs, and links to relevant YouTube clips.

Randall E. Adkins is Associate Professor and Chair of the Graduate Program in the Department of Political Science at the University of Nebraska, Omaha.

David A. Dulio is Associate Professor of Political Science at Oakland University in Rochester, MI.

Cases in Congressional Campaigns

Incumbents Playing Defense

Edited by

Randall E. Adkins
David A. Dulio

Routledge
Taylor & Francis Group

NEW YORK AND LONDON

First published 2010
by Routledge
270 Madison Avenue, New York, NY 10016

Simultaneously published in the UK
by Routledge
2 Park Square, Milton Park, Abingdon, Oxon OX14 4RN

Routledge is an imprint of the Taylor & Francis Group, an informa business

Typeset in Goudy by EvS Communication Networx, Inc.
Printed and bound in the United States of America on acid-free paper by Edwards Brothers, Inc.

Chapters 3, 4, 10, and 12 originally appeared in *The American Review of Politics*, Volume 30, Summer 2009, in a slightly different form and are used here by permission.

Library of Congress Cataloging in Publication Data
Cases in Congressional campaigns : incumbents playing defense / [edited by] Randall E. Adkins, David A. Dulio.
p. cm.
1. United States. Congress—Elections, 2008. 2. Elections—United States—History—21st century. 3. Political campaigns—United States—History—21st century. 4. United States—Politics and government—2001–2009. I. Adkins, Randall E. II. Dulio, David A.
JK19682008 .C37 2010
324.973'0931—dc22
2009027648

ISBN 10: 0-415-87387-8 (hbk)
ISBN 10: 0-415-87388-6 (pbk)
ISBN 10: 0-203-86416-6 (ebk)

ISBN 13: 978-0-415-87387-1 (hbk)
ISBN 13: 978-0-415-87388-8 (pbk)
ISBN 13: 978-0-203-86416-6 (ebk)

For Ross, Ryan, Abby, and Sophia

Contents

List of Tables

List of Figures

Acknowledgments

This book has been a truly collaborative effort from the start. It would not have been possible, however, if not for the encouragement, assistance, and support of countless individuals. First, we wish to thank the American Political Science Association's Congressional Fellowship Program (CFP), and especially the director, Jeff Biggs. The program boasts a long list of alumni who are among the best scholars in the country. In 2001, we were both fortunate to be selected to be a part of the CFP. As fellows we worked on staff for members of Congress, which allowed us to develop a much more sophisticated understanding of the institution. During our time on Capitol Hill, we also found common ground in our research interests and threatened to work together in the future. Our respect for the CFP was such that when thinking of individuals to write the chapters for this book, our first thought in many instances was of other CFP alumni.

Second, we would be remiss if we did not thank the contributors to this volume. Each one worked hard and showed a great deal of dedication to this project. They also endured our editorial queries and comments that asked them to think about and revise their chapters in addition to what they had already done. Scholars do not have to take on projects like this one, so we are very grateful they took time from their individual research agendas to help us.

We also deeply appreciate the dedication of the staff at Routledge Press. Specifically, we would like to thank Michael Kerns, the Acquisitions Editor, for his encouragement and assistance in every stage of the publication process. Michael not only supported our work, but he pushed us to make it better. His guidance improved the finished product tremendously. Editorial assistant Mary Altman and production editor Alf Symons proved to be very devoted professionals. We also wish to thank those who anonymously reviewed the book. Their comments proved very constructive and encouraged us to make a number of revisions that improved the book considerably.

Third, we wish to thank Andrew Dowdle at the University of Arkansas. Andy helped hatch the idea for this volume in the first place by suggesting that we co-edit a special edition of the journal he edits focusing on competitive congressional races in 2008. Earlier drafts of four of the chapters from this book may be found in the *American Review of Politics*, along with two other articles not included here.

At the University of Nebraska at Omaha, Adkins would foremost like to express his appreciation to the students in his campaigns and elections class who followed each of the congressional races in this volume with great passion and in great detail. David Boocker, Dean of the College of Arts and Sciences, and Loree Bykerk, Chair of the Department of Political Science, were supportive by providing release time to work on the project during the spring of 2009. Thanks are also due to Gregory Petrow for his enthusiastic and thoughtful feedback at all stages of the process.

At Oakland University, Dulio would like to thank his elections and voting behavior and political campaigns students; they have made him a better teacher and scholar through their questions and insights, and by challenging him to think about various questions related to American campaigns, many of which are at the center of this book. Dulio would also like to thank Provost Virinder Moudgil, Dean of the College of Arts and Sciences Ron Sudol, and Chair of the Political Science Department Paul Kubicek for their support of faculty research and for providing an environment in which scholars can thrive.

Our families deserve special thanks. Our homes are built through the love and commitment our families provide, and our wives and children are the rare and beautiful treasures that fill the rooms.

Finally, we hope that you, the reader, will get as much pleasure from reading this book as much as we did putting it together.

1   Playing Defense in a Year of Change

Randall E. Adkins and David A. Dulio

The 2008 election cycle will be remembered for decades because of its historic nature. After the votes were tallied, Barack Obama garnered more votes than any candidate for president in history en route to becoming the first African-American president of the United States. The story of 2008, however, is very much like an onion. It is comprised of many layers and as they are peeled back other important dynamics are revealed. For instance, Obama's victory and the larger margins for congressional Democrats in both chambers of Congress returned the Democratic Party to unified control of government. Moreover, a myriad of factors profoundly affected the election outcomes: the outgoing president had almost unprecedented low approval ratings; an economic crisis emerged after Labor Day that dominated the issue environment; both the number of registered voters and voter turnout were up dramatically, as well as many others. These, along with other dynamics, shaped the outcome of the 2008 election cycle. While the presidential race typically takes center stage in years like 2008, there were also 435 races for seats in the U.S. House of Representatives and 35 races for seats in the U.S. Senate (including two special elections to replace senators who resigned or died in office). The results of these contests were critical for the nation and for President Obama because the winners of the congressional races formed the Congress that would have to deliver the legislation to bring the change on which Obama campaigned and for which many Americans clamored.

The aftermath of the 2008 congressional elections found Democrats boasting about their new, larger majorities. Speaker of the House Nancy Pelosi (D-CA) and Majority Leader Senator Harry Reid (D-NV) were obviously pleased that they had more allies in the 111th Congress than they did in the 110th. After the votes were counted on Election Night, Nancy Pelosi said of the results, "…our increased numbers in the House better enable us to work closely with our new president for a vision for America and plan to succeed, again, as we unify the American people."[1] After a number of efforts to recount votes in very close races and hold new elections to replace those appointed to positions in the administration (or as senators replacing those appointed to positions in the administration), the partisan split in the new House of Representatives was 257 to 178. Similarly, the split was 58 to 41 in the Senate with an extended legal battle over the recount in the Minnesota race (to which we have devoted a chapter in this book) still to be decided. In other words, the sizable majorities of the Democrats in the House and Senate put them in a position to drive the issue agenda of President Obama.

Some analysts have described the 2008 election results as a "realignment,"[2] a "tectonic shift,"[3] and a "revolution."[4] The beginning of the 111th Congress in 2009 marked the first time since the two-year period between 1993 and 1994 that the Democratic Party controlled the Oval Office and both houses of Congress. Previously, control of Washington had not been unified in the hands of Democrats since a four-year stint from 1977 to 1981. Going into Election Day, however, most analysts predicted even larger majorities in both chambers than the election results produced. On Election Day, congressional Democrats fell short of their goal of a filibuster-proof Senate[5] and in the House the Democrats did not pick up the 35 additional seats some analysts thought they would.[6] In spite of the great strength at the top of the national ticket, the Democratic majorities were no larger than they were in other election cycles where the presidency changed

Table 1.1 Electoral Outcomes in Elections where the Presidency Changed Parties, 1912–2008

Year	Winner's Popular Vote Percent	Democratic Electoral College Vote	Republican Electoral College Vote	House Margin	Senate Margin
				Democrats-Republicans	
2008	52.6	365	173	257–178	58–41
2000	47.9	266	271	212–221	50–50
1992	43.0[1]	370	168	258–176	57–43
1988	53.4	111	426	259–174	55–45
1980	50.7	49	489	243–192	47–53
1976	50.1	297	240	292–143	62–38
1968	43.4	191	301	243–192	58–42
1964	61.1	486	52	295–140	68–32
1960	49.7	303	219	263–174	64–36
1952	55.1	89	442	213–221	47–48
1948	49.6	303	189	263–171	54–42
1932	57.4	472	59	313–117	59–36
1928	58.2	87	444	167–267	39–56
1924	54.0	136	382	183–247	40–54
1920	60.3	127	404	132–300	37–59
1912	41.8	435	88[2]	290–127	51–44

Note: Shaded areas represent Republican control of government.
[1] Bill Clinton won 53 percent of the two-party vote in 1992.
[2] Theodore Roosevelt won 88 electoral votes running as a third-party candidate. William Howard Taft won eight.

hands from a Republican to a Democrat. In fact, as the data in Table 1.1 show, the Democrats won more House seats in the 1912, 1932, 1960, 1976, and 1992 elections, and with the exception of 1912, at least the same number of Senate seats. Obviously, the Democrats hoped to do better.

The campaigns for the control of Congress are the focal point of this book. There will be countless volumes produced on the candidacy, campaign, and presidency of Barack Obama; we will leave those to others. The congressional races, however, should not be overlooked in the story of the 2008 election. They are part of the fabric of the election cycle and help make it so interesting.[7] The issue we wish to explore is focused on an age-old axiom in politics: incumbents usually win reelection. Most often the advantages incumbents have over their challengers are considered in terms of the hundreds of incumbents who return to office after little or no challenge in the last election. Many of these same principles can also be applied to congressional districts that the party considers a "safe" district, where the incumbent can retire knowing his or her party will almost certainly retain the seat.

The 2008 election allows us to examine incumbency in a different way. Specifically, we are interested in examining races where incumbents were fighting to save their congressional careers. Those who found themselves in a tough reelection fight in a year when the electoral dynamics were working against them and their party, and when the presidential candidate of the opposing party had great success with a message of "change" topped the list. Of course, in 2008 the most exposed incumbents were clearly Republicans. More Republicans lost in this environment than Democrats, but some of the most vulnerable Republicans managed to play good defense and win reelection.

The lessons in this book are transferable, however, to future campaign cycles, and even in different electoral environments. For example, in 2010 the Democrats have more seats to defend, some of which were won from the GOP in Republican-leaning districts; and in 2012, when President Obama is back on the ballot, there will be incumbents with turf to defend then as well.

The races that shaped the 111th Congress occurred simultaneously with the McCain and Obama presidential campaigns and were fought within the same context. The strategies of the candidates in the congressional races were also affected by the large increase in registered voters, the increased excitement among younger voters, the exit of George W. Bush from the White House, and other factors, not to mention the simple presence of Barack Obama and John McCain at the top of the ballot. How did congressional Republicans "play defense" during a bad year for the GOP? Were Republicans who won focusing on local issues in the midst of a national election? Just as important, what led to the defeat of those that lost? Was it a tidal wave of Democratic sentiment in a year when even local issues might have been nationalized? Or, was it an issue of "fit" with the district, where voters simply chose to have a Democrat represent them? These races were impacted not only by macropolitical factors driven in large part by the presidential race, but also by micropolitical factors unique to each race. The chapters that follow will help sort out what worked and what did not as Republicans played defense in this year of change.

Macrolevel Political Dynamics in 2008

At the macrolevel, the political dynamics driving the 2008 presidential election impacted individual congressional races as well. While many of these factors were simply a part of the political environment or landscape that led up to the election (such as the president's low approval ratings), others were created by those involved in the election (such as the nomination of Barack Obama), and still others were thrust upon the candidates during the campaign without much warning. These macrolevel factors deserve specific attention and are important to understanding campaigns and elections because they impact races up and down the ballot.

A Disagreeable Public Mood

In part, the dynamics of the 2008 election cycle were in place long before the first presidential caucuses or primaries in January, and before many congressional candidates even decided to run. Chief among the factors that made up the political landscape surrounding 2008 was one individual: President George W. Bush. Indeed, the outgoing president's approval ratings of 25 percent in October of 2008 were near historic lows.[8] To put this in perspective, President Richard Nixon's approval ratings were at 24 percent at the time he resigned the office following the Watergate scandal.[9] Certainly, how President Bush handled important issues like the economy, the war in Iraq, the aftermath of Hurricane Katrina, and others drove down his approval ratings. For a president who set the record for the highest public approval rating ever recorded (90% following the attacks of September 11, 2001),[10] the steady decline of his standing with the public during his second term in office is striking, even considering the numerous missteps of his administration (see Figure 1.1).

This created a context highly advantageous for Democrats seeking the presidency and also Democrats running for Congress. Much of the public clamored for a fresh start and many Democrats offered that by promising to bring change to Washington. The high disapproval ratings of President Bush and his administration became a major factor in both the presidential battle between Barack Obama and John McCain, and the competitive races that determined the makeup of the 111th Congress. Even though Democrats represented the majority in the House and Senate before the election, incumbent congressional Republicans were effectively "on their heels" throughout 2008 battling their challengers as well as they could by dismissing the unpopular president and his unpopular policy choices, to which many Republicans were tied.

The theme of "change" is a common one used by candidates of the party out of power. In fact, change is one of the most popular themes challenger candidates have used historically. For instance, Ronald Reagan turned to the camera

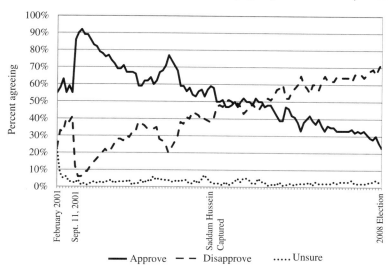

Figure 1.1 George W. Bush job approval, 2001–2008. *Source:* ABC News / Washington Post poll, various dates, data acquired from PollingReport.com, http://pollingreport.com/BushJob1.htm [accessed February 8, 2009].

during the 1980 presidential debate with incumbent President Jimmy Carter and argued for change when he said to voters:

> Next Tuesday all of you will go to the polls, will stand there in the polling place and make a decision. I think when you make that decision, it might be well if you would ask yourself, *are you better off than you were four years ago?* Is it easier for you to go and buy things in the stores than it was four years ago? Is there more or less unemployment in the country than there was four years ago? Is America as respected throughout the world as it was? Do you feel that our security is as safe, that we're as strong as we were four years ago? And if you answer all of those questions yes, why then, I think your choice is very obvious as to whom you will vote for. If you don't agree, if you don't think that this course that we've been on for the last four years is what you would like to see us follow for the next four, then I could suggest another choice that you have. This country doesn't have to be in the shape that it is in.[11]

Hence, 2008 was another year where "change" was especially effective given the dislike for the current president and many of the public policy difficulties new leaders would face. As the 2008 election cycle began in late 2007, the political environment was full of difficult issues including an unpopular war, an economy in decline, rising budget deficits, skyrocketing healthcare costs, an increasing number of individuals without health insurance, and others. With all the problems facing the nation, the public was understandably in the mood for a change. Few other measures signal the desire for change better than the question commonly asked in public opinion polls, "Do you feel things in this country are generally going in the right direction or do you feel things have pretty seriously gotten off on the wrong track?" Plainly, this poll question taps respondents' views on how the country is doing. There may be no better description of the political landscape facing candidates in 2008 than the trends that appear in Figure 1.2. While mood of the public was bad entering 2007, it only grew worse in 2008 as an unbelievable 89 percent of the public said the country was off on the wrong track in late October, with fewer than one-in-ten voters agreeing that the United States was headed in the right direction.

Combined with the president's dismal approval ratings these figures gave Democrats an initial advantage and created a context in which it would be very difficult for Republicans to be successful. A built-in theme—change—was there for the taking and the Democrats, led by Barack Obama, took that football down the field and scored a touchdown. The Obama campaign did a masterful job throughout the campaign of using the theme of change to connect with voters and to make the 2008 election less about John McCain and more about George W. Bush and his policies. Democratic congressional candidates did this as well, making President Bush a fixture in many of their stump speeches and television commercials.

During the presidential election, in both stump speeches and on television Barack Obama and his campaign persistently hammered John McCain on his ties to the sitting president. At a campaign stop in Denver, Obama said of Sena-

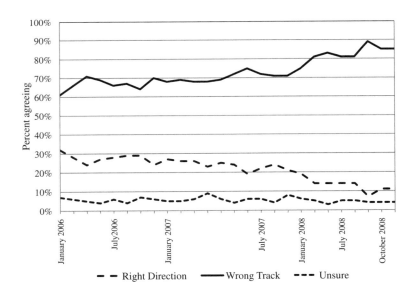

Figure 1.2 Public opinion of whether the nation ais on the "right direction" or "wrong track" 2006–2008. *Source:* CBS News poll, various dates; data acquired from PollingReport.com at http://www.pollingreport.com/right.htm [accessed February 7, 2009].

tor McCain and President Bush, "For eight years, we've seen the Bush-McCain philosophy put our country on the wrong track, and we cannot have another four years that look just like the last eight. It's time for change in Washington, and that's why I'm running for president of the United States."[12] In television commercials, the Obama campaign used their fundraising advantage to literally overwhelm the American public with their message.[13] The sitting president and his political difficulties were also a favorite topic in congressional campaigns throughout the country as Democratic challengers tied their Republican foes to President Bush through the votes they had taken in support of the president's policies. As Democrats tied Republicans to President Bush in campaign images, the Democrats' party committees—the Democratic Congressional Campaign Committee (DCCC) and the Democratic Senatorial Campaign Committee (DSCC)—also got into the act.[14] Republican candidates around the country from Michigan to Georgia and California to Connecticut found they had to play defense by defending their own record and that of an unpopular president as well.

An Economy in Turmoil

John Petrocik's theory of "issue ownership" tells us that each political party has an advantage over the other on certain issues during a campaign because the public trusts that party to better handle that issue.[15] In other words, that party "owns" that particular issue. For instance, Democrats own issues such as civil liberties and social welfare spending while Republicans own issues related to crime as well as defense spending and policy. While conventional wisdom suggests that the public believes Democrats are better able to address economic issues, Petrocik shows that the economy is not owned by either party. Rather, it is a "performance" issue where the party out of power may "lease"—that is, take short-term ownership of—an issue based on poor performance by incumbents. Because the president is typically held accountable for the economy, the poor economic performance created an opportunity for Democrats across the country to exploit. This opportunity was clear approximately a year before the election when the public was asked in a *Los Angeles Times*/Bloomberg Poll, "If the nation falls into a recession, which political party do you think would be best at restarting the country's economic growth: the Democratic Party or the Republican Party?" Forty-five percent thought the Democratic Party would do a better job, 30 percent thought the Republican Party would do a better job, and the rest were unsure.[16]

The economic meltdown that surfaced in 2008 was certainly one of the defining stories of the year. The collapse of the Federal National Mortgage Association (Fannie Mae) and the Federal Home Loan Mortgage Corporation (Freddie Mac)[17] due to the subprime mortgage crisis; the bankruptcy of financial leviathan Lehman Brothers; the liquidity issues of the large insurance company American International Group (AIG) in September; and the resulting economic problems received most of the headlines during the Fall campaign. With little doubt, these issues drove American electoral politics during the fall campaign season and continued to have an impact for many months thereafter. Even before Labor Day as the party conventions ended and the traditional campaign period heated up the economic picture was not exactly bright. In 2008, between January 1 and the end of August, the Dow Jones Industrial Average lost more than 13 percent of its value; the average cost of a gallon of gasoline went up nearly 60 cents and hit an all-time high of $4.17;[18] the unemployment rate rose a full percentage point to 6.2 percent, the highest since July 2003;[19] and payrolls lost an average of more than 80,000 jobs a month.[20]

The impact of these economic trends is hard to overstate and they only reinforced the mood of the public who desired a new direction in leadership. Of course, the state of the economy in the early phases of the campaign provided an advantage for Democrats, handing them an issue with which to build a message that would resonate with voters. The dismal economic data also allowed congressional Democrats to continue the campaign with a strategy that provided the biggest bang for their buck—tying incumbent congressional Republicans to the economic policies of President Bush. Then, the economic news actually got worse. The housing market was shocked when the federal government announced it was taking over or bailing out Fannie Mae and Freddie Mac, and a number of major multinational banking, investment, and insurance companies were found to be in financial ruin. Upon hearing this news the stock market slid even further and by Election Day it was off nearly one-third from its all-time high just one year before. Between Labor Day and Election Day unemployment also grew as the economy shed roughly one million jobs.[21]

A number of scholars have examined the political impact of these and other economic indicators. While there is some disagreement regarding their specific influence, there is no doubt that they play a part in deciding election outcomes at the presidential and congressional levels.[22] The 2008 election cycle was no different. Barack Obama rode the wave of bad economic news to victory and he was even assisted by John McCain who in the eyes of many committed a major gaffe on September 15 when he said that in spite of all the bad economic news "the fundamentals of our economy are strong." Of course, Democratic congressional candidates, especially challengers, took full advantage of the poor economic climate, using it against their Republican rivals. In fact, in most parts of the country, the economy was the only issue that mattered as Election Day approached. While the GOP still technically enjoyed ownership of a few issues—terrorism and national security, for instance—these were not issues at the top of the list of issues the public cared about at the time. Indeed, in national exit polls, 63 percent of voters said that the economy was the most important issue at the time, with Iraq (10%), health care (9%), terrorism (9%), and energy policy (7%) lagging far behind.[23]

Strategic Decision Making

The impact of President Bush's standing with the public and the nation's economic woes were felt even before candidates held their first fundraiser or aired their first television advertisement. Indeed, the congressional and presidential campaigns began many months (or in some cases years) before the public made its choices on Election Day. We know from the research of Gary Jacobson and Samuel Kernell that would-be candidates for Congress examine national trends when making their decision whether or not to run for office.[24] Among the considerations included in the calculations of potential candidates are the two factors that were arguably the most important of 2008: the economic health of the nation and the political standing of the president. At the time individuals who were thinking of running for the House or the Senate were making up their minds (the end of 2007 and the beginning of 2008), these two conditions clearly pointed in the direction of a good election cycle for Democrats. As Jacobson notes elsewhere, "if the economic situation is sufficiently dire, or if a war is sufficiently unpopular, it may become a good deal more difficult [for incumbents of the president's party] to avoid guilt by association if there is an energetic challenger continually reminding voters of the connection."[25]

For Democrats to take full advantage of the situation, candidates of both parties simply needed to behave strategically. The crux of the "strategic politician" argument is that potential candidates who might run for office examine the political landscape and decide whether it is an appropriate time to run or not. "A booming economy and a popular president...are assumed to favor the party in power; economic problems and other national failings that are blamed on the administration are costly to its congressional candidates."[26] In other words, the national context leading up to an election can and does set the stage for what happens during the campaign.

Specifically, this has a significant impact on determining the field of candidates who will run for office. The party favored by the political context will see an influx of quality candidates. Paul S. Herrnson refers to this group of individuals who have run for office previously, served as a party official, held an appointed position in government, or served as congressional staff, as "unelected politicians."[27] On the other hand, the party hurt by the political landscape typically sees an unusually large number of officeholders retire rather than face a tough reelection, leaving a field of other candidates who face, at best, long odds of winning. According to Jacobson, "Politically knowledgeable people are fully aware of the advantages of incumbency and of the long odds that challengers normally face, and they adjust their behavior accordingly."[28] When faced with a favorable environment, strategic candidates look to strike while the iron is hot if their party is favored; if their party is not favored, strategic candidates will sit out that particular election. Of course, those most able and likely to act strategically are typically those unelected politicians that Herrnson describes. What this means is that the best candidates from the favored party run while the best candidates from the other party refrain from running. This creates an unbalanced field of candidates, which sets up races between incumbents of the disadvantaged party and quality challengers of the advantaged party, and between incumbents of the advantaged party versus hopeless challengers.[29] In "nationalized" elections like 2008 this sets the table for potentially large shifts in the makeup of Congress.

Strategic behavior is not limited to candidates. Other important electoral actors also examine national tides and the prospects for their party. Included here are those who consider whether to donate money to a party or candidate. With a favorable electoral environment, a slate of quality candidates, and high hopes for winning the White House and increasing their congressional majorities, Democratic donors were much more likely to open their checkbooks than GOP donors who faced much dimmer prospects. Why would a donor give to the party or its candidates when the chances of winning were so low? In 2008 this resulted in a sizable Democratic advantage in fundraising, even though Republicans typically hold this advantage (see Tables 1.2 and 1.3). The decided advantages Democratic candidates had over their Republican rivals were also perceived by donors—both political action committees and individuals. Democratic donors were willing to give while Republicans did not want to make a bad investment.

Democratic congressional candidates were confronted with the opposite decision-making environment before the 1980 election. In 1979 the U.S. economy went into a tailspin. Following the Iranian Revolution, the new Iranian regime exported oil at lower levels, which forced a rise in prices of crisis proportions. As a result, inflation in the United States reached 10 percent and unemployment jumped to 7.1 percent. These events led to a drop in President Jimmy Carter's job approval ratings during the summer, reaching a low of 28 percent. By the beginning of the election year his approval ratings quickly doubled after a group of Islamic students and militants took over the American embassy in Iran and held 52 U.S. citizens as hostages, but the hostages were not released until after Carter left office. Thus, his job approval ratings slipped again in the spring and were in the low-30s by Labor Day.[30]

Congressional Democrats felt the pinch. The unpopular president, coupled with an economic downturn allowed the Republicans to welcome 37 new members to the House of Representatives. For House Republicans this was a net gain of 34 seats. In the Senate, with only one-third of the seats contested, Republicans picked off a whopping 12 seats from the Democrats (the Democrats took none). The results of the election meant that the GOP won control

Table 1.2 Fundraising and Expenditure Totals for Congressional Candidates, 2008

	Total Raised	Total Spent	Total from PACs	Total from Individuals
House Candidates				
Democrats	$532,443,964	$489,457,634	$195,427,082	$287,461,985
Republicans	$440,270,832	$442,450,311	$127,302,078	$240,812,538
Senate Candidates				
Democrats	$216,288,676	$218,128,127	$34,950,737	$148,180,499
Republicans	$193,612,634	$201,182,098	$45,934,331	$121,756,103

Source: Center for Responsive Politics, "Stats at a Glance," http://www.opensecrets.org/overview/index.php [accessed February 28, 2009].

Table 1.3 Party Campaign Committee Fundraising and Spending, 2008

	Total Raised	Total Spent
Democratic Congressional Campaign Committee	$176,210,540	$176,523,631
National Republican Congressional Committee	$118,324,756	$118,226,373
Democratic Senatorial Campaign Committee	$162,791,453	$162,558,225
National Republican Senatorial Committee	$94,424,743	$93,786,078

Source: Center for Responsive Politics, "Political Parties Overview," http://www.opensecrets.org/parties/index.php [accessed February 28, 2009].

of one of the two branches of Congress, in this case the Senate, for the first time since 1952.

The strategic behavior by potential candidates helped drive electoral outcomes in 2008. For instance, in Michigan's 7th Congressional District, incumbent Tim Walberg faced a tough challenge in his reelection bid from a quality challenger who raised a lot of money. In 2008, Mark Schauer, a former state Senate majority leader, raised more than Walberg ($2.2 million to $2 million) and beat the incumbent by less 2 percent of the vote. The DCCC recruited Schauer for the race because he possessed many qualities of a strong challenger: name recognition, a track record in electoral politics, and the ability to raise a lot of money. The party also "put out feelers" to Schauer in 2006 but he declined to run paving the way for Walberg's opponent in 2006, organic farmer Sharon Renier. In this contest, the underfunded and unknown challenger spent only $55,000 to Walberg's $1.2 million, but she still managed to get 46 percent of the vote. In 2006, the district did not set up as well for Democrats and Schauer stayed out of the race; when it looked like a better opportunity, he ran, and won.[31] This example points to an important lesson of national tides in congressional elections: "When a party does not field enough challengers who have the resources and skills to take full advantage of the opportunities created by national conditions, partisan swings are dampened; when it does partisan swings are enhanced. Similarly, incumbents often survive…if they avoid challengers capable of exploiting them."[32]

Democrats' Foundational Advantage

Given that more Americans identify themselves as Democrats than Republicans, the Democratic Party has traditionally enjoyed an electoral advantage.[33] Data suggest that this advantage has diminished significantly since the 1930s when the Democrats became the majority party. Elections today are more competitive and the two major parties regularly alternate control of the presidency and control of Congress. When George W. Bush was reelected in 2004, the Republicans nearly reached parity with Democrats in terms of partisan identification (see Figure 1.3). As 2005 began, however, Republicans lost the ground they had gained and by the 2006 midterm elections the Democrats had an advantage in party affiliation of about 7 percent over Republicans. Over the next two years

this advantage increased, with the exception of a slight increase in party identification for Republicans at the beginning of 2008 as the presidential primary
season started. For the remainder of 2008, however, there was a great surge in
identification with the Democratic Party. While Republicans generally lacked
enthusiasm for both their president and the party's nominee, the prolonged
campaign for the Democratic Party nomination between Senators Hillary Clinton and Barack Obama generated a form of passion among Democrats not seen
in decades. The result was the largest Democratic advantage on this measure
since 1983.

This advantage is not trivial. Although elections in the United States are
candidate-centered rather than party-centered, party identification remains a
strong predictor of voting behavior. Therefore, as the number of Americans who
called themselves Democrats increased the chances that more individuals would
be casting ballots for Democrats also increased. This advantage is also reflected
in what political pollsters call the "generic congressional ballot," a survey question asked in many polls to determine whether an individual has a partisan
preference in the upcoming congressional race. Because House and Senate races
involve hundreds of candidates from across the nation, the generic ballot asks
respondents, "If the elections for Congress were being held today, which party's
candidate would you vote for in your congressional district—[the Democratic
candidate or the Republican candidate]?" This question estimates the strength
of the two parties and suggests the likely outcome of the forthcoming congres-

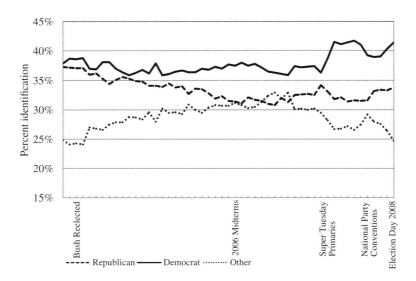

Figure 1.3 U.S. partisan identification, 2004–2008. *Source:* Rasmussen Reports, http://
www.rasmussenreports.com/public_content/politics/mood_of_america/party_affilia-
tion/party_affiliation/summary_of_party_affiliation [accessed February 8, 2009].

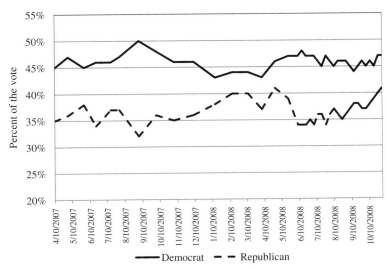

Figure 1.4 Generic congressional ballot, 2007–2008. *Source:* Rasmussen Reports http://www.rasmussenreports.com/public_content/politics/mood_of_america/congressional_ballot/generic_congressional_ballot [accessed February 8, 2009].

sional elections. Historically, Democrats typically lead generic ballot surveys of registered voters. This can occur even when Republicans win a majority of congressional races, because Republicans are more likely to turn out to vote. Again, in 2008 there was a sizable Democratic advantage (see Figure 1.4). Rasmussen Reports' measurement of this key indicator shows that the Democrats held a strong advantage with voters in congressional races across the country. Republicans narrowed the difference to as little as 4 percent in February and March of 2008 (around the same time of the increase in party identification for the GOP seen in Figure 1.3), but the Democrats pulled ahead by as much as 13 percent in July. A double-digit lead on the generic congressional ballot suggested that the Democrats were in a good position to increase their majorities. When the campaigns were in full gear during the fall of 2008, the Democrats were still regularly 6 to 8 points ahead of Republicans on the generic ballot.

Exploiting the Republican Disadvantage

While the Republicans were poorly positioned to respond to the macrolevel political dynamics of the 2008 election cycle, the Democrats were well-positioned to take advantage of the opportunity in front of them and they did. Across the country the Democratic Party, led by the Obama campaign, worked relentlessly to register new Democratic voters in the hope that they would turn out to vote for Senator Obama for president and Democratic candidates for Congress on Election Day. The Obama campaign identified several states they felt were important to win in November and spent many months there registering new Democratic voters. For example, in Nevada, Democrats were outnumbered by more than 4,000 voters in 2004, but by the end of October in 2008 they had an advantage of approximately 80,000 people.[34] In Pennsylvania the difference was even more striking. In 2000 there were roughly 500,000 more Democrats than Republicans in the state. This grew to nearly 600,000 in 2004, but it ballooned to almost 1.15 million for 2008.[35] Moreover, new Democratic registrations outpaced new GOP registrations by four to one in Colorado and six to one in North Carolina.[36] In the state of Florida, 58 percent of the 430,000 new registrants were Democrats, but only 24 percent were Republicans.[37] Of course, voter registration is not a perfect predictor because there is no guarantee that someone who registers as a member of a political party will vote for candidates of that party. For instance, in the 2004 presidential election in Florida, Republicans were outnumbered in voter registration by almost 370,000 individuals, yet President Bush won that state by more than 380,000 votes.[38] It was, however, another signal to the Democrats that this would be a good year for their party.

A Ray of Hope for the GOP

Even though most of macropolitical factors such as party identification and party registration were working in the Democrats' favor, the GOP still had a ray of hope. Voters could split their tickets by voting for a presidential candidate of one party and a congressional candidate of the other party. Even if more voters cast their ballots for Senator Obama, perhaps some would still vote for the Republican congressional candidate. A number of theories offer competing explanations for why voters split their tickets. One body of evidence suggests the characteristics of individual voters drive ticket splitting.[39] A more sophisticated argument, however, is that voters actually think about creating divided government (i.e., where Democratic Party controls one branch of government while the Republican Party controls another) before they cast their ballot.[40] The empirical support for this theory, however, is lukewarm. Nonetheless, even if all ticket splitters do not behave this way, and even if it would not produce divided government, some voters may make their vote choices with this in mind and it could have made a difference for individual GOP candidates.[41]

More recent evidence points to candidate characteristics as a driving force behind ticket splitting. Importantly, evidence suggests that incumbency plays an important role here in that incumbents can "foster ticket splitting through constituency service and pork" they bring home to the district.[42] The idea is simple: voters prefer candidates who can deliver benefits to their district, even if they are of different parties. Therefore, Republican congressional candidates in individual districts or states could still appeal to this desire for pork and potentially keep their seat.

As seen in Figure 1.5, the percentage of the public that splits their ticket has dropped from its high in the 1970s and 1980s. The level of ticket splitting is still, however, sufficient enough to elect or reelect many individuals to Congress when the president is of the other party. In the face of a likely Democratic land-

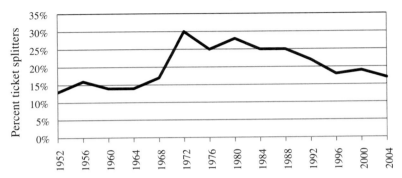

Figure 1.5 Split-ticket voting, 1952–2004. *Note:* Entries are the percentages of voters who "split" their ticket by supporting candidates of different parties for the offices indicated. Those who cast ballots for other than Democratic and Republican candidates are excluded in presidential and congressional calculations. *Source:* Table 3-12 Split-Ticket Voting, 1952–2004 (percent)." CQ Press Electronic Library, Vital Statistics on American Politics Online Edition, vsap07_tab3-12. Originally published in Harold W. Stanley and Richard G. Niemi, *Vital Statistics on American Politics 2007–2008* (Washington: CQ Press, 2008). http://library.cqpress.com.leo.lib.unomaha.edu/vsap/vsap07_tab3-12 (accessed March 3, 2009).

slide in Congress, Republicans had to make their defense to voters on a case-by-case basis in congressional districts and states across the country explaining why they deserved to be returned to Capitol Hill. To do so, Republicans needed to campaign by reminding voters what they had done for them and their districts. This type of message is standard procedure in congressional races. According to Paul S. Herrnson, incumbents:

> …seek to reinforce or expand their base of support by concentrating on those aspects of their persona that make them popular with constituents. Their messages convey images of competent, caring individuals who work tirelessly in Washington to improve the lives of the folks back home they represent. Incumbents' campaign communications often describe how they have helped constituents resolve problems, brought federal programs and projects to the district, and introduced or cosponsored popular legislation.[43]

Republican incumbents who could remind votes of what they had done in the past, had a better chance of keeping their jobs.

One additional factor that could have helped Republicans was the public approval of Congress. George W. Bush certainly had low approval numbers, but those for Congress were even worse (see Figure 1.6). Typically, these approval ratings are tied to the performance of congressional leaders, who were Democrats after the 2006 elections. Low approval ratings are nothing new, but they were even worse after Democrats took control. While GOP incumbents were certainly partially responsible for those low ratings, they did have one factor working in their favor. Fenno's Paradox illustrates that while the public may not

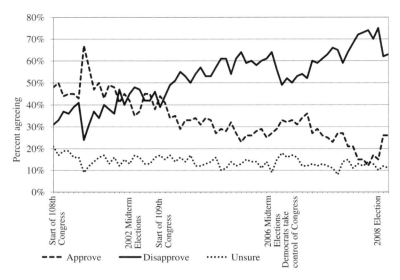

Figure 1.6 Congressional job approval, 1999–2008. *Source:* CBS News/New York Times Poll, various dates. Data retrieved from pollingreport.com http://www.pollingreport.com/CongJob1.htm (accessed February 28, 2009).

approve of the Congress as a whole, they do like their own member of Congress.[44] In other words, individual citizens seem to be saying, "My congressman isn't like all those other bums." If Republicans could use the Democratic leadership in their campaigns and tie their opponents to them, or appeal to voters by bragging about their individual accomplishments in Congress, they had a chance to fight off a strong challenger. One factor, however, muted this opportunity somewhat; empirical evidence also suggests that when incumbents face quality candidates who are well funded these incumbency effects are not as strong. As we noted earlier, this is exactly the scenario Republicans were up against in 2008—well funded and quality Democratic challengers running against GOP incumbents.

Playing Defense in a Year of "Change"

While Barack Obama won the election and the Democrats won majorities in both houses of Congress, John McCain still received more than 58 million votes (46%) and many endangered Republican congressional incumbents managed to get reelected in an election cycle where the dynamics were clearly working against them. In fact, given how strongly the national-level political indicators favored the Democrats and how poorly the Republican brand was perceived, it is surprising that the Democratic congressional victories in 2008 were not of a greater magnitude. True, Democrats recaptured the White House and increased their margins in the House and Senate, but these results must be placed in the proper context. Congressional Democrats did not meet the goals they set before Election Day. Some analysts predicted that on Election Day the Demo-

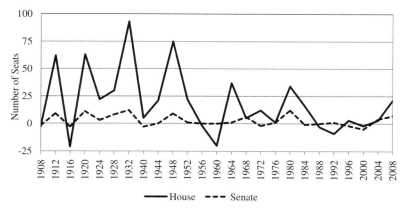

Figure 1.7 Gains and losses by the president's party in Presidential elections, 1908–2008. *Note:* The seat totals reflect the makeup of the House and Senate at the start of each Congress. Special elections that shifted party ratios between elections are not noted. Because of changes in the overall number of seats in the Senate and House, in the number of seats won by third parties, and in the number of vacancies, a Republican loss is not always matched precisely by a Democratic gain, or vice versa. Partisan seat shares at the start of each Congress need not match postelection seat shares: deaths, resignations, and special elections can cause further changes in party makeup. In the 1930 election, for example, Republicans won majority control, but when Congress organized, special elections held to fill fourteen vacancies resulted in a Democratic majority. *Source:* "Table 1-10 House and Senate Election Results, by Congress, 1788–2006." CQ Press Electronic Library, *Vital Statistics on American Politics Online Edition*, http://library.cqpress.com.leo. lib.unomaha.edu/vsap/vsap07_tab1-10. Originally published in Harold W. Stanley and Richard G. Niemi, *Vital Statistics on American Politics 2007–2008* (Washington, DC: CQ Press, 2008).

crats would add 30 to 35 or more seats in the House and attain 60 or more seats in the Senate, enough to stop a filibuster. After the votes were counted, many political analysts were underwhelmed by what the Democrats accomplished. A report in *The Hill*, a Capitol Hill newspaper, described the 19-seat gain in the House as a "blip on the screen instead of a big splash."[45] Political analyst Charlie Cook reported in the *Cook Political Report*, "...given the strength of the top of the ticket nationally, one might have thought that the victory would have been more vertically integrated."[46]

Given the political landscape, the poor perception of the Republican brand before the election, and the macropolitical factors we have noted above, Democrats were clearly hoping to ride the "coattails" of an Obama victory and increase their margins in the House and Senate. As Figure 1.7 shows, many presidents in the last century brought more new partisans to Washington with them than were there before. On the Democratic side, Woodrow Wilson's coattails in 1912 added a net of 62 more Democrats in the House and 9 in the Senate; Franklin Roosevelt's coattails in 1932 added 93 Democrats in the House and 12 in the Senate; and Harry Truman's coattails in 1948 added 75 Democrats in the House and 9 in the Senate. On the Republican side, Warren Harding's coattails in 1920 added 63 Republicans in the House and 11 in the Senate, and Ronald Reagan's coattails in 1980 added 34 in the House and 12 in the Senate. Barack Obama's election added a net of 21 new Democrats in the House and seven in the Senate. Of course, his coattails were longer than each of the presidents dating back to the 1960s (with the exception of Reagan), but they were clearly not as historic as some political analysts have suggested. In spite of the great strength of the Democratic Party at the top of the national ticket, their majorities in the 111th Congress were no larger than they were in other election cycles where the presidency changed hands from a Republican to a Democrat (see Table 1.1).

Plan of the Book

The comparative case studies contained in the chapters that follow investigate the 2008 congressional elections from a unique perspective: all of the cases in this volume examine seats that were held by some of the most vulnerable Republicans prior to November 4, 2008. As we noted earlier, this book is about how candidates of one party were able to play defense and defend their turf in a year when the deck of political factors at the national level seemed to be stacked against them.

The cases are a diverse group on several key characteristics including chamber, candidate status, and region. Cases include both House and Senate campaigns, and instances where the Republican won and was able to defend his or her turf as well as occasions when the seat changed hands. The chapters also include a rich geographic mixture with races from all regions of the country. Importantly, all of the races selected were among the most competitive (one was decided by less than 500 votes) and most expensive of the year (in one of the Senate races the candidates spent over $43 million and in one of the House races that figure was over $9 million). We believe this selection of campaigns provides just the right mixture of important characteristics that will allow us to draw some important conclusions about the 2008 congressional elections and the real value of incumbency.

While our focus is incumbency, the different campaigns analyzed in the chapters that follow also vary in terms of candidate status: in most races a GOP incumbent was running against a Democratic challenger, but one involves an open seat race in a traditionally Republican district where the incumbent was forced to retire rather than seek reelection. This is a district where, in a typical year, the incumbent would, in all likelihood, either go on to victory or would retire and the district would welcome a new member of the party; there are many similar districts around the country. On occasion, however, such districts come into play when the incumbent is forced to retire due to a scandal. So, we have devoted a chapter in this book to covering a race where the Republicans were the "incumbent party," but the Republican incumbent was forced from office. In this case, there was even more for the candidate to deal with—a difficult year for the GOP as well as an outgoing officeholder linked to scandal.

The cases that follow were written by one or a team of scholars who were "on the ground" in the district or state where the campaign occurred.[47] In many cases the individuals writing the chapter had access to one or both campaigns; in all cases, they have tracked the campaign from the beginning and have a clear sense of the dynamics of the race. This book, however, is more than a collection of essays about 12 different campaigns. Rather, the case studies allow us to examine important questions about congressional elections generally. To this end, each chapter has two important similarities. First, each has a common focus, which is to address the question of how the Republican candidate "played defense" in this dismal Republican year and eventually held or failed to hold his or her seat. Second, each chapter that follows is unified by common threads running through the case. We believe this creates a more cohesive collection that analyzes the main research question, but also creates a volume where each chapter is singing the same song even though each has a different voice. Each race does stand out in its own right, however, as the idiosyncrasies and unique aspects of the individual campaigns are brought out by the authors.

Specifically, each chapter includes an examination of the important micro- or district-level factors at work in the campaign. As the former Speaker of the House of Representatives, Tip O'Neill, once said, "All politics is local." This similar structure is designed to allow us to make comparisons between the different races. These common microlevel elements include a short description of where the campaign was waged; the demographics and past electoral trends in the district or state; whether one party typically enjoys an advantage over the other in terms of different measures of partisan strength (election outcomes, party registration, etc.). In addition, the mood of the electorate leading up to the 2008 campaign in that state or district is discussed.

Following from that, the cases include a discussion of the electoral and political context leading up to the contest under investigation. This will help us to understand why the race was competitive from the beginning. Clearly, the GOP incumbent was in electoral trouble for a reason, but these are the rare cases in modern congressional elections. Typically, incumbents seeking reelection get sent back to Washington at the alarmingly high rates of 85 or 90 percent. What was different in these cases? Was the Republican tied to President Bush, and therefore tied to his low public approval? Was the incumbent a bad "fit" for the district or state where voters felt that he or she did not represent them effectively anymore? Was the incumbent caught up in some kind of scandal? Knowing why the race started out as competitive can inform us about the result of the contest, but also the strategies and tactics employed by the GOP and their candidates to defend their turf.

Special attention is paid to the candidates in each of the races. While this book is about more than just the Republican officeholders and candidates it is important to know his or her political record. This also speaks to the question of why this officeholder landed on the endangered incumbents list. What was the incumbent's record of performance and what were his or her vulnerabilities? Did the incumbent support President Bush when voting on legislation? Did the incumbent take unpopular positions on either national or local issues? David Mayhew noted many years ago that members of Congress would likely not get in trouble with their constituents by being on the *losing* side of an issue, but they very well could get into hot water by being on the *wrong* side of an issue important to the voters.[48] In addition, were GOP candidates trying to fend off challenges by touting the vitality of the constituency service they had performed, bragging about federal dollars that had come back to the district under their watch? Moreover, as we noted above, Democrats fielded strong candidates in all of these races. Therefore, in each case special attention is paid to what got these individuals into the race this time. Were the challengers acting strategically, as Jacobson and Kernell found?[49]

The most important part of each chapter deals with how GOP candidates were playing defense against their Democratic opponents. To understand this, each case examines the strategies and tactics of the candidates in the campaign. Both sides are important here (in other words, the strategies and tactics of the Democrats as well) because one candidate's campaign can be affected by the decisions and activities of the other, and the dynamics of a race can shape its outcome. The first aspect of this piece of the puzzle has to do with messaging. What were the different candidates saying? On what were they basing their campaigns? Was the Republican talking about constituency service while avoiding national issues? Was the Democrat trying to link the Republican to President Bush or his policies? In short, what were the reasons candidates were giving voters as the reasons they should be elected. As a part of this discussion special attention is paid to the issues driving the campaign. What did voters have on their minds? Were national issues at the forefront of the race (as Democrats would have liked), or were local concerns driving the voters (as Republicans hoped)?

Also, more specific factors such as fundraising are examined; how much money did each candidate raise? Did each candidate have the resources needed to campaign effectively? Another important question is how did the candidates spend their funds? How did they communicate with voters—did they rely on television advertising, direct mail, or some other method of communication? Was this effective?

Each chapter also considers larger factors outside of the control of the individual campaigns that could have had an impact on the race. For instance, what was the impact of the presidential contest? Did Obama or McCain win the district or state? Did the presidential candidates visit the state and campaign with the congressional candidate? Were Obama's coattails long enough to allow the Democrat to ride them to Washington? The case studies also examine the role played by party organizations and outside interest groups. Was there significant activity by these outside actors in terms of spending or campaign services? If so, what activities were they involved in? Did they run TV ads, send out mail, or help with GOTV? If there were ads run, what were the messages of the groups were sending? Were they consistent with what the candidates were talking about?

Finally, each chapter offers an analysis of the factors that helped determine why the winning candidate came out on top. Was the Republican able to focus the race on local issues? Did the incumbent make use of the advantages that come with being a member of Congress? Did their electoral experience help them through the difficult reelection? On the other side, did the Democrat take advantage of the strength of Obama's victory at the top of the ticket, a general dissatisfaction with the Republican brand, or a poor job of representation by a GOP incumbent? Whether the outcomes can be explained by one of these factors or something else entirely, at the end of the next 12 chapters we will have a sample of the most competitive races and we will be able to draw some conclusions about congressional elections in this year of change. This is a topic we will address in the concluding chapter as we offer some thoughts that tie the 12 races together. In our final chapter we revisit both the macropolitical factors outlined above as well as the micropolitical analyses from each case chapter to make some generalizations about what we learned in 2008 by addressing these Republican-held districts. While the case studies in this book focus on races in 2008, this book is about more than one election cycle. The lessons uncovered by the authors of these comparative case studies will be important for scholars and students in coming congressional elections; they do not apply only to Republicans—they apply to all candidates running in difficult races. To that end, we offer some speculation on what might be ahead in 2010 and 2012. Can we expect Democrats to gain more ground, or might they be the ones who will be on the defensive?

Notes

1. http://transcripts.cnn.com/TRANSCRIPTS/0811/05/ec.04.html (accessed February 26, 2009).
2. John B. Judis, "America the Liberal," *The New Republic*, November 5, 2008, http://www.tnr.com/politics/story.html?id=c261828d-7387-4af8-9ee7-8b2922ea6df0 (accessed February 8, 2009).
3. Senator Charles Schumer (D-NY) quoted in Mort Kondrake, "Obama Needs Help in Keeping Promise to Unify Country," *Roll Call*, November 6, 2008, http://www.realclearpolitics.com/articles/2008/11/obama_needs_help_in_keeping_pr.html (accessed via RealClearPolitics.com February 8, 2009).
4. U.S. Rep. John Lewis (D-GA) quoted in Jennifer Ludden, "Obama Sails to Sweeping, Historic Victory," National Public Radio, November 5, 2008, http://www.npr.org/templates/story/story.php?storyId=96596393 (accessed February 8, 2009).
5. While Election Day did not produce the filibuster-proof margins in the Senate that Democrats coveted, Democrats would eventually gain that 60th seat. It was not because of an electoral victory, but in part because Senator Arlen Specter (PA) announced on April 28, 2009 that he would switch parties and begin to caucus with Democrats in the Senate. This, however, did not produce the final result, as Senate Democrats had to wait for the courts to decide the outcome of the Minnesota Senate contest between Norm Coleman and Al Franken; the final decision, which was in Franken's favor produced a 60–40 split in the Senate.
6. Chris Cillizza, "Friday House Line: House GOP Prospects Grow Dimmer," washingtonpost.com, October 17, 2008, http://voices.washingtonpost.com/thefix/2008/10/house_line.html (accessed February 28, 2009).

7. There are countless works on congressional elections in general and several others have used case studies to focus on specific questions regarding these contests. For congressional elections, see Gary C. Jacobson, *The Politics of Congressional Elections*, 7th ed. (New York: Longman, 2009); and Paul S. Herrnson, *Congressional Elections: Campaigning at Home and in Washington*, 5th ed. (Washington, DC: CQ Press, 2008). Those using the case study method to study congressional elections include a series of works led by David B. Magleby, the latest of which is *The Battle for Congress: Iraq, Scandal and Campaign Finance in the 2006 Elections* (Boulder, CO: Paradigm, 2008); a series of books edited by Robert E. Dewhirst and Sunil Ahuja, the latest of which is *The Roads to Congress 2006* (New York: Nova, 2007); L. Sandy Maisel and Darrell M. West, eds., *Running On Empty?: Political Discourse in Congressional Elections* (Lanham, MD: Rowman and Littlefield, 2004); James A. Thurber, ed., *The Battle for Congress: Consultants, Candidates, and Voters*, (Washington, DC: Brookings Institution Press, 2001); Michael A. Bailey, Ronald A. Faucheux, Paul S. Herrnson, and Clyde Wilcox, *Campaigns and Elections: Contemporary Case Studies* (Washington, DC: CQ Press, 2000).

8. http://www.gallup.com/poll/1723/Presidential-Job-Approval-Depth.aspx (accessed February 24, 2009).

9. http://www.gallup.com/poll/113770/Bush-Presidency-Closes-34-Approval-61-Disapproval.aspx (accessed February 24, 2009).

10. http://www.gallup.com/poll/1723/Presidential-Job-Approval-Depth.aspx (accessed February 24, 2009).

11. Emphasis added; http://www.debates.org/pages/trans80b.html (accessed February 24, 2009).

12. http://www.washingtontimes.com/news/2008/oct/26/obama-mccain-bush-have-whole-lot-common/print/ ([accessed February 24, 2009).

13. Examples of presidential ads include: http://www.youtube.com/watch?v=GV_ury-FRPjY; http://www.youtube.com/watch?v=8xukbiS8q9s (accessed February 6, 2009).

14. Examples at the congressional level include: http://www.youtube.com/watch?v=conf1mnABc8; http://www.youtube.com/watch?v=Qc7ghbCrR-c; http://www.youtube.com/watch?v=gpIVzbJd5R0; http://www.youtube.com/watch?v=9ySzSq8HFoY; http://www.youtube.com/watch?v=tpyc7gXzu8U; http://www.youtube.com/watch? v=UnqbuMsD_0; http://www.youtube.com/watch?v=B-ZNDs-PGdk; http://www.youtube.com/watch?v=OmaHTcdJFjI; http://www.youtube.com/watch?v=NHDoPzBRpC8; http://www.youtube.com/watch?v=Qgpli4Vsy-M (accessed February 6, 2009).

15. John R. Petrocik, "Issue Ownership in Presidential Elections, with a 1980 Case Study," *American Journal of Political Science* 40 (1996): 825–50.

16. *Los Angeles Times*/Bloomberg Poll. November 30–December 3, 2007. N = 1,467 adults nationwide. MoE ± 3. http://www.pollingreport.com/consumer2.htm (accessed February 24, 2009).

17. These are two government sponsored enterprises designed to play a role in the mortgage securities market. Fannie Mae was chartered by Congress in 1968 but dates back to 1938 when it was founded during the Great Depression. Its charge is to purchase and securitize mortgages so that funds are always available to other institutions to lend money to home buyers. Freddie Mac was established in 1970 to expand the secondary mortgage market; its purchases of mortgages increase the supply of money available for home purchases.

18. U. S. Energy Information Administration, http://www.eia.doe.gov/oil_gas/petroleum/data_publications/wrgp/mogas_history.html (accessed February 6, 2009).

19. U.S. Bureau of Labor Statistics, http://data.bls.gov/PDQ/servlet/SurveyOutputServlet?data_tool=latest_numbers&series_id=LNS14000000 (accessed February 6, 2009).

20. Isabelle Clary, "2008 Job Losses Most Since 1945," *Pensions & Investments* (January 9, 2009), http://www.pionline.com/apps/pbcs.dll/article?AID=/20090109/DAILY/901099993 (accessed February 6, 2009).

21. Isabelle Clary, "2008 Job Losses."

22. Gerald Kramer, "Short-Term Fluctuations in U.S. Voting Behavior, 1896–1964." *American Political Science Review* 65 (1971): 131–43; George J. Stigler, "Economic Competition and Political Competition," *Public Choice* 13 (September 1972): 91–106; Edward R. Tufte, *Political Control of the Economy* (Princeton, NJ: Princeton University Press, 1978); Douglas A. Hibbs, Jr., "On the Demand for Economic Outcomes," *Journal of Politics* 44 (1982: 426–62; Brian Newman and Charles Ostrom, Jr. "Explaining Seat Changes in the U.S. House of Representatives, 1950–98," *Legislative Studies Quarterly* 27, no. 3 (August 2002): 383–405.

23. Exit poll data taken from CNN.com http://www.cnn.com/ELECTION/2008/results/polls/#val=USP00p6 (accessed June 24, 2009).

24. Gary C. Jacobson and Samuel Kernell, *Strategy and Choice in Congressional Elections* (New Haven, CT: Yale University Press, 1983).

25. Jacobson, *Politics of Congressional Elections*, 175.

26 Ibid., 169.

27. Herrnson, *Congressional Elections*, 42.

28. Jacobson, *Politics of Congressional Elections*, 42.

29. *Hopeless challenger* is another term coined by Herrnson to describe those who have no real shot of winning.

30. http://webapps.ropercenter.uconn.edu/CFIDE/roper/presidential/webroot/presidential_rating_detail.cfm?allRate=True&presidentName=Carter (accessed June 15, 2009).

31. The story of the 2006 and 2008 campaigns in Michigan's 7th District can be found in David A. Dulio and John S. Klemanski, "Incumbency Is No Advantage: Michigan's 7th Congressional District," *American Review of Politics* 30 (Summer 2009) pp. 189–212.

32. Jacobson, *Politics of Congressional Elections*, 175.

33. There is a great debate in the political science literature over how to measure party identification, however. One school of thought argues that to get a true measure of party id, one must include "leaners"— those individuals who do not report a partisan attachment when first asked, but do so when asked if they "lean" toward one party or the other; the idea being that there is latent partisanship within these individuals which just needs to be coaxed out. Another group of scholars argues that leaners should not be included. Either way, what can be agreed upon is that over time there have been more Democrats than Republicans, no matter how partisan attachment was measured.

34. Peter Nicholas, "New Registrations Favor Democrats," *Los Angeles Times*, October 6, 2008, A6.

35. Ibid.

36. Alec MacGillis and Alice Crites, "Registration Gains Favor Democrats," *Washington Post*, October 6, 2008, A1.

37. Michael C. Bender, "430,000 New Voters Register in Florida," *Palm Beach Post*, October 4, 2008, http://www.palmbeachpost.com/state/content/state/epaper/2008/10/04/1004_newvoters.html (accessed February 7, 2009).

38. Nicholas, "New Registrations Favor Democrats."

39. Paul Allen Beck, Lawrence Baum, Aage R. Clausen, and Charles E. Smith, Jr., "Patterns and Sources of Ticket Splitting in Subpresidential Voting," *American Political Science Review* 86, no. 4 (1992): 916–28; Richard Born, "Congressional Incumbency and the Rise of Split-Ticket Voting," *Legislative Studies Quarterly* 25, no. 3 (2000): 365–87; Joe Soss and David T. Canon. "Partisan Divisions and

Voting Decisions: US Senators, Governors, and the Rise of a Divided Federal Government," *Political Research Quarterly* 48, no. 2 (1995): 253–74.

40. Alberto Alesina and Howard Rosenthal. "Partisan Cycles in Congressional Elections and the Macroeconomy," *American Political Science Review* 83 (1989): 373–98; Alberto Alesina and Howard Rosenthal, *Partisan Politics, Divided Government, and the Economy* (New York: Cambridge University Press, 1995); Alberto Alesina and Howard Rosenthal, "A Theory of Divided Government," *Econometrica* 64 (1996): 1311–41; Morris P. Fiorina, "The Reagan Years: Turning Toward the Right or Groping Toward the Middle?" In *The Resurgence of Conservatism in Anglo-American Democracies*, ed. Barry Cooper, Allan Kornberg, and William Mishler (Durham, NC: Duke University Press, 1988); Morris P. Fiorina *Divided Government*, 2nd ed. (Boston: Allyn and Bacon, 1996), 430–60; James C. Garrand and Marci Glascock Lichtl, "Explaining Divided Government in the United States: Testing an Intentional Model of Split-Ticket Voting," *British Journal of Political Science* 30, no. 1(2000): 173–91; Daniel Ingberman and John Villani, "An Institutional Theory of Divided Government and Party Polarization," *American Journal of Political Science* 37, no. 2 (1993):429–71; Walter R. Mebane, Jr., "Coordination, Moderation, and Institutional Balancing in American Presidential and House Elections," *American Political Science Review* 94, no. 1 (2000): 37–57.

41. In fact, near the end of the campaign, John McCain made this exact point. Knowing that the Democrats would hold the House and Senate, he argued the country needed divided government and a Republican in the White House to veto legislation coming from the Congress.

42. Douglas D. Roscoe, "The Choosers or the Choices? Voter Characteristics and the Structure of Electoral Competition as Explanations for Ticket Splitting," *Journal of Politics* 65, no. 4 (November 2003): 1147–64.

43. Herrnson, *Congressional Elections*, 210.

44. Richard F. Fenno, Jr., "If, as Ralph Nader says, Congress is 'The Broken Branch,' How Come We Love Our Congressmen So Much?" In *Congress in Change: Evolution and Reform* ed., Norman J. Ornstein (New York: Praeger, 1975), 277–87.

45. Aaron Blake, "Dems' 19-Seat Gain Not Making Splash," *The Hill*, November 5, 2008, http://thehill.com/leading-the-news/dems-19-seat-gain-not-making-splash-2008-11-05.html (accessed February 8, 2009). See also, Mort Kondrake, "Obama Needs Help in Keeping Promise to Unify Country." Note: This story was written the day following the election. The Democrats ended up picking up 21 seats in total.

46. Charlie Cook, *Cook Political Report*, http://www.cookpolitical.com/node/3607 (accessed November 25, 2008).

47. There are two exceptions here: the Shays/Himes race for the 4th Congressional District of Connecticut and the McClintock/Brown race in California's 4th congressional district. The Shay/Himes case was written by Victoria Farrar-Myers who was not in the district at the time of the campaign; however, she had a unique perspective in that she previously worked in Rep. Shays's congressional office as an American Political Science Association Congressional Fellow. Colton Campbell who wrote the case on McClintock/Brown was also not in the district at the time of the campaign, but he previously worked for Congressman Mike Thompson in the neighboring 1st Congressional District which gives him an intimate knowledge of the area.

48. David R. Mayhew, *Congress: The Electoral Connection* (New Haven, CT: Yale University Press, 1973).

49. Jacobson and Kernell, *Strategy and Choice in Congressional Elections*.

2   Sinking in "The Perfect Storm"

Knollenberg vs. Peters in Michigan's Ninth Congressional District

David A. Dulio and John S. Klemanski

Between 1993 and 2009, Michigan's 9th Congressional District was represented by Republican Joe Knollenberg. This kind of stability in representation is typical of many U.S. House districts, where safe seats are common and challengers often lose to incumbents by double-digit margins. By 2006, many incumbent House Republicans across the United States had a difficult time with reelection because of national-level issues. Voters were blaming President Bush and the Republican Party in general, for problems at home with the economy, along with a frustrating war in Iraq.[1] This trend occurred in the Michigan 9th District as well. While Representative Knollenberg had little trouble with reelection prior to 2006, he won a surprisingly close race (52 to 46%) that year against relatively unknown and underfunded Democrat Nancy Skinner. This race revealed Knollenberg's vulnerability in the district and set the stage for an increased Democratic effort to challenge him in 2008.

In the 2008 election, voters in Michigan's 9th District contributed to the Democratic Party's expansion of their majority in the House by electing Democrat Gary Peters over the eight-term incumbent. While macropolitical and economic factors appeared to dominate the tone of the campaign, there also were factors specific to the candidates and the district that helped contribute to Rep. Knollenberg's loss in 2008. On election night the defeated incumbent suggested that "a perfect storm" of several different elements contributed to his loss.[2] In order to better understand how a Democratic challenger beat an incumbent Republican in this election, we will examine how those factors combined to sink Representative Knollenberg's chances for victory.

The Michigan 9th U.S. House District

Michigan's 9th Congressional District comprises about 60 percent of Oakland County, which lies northwest of the city of Detroit. The local economy, especially those activities related to the automobile industry, has suffered over the past 20 years. Despite many changes in the automobile industry since the 1970s, the district's economy attempted to keep pace with new technologies that are so much a part of the "new economy," and more specifically those being adopted by auto manufacturers. Auburn Hills is the location of many high tech firms doing business with automobile companies, as well as the Chrysler Corporation's world headquarters. A little further to the south, Troy serves as host community to "Automation Alley," a collaborative effort of local governments, higher education institutions, and businesses in the metropolitan Detroit area that conducts trade missions, markets area businesses on an international scale, and serves as a business accelerator and incubator designed to support and encourage high tech entrepreneurship.

In 2007, 80 percent of the district's population was White, an estimated 10 percent was Black, about 7 percent of the population was Asian, and about 3 percent was Hispanic. The district's demographics have changed since 2000, with increasing diversity in race and ethnicity in cities such as Farmington Hills and West Bloomfield. The district's unemployment rate in 2007 was 6.6 percent, with 5.4 percent of the population living under the poverty level.[3]

Oakland County is the most affluent and highly educated county in the state of Michigan and it often makes the list of wealthiest counties in the United States. In 2007, it was the fourth wealthiest county with a population of 1 million or more. Median household income figures illustrate the wealth of some of the district's communities. Half of the district's 24 communities in 2007 had median household incomes of at least $88,000.[4] Almost half (47.1%) of the district's population 25 years and older had a bachelor's degree or higher.[5] About half (49.6%) of those living in the 9th District are considered to be in management, professional, and related occupations.[6] Many of the district's residents became wealthy from the automobile industry, and the conservative tilt in the district over the years is typical of professional and white collar support for the party.

While the district had elected Republican Joe Knollenberg to Congress since 1992, it marginally supported George W. Bush in 2000 (51 to 47%) and 2004 (51 to 49%). Recent changes have made the 9th District more competitive. Redistricting after 2000 meant that 60 percent of the district was new to Knollenberg. More importantly, changing demographics have meant that the district has trended Democratic since 2000 as African Americans, blue-collar workers, and members of other traditionally Democratic groups moved into the district. National politics and the macrofactors of the national economy also began to play a major role in the district's politics beginning with the 2000 election.

The 2006 Election and Aftermath

Joe Knollenberg worked in the insurance industry prior to running for Congress in 1992, but also served as campaign manager for Republican U.S. Representative William Broomfield, who had represented the area for 34 years. Broomfield announced his retirement prior to the 1992 election, and tapped Joe Knollenberg as his successor. Knollenberg won that first primary election with 43 percent of the vote and then coasted to an easy general election victory. He then went on to similar victories in the each election until 2006. Representative Knollenberg's lowest percentage in any of these elections was 56 percent (in 2000), and most often he won with over 60 percent of the vote.

Throughout his career, Knollenberg served his district without much controversy or fanfare, and would be considered a "workhorse" in the House. He served on the Appropriations Committee, allowing him to have great power in the House and deliver, even if behind the scenes, for the district. Knollenberg was an advocate for the automobile industry by trying to ease Corporate Average Fuel Economy (CAFE) standards, but he also was a supporter of the North American Free Trade Agreement (NAFTA), which many auto workers and labor unions opposed.

With only a few exceptions, Knollenberg exhibited a dependably conservative voting record in Congress (see Table 2.1). He received high ratings from the American Conservative Union (ACU) with scores consistently in the 80s, and low ratings from Americans for Democratic Action (ADA) with scores near zero.[7] Knollenberg's high party unity scores illustrate that he was also a reliable vote for his party throughout his career. Moreover, he showed little support for President Clinton, but great support for President Bush.[8] Notably for the district, Knollenberg opposed Bush on increased steel tariffs in 2002, again in support of automobile manufacturers who would have faced much higher steel prices if the tariff had passed.

Table 2.1 Congressional Vote Scores for Joe Knollenberg, 1993–2008

Year	American Conservative Union	Americans for Democratic Action	Presidential Support	Party Unity
2008	72	40	60	90
2007	84	20	74	87
2006	75	5	95	97
2005	84	0	89	95
2004	84	5	88	94
2003	84	5	100	97
2002	88	0	97	96
2001	92	0	98	99
2000	80	0	32	92
1999	80	5	30	90
1998	96	0	24	94
1997	76	10	21	90
1996	95	0	38	93
1995	88	0	23	95
1994	100	0	44	95
1993	96	5	29	94

Source: 1993–2006 scores from various editions of CQ's *Politics in America;* 2007–2008 American Conservative Union (ACU) and Americans for Democratic Action (ADA) scores from the organization Web sites; 2007–2008 party unity and presidential support scores from CQ *Weekly Report.*

In the 2006 general election, Knollenberg was opposed by radio talk show host Nancy Skinner. Skinner was a somewhat unusual choice for the Democrats and it is likely that the Democratic Party leadership still considered Knollenberg unbeatable and therefore did little in terms of recruiting a quality challenger. Skinner spent about $400,000 in the 2006 campaign, but that amount paled in comparison to Knollenberg's $3.1 million, much of which was spent in the final weeks after the race had tightened. Despite those advantages, Knollenberg only won by 6 points (52 to 46%). As with many other districts across the U.S., the closeness of this election suggested a vulnerability that both parties noted with great interest in terms of the 2008 election.

Between the 2006 and 2008 elections, Knollenberg attempted to respond to this vulnerability both in his campaign strategy and with his policy positions. Early on, he hired a new campaign manager, media consultant, and pollster, and generally launched his 2008 campaign with a more sophisticated approach than had been present in past races. Moreover, Knollenberg also made changes to how he acted in his role as a member of the House. Knollenberg noted:

> I began to look at some things a little differently.... Did I start changing my attitude to some extent? Yes, but not in a major way. But there were some things that we could vote for that we had traditionally been voting against, or maybe not giving a whole lot of support. Some things we tried to single out...I did vote for the minimum wage...I voted against big oil in '07...the subsidies, the incentives for the oil industry.[9]

This different approach showed in Knollenberg's vote scores after 2006. Most notably, his ADA scores went from 5 in 2006 to 20 in 2007 and then to 40 in 2008; and his support for President Bush plummeted from 95 in 2006 to 60 in 2008. This is a clear signal that Knollenberg knew his voting record—especially his support for the president—might hurt him in the next election and this was his effort to change that.

By the end of 2007, the 9th District was seen as a prime target for the Democratic Congressional Campaign Committee (DCCC). By this time, the DCCC had roughly 40 GOP-held seats on its list of most vulnerable targets and Joe Knollenberg was near the top. The DCCC was looking for a strong challenger, one with experience, who ideally had some name recognition in the district, and who had a broad appeal to voters. Gary Peters described how he came to enter the 2008 race:

> I [had] always looked at running for this congressional seat.... I had represented a good part of the district as a state senator.... I thought about running in 2006—Rahm Emanuel was recruiting me in 2006.... We decided it wasn't right, primarily because of our family.... When 2008 came around, they called me again and asked if I would run for the seat.... I started talking to key people—my own supporters and key people in the district and the party.... The response was all very positive.[10]

Peters had served as a state senator representing a district wholly within the 9th Congressional District (he had also served as state lottery commissioner). Beyond this, Peters's resume made him look like attractive candidate for the 9th in the existing political climate. Peters holds an MBA degree and worked for many years in the private sector as a financial advisor. He also served as a U.S. Naval Reserve officer during the Persian Gulf War and volunteered for duty again after September 11, 2001. As Peters's campaign manager Julie Petrick noted, this background made him "a credible alternative" to the incumbent.[11]

The Strategic and Issue Environments

Joe Knollenberg faced an early and likely unforeseen problem at the start of the campaign. Polling by the campaign in early 2007 showed that the candidate was not well defined in the minds of the voters. According to Campaign Manager Mike Brownfield,

> ...Congressman Knollenberg was largely undefined in the minds of the voters in the district. His name identification was pretty high, as you would expect with a 15-year incumbent.... But there wasn't some sense that... this is who he is, this is what he does.... He wasn't defined, which is terribly dangerous for any incumbent because that leaves him wide open to being defined [by the opposition].[12]

Knollenberg and his team spent much of the first year after the close election in 2006 trying to rectify this situation and eradicate this vulnerability. Early polling for the Peters campaign showed similar results, finding that Knollenberg "had high name ID, but people didn't really know what he stood for...and that shows some vulnerability."[13]

The strategic environment in the 9th District at the start of the 2008 general election campaign reflected these problems. The election was very competitive for two reasons. First, those living in the 9th District were disgruntled with the current leadership at the national level. In a mid-August poll of district residents, 73 percent of likely voters said that they felt the country was on "the wrong track," and 82 percent said the same about things in Michigan. The job approval ratings of President Bush as well as those of Democratic Governor Jennifer Granholm were dismal: Bush had a 28 percent job approval rating while Granholm's was strikingly lower at 26 percent. While the public's discontent was bipartisan, the nature of the contest did give a slight advantage to Gary Peters because the focus was on President Bush and deteriorating economic conditions. As others have noted, "economic trends and presidential popularity are powerful political tides" in congressional political campaigns.[14]

Second, Joe Knollenberg faced a difficulty that hit closer to home in the lead-up to the fall campaign: his own low job approval ratings. In mid-August, only 35 percent of likely voters in the district gave Knollenberg a positive rating. Even Republicans were only lukewarm about their congressman at this point in the campaign—only 56 percent said he was doing an "excellent" or "good" job. Moreover, Knollenberg's favorability rating was only at 45 percent. Finally, in an early ballot test, Knollenberg led Peters, but only by a slim 43 to 36 percent margin. Again, even Republicans were not showing the support the candidate would have liked: only 74 percent said Knollenberg would be their choice. More importantly, an incumbent with less than 50 percent support at this point in the race should be worried about the fall election.[15]

These facts of the political environment were all very good news for Gary Peters. He was running against an incumbent who was not very popular in the district, in a year when his opponent's party was mired in its own difficulties, and when his opponent could be closely tied to an unpopular president. Typically, these factors would create a scenario where a challenger with Gary Peters's background would be able to pounce and have a good chance of defeating the incumbent. Peters, however, faced his own difficulties. Despite his previous public service, a full 56 percent of likely voters, and 53 percent of Democrats, had no recollection of his name when asked about him in the mid-August poll.[16] In spite of this, there was good news for Peters. While he trailed Knollenberg in the mid-August poll ballot test, when respondents in that poll were given the candidates' biographies, Peters led by a margin of 43 to 39 percent. These early polling results showed that Peters was in a position to close the gap if he could tell voters his story.

Residents of Michigan's 9th Congressional District cared about one issue during this campaign: the economy. Michiganders had been watching jobs disappear for years while the national economy was still creating them, and their state was the only state with a shrinking economy in 2006. This held true on Election Day in Michigan as well; statewide exit polls showed that 64 percent of voters said the economy was the most important issue, with no other issue registering over 10 percent.[17]

Candidate Strategy and Issues

To win in 2008, both Joe Knollenberg and Gary Peters had to take on the issues that were most important to the voters. John Petrocik's theory of issue ownership tells us that the different parties "own" certain issues because the public trusts that party to handle the issue better than the other party.[18] Now, in a typical election there might be a number of different issues that a sizable portion of the electorate has at the top of their priority list—such as health care, education, national security, and taxes. This type of issue environment would create a scenario where candidates of both parties could campaign on issues that their particular party "owns." For Democrats this means issues such as civil liberties and social welfare spending, and for Republicans it means issues related to crime, defense spending and policy, and taxes.

In this atypical election cycle in the 9th District there were only two issues on the minds of voters—the economy and jobs. The economy, according to Petrocik, is not a Democrat- or Republican-owned issue. Rather, it is what he calls a "performance issue," where neither party owns the issue but one party can take out a short term "lease" on the issue based on how the party in power had performed. Clearly, the public across the nation placed blame with Republicans, and specifically President Bush, for the declining state of the economy. On balance in 2008, Gary Peters should have been able to take advantage of the economy as an issue since he was from the party out of power and the public was unhappy with Republican leadership on the issue.

Before they tackled this main issue, however, both candidates had other obstacles to overcome. Joe Knollenberg needed to define himself to voters that knew his name, and Gary Peters needed to gain the name recognition that Knollenberg already enjoyed.

Knollenberg Becomes the Big 3's Congressman

To define himself in the district, Joe Knollenberg developed a strategy that he thought would connect with his constituents. Not long after the 2006 election, Knollenberg tried to increase his profile as a defender of the Big 3 auto companies. The strategy was for him to get out in front of issues such as steel tariffs and CAFE standards. According to Campaign Manager Brownfield:

> The congressman was going to get out strong on steel tariffs.... The president was for steel tariffs, which would help the steel industry, but conversely would harm the auto suppliers in southeast Michigan. So Joe beat back the steel tariffs, [and they] didn't go through. The CAFE standards was a big drum he was beating loudly. With the new energy bill coming up this was something that was going to be included, so he was fighting on that.[19]

In addition to being issues that hit home with the district, the issue of tariffs had the added benefit of giving Knollenberg the opportunity to break from the president on a key issue. Knollenberg also introduced the New Bridging Industry and Government through Hi-tech Research on Energy Efficiency (or New Big Three Act), which would have rewritten the tax code to give the auto companies more annual tax rebates as they spent billions to meet the new fuel economy standards. The bill was praised by all three auto makers as a way to help to their struggling industry.[20] Unfortunately for the Knollenberg reelection effort, this strategy did not work as intended. After a year, the campaign found that the message was not resonating with voters. Knollenberg had to change defensive strategies.

Knollenberg Adjusts the Campaign's Messaging

Starting in early 2008, the Knollenberg campaign focused on a different priority—constituent service. In short, the message of the campaign was "Joe delivers" for the 9th District. The campaign focused on the fact that Congressman Knollenberg had been chairman and then ranking minority member on the House Appropriations Subcommittee on Transportation. The campaign had a long list of projects for which Knollenberg had been able to secure funding and they used that list to illustrate the "added value" Knollenberg brought to the district.[21] Reminding voters of the benefits to the district brought by the incumbent is a common strategy that incumbents use in their campaigns; there is strong evidence that it pays dividends to incumbents in House elections.[22]

There was another factor in using this message as well. According to Mike Brownfield, it was "to get away from being a partisan" because they knew they "couldn't win the race being a partisan Republican."[23] This is an interesting aspect of the campaign's message development. Petrocik's theory of issue ownership does not explicitly assume that a candidate will be partisan in the use of an issue on which their party has an advantage. But, by focusing on an issue that voters view as being better handled by one of the two parties, there is a partisan flavor to some degree since an important component of any campaign message is contrast. Pointing out how one candidate is better on taxes, for example, must include how the candidate from the other party is not preferable. Sticking to constituency service, however, can provide contrast without being partisan. The Knollenberg campaign was able to tout his experience and what he delivered for the district and create a contrast with his opponent while not appearing to be just another partisan.

The Knollenberg campaign utilized several different communication methods to spread their message including television ads, direct mail, and phone calls. The campaign aired five different television ads in total, and these were divided into three phases. The first phase was designed to boost Knollenberg's positives in the district and began in late September on cable television. The first ad was a testimonial from a mother of a special needs child, which lauded Congressman Knollenberg's work in securing funding for a local organization that helps families with special needs children. In addition to the message about the federal money coming to the district, the key part of the ad was near the end, when the mother said: "As a Democrat, I am supporting Joe Knollenberg. He is a person who fights for the community. Congressman Knollenberg is a person who cares about people."[24] Another ad touted federal funding ($7.5 million) that Knollenberg had secured for the Karmanos Cancer Center. According to Mike Brownfield, the thinking behind this ad was that several key groups (mainly women) might be susceptible to the early negative ads that were being run by Peters as well as outside groups (see below). And, "If we could build a firewall with positives aimed at that demographic, we could help hedge against those attacks."[25]

The second phase of ads was confined to one spot that was run "in heavy rotation on network and cable was focused on the number one issue in the election cycle—jobs in Michigan."[26] The ad also featured a very well known and popular figure in county politics, County Executive L. Brooks Patterson and contained the following audio:

> [Narrator]: Our economy needs new high-tech jobs in growth industries. That's why Congressman Joe Knollenberg is teaming with Brooks Patterson to bring these jobs to Oakland County.
>
> [L. Brooks Patterson]: Joe has been there. When we talked about Automation Alley, Joe was quick to respond. Joe was quick to pass legislation to

create a healthy environment that attacks investment in jobs in southeast Michigan. He's been the go to guy.

[Narrator]: Joe Knollenberg and Brooks Patterson. Creating jobs for Oakland County.[27]

The campaign's goal was to show that "Congressman Knollenberg could work with local leaders to deliver real job results."[28]

The final phase of the ad campaign, run for the last two weeks of the campaign, took on the opponent in a tough way with attack ads that went after Peters's policy stances as well as his character. The first of these ads discussed a "government-run health care plan" supported by Peters "that Barack Obama has called 'extreme' and 'wrong'" and alleged it would raise taxes and provide health care benefits to illegal aliens.[29] The message in the ad tested very well in polling done by the campaign.[30] The final ad attacked Peters for wanting to raise taxes during a recession, for being a "Wall Street big shot" who was "sued for discrimination," for making it easier for "convicted criminals to profit from gambling," and for his faculty position at Central Michigan University where he earned "$700 an hour" while "college costs rise."[31] This ad was "was designed to drive up Peters' personal negatives" in the hopes of creating doubt about his ability to serve in Congress.[32]

Gary Peters Plays to his Strengths

Gary Peters took a much more conventional approach in terms of his issue focus during the fall campaign. His campaign tried to highlight the economic troubles and blame them on an unpopular president. Just as important were the Peters campaign's efforts to explicitly tie Knollenberg to George W. Bush. This was done early in the campaign and with one issue in particular. In 2007, Knollenberg voted against a bill that would have provided health insurance to children—the State Children's Health Insurance Program (SCHIP)—and voted to uphold the president's veto of that legislation.[33]

The Peters campaign and national Democrats through the DCCC went hard after Knollenberg on this issue. DCCC Chair Chris Van Hollen (D-MD) said, "Vulnerable Republicans who continue to vote in lock-step with George Bush against SCHIP will be held accountable by their constituents."[34] As the campaign entered 2008, "Van Hollen and Peters made clear the strategy they [would] follow: link Knollenberg to controversial Bush administration policies—such as support for the Iraq war, veto of [SCHIP] and approval of free-trade treaties."[35] The impact of President Bush in this race was felt deeply by the Knollenberg campaign; Congressman Knollenberg described the importance of Bush very succinctly: "My belief is that Bush was a big problem."[36]

Gary Peters's lack of name recognition earlier in the campaign was solved with heavy spending on television and mail, as well as an aggressive door-to-door schedule that targeted independent voters. The team used a relatively high tech approach to collecting information while they walked door-to-door. Peters described this approach:

We targeted by household, not by community. We were in every community and every street targeting independent and swing voters....We used Palm Pilots to collect information about voters and it was good information... and we were seeing what was happening every day. We could see how our economy message was hitting just at the right point.... I'm a big believer that our field campaign was ...effective for us.[37]

The Peters campaign also aired several television commercials throughout the campaign. Early ads helped define the candidate by focusing on his background and roots in the district, as well as the important issues of the day, such as his work on middle class tax cuts in the state Senate. With these ads, the Peters campaign was able to introduce the candidate, hit on a major issue of the campaign, and connect the two by noting Peters's background in finance as well as the ever-popular issue of middle class tax cuts.

The Peters campaign also retaliated against the attack advertising that came from the Knollenberg campaign at the end of the race. The campaign was trying to hold down their candidate's negatives and drive up Knollenberg's at the same time with an ad claiming Knollenberg had lied in his ad, and that he was "smearing" Peters to "cover up his own record—voting with Bush 90 percent of the time for unfair trade deals, tax breaks to corporations sending jobs overseas, for a failed economy that cost Michigan over 400,000 jobs. It's time for a change."[38] This ad continued the onslaught of attacks against Knollenberg for voting with President Bush and hit on common Democratic messages on outsourcing and the troubled economy; the ad also featured a major theme many Democrats utilized during 2008—change. This allowed the campaign to latch onto the positive feelings for Barack Obama and increase their chances of taking advantage of any coattail effects that might be in place.

The candidates had one debate[39] where they clashed on the two candidates' main themes—experience vs. change. "Knollenberg built a case on experience and seniority, suggesting his position as chairman of a key appropriations committee has brought important benefits to the district."[40] On the other hand, he also invoked the Democratic mantra of change, stating: "We need to bring about change that will improve lives of people in Oakland County, and that's exactly what I've done."[41] Importantly, Peters used the platform to tout his private-sector experience in investment banking, arguing that it prepared him to immediately deal with the financial crisis that was raging at the time and help lead the economic recovery. If elected, Peters said he would seek a seat on the House's Committee on Financial Services, so he could help enact new regulations on Wall Street.

Interestingly, one back-and-forth during the debate reflected the issue environment and the importance of the economy as a "performance issue." During the debate, Knollenberg pressed Peters on how he would vote on tax policy, and specifically if he would vote for higher taxes. Peters resisted answering, knowing that if he backed the Democratic position of rolling back the Bush tax cuts for those making $250,000 a year, he would run the risk of irritating voters who fit in that tax bracket, which is a sizable portion of the electorate in this affluent district. As *Detroit News* reporter Gordon Trowbridge noted, "In a normal political environment, that lack of specificity...might have created some doubt in the minds of some voters. But in this situation, where the Republican Party had been discredited in terms of its ability to run the economy, and [Peters] could present [himself] as a...former investment counselor, image becomes the message in a way."[42]

Money in the Michigan 9th

Both Joe Knollenberg and Gary Peters were well-funded for their contest in 2008. In total, Knollenberg raised $3,774,155 while Peters collected $2,549,935.[43] The totals reflect a common outcome of the fundraising race in congressional elections—incumbents raise far more than challengers. Unlike other challenger candidates, Gary Peters was far from underfunded; both had enough resources to wage a very competitive campaign. Nathan Gonzales of the nonpartisan *Rothenberg Political Report* noted in mid-2008, "It's clear this race won't be won or lost because of a lack of money. Both candidates are going to have plenty of money. It's going to be a battle of whose message resonates with voters the best."[44]

Knollenberg had a head start in fundraising for 2008 because he had money left over from his 2006 race. Gary Peters did not decide to get into the race and start raising money until mid-2007. By the time Peters entered the race, Knollenberg had raised over $1 million for the race and had nearly $900,000 in available resources. Peters raised nearly $400,000 in all of 2007, which still left him far behind Knollenberg.

The quick pace of the Knollenberg fundraising operation—raising $750,000 by the middle of 2007—is typical of incumbents, who begin to build their war chests early in the hopes of scaring off challengers; the thinking is that if the incumbent raises large sums early, a challenger will stay out of the race knowing it would be unlikely he or she could match that level of fundraising. In 2008, this was not the case, however; Knollenberg's $600,000 in cash on hand at the time was not enough to scare off a challenge from Gary Peters. Given the context of 2008, Peters knew that he could compete financially with Knollenberg.

Once 2008 began, however, Peters started to make progress in the endless pursuit of resources that is common in congressional campaigns, as he nearly matched Knollenberg in fundraising in the first quarter of the year. Peters made major progress in catching up to his opponent during the summer months of 2008; by mid-July he had raised over $1.3 million and had $1 million in cash on hand. Knollenberg still had the upper hand, however, as he was sitting on nearly $2 million in available cash. Between mid-July and the end of September, Peters had his best fundraising effort as he raised over $600,000 (this was the only fundraising period in which his fundraising outdid that of his opponent).

Until the summer of 2008, both candidates kept adding to their campaign coffers. But once the general election campaign began, Gary Peters started an aggressive campaign that spent a large amount of his campaign resources, while Joe Knollenberg kept adding to his available cash. It was not until the very end that the Knollenberg campaign started to burn through their money.

This, in part, reflects the strategy of each campaign. The Knollenberg campaign knew that they would be up against a set of difficult forces as the race entered its final phases and they chose to sit on their resources until the last minute—much of this went to late ad buys for television advertising and other campaign communications. Over the course of the campaign, the Knollenberg campaign spent roughly $2.5 million on television advertising, $400,000 on direct mail, and $30,000 on phone calls.[45] The Peters campaign, however, spent more early. This reflects their need to increase the candidate's name identification. Early spending may also have been a function of other resources that were coming to the race from outside groups (more on this below) which would have allowed the Peters campaign to spend their funds and wait for help from friends later.

The presence of noncandidate money in the 9th Congressional District was a near certainty even before Gary Peters got in the race. Not long after the 2006 elections were over, the DCCC began looking ahead to 2008 and the 9th was one district they thought they could capture. Once 2008 began, the DCCC ramped up its assistance to Gary Peters. DCCC chairman Chris Van Hollen (D-MD) came to the district to help Peters raise money in February 2008, as did Rep. Rahm Emanuel (D-IL) and House Majority Leader Steny Hoyer (D-MD). Not long after, in March, Peters was added to the DCCC's "Red to Blue" fundraising program, which also helped Peters raise money; in 2006, the program helped 56 candidates raise a total of $22.6 million, or $404,000 per campaign.[46] The real help from the DCCC, however, came as the campaign was coming to an end. Van Hollen promised "maximum effort" to help the Peters campaign in the final three weeks.[47] Much of this would come in the form of television ads which hit on the familiar and predictable themes including Knollenberg's support of President Bush's agenda, job losses, and the federal deficit.

The party also ran a contrast ad in the final days of the campaign that still attacked Knollenberg but also touted Gary Peters:

> Eight years of George Bush and Joe Knollenberg. They rewarded companies that shipped our jobs overseas, while Michigan has lost 250,000 manufacturing jobs. Bush and Knollenberg, they have spent $500 billion rebuilding Iraq and handed us a $10 trillion federal debt. It's time for leaders who will invest in Michigan again and get our economy moving. That's Gary Peters. The change Michigan needs.[48]

The DCCC spent roughly $750,000 in September alone, and $1.6 million in total, on television ads and direct mail.[49]

Party money was also a story on the other side of the race, but not for the large amount that was spent. Rather than providing a late infusion of support, the National Republican Congressional Committee (NRCC) decided to pull the money it had allotted for television ads in the 9th District late in the game. By mid-October, "The NRCC canceled one buy from October 14–20 for $150,000, and another October 21–27 for almost $170,000."[50] And a week later they canceled another ad buy for $314,000. In short, that was over $600,000 that could have helped Knollenberg in the last few weeks. At the end of the election cycle, the NRCC had to make difficult choices about where to spend its money and there were many endangered Republicans in addition to Knollenberg, and not enough dollars to help them all. Plus, recall the fundraising figures above that showed Knollenberg still had a sizable cash-on-hand figure. In this case, Joe Knollenberg's successful fundraising may have come back to hurt him. No one will know if Knollenberg would have won if the NRCC had spent that money, but it could not have hurt his efforts.

In addition to the party money that was spent in the 9th District, a number of interest groups also spent large sums in efforts to see one candidate come out on top. Early in the race, the League of Conservation Voters (LCV) got involved when it endorsed Peters. This was no surprise given that the LCV had named Knollenberg to its "Dirty Dozen" lawmakers that the group opposed for their votes on environmental issues. Some of the groups that were active included: the Service Employees International Union (SEIU), which spent about $78,000 on mailings attacking Knollenberg; Patriot Majority Midwest, which spent $450,000 on television ads attacking Knollenberg; the National Association of Realtors, which spent more than $500,000 on an ad in support of Knollenberg; and the National Rifle Association's Victory Fund, which spent $6,000 on a billboard for Knollenberg.[51]

The ads run against Knollenberg from outside groups were very much on message with what the Peters campaign and the DCCC were saying at the time. Consider an ad from Patriot Majority Midwest, a group supported by labor unions, against Knollenberg:

> It's a shame. Gas prices are hurting everyone, but our congressman, Joe Knollenberg, is part of the problem in Washington. Knollenberg voted for billions in special tax breaks for big oil companies, not once, not twice, but four times. We're getting clobbered at the pump, but Knollenberg voted to help the oil companies instead of us. Tell Congressman Knollenberg to stop siding with big oil.[52]

Sometimes, when outside groups get involved in campaigns, however, they can take the campaign they are trying to help off message by focusing on issues that are not on the minds of voters. One group—the Humane Society of the United States—fell into this category. This group spent about $400,000 on a very memorable ad attacking Knollenberg. Along with disturbing visual images, the ad included the following audio:

> Joe Knollenberg has one of the worse records on animal cruelty in the country. He voted against preventing sick cows from entering our food supply. He voted to allow the killing of threatened polar bears and the slaughtering of American horses. Joe Knollenberg even voted against enforcing the law used to stop dog fighting. It's time for a new congressman.[53]

For the Knollenberg campaign, the ad came out of nowhere as the Humane Society had never gotten involved in a congressional race in this way. The timing of the ad late in the race as well as the substance and financial factors made it difficult for the campaign to respond to the attacks. As Mike Brownfield lamented,

> Alright, so this ad comes out…how do you respond? Our money is tied up in doing ads that are positive about Joe and ads that are attacking Peters. We don't have the money to do three different ads, so the question is "do you start responding to everything?"…So ultimately we responded with…a radio ad, but the size of the buy, and the impact of the ad, was so strong… it was such a vicious ad it was really impactful…. If we [go] to "Joe Knollenberg doesn't hate animals," even if we put that ad on TV, then people are thinking, "Does Joe Knollenberg hate animals?"[54]

The Knollenberg campaign not only had to play defense against Gary Peters, the DCCC, and other familiar Democratic groups, but a new foe that took them by surprise and to whom they had trouble responding.

The Impact of the Presidential Race

For the last several presidential election cycles, Michigan has been one of the "battleground" states that the presidential campaigns targeted with resources that included money, volunteers and staff, and candidate visits. These important resources can bring paid media campaigns that spread a party message, workers for get-out-the-vote efforts and other mobilization activities close to Election Day, and enthusiasm for the party's base. Voters in Michigan were set for the more of the same in 2008. The candidates in the 9th District were hoping to benefit from the presence of their party's standard bearer.

For much of the summer and into the fall this was the case. Both presidential candidates were active with television ads, voter contact efforts, and other activities across the state and in Oakland County. The candidates also made visits to the state expecting it to once again be a tough battle for the state's 17 electoral votes. In fact, Oakland County historically has been thought to be a bellwether county for presidential elections. Therefore, there was a lot of attention around the 9th District race. This all changed in the first week of October when the McCain campaign announced it was pulling its resources from the state of Michigan to increase spending in other competitive states.

Democrats were hoping that they could take advantage of what they called the "Obama effect"—higher turnout among African-Americans and young voters as well as independents. In the 9th District, the city of Pontiac was a center of attention because of its large African-American population. In a rare involvement in a congressional race, Obama also lent his voice to a radio ad for Peters.

The McCain campaign's decision to pull out of the state had an important impact on the race in the 9th District. As Knollenberg recounted, "It's like telling the world, 'the hell with it….' And that really did not help at all."[55] Now, instead of both candidates rallying support and trying to energize the base, only the Obama campaign was left in Michigan. The resources that could have helped Joe Knollenberg while John McCain battled to win statewide were gone. The Obama campaign, buoyed by their tremendous advantage in campaign resources, stayed active in Michigan. They stayed on the air and kept much of their staff in the state, thus keeping up the excitement in the Democratic base and indirectly supporting Democratic candidates down the ticket.[56]

How much of an impact the withdrawal had on the Election Day outcome is debatable. The Knollenberg campaign would certainly say it hampered their efforts to get Republican voters to the polls. The district turnout data appear to support that view. One analyst, however, sees McCain pulling out as having an impact on the margins only: "There may have been some Republican voters who would have gotten to the polls to vote for [Knollenberg] on Election Day that didn't, but the sense that I got was that Republicans were largely resigned to losing that seat even before McCain's decision…I think it mattered in the [vote totals] but I'm not sure…it mattered to the outcome."[57]

Concluding Thoughts

After the votes were counted, Joe Knollenberg lost his reelection bid by more than 30,000 votes (about 10 percentage points). What explains his defeat? According to Knollenberg, it was a "perfect storm" of factors that came together at the same time. Included in these factors were Barack Obama's popularity, a great deal of money from outside the district that was spent to attack him and his record, and a terrible year for President Bush and the GOP brand generally. As Knollenberg concluded:

> I really think it was a tsunami, I think it was a perfect storm and I don't think anyone could have stopped it. I don't think money would have been enough to stop it.… I also wouldn't want people to think that I'm bitter. How can you be bitter? You can be angry, be upset, but you can't be bitter about it.… Sixteen years, in my judgment, is a good ride.… I didn't anticipate this, but I knew it was going to be a tough election, no question about that.[58]

Knollenberg's campaign manager also acknowledges macrofactors as primarily responsible for their loss in 2008: "That was the entire problem.… He was running against the national atmosphere.… Every issue that was lodged against the congressman was a national issue that was attached to him."[59]

One important question that impacts the results, and that also has to do with the national factors in play at the time, is Gary Peters's decision to enter the race. As noted in chapter 1, the best challengers are strategic actors and they know when it is a good time to run and when they should sit on the sidelines. Gary Peters is one of those strategic politicians. If the national tides that were present before the 2008 cycle got into full swing had not been there, would Gary Peters have run? As reporter Gordon Trowbridge pointed out:

All things being equal, the incumbents win. Somebody like Knollenberg who is considered [to be] somewhat effective as a legislator, [and has] no hints of scandal or misdeeds around him—in a normal political environment someone with a long history of winning elections in the district, you would figure…[he] would be favored in that race, but obviously all things were not equal in 2008 and those outside factors [were important].[60]

In the end, it appears that Joe Knollenberg was right in his assessment—it was a perfect storm of factors that led to his defeat. The changing nature of the district, national issues and the terrible environment for his party, along with the quality of the candidates running (Peters and Barack Obama) were all part of this gathering storm. From his vantage point, Gary Peters was able to take advantage of the political environment and was in the right place at the right time. Whether he can hold on to his seat remains to be seen. The 9th District is far from a safe seat for Democrats—it must be considered a competitive district for 2010. Should the national environment shift with respect to party performance, things might change again in the 9th. Election analyst Charlie Cook of the *Cook Political Report* rates the district as one that is in the "lean Democrat" column, likely because a Democrat will now be able to take advantage of the perks of incumbency. A strong signal that Peters is not taking his reelection for granted is his fundraising activities immediately after the 2008 cycle in 2009; in the first quarter of fundraising for 2010, he had raised more than $430,000, which ranked second among freshmen who had won a seat held by the other party in 2008.[61] How difficult it is for Gary Peters to play defense in 2010 will depend on a number of factors, including many of those that led to Joe Knollenberg's defeat in 2008.

Notes

1. Paul R. Abramson, John H. Aldrich, and David W. Rohde, *Change and Continuity in the 2004 and 2006 Elections* (Washington, DC: CQ Press, 2007).; Paul S. Herrnson and James M. Curry, "Issue Voting in the 2006 Elections for the U.S. House of Representatives," in Lawrence C. Dodd and Bruce I. Oppenheimer, eds., *Congress Reconsidered*, 9th ed. (Washington, DC: CQ Press, 2009), 97–118.
2. Kathleen Gray, "Knollenberg Loses Seat, Blames 'Perfect Storm,'" *Detroit News*, November 5, 2008, http://www.freep.com/article/20081105/NEWS15/311050004/ (accessed June 9, 2009).
3. Fast Facts for Congress, http://www.fastfacts.census.gov/servlet/CWSADPT Table?geo_id=50000US2609&ds_name=ACS (accessed May 20, 2009).
4. http://www.oakgov.com/peds/info_pub/community_profiles_index.html (accessed June 22, 2009).
5. Fast Facts for Congress, http://www.fastfacts.census.gov/servlet/CWSADPT Table?geo_id=50000US2609&ds_name=ACS (accessed May 20, 2009).
6. U.S. Census Bureau, *American Community Survey, 2005–2007.*
7. The ACU tracks a series of votes on a wide variety of issues by all members of Congress; the vote scores (with a maximum of 100) indicate how well a member's votes on the floor of the House match with a conservative agenda (see http://www. acuratings.org/). The ADA is a liberal organization that does much the same thing but they use a series of 20 "key" votes to rate each member; each of these votes is

worth 5 points and when aggregated is their "Liberal Quotient," http://www.adaction.org/pages/publications/voting-records.php.

8. Party unity scores are defined by *Congressional Quarterly* as "The frequency with which they vote with their party, on occasions when a majority of Republicans oppose a majority of Democrats"; presidential support scores reflect "The frequency with which lawmakers vote with the president when he clearly indicates his preferences," http://innovation.cq.com/multimedia/cqvotestudies08 (accessed June 29, 2009).

9. Congressman Joe Knollenberg, personal interview, April 30, 2009.

10. Representative Gary Peters, personal interview, May 15, 2009.

11. Julie Petrick, telephone interview, May 4, 2009.

12. Mike Brownfield, personal interview, April 15, 2009.

13. Representative Gary Peters, personal interview, May 15, 2009.

14. Daniel M. Shea and Michael John Burton, *Campaign Craft: The Strategies, Tactics, and Art of Political Campaign Management*, 3rd ed. (Westport, CT: Praeger, 2006), 41; see also Gary C. Jacobson and Samuel Kernell, *Strategy and Choice in Congressional Elections* (New Haven, CT: Yale University Press, 1983).

15. Polling data in this paragraph comes from an EPIC-MRA poll conducted with likely voters, August 18–21, 2008. Data were supplied by EPIC-MRA's president Bernie Porn.

16. Polling data in this paragraph are from the EPIC-MRA survey noted above.

17. Exit poll data taken from http://www.cnn.com/ELECTION/2008/results/polls/#val=MIP00p1 (accessed April 24, 2009).

18. John R. Petrocik, "Issue Ownership in Presidential Elections, with a 1980 Case Study," *American Journal of Political Science* 40 (1996): 825–50.

19. Mike Brownfield, personal interview, April 15, 2009.

20. David Shepardson, "Knollenberg Proposes $1.2B Aid for Big 3," *Detroit News*, August, 8, 2007, http://www.detroitnews.com/apps/pbcs.dll/article?AID=/20080430/AUTO01/804300358/1001/BIZ (accessed April 24, 2009).

21. Mike Brownfield, personal interview, April 15, 2009.

22. John A. Ferejohn, *Pork Barrel Politics: Rivers and Harbors Legislation: 1947–1968* (Stanford, CA: Stanford University Press, 1974); Steven D. Levitt and James M. Snyder, Jr., "The Impact of Federal Spending on House Election Outcomes," *Journal of Political Economy* 105 (1997): 30–53.

23. Mike Brownfield, personal interview, April 15, 2009.

24. http://video.google.com/videoplay?docid=3682965021985479761&hl=en.

25. Mike Brownfield, e-mail to authors on April 16, 2009.

26. Ibid.

27. http://video.google.com/videoplay?docid=7971432182981463726&hl=en.

28. Mike Brownfield, e-mail to authors on April 16, 2009.

29. http://video.google.com/videoplay?docid=2976908359157594799&hl=en.

30. Mike Brownfield, e-mail to authors on April 16, 2009.

31. http://video.google.com/videoplay?docid=2279869798790965803&hl=en.

32. Mike Brownfield, e-mail to authors on April 16, 2009.

33. As happens many times in campaigns, votes can be taken out of context. The Knollenberg campaign claimed that it was the victim of such actions on this vote. Mike Brownfield notes that Knollenberg did vote against a version of the SCHIP bill, but that he did so because it contained a provision that would have provided benefits to illegal aliens. Knollenberg also notes that the version he voted against nearly doubled the income level for those who would qualify for the program from roughly $40,000 per year to over $80,000. Brownfield also points out that Knollenberg cosponsored another version of the bill; Mike Brownfield, personal interview, April 15, 2009; Joe Knollenberg, personal interview, April 30, 2009.

34. David M. Drucker, "DCCC: SCHIP Hurts GOP," *Roll Call*, November 6, 2007, http://www.rollcall.com/issues/53_55/news/20863-1.html?CMP=OTC-RSS

(accessed April 24, 2009); see also, Gordon Trowbridge, "Top Michigan Dems Unite behind Peters, Schauer for Congress," *Detroit News*, November 9, 2007.

35. Gordon Trowbridge, "Dems Step Up Efforts to Unseat Knollenberg—Democratic Candidate Gary Peters, Party Leader Join Forces at Local Rally In Bid to Oust GOP Veteran," *Detroit News*, February 21, 2008, B5.
36. Congressman Joe Knollenberg, personal interview, April 30, 2009.
37. Representative Gary Peters, personal interview, May 15, 2009.
38. http://www.youtube.com/watch?v=wo8P3yxOs30
39. The debate also included the other two candidates in the race—Jack Kevorkian, the assisted suicide advocate, and Green Party candidate, Doug Campbell. These two candidates had, at best, a marginal impact on the race.
40. Gordon Trowbridge and Deb Price, "Congressional Candidates Knollenberg, Peters Clash over Taxes, Economy in Debate," *Detroit News*, October 17, 2008, ttp://www.detnews.com/apps/pbcs.dll/article?AID=/20081016/POLITICS/810160480/1020 (accessed April 27, 2009).
41. Ibid.
42. Gordon Trowbridge, telephone interview, April 22, 2009.
43. Source: Center for Responsive Politics, "2008 Race: Michigan District 09," http://www.opensecrets.org/races/summary.php?cycle=2008&id=MI09 (accessed April 28, 2009).
44. Quoted in Deb Price, "Congressional Races Rake in Contributions," *Detroit News*, July 25, 2008, B1.
45. Figures from authors' interview with Mike Brownfield cited above and from from Federal Election Commission data.
46. Jennifer Chalmers, "Kevorkian to Try Politics—The Assisted Suicide Advocate Has Taken Out Petitions to Run For Congress as Independent," *Detroit News*, March 13, 2008, B2.
47. Gordon Trowbridge, "2 Dems Move Up In Race for Congress," *Detroit News*, October 15, 2008, p. B2.
48. http://www.youtube.com/watch?v=k-iFHaCz6Ck.
49. Kathy Barks Hoffman, "Dems Outspent GOP Candidates—Parties, Interest Groups, Upped the Ante," *Grand Rapids Press*, November 12, 2008, B2.
50. *The Hill*, "NRCC Pulls $320k in Michigan Congressional Race," http://briefingroom.thehill.com/2008/10/16/nrcc-pulls-320k-in-michigan-congressional-race/ (accessed April 28, 2009).
51. Deb Price, "Challengers Outraise Knollenberg, Walberg in Congressional Races," *Detroit News*, October 16, 2008, http://www.detnews.com/apps/pbcs.dll/article?AID=/20081015/METRO/810150447/1022/rss10 (accessed April 28, 2009).
52. http://www.youtube.com/watch?v=3JBz5cIILIU.
53. http://www.youtube.com/watch?v=RCDT60e7rVw.
54. Mike Brownfield, personal interview, April 15, 2009.
55. Congressman Joe Knollenberg, personal interview, April 30, 2009.
56. Ken Brock, Democratic campaing strategist, personal interview, March 12, 2009.
57. Gordon Trowbridge, telephone interview, April 22, 2009.
58. Congressman Joe Knollenberg, personal interview, April 30, 2009.
59. Mike Brownfield, personal interview April 15, 2009.
60. Gordon Trowbridge, telephone interview, April 22, 2009.
61. Gordon Trowbridge, "Mich. Congressional Freshmen Get Good Fundraising Start," *Detroit News*, April 16, 2009, http://www.detnews.com/article/20090416/POLITICS02/904160380/1024/POLITICS03/Mich.+congressional+freshmen+get+good+fundraising+start (accessed April 28, 2009).

3 All Politics Is *Still* Local
McConnell vs. Lunsford in Kentucky's Senate Race

Jasmine Farrier

The political drama of Kentucky Senator Mitch McConnell's 2008 reelection was not his eventual fifth victory, which was predictable, but the fact that he won by only 6 percent of the vote. Senator McConnell spent over $20 million (including $2 million in loans in the final stretch) to defend his seat against a self-financed businessman who spent $11 million and had never held an elected post. The fact that this race was the second most expensive in the country in 2008 suggests that his seat was in real danger for the first time in decades and McConnell knew it.[1] His first two elections in 1984 and 1990 were very close, but as he ascended in statewide and national prominence his next two elections were landslides. While 2008 had special twists, this type of sudden vulnerability was not unique to Senator McConnell. In fact, this "bumpy-smooth-bumpy" electoral trajectory happens in many congressional careers. Paul S. Herrnson writes, "[a]lthough incumbents generally derive tremendous advantages from the strategic environment, the political setting in a given year can pose obstacles for some, resulting in significant numbers losing their seats."[2]

McConnell versus Lunsford was a meaningful contest for many reasons that spring from Kentucky's complex political environment but also transcend it. On the one hand, the election appears to be a straightforward story about the power of incumbency, political demographics, and maintaining large war chests. Looking deeper, McConnell's reelection highlights how senators balance their responsibilities—statewide representative of diverse interests, national policy maker, and partisan—and communicate their choices to voters when these duties come into conflict.[3] The full story has several interconnected components, which centered on the ways Senator McConnell has used his position in the Senate to bring federal dollars to a variety of industries and regions in Kentucky. In addition, the state's political environment was not as open to "change" in 2008, in the form of Barack Obama, as other states.[4]

The People and the Politics of the Bluegrass State

In many ways, Kentucky is square in the demographic mainstream of the current Republican Party. It is more racially and ethnically homogenous than national averages (88% of the voters in Kentucky are White, 7.7% are Black, and 2.2%

are Hispanic), and the state has lower median education and income levels.[5] While maintaining its national image of bourbon distilleries, horse breeding, and tobacco farms, the largest employers in the state over the past decades have shifted toward health care-related services, retail businesses, and auto manufacturing, including domestic and foreign brands that expanded production to Southern states.[6]

Like neighboring Midwestern and Southern states, Kentucky is split internally between urban and rural voters, with the latter favoring Republicans by increasing margins and the reverse being true in the cities. In 2008, Senator McConnell lost the counties that contained the biggest cities in Kentucky, Louisville and Lexington (the latter for the first time). Barack Obama won both of those counties. Yet as a state, Kentucky is closer to the contemporary averages of the Republican Party on a variety of "culture war" issues in recent decades. Almost 37 percent of Kentucky's population describes itself as "evangelical Protestant," which places the Commonwealth sixth highest in the nation— Arkansas leads with 43 percent and Rhode Island is last with 1.5 percent.[7] In a separate aggregate 2004–2006 Gallup poll report, Kentucky ranked 12th in the nation for church attendance, with 48 percent responding that they attend once a week or almost every week.[8] Majority opinion in Kentucky is very close to the Republican National Committee's (RNC) "Values" platform on abortion, gay marriage, and guns.[9]

At the same time, even though Kentucky is not a high profile "swing state" and was not courted heavily by presidential candidates in 2004 and 2008, it has shown complex electoral patterns since the 1970s. On the presidential level, Kentuckians preferred fellow Southerners Carter and Clinton, but otherwise started leaning Republican with Richard Nixon in 1968. Yet, given its statewide registration figures, Kentucky must still be considered a Democratic-leaning state, 57 percent to the Republicans' 36 percent. Kentucky also only elected a single, one-term Republican governor from 2003 to 2007 after decades of Democrats. For the past 10 years, the state legislature was split with the state Senate dominated by Republicans, and the state House of Representatives dominated by Democrats.[10] Democrats have been on the rebound since 2007 with the election of Governor Steve Beshear and a nearly complete party sweep of independently elected cabinet offices.[11]

While the causes and evidence of split-ticket voting decisions are complex,[12] these different national and statewide electoral results in Kentucky imply that statewide candidates must work harder and more personally for votes. For example, in 2004, George W. Bush won Kentucky by 20 percent over John Kerry and voters went 3:1 in favor of a gay marriage ban in the state Constitution. On the other hand, Kentucky's junior Senator, Jim Bunning, also a conservative Republican, won reelection by just 2 percent against a little-known Democratic state senator. Although a less dramatic difference in 2008, John McCain won almost 300,000 more votes than Barack Obama (57 to 41%). Senator McConnell's victory, however, was just a third of that margin, with almost 107,000 votes more than Lunsford (53 to 47%).[13]

Senator McConnell obviously did not have to worry about an Obama coattail effect in 2008 and probably benefited in reverse. With a relatively low African-American population (under 8%) and widespread assumption of racism among Kentucky's White rural voters, all of the campaign officials interviewed said unequivocally and unsolicited that Bruce Lunsford suffered by being one spot below Barack Obama on the ballot instead of Hillary Clinton (who won the Kentucky primary easily in May of 2008).

While McConnell would have had a tougher reelection in 2008 even with a Democrat who was more popular in the state heading the ballot, Kentucky's political culture allowed him to be judged on his own merits, outside a state and national party environment that was increasingly hostile to Republicans. McConnell had become, in the words of several political insiders, "his own institution."

Electoral and Political Context of the 2008 Election Cycle

McConnell's sudden vulnerability had little to do with statewide issues. There was no particular scandal at home involving Kentucky's senior Senator and there was no widespread sense that other than being a Republican in a bad moment for Republicans that he was a bad "fit" for Kentucky. McConnell would not have been challenged as effectively as he was in 2008, however, if the Republican Party and President Bush were not held so low in popular opinion. In Kentucky, President Bush's approval rating declined steadily from 2005 to 2008. His monthly approval rating hovered in the high to low 40s in 2005, the low 40s to high 30s in 2006, and then stayed in the 30s for both 2007 and 2008, with the exception of two months that reached 41 percent approval.[14] Interestingly, one of Lunsford's advisors said in an interview that the Democrats needed to keep in mind that Kentucky did vote for President Bush twice and thus the campaign needed to tread a delicate line between exploiting the GOP downturn while still understanding the mentality of a fundamentally conservative state. Bush-bashing was necessary, but it might turn off prized independent voters whose political choices were more complex and personal than the Democrats could expect.

The Incumbent: Republican Mitch McConnell

Senator McConnell was not dragged into politics. He said the night of his 2008 election that "[c]ampaigns like this force you to work harder, and they remind you what a privilege it is to serve. But public service has always been a special privilege for me. Growing up, most kids want to be baseball players. I wanted to be a U.S. Senator."[15] Addison Mitch McConnell, Jr. was born in Alabama, where he received treatment for polio as a child, but was largely raised and educated in Kentucky. McConnell showed early political ambition by winning three positions as some form of student body president: in high school in Louisville, as an undergraduate at the University of Louisville, and then president of the Student Bar Association at the University of Kentucky Law School. After he completed law school, McConnell worked for two liberal/moderate Republican Senators from Kentucky: John Sherman Cooper and Marlow Cook. McConnell then became a deputy assistant attorney general under President Gerald Ford. His first elected position in Kentucky was serving as County Judge-Executive in Jefferson County, which includes Louisville—the state's most populous and liberal county—from 1978 to 1984. McConnell's two Senate mentors also held this once-powerful post (now defunct due to county government reorganization).[16]

The start of McConnell's Senate career was in 1984, when he squeaked ahead of two-time Democratic Senate incumbent Walter "Dee" Huddleston *by less than one-half of one percentage point* and became the first Republican to win a Senate seat from Kentucky in almost 20 years. McConnell won in an upset in part by riding President Reagan's long coattails, and winning Louisville and Lexington. In addition, the election was quickly sewn into Kentucky lore in a humorous "hound dog" television ad campaign that showed a "search" for the incumbent Huddleston, who McConnell argued missed too many votes in Washington to be a potent voice for the state. Since then, McConnell's career theme was consistent: be present on Capitol Hill, climb the ladder, and deliver the goods.[17]

Over two and a half decades in the Senate, McConnell climbed the ranks on the Agriculture, Nutrition and Forestry, and Appropriations Committees as well as the party leadership ladder. In 2002, he was elected to be Assistant Majority Leader and after the Republicans were relegated to the minority after the 2006 election he was promoted to Minority Leader, which he retained after the 2008 election. Among other national policy stances, he supported agricultural policy, especially federal payouts for tobacco farmers' transition into other crops, and appropriations for Kentucky's universities, infrastructure, and community centers across the state.[18] In Washington, McConnell has long been considered a conservative Republican motivated by an ambitious pragmatism rather than ideological fervor on any one issue, the one exception being his near absolutist stance on First Amendment issues. His ideological and party vote scores, however, have been consistently conservative through the Clinton and George W. Bush administrations (see Table 3.1). McConnell's presidential support scores were consistent with this pattern—his support for Clinton was much lower than for Bush. During the Bush years, McConnell voted with his party on most culture war issues, taxation, and the war on terror, but never wavered from bringing home federal dollars (even while repositioning himself as a deficit hawk in 2009).[19]

Despite this conservative record, and clear loyalty to President George W. Bush, in 2008 Senator McConnell always played up his political position—rather than his political ideology—to the people of Kentucky. Senator McConnell's defense during the year of "change" turned the recession and accompanying anti-Republican tide on its head. His main argument was that the Commonwealth would benefit from his power and prestige, regardless of who won the White House and which party held the majority in Congress. While John McCain campaigned against federal spending earmarks during his presidential run, McConnell touted in detail his efforts to deliver benefits to his constituents, with the underlying message that the Senator put Kentucky first.[20] In this way,

Table 3.1 Congressional Vote Scores for Mitch McConnell, 1993–2008

Year	American Conservative Union	Americans for Democratic Action	Presidential Support	Party Unity
2008	80	20	76	97
2007	92	10	86	95
2006	84	5	91	96
2005	100	5	93	99
2004	96	15	98	99
2003	84	10	100	99
2002	100	0	96	97
2001	96	5	97	98
2000	100	5	42	99
1999	84	0	33	95
1998	92	0	39	95
1997	88	5	59	97
1996	95	10	39	95
1995	91	0	24	95
1994	92	5	37	92
1993	79	15	28	94

Source: 1993-2006 scores from various editions of CQ's *Politics in America;* 2007–2008 American Conservative Union (ACU) and Americans for Democratic Action (ADA) scores from the organization Web sites; 2007–2008 party unity and presidential support scores from *CQ Weekly Report.*

McConnell turned his main liability—being a key member of the Republican Washington establishment—into an asset by distancing himself from President Bush, Republicans in Congress, and his own party's presidential candidate, all the while maintaining and promoting his stature as the most important Republican in Congress in 2008 (and probably the most important Republican in all of Washington in 2009).[21]

The Challenger: Democrat Bruce Lunsford

Bruce Lunsford is a Kentucky native who has lived in-state most of his life and, like McConnell, earned degrees from its public institutions: the University of Kentucky for his undergraduate degree and Northern Kentucky University for his law degree. In the late 1970s, Lunsford was active in the state Democratic Party as Treasurer and had high-profile roles in the campaign and administration of Democratic Governor John Y. Brown Jr., who remained close to the candidate in 2008. Lunsford was appointed by Brown as the state's first Commerce Secretary and had a large hand in developing the Northern Kentucky airport near Cincinnati as a Delta hub, which helped revitalize that region of the state. Lunsford is also a certified public accountant, who in the 1980s founded a large nursing home and health care company, currently known as Kindred Healthcare.

While no longer owned by him, this company's history in its earlier forms proved a consistent burden when Lunsford decided to enter politics. In the late 1990s, Lunsford's company, then known as Vencor, was involved in a federal civil suit over alleged wrongdoing. Meanwhile, throughout this time, Lunsford gave millions to both Democratic and Republican Party candidates and committees, which probably did not help him win over the Democratic establishment. In his defense, these past actions reflected what one advisor called Lunsford's "bipartisan" and "problem-driven" mindset that served Lunsford well in his business ventures. At the time he ran for Senate in 2008, Lunsford's current business interests were less controversial, including a private investment firm, horse racing, and independent film production.[22]

While Lunsford had no discernible record as a policy advocate, in 2003 he ran in the Democratic gubernatorial primary and spent about $8 million of his own money. This raised some eyebrows, but not as much as his other political maneuvers. First, after Democratic rival Ben Chandler, then-state Attorney General and son of a former governor, raised the Vencor settlement issues in an ad campaign, Lunsford dropped out at the last minute and endorsed Democrat Jody Richards, speaker of the state House. Chandler won the primary and Lunsford then endorsed the Republican nominee, Congressman Ernie Fletcher, who won in November. Lunsford then served on Fletcher's transition committee. In interviews and media accounts, this "betrayal" of Democrats in 2003 is considered Lunsford's main "baggage"—even more so than his complex heath care businesses.

In 2007, three Democratic tickets of governor/lieutenant governor contested the primary and Lunsford's ticket came in second. His partisan loyalties were considered thin and malleable by some Democrats and Republicans that year, based on his behavior four years earlier and the fact that the same Republican Governor Fletcher was running for reelection.[23] In 2008, the primary choice was mainly between Lunsford and a lower-profile Democratic businessman who had more establishment support; Lunsford won with 51 percent.[24] One Lunsford advisor said that these past statewide runs certainly helped the candidate's name recognition, but perhaps in a year of "change" Lunsford was not a sufficiently fresh face to unloose Senator McConnell's considerable hold on Kentucky's political culture.

Strategies and Tactics in the Campaign

Senator McConnell is a prodigious fundraiser and fierce campaigner known for attacking challengers on personal and political vulnerabilities. McConnell has a reputation in Kentucky for defining his opponents negatively early, and 2008 was no different. McConnell simply asked, "Who is Bruce Lunsford?" and made Lunsford's business success, personal wealth, and homes in multiple states all look to be mysterious and nonrepresentative of Kentucky's interests.[25] Bruce

Lunsford was not able to overcome this negativity despite the fact that Senator McConnell's own approval fell throughout the fall as the economy worsened and Republicans nationally (including John McCain) suffered one political blow after another.[26] Using television ads tailored to each part of the state, direct mail, and a two-week final bus tour making over 60 campaign appearances in small towns, McConnell defended his unique position in Washington, while keeping the heat on Lunsford and repeatedly saying only he knew how to deliver.

During the campaign Lunsford tried to paint his personal and business history as a Horatio Alger story of rags to riches: a blue collar and agricultural family produced an entrepreneurial success that benefited Kentucky. McConnell, however, painted Lunsford's complex business interests as being built on greed and ethical lapses. McConnell's campaign also tried to portray Bruce Lunsford as a wealthy outsider, highlighting his homes and business ventures outside of Kentucky.[27] Despite his rocky relations with other prominent Democrats, Lunsford tried to minimize these liabilities with endorsements from the state's four previous Democratic governors in a television ad touting his job creation in Kentucky.[28] Lunsford also made several appearances with important Democrats, such as Louisville-area congressman John Yarmuth and mayor Jerry Abramson, as well as state attorney general Jack Conway, all of whom were not particularly well-known or liked by rural voters.[29]

Lunsford's portrayal of himself as a populist was in constant competition with McConnell's repeated description of him as a wealthy and shady businessman.[30] In a surprising attack ad that focused on the lesser-known spin-off of Lunsford's health care company, McConnell accused Lunsford of neglecting veterans' medical care. This dramatic and negative image stuck.[31] Strategists on both sides said McConnell did not need to, or care to, exploit other business vulnerabilities of Lunsford's related to the late 1990s bankruptcy and federal civil suit, in part because McConnell's wife Elaine Chao sat on one of those company's boards. Even as one of McConnell's advisors said in an interview that his campaign team had shown restraint against Lunsford, a Lunsford advisor described the attacks on his business record as part of McConnell's long utilization of "the politics of personal destruction."

In late 2007, national antiwar groups began airing ads against Senator McConnell's support for President Bush and the Iraq war.[32] Bruce Lunsford picked up on this strategy and attacked Senator McConnell most consistently on his close connection to the national Republican Party and the policies of outgoing President Bush, both obvious targets in 2008. This was the most important and successful message of Lunsford's campaign, according to all the sources interviewed. He was less successful in challenging McConnell's assertions about his appropriations prowess; Lunsford tried to argue he could deliver more federal money and services to Kentucky than McConnell and that McConnell overstated the amount of federal dollars he brought to Kentucky. All of the campaign professionals interviewed agreed this strategy did not work.

Those interviewed also added that they were surprised that Lunsford did not successfully exploit McConnell's clear help for President Bush in securing the first finance industry bailout in October 2008, which was not popular in Kentucky. According to one poll, Lunsford was supported by 61 percent of voters who rated the economy as the top issue in the fall election.[33] Part of the reason for Lunsford's tepid response was, according to sources on both sides of the race, that he did not articulate his own position on the bailout and seemed privately and publicly unsure how he would have voted had he been in the Senate.[34] In a television ad, for example, Lunsford alluded to this issue as well as the conviction of McConnell's close colleague Sen. Ted Stevens (R-AK), but did not hit them very hard.[35] In the end, Lunsford's arguments and strategies failed to undermine McConnell's main argument of being deeply useful to Kentucky.

While Lunsford tried to paint Senator McConnell as being tied to Bush's hip, such efforts were undermined by McConnell's party separation strategy. Research on congressional elections shows that high levels of partisan voting in Congress often results in a potent strategy for challengers in certain circumstances.[36] According to strategists on both sides, 2008 was the most favorable political environment for Democrats to win McConnell's seat but Lunsford was not the person to do it. On the other hand, McConnell presented himself as much more than President Bush's "water boy" in the words of one political reporter; he had his own reputation to lean on. Under some political conditions that punish incumbents, this description would be a liability, but that argument did not stick in 2008 against McConnell. This outcome is familiar in U.S. politics as loyalty to incumbents can transcend partisan loyalty or criticism.[37] At the same time, exit polls in Kentucky show that on several questions related to the economy, the worse people saw the situation to be, the greater the support they had for Bruce Lunsford. Those who were most worried about terrorism and the war in Iraq showed greater support for Mitch McConnell.[38]

McConnell's campaign was primarily about his own strengths and secondarily about Lunsford's weaknesses. He tailored several similar television ads to each part of the state to explain how much and where the money went to benefit Louisville, Central Kentucky, and Northern Kentucky.

Lunsford, interestingly, was not the central point of 2008 even within his own campaign; rather, the battle cry of the Democrats was "Ditch Mitch." Jennifer Duffy, of the nonpartisan *Cook Political Report*, reported that Lunsford was the fourth or fifth choice of statewide Democrats for 2008, but only Lunsford had the personal funds to make the race interesting.[39] One Kentucky Democratic insider who was a field organizer for Lunsford said there was not much love lost between Lunsford and his soldiers in the field. This person personally expressed a personal dislike for Lunsford as a candidate and described the campaign manager Bradley Katz's strategy of "A.A."—Lunsford was an "acceptable alternative" to McConnell and should be presented as such to voters. A Republican strategist involved in the McConnell campaign noticed at opposition rallies there were seas of "Ditch Mitch" T-shirts and signs, not "Lunsford for Senate." Even one of Lunsford's own top advisors agreed that a snappy answer to the crucial question "Why vote for Lunsford?" eluded the campaign.

The Horserace

The horserace in Kentucky did not get interesting until the final stretch of the long campaign. Early on, national political analysts who followed public opinion closely showed McConnell comfortably ahead.[40] Bruce Lunsford only narrowed the gap significantly toward the end. For example, Larry Sabato's Crystal Ball Web site entries over the course of the 2008 election showed weaker support for McConnell as the year progressed.[36]

As economic news worsened from late summer through the end of the race, however, the most important issue in Kentucky was jobs. Exit polls clearly show that the economy mattered most to Kentuckians in the fall of 2008—59 percent of all voters cited this as the most important issue—and McConnell's voting record in support of President Bush's fiscal policies made him vulnerable.[41] While Republicans suffered in this environment, McConnell's longstanding ability to get earmarks for Kentucky's universities, infrastructure, farmers, and urban areas was a fitting message at this time. Although the Iraq war was an important issue in the early part of the presidential campaign, Lunsford could not have exploited it as well as the economic downturn because Kentuckians still supported the war more than most other states.

Lunsford's support peaked twice—once in May after he won the primary and, more tellingly, in the middle of October when the first Wall Street bailout dominated the news. In October, Senator McConnell still held a 51 percent to 44 percent lead on Lunsford, with 5 percent undecided, according to an October 28 poll of voters in the state.[42] Just the previous week, McConnell was ahead by several points, however. As the fall continued, the race went up and down, but McConnell's baseline of support continued to range from the mid-40s to the low 50s, which kept him in the lead even as Lunsford gained steadily from the high 30s to the high 40s.[43]

Money: Record-Breaking War Chests

Mitch McConnell built a substantial war chest well in advance of the fall campaign, as he had done in previous races, and had $7.7 million on hand at the time Lunsford won the primary in May (see Table 3.2). According to the Center for Responsive Politics, McConnell's contributions from political action committees (PACs) were around a quarter of his total financing while Lunsford's were much less—around 4 percent—which is typical for incumbents and challengers, respectively. McConnell's campaign war chest was dominated by individual contributions, which made up 60 percent of his total funds, with about 16 percent coming from self-financed contributions and $2 million in bank loans. When polls showed the race tightening beginning in late September, these loans got a lot of local press attention as McConnell financed a blizzard of new television ads in the final weeks of the campaign in response to the Democratic Senatorial Campaign Committee's (DSCC) infusion of ads and money in support of Lunsford.[44]

Table 3.2 Campaign Finance Data for Kentucky Senate Seat, 1984–2008

Year	Disbursements		Receipts		Vote percent	
	McConnell	Opponent	McConnell	Opponent	McConnell	Opponent
2008	$21,334,523	$10,801,203	$20,991,678	$10,883,172	53	47
2002	$5,241,832	$2,189,846	$4,735,540	$2,239,125	65	35
1996	$4,669,642	$2,073, 794	$3,840,374	$1,879,343	55	43
1990	$5,074,187	$2,927,624	$4,073,583	$2,571.559	52	48
1984	$1,776,128	$2,380,239	$1,591,303	$2,189,001	50	50

Source: http://www.opensecrets.org/races/summary.php?id=KYS1&cycle=2008 [accessed on June 2, 2009]; CQ's *Politics in America* (Washington: Congressional Quarterly, Inc., 2006; 1998, 1992, and 1986)

Lunsford's campaign raised over $7 million on its own. Individual contributions to Lunsford's campaign only totaled 16 percent of his total with the bulk (80%) of his cash coming from loans made by Lunsford to his campaign. Beyond his own campaign's resources, Lunsford benefited from almost $3.5 million from the DSCC. This ranked eighth out of 18 races supported by the party, which spent anywhere between $1.5 to 12.5 million in independent expenditures. Notably, independent expenditures from the National Republican Senatorial Committee were negligible.[45] This is no surprise, however, given the huge resource advantage McConnell enjoyed. The Kentucky Senate race was the most expensive in state history and, at more than $31 million for both sides, was the nation's second most expensive Senate race, according to the Center for Responsive Politics, with the Minnesota Senate contest (covered elsewhere in this volume) at the top.[46]

The totals on both sides imply McConnell knew he was in trouble in 2008. While it is not uncommon for powerful incumbents to raise a lot of money, what does raise eyebrows is when they *spend* a similar amount. This is a signal that the incumbent is more concerned than normal about his or her chances. For Mitch McConnell, this was a wise strategy and helped secure his reelection. One Louisville columnist in his year-end summary of political life in the state in 2008 explained that all of McConnell's funds, especially the extra $2 million, were necessary and well-used. "Polls showed McConnell and Lunsford about neck-and-neck a month before the election, but McConnell used the millions he raised and borrowed wisely and was able to pull out a 6-point win."[47]

Impact of the 2008 Presidential Contest

Kentucky was never in play at the presidential level. So it is not surprising the state barely got a dozen total visits from the Democratic and Republican candidates combined. Barack and Michelle Obama each visited only once (just before the May 20 primary). Hillary, Bill, and Chelsea Clinton, however, visited several parts of the state before the primary, which Clinton won by a large margin as predicted. In the early part of the campaign, Sen. McCain visited Kentucky twice—in April as part of his "poverty tour" and in May to address the National Rifle Association convention in Louisville.[48] In the general election, McCain visited once more. Vice presidential candidate Joe Biden also visited Kentucky just once, in September, for a fundraising dinner. Sarah Palin never visited Kentucky at all; however, both vice presidential candidates visited nearby Indiana in the fall and received news coverage and visitors from across the Ohio River in Louisville.[49] The Obama campaign had some presence in the largest metropolitan areas in the weeks before the primary, but no dominant force before the general election. Obama's campaign had a Kentucky page on his general election Web site, but it was not personalized to the state in any dramatic manner.[50]

The most obvious fact about Kentucky's presence in the 2008 presidential election drama was that Kentucky was pegged as a solid GOP state throughout the entire cycle, especially after Barack Obama won the nomination. Kentucky was one of only seven states that did not hand Obama either a primary or general election victory.[51] Significant shifts occurred in Kentucky at the end of the race that favored McCain, even as his fortunes suffered elsewhere. Over the month of October, McCain increased his support from an 8 to 10 to 12 percentage lead over Barack Obama, ending the month up 55 to 43, which was his highest showing against Obama for five months, according to Rasmussen Reports. Part of this jump was attributed to unaffiliated voters leaning heaving toward McCain. In late October, Rasmussen polling in Kentucky showed McCain leading by just 4 points among men in Kentucky. Just five days before Election Day this jumped to 58 percent to 39 percent among men (compared to 52 percent to 47 percent among women). A lopsided racial disparity continued, with White voters choosing McCain over Obama by a 59 percent to 40 percent margin and Black voters overwhelmingly backing Obama, 90 percent to 10 percent. Bucking the national trends at the end of the presidential race, Kentucky voters trusted McCain over Obama by 11 points on the economy. Unaffiliated voters in the state trusted the Republican even more, 55 percent to 37 percent. Voters in Kentucky also gave McCain the edge on national security by 22 points.[52]

As noted above, these numbers did not reflect a great affection for McCain as much as a deep dislike or distrust of Obama that negatively impacted Bruce Lunsford's chances. One senior field organizer for Lunsford said in an interview that campaign phone and door-to-door workers were explicitly instructed to downplay Lunsford's affiliation with Obama as much as possible if asked. The prevailing mode in the Lunsford campaign was to completely avoid mentioning or discussing the presidential nominee. Lunsford's extensive television advertising campaign did not mention Barack Obama or feature his image, words, or other evidence of any form of coattails strategy.

In television news interviews, Lunsford argued repeatedly that voters could separate the offices on the ballot as they had done in the past. Each of the campaign professionals interviewed for this article suggested (unsolicited) that race played a large factor in most rural counties' voting behavior and if Hillary Rodham Clinton had been the Democratic nominee, she might have won Kentucky or at least gotten closer to winning than Obama. Likewise, if Lunsford had been listed below Clinton on the ballot, he probably would have fared better and could have even won.

Why McConnell Wins by a Length

McConnell's victory speech the night of his reelection began with a quotation. "Winston Churchill once said that the most exhilarating feeling in life is to be shot at—and missed. After the last few months, I think what he really meant to say is that there's nothing more exhausting. This election has been both."[53] The race was intense and expensive because McConnell had to prove himself worthy of the seat for the first time in decades and Republicans nationally had to "play defense" in the wake of the unpopular outgoing president. Although this race, like all others, is best understood in the state's multilayered political and cultural contexts, there are aspects of the race that lend insights into voting and political behavior more generally.

In 2008, it seems Kentucky voters punished Senator McConnell more than Senator McCain for being a Republican loyal to the signature policies of President Bush. As the data in Table 3.3 demonstrate, McConnell ran behind the Republican presidential nominee in rural areas, micropolitan areas, and all metropolitan areas other than the city of Louisville. In fact, McConnell's victory margin was larger than McCain's in only four of 120 counties in Kentucky. At the same time, according to the state party political strategists and news analysts interviewed, McCain's high margin of victory did not imply high levels of support for him personally or the party but rather fear and distrust of Barack Obama. Both McCain and McConnell struggled to distance themselves from President Bush and their burdens had different origins and consequences for the election. All seven insiders agreed that McConnell's position as party leader made his floor votes and public rhetorical support crucial to the President's legislative goals for both terms. The trick for McConnell was to temporarily divorce

Table 3.3 Kentucky Election Results by Geographic Area, 2008

Region	Counties	McCain	McConnell	Difference
City of Louisville	1 (Jefferson)	43.5%	44.3%	(0.8%)
City of Lexington	1 (Fayette)	46.9%	45.9%	1.1%
Other metropolitan areas	33	60.4%	57.5%	2.9%
Micropolitan areas	26	64.1%	55.8%	8.3%
Rural areas	59	63.0%	53.8%	9.2%

Note: Metropolitan areas have at least one urban cluster with 50,000 or more persons. Micropolitan areas have at least one urban cluster with 10,000 or more persons. Negative numbers in *parentheses*.

Source: Compiled by the author from www.census.gov/population/www/metroareas/lists/2007/List1.txt and www.elect.ky.gov/results/2008gen.htm [accessed on June 2, 2009].

himself from this policy loyalty that enabled him to climb the party ladder and convince voters that the Commonwealth was always his first priority.

In Kentucky, McConnell swam successfully against the national tide because he spoke the language of representation: Kentucky is a poor state and relies openly on federal assistance in both urban and rural areas, from the state universities' elite researchers to unemployed blue-collar families to financially insecure farmers. McConnell's Washington career and campaign themes have long centered on political clout for Kentucky. Separating himself from the woes of his party, McConnell's personal brand is defined by an economic connection to all parts of the state. This relationship is continuous, demanding, and sets clear rules for each side: support for McConnell will result in some form of federal assistance.[54] McConnell put it bluntly: "The guy running against me, if he was successful, would be a rookie. Do you want to send Kentucky to the back bench with little or no influence?"[55] This very line of thinking, however, reveals a potential vulnerability if he is perceived as not sticking to his promises. A week after the election, an editorial in *The Hazard Herald* reminded McConnell not to forget the economically disadvantaged East.

> While we realize that Sen. McConnell has a number of duties to attend to in Washington while being the leader of his party in the Senate, there are a myriad of responsibilities right here in his own state that need attending to as well.... The senator from Louisville campaigned on the power he wields in Washington, and he has again gained the majority of votes from his home state. Now is not the time to rest with the knowledge that another six years have been gained, but to put into action the words heard on the campaign trail. The people deserve no less.[56]

In this story of power and representation, there is also a lesson for political challengers. Lunsford did better than any other challenger to McConnell since his first reelection in 1990, but left some wondering if he had turned over every stone. Lunsford did not attack McConnell's vulnerabilities and he had to play defense himself because his prior business practices were a distracting issue. In an election postmortem, a columnist for the *Lexington Herald-Leader* said Lunsford failed to hammer McConnell on three specific issues: McConnell's close relationship with the deeply unpopular (even for Kentucky) President Bush; McConnell's unhesitant support for the $700 billion October financial industry bailout; and McConnell's personal and political closeness to Senator Ted Stevens, who at that time had recently been convicted of three federal felony counts just before the election.[57]

Top strategists on both sides said in interviews that Lunsford's main reason for running was his "ego" and need to erase the previous losses. Lunsford looked to be an appealing candidate: he had personal wealth that he could use to fund the campaign (this also helped his popularity with state and national Democrats) and he had some inborn political skills (he was smart, charming, and remembers names very well). The consensus during and after the 2008 race, however, was that Bruce Lunsford did not provide the strongest possible threat to Senator McConnell. Apparently, more established Kentucky Democrats were waiting until the more vulnerable Senator Bunning ran for reelection in 2010. Personal wealth, a bipartisan political history, and good timing appeared not to be a match against a dyed-in-wool politician.

McConnell fought off Lunsford by emphasizing his credentials as a representative and downplaying his national connections. He admitted as much after the election was over, seemingly thankful that he survived the tough election year. Senator McConnell said in January, 2009, on the *Today Show*: "Well, I was a strong supporter of the President [Bush], but presidential unpopularity is bad for the president's party. We suffered losses in '06 and '08. We wish President Bush well. But frankly, [in 2010] we will not have to be carrying that sort of political burden that we carried the last two elections."[58] Luck and timing played into it too: if Bunning and McConnell's election schedule had been reversed, with McConnell running for reelection in 2004 and Bunning in 2008, Bunning would likely be out.

Above all else, the campaign professionals interviewed agreed that McConnell is deeply tuned in to his strengths and weaknesses. Rural and small town voters know he is not one of them—not a farmer or the son of a coal miner, and does not have extensive military experience. Since his first statewide election in 1984, McConnell is associated with Louisville in the minds of many rural Kentucky voters. He does not have a symbolic/descriptive representative mindset—nor do they.[59] These voters are old fashioned enough to want the candidate to justify his record and come ask them face-to-face for support. In 2008, McConnell went county by county on the stump. It is about substance: What did you do for me lately? Nationally, Democrats were hoping to unseat the party leader, as happened to Senator Tom Daschle (D-SD) in 2004 and Rep. Tom Foley (D-WA) in 1994. McConnell was tuned into that vulnerability when he said on the campaign trail: "unlike six years ago, it's not going to be a coronation. It was fun getting 65 percent of the vote and carrying 113 out of 120 counties [in 2002]. That was then, and this is now. And what is different is that your senator is a lot bigger target than he used to be."[60]

Notes

1. Gary C. Jacobson, *Money in Congressional Elections* (New Haven, CT: Yale University Press, 1980) and Gary C. Jacobson, "Money and Votes Reconsidered: Congressional Elections, 1972–1982," *Public Choice* 47 (1985): 7–62.
2. Paul S. Herrnson, *Congressional Elections: Campaigning at Home and in Washington*, 4th ed. (Washington, DC: CQ Press, 2004), 29.
3. For a comprehensive review of key concepts and literature in the study of representation see http://plato.stanford.edu/entries/political-representation/.
4. To make these arguments, I rely on public data, media reports, and interviews with seven people knowledgeable about the race (two closely involved with Kentucky Republicans and Senator McConnell, three with Democrats and Lunsford, and two veteran statewide political reporters, each affiliated with one of the two largest-circulation newspapers).

5. Census Bureau, State and County QuickFacts, http://quickfacts.census.gov/qfd/states/21000.html (accessed January 30, 2009).

6. U.S. Census Bureau, Statistics of U.S. Businesses, 2001, Kentucky, http://www.census.gov/epcd/susb/2001/ky/KY--.HTM#table3 (accessed June 7, 2009); see also http://www.statemaster.com/state/KY-kentucky/ind-industry (accessed June 7, 2009).

7. The Association of Religion Data Archives, Evangelical Protestant States (2000), http://www.thearda.com/QuickLists/QuickList_64.asp.

8. Frank Newport, "Church Attendance Lowest in New England, Highest in South," Gallup, http://www.gallup.com/poll/22579/Church-Attendance-Lowest-New-England-Highest-South.aspx.

9. See Republican National Committee, 2008 Platform, "Values" Section, http://www.gop.com/2008Platform/Values.htm; Guttmacher Institute, *State Facts about Abortion: Kentucky*, http://www.guttmacher.org/pubs/sfaa/kentucky.html; CNN.com Election Results: Ballot Measures, November, 2004, http://www.cnn.com/ELECTION/2004/pages/results/ballot.measures/; Brady Campaign to Prevent Gun Violence, *Kentucky Gun Laws: Brady State Scorecard 2008*, http://www.stategunlaws.org/viewstate.php?st=KY; Behavioral Risk Factor Surveillance System study, as reported in the *Washington Post*, May 26, 2006, http://www.washingtonpost.com/wp-srv/health/interactives/guns/ownership.html.

10. http://www.lrc.ky.gov/orgadm.htm (accessed April 13, 2009).

11. SurveyUSA, Survey News Poll 11478, December, 2006, "Do You Approve or Disapprove the Job Ernie Fletcher is doing as Governor?" http://www.surveyusa.com/client/PollReport.aspx?g=a3755e2c-daa4-4239-a0f0-748f3d0ae28e.

12. For a recent overview of split-ticket voting studies, see Jeffrey A. Karp and Marshall W. Garland, "Ideological Ambiguity and Split Ticket Voting," *Political Research Quarterly* 60(2007): 722–32.

13. See http://elect.ky.gov/NR/rdonlyres/1283C01A-3F26-4821-8336-5878446F15E4/173402/STATE.TXT for official Kentucky election outcomes and http://www.cnn.com/ELECTION/2008/results/individual/#mapSKY for additional data.

14. SurveyUSA, Presidential Approval, Adults in Kentucky, May, 2005 through December, 2008, http://www.surveyusa.com/client/PollTrack.aspx?g=eaaa48ca-8770-4081-b879-faaced5ac45a.

15. Text of Senator McConnell's election night victory speech, http://www.wave3.com/Global/story.asp?S=9294377.

16. Ourcampaigns.com for details about Senator McConnell's political resume, http://www.ourcampaigns.com/CandidateDetail.html?CandidateID=41

17. The "hounds" ad campaign went immediately and deeply into Kentucky political lore—so much so that Bruce Lunsford's campaign in 2008 used the exact concept against Sen. McConnell, down to the running dogs, a bearded man in a flannel shirt holding the leashes, and a suited man representing the incumbent going up a tree. See two different "bloodhound" ads from the 1984 campaign, http://www.youtube.com/watch?v=_K4KOhlZR9s and http://www.youtube.com/watch?v=T4-4EPc2xvU; Lunsford's reversal of the bloodhound trail in 2008 can be seen at http://www.youtube.com/watch?v=rC8QSGvRDLE.

18. For a variety of vote and issue positions, see http://www.sourcewatch.org/index.php?title=Mitch_McConnell.

19. Halimah Abdullah, "Profile of Mitch McConnell: Versed in the Ways of Power," *Lexington Herald-Leader* (KY), October 21, 2008, http://www.kentucky.com/181/story/562661.html.

20. See for example different spots that showcased federal appropriations for Louisville, http://www.youtube.com/watch?v=PFgRKl9-MIM); Northern Kentucky, http://www.youtube.com/watch?v=Rbi265Q8omE, and Central Kentucky, http://www.youtube.com/watch?v=mi-_aZz5oGw.

21. This kind of delicate dance between national partisanship and district focus in Congress is a key to long-term electoral and political success (e.g., David R. Mayhew, *Congress: The Electoral Connection* (New Haven, CT: Yale University Press, 1974).

22. http://www.ontheissues.org/senate/Bruce_Lunsford.htm.

23. Patrick Crowly, "Lunsford's Party Loyalty May be Issue," *Kentucky Enquirer*, February 26, 2007, posted at http://news.cincinnati.com/apps/pbcs.dll/article?AID=/20070226/NEWS0103/702260362/1077/COL02.

24. http://www.ontheissues.org/senate/Bruce_Lunsford.htm.

25. http://www.youtube.com/watch?v=_KHCcLHooVM.

26. For McConnell approval data, see http://www.ourcampaigns.com/Candidate Detail.html?CandidateID=41&ShowAllPoll=Y; Rasmussen Reports, October28, 2008, http://www.rasmussenreports.com/public_content/politics/election_20082/2008_senate_elections/kentucky/election_2008_kentucky_senate.

27. Jack Brammer, "Profile of Bruce Lunsford: Real Rags-to-Riches Tale," *Lexington Herald-Leader* (KY), October 20, 2008, http://www.kentucky.com/181/story/561558.html.

28. http://www.youtube.com/watch?v=vPqL0Yd_j-s

29. Trey Pollard, "Top Democrats Praise Lunsford in Louisville," PolitickerKy.com, June 13, 2008, http://www.politicker.com/kentucky/6488/top-democrats-praise-lunsford-louisville.

30. Jill Laster, "Candidate Profile: Bruce Lunsford," *Kentucky Kernel*, October 30, 2008, http://kykernel.com/2008/10/30/candidate-profile-bruce-lunsford/.

31. http://www.youtube.com/watch?v=0JVJIvSfxIQ.

32. http://www.youtube.com/watch?v=FkG4JpXGXoA.

33. Rasmussen Reports, 2008 Election: Kentucky Presidential Election, October 28, 2008, http://www.rasmussenreports.com/public_content/politics/election_20082/2008_presidential_election/kentucky/election_2008_kentucky_presidential_election.

34. However, one of Lunsford's advisors said in an interview that the legislation was too complex for Lunsford to be pushed into a quick decision and defended his need to digest the bills that were controversial in the state. After all, the advisor said, Bunning and McConnell voted in the opposite manner and Louisville's Democratic congressman John Yarmuth changed his mind from "no" on the first vote to "yes" on the second.

35. http://www.youtube.com/watch?v=jidL3Q_JbeA.

36. Jamie L. Carson, "Strategy, Selection, and Candidate Competition in U.S. House and Senate Elections," *The Journal of Politics* 67(2005): 1–28.

37. See William J. Keefe and Marc J. Hetherington, *Parties, Politics, and Public Policy in America*, 9th ed. (Washington, DC: CQ Press, 2003).

38. Kentucky exit poll data taken from CNN.com, http://www.cnn.com/ELECTION/2008/results/polls/#KYS01p1 (accessed June 10, 2009).

39. Halimah Abdulla, "Election Precedent Set—Senate, Presidential Fund-Raising Break Records," *Lexington Herald-Leader* (KY), November 9, 2008.

40. Real Clear Politics, Kentucky Senate 2008, http://www.realclearpolitics.com/epolls/2008/senate/ky/kentucky_senate-917.html.

41. Kentucky exit poll data taken from CNN.com,http://www.cnn.com/ELECTION/2008/results/polls/#val=KYS01p1 (accessed June 10, 2009).

42. Rasmussen Reports, October28, 2008, http://www.rasmussenreports.com/public_content/politics/election_20082/2008_senate_elections/kentucky/election_2008_kentucky_senate

43. See a summary of polling data in Real Clear Politics, Kentucky Senate 2008, http://www.realclearpolitics.com/epolls/2008/senate/ky/kentucky_senate-917.html (accessed February 9, 2009).

44. Joseph Gerth, "McConnell $2 Million in Debt," *The Courier-Journal* (Louisville, KY), December 7, 2008.

45. A First Look at Money in the House and Senate Elections, November 6, 2008, Campaign Finance Institute, George Washington University, Table 6: All Senate Races, 2008, http://www.cfinst.org/congress/pdf/Table6_PostElec.pdf; A First Look at Money in the House and Senate Elections, November 6, 2008, Campaign Finance Institute, George Washington University, Table 7: Independent Expenditures by National Party Committees in the 2008 Congressional General Election (Reported through November 3, 2008), http://www.cfinst.org/congress/pdf/Table7_PostElec.pdf.

46. Halimah Abdullah, "McConnell Campaign in Debt—Nearly $2 Million Borrowed for 2008 Run," *Lexington Herald-Leader* (KY), December 10, 2008.

47. Joseph Gerth, "Political Notebook: A Look Back at What 2008 Brought Kentucky," *The Courier-Journal* (Louisville, KY), December 29, 2008.

48. For news summaries of both visits, see http://www.reuters.com/article/topNews/idUSN2343192120080423 and http://www.youtube.com/watch?v=juwXH3P0NXg.

49. http://www.gwu.edu/~action/2008/obama/bidenstatevisits.html; http://www.gwu.edu/~action/2008/mccain/palinstatevisits.html.

50. http://my.barackobama.com/page/content/kyhome .

51. Joseph Gerth, "Political Notebook: A Look Back at What 2008 Brought Kentucky," *The Courier-Journal* (Louisville, KY), December 29, 2008.

52. *Rasmussen Reports, 2008 Election: Kentucky Presidential Election*, October 28, 2008, http://www.rasmussenreports.com/public_content/politics/election_20082/2008_presidential_election/kentucky/election_2008_kentucky_presidential_election.

53. Text of Senator McConnell's election night victory speech, http://www.wave3.com/Global/story.asp?S=9294377.

54. Jill Laster, "Candidate Profile: Mitch McConnell," *Kentucky Kernel*, October 30, 2008, http://kykernel.com/2008/10/30/candidate-profile-mitch-mcconnell/#more-7325 .

55. Jack Brammer and Beth Musgrave, "McConnell Blames Tight Race on Left," *Lexington Herald-Leader* (KY), October 21, 2008, http://www.kentucky.com/181/story/562710.html.

56. Editorial, "It's Time to Use Some of that Clout," *The Hazard Herald* (KY), November 12, 2008.

57. Larry Dale Keeling, "Lunsford, Dems Missed Chance to 'Ditch Mitch'—Didn't Hit McConnell on Bush, Economy, Stevens," *Lexington Herald-Leader* (KY), November 9, 2008.

58. http://thinkprogress.org/2009/01/27/mcconnell-bush-burden/.

59. Hanna Pitkin, *The Concept of Representation* (Berkeley: University of California Press, 1967).

60. Jack Brammer and Beth Musgrave, "McConnell Blames Tight Race on Left," *Lexington Herald-Leader* (KY), October 21, 2008, http://www.kentucky.com/181/story/562710.html.

4 Running Scared from the Hill and at Home
Kirk vs. Seals in Illinois's Tenth Congressional District

Wayne P. Steger

By all accounts, 2008 was supposed to be a tough year for Republican incumbents trying to retain their seats. Nationally, Republicans were saddled with an unpopular Republican president, increasingly unpopular wars, high gas prices, a looming recession, and growing budget deficits. Polls indicated widespread public dissatisfaction with the status quo on a wide range of issues and substantial support for "change." The local context also favored Democrats in Illinois, where Democrats had gained control of both chambers of the state legislature and all state-wide elected offices. Further, this particular district lies just 30 miles north of Chicago, the epicenter of Barack Obama's political base. That location translated into a substantial advantage in media coverage for the Democratic presidential nominee and considerable excitement among Democratic activists and voters throughout the area.

In 2008, most congressional elections in Illinois reflected the expected boost for Democratic candidates. Across all 19 congressional districts in Illinois, Barack Obama averaged more than 6.6 percent more of the presidential vote in 2008 than had Democratic presidential candidate John Kerry in 2004. Obama won a majority of the presidential vote in 16 of the 19 Illinois congressional districts, including the 10th District where he received more than 61 percent of the vote. The Democratic surge behind Obama seems to have had coattails in most congressional districts in Illinois, but especially in traditionally Republican districts where Democrats had the most to gain. Across the state, Democratic congressional candidates in Republican-controlled districts increased their vote share by an average of 22.2 percent over their vote share in 2004. In the end, Democrats picked up two congressional seats in traditionally Republican areas in the Chicago exurbs that had been vacated by Republican incumbents.[1]

One of those pickups, however, was not in the 10th District. The incumbent, Mark Kirk, was considered vulnerable after he won with only 53 percent of the vote against a relatively unknown challenger in 2006. Although the candidate running against Kirk, Dan Seals, was not a quality challenger in the usual sense, he posed a serious challenge to Kirk.[2] Seals entered the 2008 campaign with substantial name recognition, experience, and organization after having almost upset Kirk in the 2006 election. He also had the financial backing of the Democratic Congressional Campaign Committee (DCCC), something he lacked in his 2006 campaign. That the DCCC targeted the race is itself an indication that Washington handicappers saw this as a seat that could be won. Indeed, the *Cook Political Report*'s Partisan Voting Index (PVI), a measure of how strongly a congressional district leans toward one political party compared to the nation as a whole, rated the 10th District as D+4.[3] One week before the election, *Congressional Quarterly* declared there was "no clear favorite."[4]

Given the surge in the Democratic vote across the state, how did Mark Kirk manage to prevail again? Several factors are relevant. First, Kirk took advantage of the decentralized, pragmatic nature of American political parties that enables incumbents to deviate from party positions on issues for which local constituency preferences are not aligned with the national party line. Second, Mark Kirk typified an incumbent who was "running scared" in a swing district. Incumbents like Kirk win because they work hard to get reelected and they use their offices effectively to promote constituency interests and preferences. Contrary to many races of this type, money did not seem to be a critical factor and the battle was decided because of other factors.

The 10th Congressional District and the 2008 Elections

Given all the circumstances suggesting an upset, why did the incumbent Mark Kirk do as well in 2008 as he had in 2006? In part, the result owes to the characteristics of the voters in the district. Historically, the 10th District has been a safe seat for the Republicans. Only one Democrat had won the district since 1886, and that occurred in the wake of Watergate in 1974. However, while being historically Republican, the 10th District does not fall neatly into the stereotypes of a "Republican" or "Democratic" district. Rather, the district is a stereotypical swing district by voter characteristics and behavior. This is important because split-ticket voting remains common in moderate or swing districts like the 10th District, where a significant portion of voters have cross-pressured preferences for policy.

The district has split for the Republican candidate in the congressional elections while voting increasingly Democratic at the presidential level. The Republican incumbent, Mark Kirk, ran ahead of his party's presidential candidate in each of the last three presidential elections. Kirk ran 4 percentage points ahead of George W. Bush in 2000 and 17 percentage points ahead of him in 2004. In 2008, Kirk ran 15 percentage points ahead of John McCain. In other words, Kirk has continued to win while Democratic presidential candidates have run increasingly well in the district.

Ticket-splitting appears to result mainly from incumbency and cross-pressured voters holding candidate evaluations at odds with their partisan leanings.[5] The 10th District is often characterized as a swing district with "moderate" preferences—right of center on economics but left of center on social or cultural issues—exactly the kind of mix that could be expected to give rise to split-ticket voting. A number of Fortune 500 Companies are headquartered in the district including pharmaceutical, computer, corporate consulting, manufacturing, and food companies, along with the Great Lakes Naval Station. The 10th District is wealthy and well educated, ranked 21st of all congressional districts in terms of wealth with a median household income of $78,269 (as of 2006). Almost 48 percent of the district's adult population has a college or graduate degree and a majority of adults work in management, professional, or office occupations.[6] The district also has substantial immigrant populations from Eastern Europe as well as Asia and Latin America; this is critical for understanding local electoral outcomes as immigrants tend to have weaker ties to either political party. In addition, the 10th District also is home to one of the larger Jewish populations in the United States. Taxes, education, the environment, civil liberties, defense, and foreign policy toward Israel and the Middle East have been perennially salient issues in recent congressional campaigns. The socioeconomic and demographic composition of the district means that neither party has a lock on the loyalties of voters. So, frequent split-ticket voting is not surprising. Moreover, both parties own issues that appeal to voters in the district and both parties could assemble winning coalitions in the 10th District.

Candidate Strategies: Framing the Vote Choice through a National versus Local Lens

Both candidates pursued issue positions to attract votes and each sought to define the other as out of touch with district constituencies on key issues. The incumbent, Mark Kirk, tailored his issue positions to an economically conservative and socially moderate constituency, while portraying his Democratic opponent as a tax and spend liberal. The Democratic challenger, Dan Seals, adopted a strategy common to many Democratic challengers across the country in 2008. Seals sought to tie his fortune to Barack Obama and a message that emphasized change, while tying Mark Kirk to the Republican Administration of George W. Bush.[7] Seal's advertisements, mailings, and press releases encouraged voters to view a vote for Kirk as a vote for "more of the same." Seal's strategy, however, did not appear to resonate with a majority of voters in the 10th District. The incumbent had already established a solid reputation as a moderate, and he created even more separation between himself and his party in Washington, DC between the 2006 and 2008 elections.

Mark Kirk had long cultivated an image of a "moderate" Republican through a mix of economic conservatism and moderate social positions. Both the Americans for Democratic Action (ADA) and the American Conservative Union (ACU) consistently identified Kirk as a moderate in Congress (see Table 4.1). Throughout his congressional career, Kirk has often deviated from his party's position on roll call votes. Kirk's party unity scores averaged about 8 percentage points lower than the average Republican in Congress and more than 10 percentage points lower than the average Republican representative from Illinois from 2001 to 2008. That Kirk was generally less supportive of his party's positions is consistent with his independent image and reflects the mixture of values held by his constituents. Kirk also was less supportive of President George W.

Bush's positions on roll call votes than the average Republican in Congress or even the average Republican from Illinois. From 2001 to 2008, Kirk supported President Bush's positions over 12 percentage points less often in comparison to either group. The moderate voting record made less credible Seal's claims that a vote for Kirk is a vote for "more of the same" or a vote "for Bush."

Kirk not only established a moderate record in Congress, he sought to create greater separation from his party and his president after his close call in the 2006 election. Kirk's party unity score dropped from an average of 79.5 percent in the 109th Congress to 71.5 percent in the 110th Congress (2007–08). This figure understates Kirk's efforts to distance himself from the national party as the election approached, since he voted with his party only 66 percent of the time prior to the election in 2008.[8] Kirk's support for President Bush's position on roll call votes dropped from an average of 73.5 percent in the 109th Congress to an average of 47 percent in the 110th Congress (see Table 4.1). Kirk supported President Bush's position on only 39 percent of roll call votes before the 2008 election.[9] Kirk's voting record indicates that he voted with an eye on voters back home—he became less supportive of President Bush as the president's job approval ratings declined (see Figure 4.1). This is consistent with John Kingdon's observation that incumbents typically become less supportive of their party's president as the president's approval ratings drop.[10]

The campaign itself largely reinforced the moderate image that Kirk had cultivated and deflected Seal's charges that Kirk represented more of the same. While Seals sought to nationalize the electoral focus, Kirk kept the focus local and emphasized his contributions to his district.[11] Kirk's voting record, Web page, direct mail, and advertisements emphasized issue positions and priorities that cut across party lines. Kirk supported tax cuts and opposed tax increases, which played well in one of the most affluent districts in the country. The 10th

Table 4.1 Congressional Vote Scores for Mark Kirk, 2001–2008

Year	American Conservative Union	Americans for Democratic Action	Presidential Support	Party Unity
2008	48	55	53	73
2007	40	40	41	70
2006	54	45	80	79
2005	36	30	67	80
2004	63	45	63	84
2003	63	10	81	87
2002	76	20	85	85
2001	48	25	74	85

Source: 2001–2006 scores from various editions of *CQ's Politics in America*; 2007–2008 American Conservative Union (ACU) and Americans for Democratic Action (ADA) scores from the organization Web sites; 2007–2008 party unity and presidential support scores from *CQ Weekly Report.*

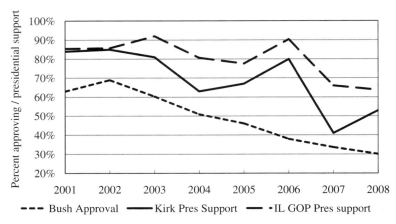

Figure 4.1 Presidential support scores of Mark Kirk, the average scores of Illinois Republican Representatives, and annually averaged presidential approval ratings, 2001–2008.
Source: Congressional Quarterly Party Support Scores, Gallup Polls, various dates.

District is home to a naval reserve base and a veterans' hospital, and Kirk consistently supported more spending on defense and veterans' health care. The district has a large number of well-educated, environmentally conscious voters and
Kirk was active in proposing legislation regarding the environmental condition
of Lake Michigan. He also backed a mixture of liberal and conservative policies
on energy supplies. Kirk supported increasing oil supplies, including offshore
drilling, but opposed opening the Arctic National Wildlife Refuge (ANWR) to
drilling. In addition, he supported increasing fuel efficiency standards and alternative energy sources. This mix of positions plays well with an environmentally
conscious population that logs a lot of miles in automobiles. Kirk also secured
federal funding for education and highways, which are both important given the
district's demographic and traffic. Additionally, he has been an avid supporter of
Israel and has taken a hard line on terrorism, Iran, and Iraq in the Middle East,
which plays well with the large Jewish population in the district.

Kirk took issue positions that reflect a complex balancing of various, sometimes conflicting preferences of his different constituencies. He developed a
centrist position on abortion by supporting rules bringing restrictive bills or
amendments to the floor, which is important for social conservatives in the
Republican Party, but voted against those measures on roll call votes, which
is apparently preferred by the majority of voters in the district. Again, showing
his tendencies to break with his party, Kirk supported gun control at home.
Kirk also hewed a complex position on the economy, as he supported lower
income and capital gains taxes and less spending on social welfare (the 10th
District ranked 432 in direct federal payments to individuals), and advocated
less government regulation of business. He also voted for the federal bailout of

the banking industry while calling for FBI investigations of corporate management.[12] These kinds of mixed positions reflect a nuanced understanding of what will be politically popular in this district.

Kirk's biggest potential problem in 2008 may have been his support for the Iraq War, which had become unpopular in the district. After supporting the war for several years, Kirk modified his position following his close call in the 2006 election. Kirk was among a group of congressional Republicans who warned President Bush of crumbling public support for the war.[13] He also broke with his party and president by endorsing a withdrawal of troops in 2007.[14] This position put him at odds with both President Bush and GOP presidential candidate John McCain who were calling for a troop surge in Iraq. The switch enabled Kirk to mute criticism of his support for the war and reduced his association with an increasingly unpopular president.

Incumbents like Kirk begin the campaign already having established name recognition, an image, a campaign organization, networks of supporters, and a winning coalition from the prior election. Challengers face the tougher task. They need to establish name recognition, cultivate a favorable image, usually from scratch, and they have to give voters a reason to reject the incumbent. In 2008, Dan Seals tried to give voters several reasons to reject Kirk. First and foremost, Seals sought to nationalize the election by associating Kirk with George W. Bush and the Republican Party. Second, Seals sought to attack Kirk on the Iraq War, for which Kirk had been a strong supporter. As noted above, however, Kirk successfully distanced himself from both George W. Bush and the Republican Party in Washington by defecting from the party line on issues that were salient in the district. By shifting positions on the Iraq War and engaging in populist outrage at high energy costs and corporate malfeasance and greed in the financial sector, Kirk denied his opponent several critical issues.

While national trends worked against the Republicans and John McCain at the national level, decentralized political parties and the collective authority of Congress enable individual incumbents to escape blame for unpopular policies and to take credit selectively for those that are popular with their voters in their districts. The collective but fragmented structure and processes of Congress make it difficult to attribute credit and blame for national conditions. The congressional parties prefer their members in Congress to follow the party line, but allow partisan members to deviate from the party line when it is electorally advantageous to do so.[15] The autonomy of individual legislators enables them to tailor their issue positions to local constituencies rather than those of the political party he or she affiliates with. To that end, Kirk's behavior typified a candidate-centered campaign in Washington and in the district. The result was an incumbent largely insulated from national trends adversely affecting the Republican Party. By separating himself from the Republican Party and distancing himself from his party's unpopular president, Kirk avoided drowning in a national Democratic tide.

Benefits and Services Only an Incumbent Can Provide

Mark Kirk is a classic career politician, having spent most of his adult life in congressional politics—first as a staffer and then chief of staff for former 10th District Representative John Porter. Though other goals matter to career politicians, reelection is an instrumental, intermediary step for the attainment of other goals.[16] While members seek reelection, they are almost always uneasy and uncertain about their reelection prospects.[17] Even large electoral margins in a previous election do not imply safety in a volatile electorate loosely anchored by partisan loyalties, such as those in swing districts.[18] Kirk typifies an incumbent whose reelection in 2008 owed in part to his behavior in office. Simply put, he ran scared.[19] Like other incumbents, he won reelection in part by taking care of his constituents—securing benefits and services for constituents, communicating with constituents, and raising money in preparation for a serious electoral challenge.[20] His opponent, Dan Seals, lacked experience in elective office and could not point to comparable accomplishments or services for the constituents of the district.

Incumbents have a substantial advantage in gathering information on constituent preferences through their congressional staffs, which operate as efficient and effective intelligence operations generating dual-use information for both legislative and campaign activities.[21] Legislators use such information for deciding how to vote on issues, what bills to sponsor, and what services to provide constituents. Knowledge of constituent concerns also informs campaign strategy, messages and images, and identifying and targeting audiences for stylized communications.

Congress as an institution accommodates members' desire to visit their constituencies by providing them with ample travel budgets and by scheduling most legislative business between Tuesday and Thursday.[22] This kind of personal outreach on official business is another dual function of the office. Legislators like Kirk solicit requests for assistance, listen to complaints, and get constituent input on policy. They also use the opportunity to explain or justify their activities in Washington in order to shore up support among loyalists, consult with their friends and allies, advertise and claim credit for programs benefiting the district, and cultivate an image of "competence, empathy, and identification as being 'one of us.'"[23] Kirk was clearly actively campaigning from the soapbox of the office during 2008. He made numerous public appearances and announcements through the summer and fall of 2008 proclaiming his success in delivering benefits for specific projects (funds for cleaning up a local harbor, Lake Michigan, education, transportation, and the Veterans Affairs hospital in the district).

Bringing money to the district is another advantage that incumbents use to help themselves in their reelections,[24] and Mark Kirk was a successful procurer of federal funds for his district, using his position on the House Appropriations Committee to help secure more contracts during election years. Election years are easy to identify in terms of federal contracts, as the 10th District ranked 126th among congressional districts receiving federal funds in 2008 compared

to 147th in 2007, 80th in 2006, 180th in 2005, and 89th in 2004.[25] While advocating less government and balanced budgets in his speeches, direct mail, and
on his Web site, Kirk used his position on the House Appropriations Committee
to fight for and secure funding for small to massive local projects for education,
immigrant programs, environmental cleanup, mass transit, highway transportation, local monies for Homeland Security at O'Hare airport, and most notably,
a massive Department of Defense–Veterans Administration hospital in the district (an expansion worth $130 million). Notably, each project yielded favorable
coverage in local news media; this kind of earned media response can be critical
in a tight congressional race, especially in a media market as expensive as Chicago (see below).

Finally, Kirk's congressional office is known for effective constituency service.[26] Members have provided themselves with enough staff support, both in
their Washington office and in their district or state offices, to provide services
to constituents that supply significant electoral benefit for legislators, even
though the number of people serviced varies considerably across districts and
states.[27] Though most congressional staffers take care to separate governing and
campaign work, congressional offices have an inseparable dual functionality.
Efforts to serve constituents have inevitable implications for the campaign and
election. Incumbents and their staffs research their constituencies, they create
and distribute programs and services tailored to the demands of their constituents, and they advertise themselves to their various constituencies. Kirk's staff is
well known for being responsive to constituents and Kirk has an active presence
in the district, all of which is a tremendous advantage come election time.[28]

Information in the Campaign

Kirk used the resources of office, such as the franking privilege, his office Web
site, and numerous press releases to explain his activities in Washington, take
credit for programs in the district, and offer services to his constituents; many
of these were featured in stories by the local press. Compared to other Illinois
Representatives, Kirk had more appearances on *Chicago Tonight*, a well watched
Chicago public television program, and other local TV and radio news programs; he also enjoyed repeated coverage in the Chicago metro- and suburban
newspapers. Kirk's exposure on TV, radio, and in print media exceeded that of
his opponent, Dan Seals, whose coverage was largely limited to stories on the
closeness of the race and for a single campaign event in which his campaign
provided cheap gas to voters.[29] These stories, however, were not all favorable as
Seals's gas giveaway caused a traffic jam.

Kirk's campaign used a mixture of heavy direct mail, radio and television
advertising, which matched the paid advertising of the Democratic challenger
and outside groups.[30] Kirk spent $1.4 million on media expenditures for the
2008 campaign, which is about what the average House Republican incumbent
spent for their entire campaign.[31] Once independent expenditures are taken
into account, the Seals campaign roughly matched the media spending by Kirk.

With this level of spending, both campaigns had ample opportunity to present their case to voters. As noted earlier, however, the messages in the local news media largely reinforced the image that Kirk sought to portray and generally ran contrary to the message portrayed by the Seals campaign.

Both campaigns emphasized issues that were salient to the constituency. Both candidates' campaign communications sought to portray themselves as supporting policies that would grow the economy while attacking the other for misguided economic policies.[32] Both sides, for example, condemned terrorist attacks on Israel, pledged strong support for Israel, and advocated a tough foreign policy toward Iran. Both sides used direct mail and television ads that related to health care, veterans' health care, energy, education, and the environment. While presidential campaigns tend to emphasize issues owned by their political party,[33] the congressional campaign in the district featured both campaigns focusing on issues that were important to constituents as well as those owned by their respective political parties, again reflecting the mixed issue preferences of voters in the 10th District.

Like other close congressional races, both sides engaged in a mixture of positive and negative advertising during the campaign. All incumbents face potential opponents who will seek to undermine their image with negative advertising, and the Seals campaign was no different. For instance, Seals was highly critical of Kirk's support for the Bush administration, particularly in regard to the war in Iraq as a misguided, mismanaged, and costly mistake. The Seals campaign also criticized Kirk on a range of issues that are "owned" by the Democratic Party (see chapter 1). For example, the campaign attacked Kirk for opposing equal pay for women and the extension of unemployment benefits in 2008, and for supporting a plan to partially privatize Social Security. The campaign also sought to undermine Kirk's image as environmentally friendly with ads and mailings associating Kirk with President Bush as well as oil companies. Interestingly, the Seals campaign also hit Kirk on issues typically perceived as owned by the Republicans. For example, the Seals campaign ads repeatedly referred to wasteful spending and economic policies that have "hurt the economy," picking up on the issues of the federal budget and spending, two issues Republican candidates have relied on for decades.

For his part, Kirk essentially tried to link Seals to fears that a Democratic president and Congress would increase taxes. In a move also consistent with the issue ownership theory, the Kirk campaign accused the Democrat of supporting higher taxes, especially capital gains taxes—an important concern given the affluence of the district. They also accused Seals of supporting greater regulation of small businesses, weakening veterans' health benefits, and of gimmickry on energy policy. Kirk even criticized Seals' ethics and thereby associated him by common label with the widely-perceived corruption of Cook County Democrats and Governor Rod Blagojevich who was under investigation by the U.S. Justice Department before the election.[34]

With two campaigns otherwise closely matched in paid media, earned media was a critical factor in this race. The flow of information during the campaign through the news media tended to contradict the Seals information strategy and reinforced Kirk's message. As an incumbent, Kirk was able to gain repeated favorable exposure in the media for securing federal funds to clean up PCBs (polychlorinated biphenyls) in Lake Michigan, opposing mercury pollution by a British Petroleum refinery in Indiana, and for extending tax credits for alternative energy development and energy conservation.[35] This support for legislation on the environment received repeated coverage in suburban newspapers. Kirk also received favorable coverage for securing funds for literacy programs for immigrants (who constitute 18% of the district's population) and for sponsoring amendments to weaken the No Child Left Behind Act.[36] Kirk received favorable news coverage on gun control for sponsoring legislation to restore the ban on assault weapons.[37] Local news was quick to cover his efforts to gain funding for the North Chicago VA Hospital, a joint Department of Defense–VA hospital in the district.[38] Kirk also gained coverage for his activities on the House Appropriations Committee where he pushed for more funding for FBI agents to investigate financial crimes, for mass and highway transit in the district, public education, and homeland security.[39] Finally, ethnic and local newspapers covered Kirk favorably for his support for sharing data with Israel from early warning satellites in Europe.[40] In short, Kirk frequently received favorable news coverage in the local print media, and on radio and TV news programs, often for appearances and announcements of programs or projects secured for the district. The incumbent used his position in Congress to secure the exposure and favorable coverage that typically advantages incumbents in congressional elections.

All of the major newspapers for the area endorsed the incumbent, including both major city newspapers and four suburban papers. The Republican-leaning *Chicago Tribune* endorsed Kirk noting that he is, "one of the most thoughtful, independent and effective members of the House. Kirk is a leader on environmental issues.... He is a strong advocate for embryonic stem-cell research. He's a workhorse on local concerns, known for having a diligent staff. Voters should look beyond partisanship and embrace their pragmatic, get-it-done congressman."[41]

The *Chicago Sun Times* called Kirk, "hard working, very knowledgeable, fiercely independent, dedicated to bipartisan action, and an effective contributor to resolving the nation's and his district's problems."[42] These newspaper endorsements matched well the image that the incumbent sought to cultivate and the messaging that he used through the campaign. The challenger, by contrast, received less news coverage and a solitary endorsement by a local paper despite being recognized as a capable candidate in all of the newspapers.[43]

Endorsements of Kirk reflected his economically conservative and socially moderate issue positions. Reflecting his positions on economic policy, taxes, and balanced budgets, Kirk received endorsements by economically conservative groups like the U.S. Chamber of Commerce and the National Federation of Independent Business. For his positions on defense and veterans' issues, Kirk garnered the endorsement of the Veterans of Foreign Wars. Although unusual for a Republican, Kirk received numerous endorsements from environmental groups including the Sierra Club, the Humane Society, League of Conservation Voters, and the National Wildlife Federation. He was even endorsed by a variety of other groups typically associated with liberal causes including Planned Parenthood, the Brady Campaign to Prevent Gun Violence, the Illinois Education Association, the National Education Association, and the Human Rights Campaign. Finally, Kirk was endorsed by Jewish groups for his positions on Israel and the Middle East.[44] In contrast, his opponent, Dan Seals, received endorsements mainly from liberal groups including a number of unions, the National Organization for Women, and a few others advocating various social welfare programs.[45] Like other aspects of the campaign, these endorsements fit with the message Kirk wanted voters to hear, especially that Seals was a typical Democratic liberal.

A Note on Money: The "Mother's Milk" of a Campaign?

Conducting a continuous campaign is expensive. While the monetary advantage of incumbents is often identified as a critical factor in explaining the success rates and electoral margins of incumbents,[46] money is a necessary but not sufficient condition for winning congressional elections. The asymmetry is that money allows candidates to compete for votes by enabling them to make their case before voters, but it does not ensure that voters will like what they see, hear, or read. The imbalances in campaign finance that we often see between incumbent and challenger spending are in large part a consequence of the relative chances of victory for the candidates. Candidates who have the characteristics that make them appealing to voters, and likely to win as a result, are the candidates who are able to raise money. Candidates who lack either the characteristics that appeal to voters or are perceived as unlikely to win are generally unable to raise much money. The interesting cases are those in which both candidates are well funded, as occurred in the 2008 congressional election in the 10th District.

While Kirk had an advantage in candidate spending, Dan Seals benefited from greater national party support. Overall, there was little difference in the spending and both sides had sufficient financial resources to make their case to voters in the 10th District. Table 4.2 shows fundraising and spending patterns in the last six elections. Though based on only six elections, there is a moderate correlation between candidates' campaign spending in the 10th District and candidates' vote shares. What seems to matter is the financial advantage of the incumbent relative to the challenger. The correlation between the ratio of incumbent to challenger spending on one hand and the ratio of incumbent to challenger vote share is $r = .415$. Kirk had a financial advantage in each of his elections, with the advantage being greatest in 2004 when Kirk faced only nominal opposition. Correlations, however, mask important variations. Kirk's spending advantage over his Democratic rival actually decreased from 2006 to 2008. Kirk outspent Dan Seals by a ratio of 1.87 to 1 in 2006, but only by a ratio of 1.53 to 1 in 2008. Kirk spent 87 percent more than Seals while gaining about

Table 4.2 Campaign Finance Data for Illinois' 10th District, 2000–2008

Year	Receipts		Disbursements		Vote	
	Kirk	Challenger	Kirk	Challenger	Kirk	Challenger
2008	$5,451,604	$3,532,528	$5,445,659	$3,566,123	52.6%	47.4%
2006	$3,168,367	$1,918,167	$3,512,971	$1,882,795	53.4%	46.6%
2004	$1,747,924	$95,992	$1,653,529	$88,520	64.1%	35.9%
2002	$1,705,510	$477,584	$1,436,056	$473,270	68.8%	31.2%
2000	$2,068,719	$1,975,304	$2,016,292	$1,967,426	51.2%	48.8%

Source: http://www.opensecrets.org/races/summary.php?id=IL10&cycle=2008 [accessed on June 4, 2009].

14 percent more of the vote in 2006; while spending 53 percent more than Seals in 2008 while gaining 11 percent more of the vote than Seals. Just taking into account candidate spending, Kirk's vote share stayed constant even as his financial advantage decreased relative to that of his challenger.

Further, the difference in spending is even less in 2008 once we take into account independent spending in support or in opposition to the candidates. According to the Center for Responsive Politics, the DCCC and other groups spent $1,030,368 in support of Dan Seals's candidacy and $1,033,180 in opposition to Mark Kirk. The National Republican Congressional Committee (NRCC) and other groups spent only $198,346 in support of Mark Kirk and nothing in opposition to Dan Seals. If these figures are added to the spending amounts of the candidates, then spending by or in support of Kirk totaled $5,644,005; while spending by or in support of Seals (or in opposition to Kirk) totaled $5,629,671. In effect, the amounts of money spent in this campaign were almost identical for the two candidates. While there are no comparable figures available for 2006, neither party committee targeted the race in 2006, which suggests that independent expenditures were negligible in that year.

Thus, while campaign spending is important, it does not fully or even marginally explain the rise in vote shares by the incumbent Mark Kirk. That is a remarkable inference when we recall that most of the exogenous factors of the state and national tides favored the Democratic challenger. Certainly money matters, otherwise candidates would not spend so much time and energy raising it, but variations in fundraising and spending do not account for much of the change in the vote from 2006 to 2008. Rather, the amounts of money raised do indicate a change in candidate behavior that likely does matter. Kirk raised substantially more funds when he faced a tougher election and reelection campaign (see Table 4.2).

If we take the 2000 race as a baseline—when the seat was open and most vulnerable to a change in party control, then we can gain insights into the behavior of the incumbent. Kirk raised about $2 million during his first congressional campaign—much of which was spent in the Republican primary against a well-funded field of politicians eager to replace the retiring John Porter. Kirk raised about $1.7 million in each of the two next cycles while facing moderately and poorly funded challengers in the two races, respectively. Kirk raised substantially larger sums in 2006 when he faced a strong challenge by Dan Seals, consistent with the hypotheses that challenger spending drives incumbent spending. Kirk was highly aggressive in raising funds following his close call in 2006, raising $5,451,604 for his 2008 campaign. Further, Kirk expanded his fundraising extensively going into 2008—raising more funds earlier, raising more funds out of state, and raising more funds from political action committees. These patterns indicate an incumbent who anticipated a tough reelection fight in 2008 and who adapted his behavior by engaging in substantial fundraising efforts. Mark Kirk's fundraising and spending patterns fit the profile of an incumbent who believed he was safe (from 2000 to 2004) and suddenly faced a tougher race in 2006 and 2008. It seems likely that the increased effort to defend the seat—represented in the financial figures—matters at least as much or more than the actual funds themselves.

Conclusions

In sum, Mark Kirk was an incumbent who ran scared. His actions in office and in the district were critical to his reelection in 2008. Mark Kirk successfully defended his seat largely because he did what incumbents do well. He and his staff paid close attention to their constituents and used that information to propose (and take credit for proposing) legislation on issues salient to constituents. He also deviated from his political party and president on issues salient to his constituents. While maintaining a relatively moderate voting record in Congress, he increasingly deviated from his party's positions in Congress after his close call in the 2006 election. Finally, he actively used his position on the Appropriations Committee to steer money into his district for a range of projects. All of these activities reinforced an image of a hard-working incumbent, in touch with his constituents, and willing to act as an "independent voice" in Washington. These activities also undermined the central claim of the challenger's campaign—that a vote for Mark Kirk would be a vote for continuation of Republican policies in Washington. The campaign itself was hard fought over the airwaves, in the media, and on the ground. Both sides spent over $5 million on the campaign (including independent expenditures in support or opposition to one of the candidates). As a close race, the campaign drew a larger than normal amount of local and national media coverage, the content of which generally reinforced the imaging and messages of the incumbent while tending to undermine that of the challenger. While national conditions were a major force in the 2008 congressional races across the country, in the battle for the 10th District, local dynamics dominated the campaign and made the difference for this vulnerable incumbent.

Notes

1. Democrats won the 8th District in 2004, which had been represented by a Republican since 1962. Democrats won the 14th District in a special election in March of 2008 to replace retiring former Speaker of the House, Dennis Hastert. Democrats also were poised to win the 11th District where Republican incumbent, Jerry Weller, was retiring.
2. Seals had never held elected office. Quality or strong challengers are typically elected officials with a constituency that overlaps that of the incumbent; see, Peverill Squire, "Challenger Quality and Voting Behavior in Senate Elections," *Legislative Studies Quarterly* 17 (1992): 247–63.
3. The index for each congressional district is the average of the district vote for the president in the prior two elections compared to the national presidential vote. See, *Cook Political Report*, PVI for the 110th Congress, http://www.cookpolitical. com/sites/default/files/pvichart.pdf.
4. *CQ News Online*, October 27, 2008.
5. See, for example, Franco Mattei and John S. Howes, "Competing Explanations of Split-Ticket Voting in American National Elections," *American Politics Research* 28 (2000): 379–407.
6. Data derived from the 2000 U. S. Census. http://www.nipc.org/forecasting/GDP-cds/CD_108_DP1234_2000.pdf
7. The Associated Press State and Local Wire, September 29, 2008.
8. *Crain's Chicago Business*. October 15, 2008.
9. Ibid.
10. See, for example, John W. Kingdon, *Congressmen's Voting Decisions*, 3rd ed. (Ann Arbor: University of Michigan Press, 1989).
11. Associated Press State and Local News Wire, November 11, 2008.
12. WGN Radio, September 22, 2008.
13. *New York Times*, May 30, 2007.
14. Chicago Public Radio, September 12, 2007.
15. Kingdon, 1989, Congressmen's Voting Decisions.
16. David R. Mayhew, *Congress: the Electoral Connection* (New Haven, CT: Yale University Press, 1974).
17. See, for example, Richard F. Fenno, Jr., *Home Style: House Members in Their Districts* (Boston: Little, Brown, 1978), and Thomas Mann, *Unsafe at Any Margin: Interpreting Congressional Elections* (Washington DC: American Enterprise Institute, 1978).
18. See, for example, Gary C. Jacobson, *The Politics of Congressional Elections*, 3rd ed. (New York: HarperCollins, 1992).
19. See, for example, Anthony King, *Running Scared: Why American Politicians Campaign Too Much and Govern Too Little* (New York: Free Press, 1997).
20. See, for example, Jacobson, *Politics of Congressional Elections*, and Paul S. Herrnson, *Congressional Elections: Campaigning at Home and in Washington*, 2nd ed. (Washington DC: CQ Press, 1997).
21. See, for example, Wayne P. Steger, "The Permanent Campaign: Marketing As a Governing Tool," in *Handbook of Political Marketing*, ed. Bruce I. Newman, 661–84.(Thousand Oaks, CA: Sage,1999).
22. See, for example, Fenno, Jr., *Home Style* and King, *Running Scared*.
23. Fenno, ibid., 153.
24. John A. Ferejohn, *Pork Barrel Politics: Rivers and Harbors Legislation: 1947–1968* (Stanford, CA: Stanford University Press, 1974); Steven D. Levitt and James M. Snyder, Jr., "The Impact of Federal Spending on House Election Outcomes," *Journal of Political Economy* 105 (1997): 30–53.

25. http://www.usaspending.gov/fpds/index.php?reptype=a
26. *Lake County News Sun*, October 4, 2008.
27. See, for example, Bruce Cain, John Ferejohn, and Morris Fiorina, *The Personal Vote: Constituency Service and Electoral Independence* (Cambridge, MA: Harvard University Press, 1987); and John R. Johannes, *To Serve the People: Congress and Constituency Service* (Lincoln: University of Nebraska Press, 1984).
28. *Lake County News Sun*, October 4, 2008.
29. See, for example, *Cook Political Report*, September 25, 2008.
30. The Kirk campaign outspent the Seals campaign on TV advertising, but probably not the combined TV advertising of Seals and ads run by the DCCC and other groups.
31. http://www.opensecrets.org
32. The following examples were drawn from the Kirk and Seals campaign press releases and video streams of the ads run by the two campaigns, http://dansealsforcongress.com and http://www.kirkforcongress.com.
33. John R. Petrocik, "Issue Ownership in Presidential Elections, with a 1980 Case Study," *American Journal of Political Science* 40 (1996): 825–50.
34. *Chicago Sun Times*, August 31, 2008; *Chicago Daily Herald*, October 6, 2008.
35. *Daily Herald*, October 29, 2008; *Pioneer Press*, October 9, 2008; ABC 7 Chicago, August 26, 2008; WBBM 780 Radio, July 8, 2008; CBC 2 Chicago, June 24 2008.
36. *Daily Herald*, June 9, 2008.
37. *Daily Herald*, August 19, 2008; *Pioneer Press*, June 19, 2008.
38. *Pioneer Press*, October 9, 2008.
39. *New York Times*, October 20, 2008; *Daily Herald*, October 19, 2008; *Crain's Chicago Business*, February 21, 2008.
40. *Ha'aretz*, September 27, 2008; *Wall Street Journal*, September 10, 2008.
41. *Chicago Tribune*, October 21, 2008.
42. *Chicago Sun Times*, October 13, 2008.
43. The *Journal and Topics* newspaper endorsed Seals on October 29, being critical of Kirk for voting against a bill for equal pay for women and for negative advertising.
44. See Kirk's Web site, http://www.kirkforcongress.com (accessed January 5, 2009).
45. See Seals's Web site, http://www.dansealsforcongress.com (accessed January 10, 2009).
46. See, for example, Jacobson, *Politics of Congressional Elections*.

5 Defending Principles against a Tsunami

Shays vs. Himes in Connecticut's Fourth Congressional District

Victoria A. Farrar-Myers

> I'm willing to lose the next election; you have to be willing to lose it in order to deserve winning.
>
> —*Representative Christopher Shays, July 2008*[1]

While he was known as the last Republican member of the U.S. House of Representatives from New England still standing, while he labeled himself as an "endangered species,"[2] and while the national Democratic Party targeted his seat for the 2008 election, Chris Shays did not approach his race against Jim Himes by simply trying to defend his job. Instead, he did what he always did—he defended his values. He placed those values and his 21 years in Congress before the voters of Connecticut's 4th District and asked them to renew his contract with them for another two years.[3] The voting constituency in 2008, however, was no longer comprised of the same people that hired Shays originally, or even of those who had renewed his contract just two years earlier.

Many factors contribute to the story of the Shays–Himes race, ranging from partisan trends at the macrolevel, to Shays's unique position as a moderate but dedicated Republican who at times battled more with his party's leadership than with Democrats, to the effectiveness of Himes's campaign and message. In the end, however, the outcome of the race was a classic story of mobilizing voters and winning the ground game. Chris Shays was indeed willing to lose the 2008 election and played to win instead of playing not to lose. While his message still resonated positively with many voters in the 4th District, it was not enough to sway a large swell of newly registered Democratic voters who appeared in the district to support Barack Obama.

The Fourth District: A Wealthy District…and Bridgeport

Connecticut's 4th District has been described as "a fabled House district running up the coast in wealthy Fairfield County, just north of New York City. It's where Wall Street sleeps, where Congresswoman Clare Booth Luce denounced Franklin Roosevelt in the 1940s and where Republicans have held sway for the past 40 years—21 under Rep. Christopher Shays."[4] On many traditional demographic variables, however, the district does not vary from national averages. For example, 76.7 percent of the district's residents are White, 15.0 percent Hispanic or Latino, and 11.3 percent African American, as compared to national averages of 74.1 percent, 14.7 percent, and 11.3 percent respectively. Similarly, the district is close to the national average for age (38.9 median district age compared to 36.4 nationally).

What makes Connecticut's 4th District stand out is that it is the wealthiest district in one of the wealthiest states in the nation. The district's median household income, median family income, and per capita income are all between 163 percent and 195 percent of the national average. The median value of owner-occupied homes in the district is over three times the national median value.

These aggregate numbers, though, mask the distribution of the wealth throughout the 4th District. Of the 17 municipalities that comprise the district,[5] most have median household incomes *in excess of* two times (Easton, Fairfield, Greenwich, Monroe, Redding, Ridgefield, and Westport) or three times (Darien, New Canaan, Weston, and Wilton) the national average. Most of the rest of the district, including the second and third largest cities (Stamford with a population of approximately 118,000 and Norwalk with approximately 81,000), also exceed the national median household income by significant margins.

In stark contrast to the wealth throughout the rest of the district, however, stands the district's largest city of Bridgeport—approximately 130,000 or 19 percent of the district. With a declining industrial economic base, Bridgeport's median household income is less than 80 percent of the national average, and more than 17.1 percent of families and 19.2 percent of individuals live in poverty (compared to national averages of 9.8 percent and 13.3 percent). In addition, Bridgeport is more racially diverse and younger, and has a lower percentage of adults who have at least a bachelor's degree than the rest of the district.[6]

Politically, southwest Connecticut has had a history of supporting Yankee Republicans, "politicians in the mold of [Theodore] Roosevelt and Rockefeller: socially tolerant, environmentally enthusiastic, people who like government to keep its wallet close to its vest and its hands out of social issues like abortion and, in recent years, same-sex marriage."[7] The 4th District elected Yankee Republicans to the House of Representatives for 40 years, starting with Lowell Weicker in 1968, followed by Stewart McKinney until his death in 1987, and then Christopher Shays. Despite this congressional tradition of Yankee Republicanism, at the presidential level Democratic candidates Al Gore and John Kerry beat Republican George W. Bush in the district in 2000 and 2004 respectively.

Incumbent Chris Shays: A Yankee Republican

Even before entering Congress, Shays was known for standing up for and holding true to his principles. As a conscientious objector to the Vietnam War, he along with his wife joined the Peace Corps and lived in Fiji from 1968 to 1970. While in the Connecticut state House of Representatives after first being elected in 1974, he fought against abuses in the state probate system and was even jailed by a judge for criticizing the level of corruption in the state's judicial system.[8]

Already an established incumbent by the time of the 1994 midterm elections, Shays signed the GOP's "Contract with America" and was the primary sponsor of the Congressional Accountability Act of 1995, which was the first bill that the new House Republican majority passed in 1995. He saw the Republican Party as being the party of governmental reform and the principles of the Contract as supporting that vision. He viewed the GOP as being, or at least thought it should be, broad enough to include moderates like him as well as the conservatives who held the party leadership positions in Congress. Shays, true to this belief, supported Speaker Newt Gingrich, and even tipped him off about a potential coup against him in 1997 by more conservative members among the House Republicans.

Shays emerged as a national political figure, though, because of his willingness to take positions and pursue issues opposed by the conservative wing of the Republican Party. Most notably, Shays became an issue leader in the area of campaign finance reform, and as primary sponsor of the House version of the McCain–Feingold bill he became linked with John McCain on this issue. Shays's pursuit of campaign finance legislation led to the House passing bills in both the 105th and 106th Congresses, only to see the bills die in the Senate. His efforts, however, strained his relationship with Gingrich and forced him to break with his party leaders, who opposed the bill both as a matter of policy and by using numerous procedural devices to block the bill. For example, Shays was highly criticized within the party when in 1998 he signed a highly visible discharge petition to force campaign finance legislation to a floor vote and to take control of the process out of the Republican leadership's hands. Although Senator John McCain had become the public face of the issue of campaign finance reform by the time of the passage of the Bipartisan Campaign Reform Act in 2002, the issue quite likely would not have been able to continue on the public agenda without Shays's successes in the House in the late 1990s.[9]

Campaign finance reform was not the only issue on which Shays differed from the more conservative party base: he voted against the impeachment of President Bill Clinton; is pro-choice on abortion; supported minimum wage increases; is an ardent environmentalist; and was the first Republican House member to call for Tom DeLay to resign as Republican House Majority Leader in the wake of an ethics scandal, among other issues. When Newt Gingrich stepped down as Speaker, Shays lost the political cover that Gingrich afforded him within the party. Without it, Shays became subject to intraparty attacks, such as being bypassed for the chairmanship of the House Government Reform Committee even though he was ranking party member on the committee, and facing a primary challenge for his seat in 2000 when he was attacked for being too liberal.

Various key voting scores bear out Shays's more moderate voting record over the course of his congressional career (see Table 5.1). His career average voting score from the American Conservative Union (41%) was significantly lower than his career average Americans for Democratic Action vote score (55%). On party unity votes, which *Congressional Quarterly* defines as votes on which a majority of voting Democrats opposed a majority of voting Republicans, Shays voted with his Republican partisans only about two-thirds of the time (66%). His career average *Congressional Quarterly* presidential support score was lower under Republican presidents (50.8%) than it was during Bill Clinton's administration (52.1%). In fact, Shays's 2007 presidential support score of 33 percent was actually lower than Barack Obama (40%), Edward Kennedy (40%), and Hillary Clinton (35%), a point noted in Shays's campaign literature.

Despite his public differences with, and criticisms of, the Republicans' conservative wing, he remained dedicated to the party and the principles for

Table 5.1 Congressional Vote Scores for Christopher Shays, 1988–2008

Year	American Conservative Union	Americans for Democratic Action	Presidential Support	Party Unity
2008	32	75	34	68
2007	20	55	33	67
2006	36	55	53	57
2005	20	65	57	67
2004	38	70	59	69
2003	52	30	67	78
2002	76	20	82	80
2001	32	35	65	75
2000	60	40	49	71
1999	44	55	48	66
1998	40	45	57	58
1997	56	55	55	66
1996	60	30	53	69
1995	40	40	44	71
1994	38	55	56	67
1993	58	60	55	63
1992	40	65	40	62
1991	50	60	58	65
1990	25	72	34	60
1989	29	85	36	54
1988	24	90	42	59

Note: Since Shays was sworn into office in September 1987, he did not vote in all votes used in determining the various scores for that year, so data from 1987, even if available, is omitted.

Source: 1988-2006 scores from various editions of *CQ's Politics in America*; 2007-2008 American Conservative Union (ACU) and Americans for Democratic Action (ADA) scores from the organization Web sites; 2007-2008 party unity and presidential support scores from *CQ Weekly Report.*

which he believed it stood. He served on the House Oversight and Govern-ment Reform, Financial Services, and Homeland Security committees. As the Republican majority in the House started to narrow in the early 2000s, Shays served as an important swing vote which the party leadership needed in order to ensure victory on close roll call votes. Perhaps most significantly as it relates to Shays's defeat in 2008, Shays voted for the resolution authorizing the Iraq War and maintained support for the war effort at least well into 2006 (although he later criticized the Bush administration's handling of the war and acknowledged that he regretted voting for the initial resolution).[10]

Shays epitomized Yankee Republicanism, both in terms of ideals and in the political pros and cons of adhering to those ideals. When successful, he was praised for independence and bipartisanship; during his early battles on cam-paign finance reform he was even referred to as a "hero" and once depicted in a local paper in Connecticut as "SuperShays" complete with tights and cape.[11] By falling in the middle of the political spectrum, however, Shays was open to attack from both parties: by Republicans for being too independent and not adhering to conservative positions, and Democrats for being someone "who votes with the Republicans when they need him and votes with Democrats when they don't."[12] Shays's success and national prominence helped him last longer than any other Yankee Republican serving in the House. When the Republicans became the majority party following the 1994 elections, Shays was one of eight Republicans elected from New England.[13] This number started to dwindle in the next election. When the Democrats regained control in the 2006 elections, the other four New England Republicans who were still in the House at the time were swept away along with the Republicans' majority status, leaving Shays as the only Republican among the region's 22 House members.

Democrat Jim Himes: Shays's Opponent Emerges

Although Jim Himes decided in February 2007 that defeating Shays in 2008 "would be hard, but not impossible," he decided to take up the challenge.[14] Himes cited his disapproval of President Bush's policies as a primary factor in his decision to run for Congress. Endorsed early by Democratic Party leaders, Himes easily won an August 2008 primary against a political unknown who had no real campaign organization or funds.

Himes's political experience was limited to holding various board and com-missioner positions in Greenwich, but his private business experience gave him a background that would serve him well in the 2008 election. A Harvard gradu-ate and former Rhodes Scholar, Himes had a 12-year career at Goldman Sachs, the international investment banking and securities firm, working in its Latin America, mergers and acquisitions, and technology groups. He left Goldman Sachs interested in finding ways to fight poverty with business-oriented solu-tions, and ended up running the New York City branch of a nonprofit financier of low-income housing where he helped develop a $230 million acquisition fund to assist developers of low-income housing. As the *New York Times* concluded based on comments from a Democratic leader in the district, "In the campaign, Mr. Himes's résumé proved fortunate; the financial crisis played to his background as an investment banker who had spent years in housing finance. His Wall Street experience also made him a safe choice for the moneyed voters of Fairfield County."[15]

Fundraising in the Land of the Moneyed Voters of Fairfield County

To successfully challenge Shays, Himes needed to be financially competitive with the incumbent. As shown in Table 5.2, Shays had been able to maintain a fundraising advantage over his Democratic challengers in recent elections. Himes, however, bucked this trend and, more importantly, proved that he was a competitive fundraiser early. By the end of 2007, a full 10 months before the general election, Himes had raised $937,630 as compared to Shays's $1,159,836. As shown in Table 5.2, Himes stayed close to Shays in fundraising throughout the campaign, although he did loan his campaign $350,000 in the last few weeks before the election.[16] In the end, Shays raised $3,774,745 in contributions, but was matched by the $3,940,034 in funds raised by Himes (including the loans). Both candidates used all available funds during their campaigns and ended the election cycles with slight debts.[17]

Himes's former Goldman Sachs job positioned him to be able to raise nearly $570,000 from the securities and investment industry. Given Shays's own background and service on the Committee on Financial Services, however, he was also able to raise significant funds—nearly $470,000—from this sector. Himes and Shays were second and third respectively on the list of House candidates who received the largest amount of contributions from the securities and investment industry.[18]

Table 5.2 Campaign Finance Data for Connecticut's 4th District, 2000–2008

Date/Year	Shays Amount	Challenger	Challenger Amount
Previous Elections			
2000	$943,798	Stephanie Sanchez	$172,155
2002	$975,551	Stephanie Sanchez	$110,699
2004	$2,233,286	Diane Ferrell	$1,542,410
2006	$3,827,216	Diane Ferrell	$2,961,500
2007–2008 Election Cycle			
As of December 31, 2007	$1,159,836	Jim Himes	$937,630
As of September 30, 2008	$3,101,622	Jim Himes	$2,848,142
As of October 15, 2008	$3,312,846	Jim Himes	$2,978,196
End of Campaign	$3,774,745	Jim Himes	$3,940,034

Source: Previous Elections data — Opensecrets.org; 2007–2008 Election Cycle — compiled by author from data available from the Federal Election Commission (www.fec.gov).

The Democratic Congressional Campaign Committee (DCCC) targeted the Shays–Himes race early in the campaign cycle and spent over $1.3 million in independent expenditures. About half was spent to promote Himes with half used in opposition to Shays.[19] By comparison, the National Republican Congressional Committee (NRCC) spent only $2,600 on the Shays–Himes race, although in large part because Shays asked the NRCC not to spend funds on ads in his district given that he did not think they worked with his constituents. The National Association of Realtors, however, spent over $1 million in independent expenditures in the election to support Shays, who was one of four Republicans and five Democrats that the Realtors supported by making at least $300,000 in independent expenditures.[20] A spokesman for the Realtors PAC indicated that Shays was chosen for his support of Federal Housing Administration (FHA) reform and other issues.[21]

The Realtors' support for Shays received some scrutiny after a *New York Post* story implied that the Realtors' expenditures were connected to Shays "quietly pushing to overturn a recently implemented White House ban on Federal Housing Administration mortgages made with seller-financed down payments."[22] Although the story produced much fodder for Democratic-leaning blogs, it was put to rest when Democratic Representative Maxine Waters of California visited the 4th District to campaign for Jim Himes. Like Shays, Waters was a cosponsor of the legislation in question, and noted that community groups pushed the legislation because they sought to expand access to housing to low-income individuals.[23]

All in all, Himes had the financial resources to compete with Shays in what was one of the more expensive House races in 2008. He also had the financial support of his national party behind him. Himes's fundraising success and support allowed him to focus on running his campaign to unseat Shays.

The Campaign: A Substantive Dialogue on the Issues

Although Jim Himes had been Shays's presumptive challenger for quite some time, the Shays–Himes race did not begin in earnest until after Himes officially received his party's nomination in August 2008. When Sacred Heart University published the first objective poll regarding the Shays–Himes race, based on interviews conducted from September 22 to 25, 2008, Himes was still facing the "hard but not impossible" task of overcoming a 10-point margin favoring the incumbent. The poll showed that 29 percent of the respondents were still undecided, however, thus giving Himes the ability to overcome this deficit.

Himes's initial electoral strategy in 2008 looked very similar to the ones waged by Shays's Democratic opponent in 2004 and 2006, former Westport First Selectwoman Diane Ferrell. Shays had never been seriously challenged by a Democratic opponent prior to the 2004 election. His relatively narrow margins of victory in 2004 (52.4% of the vote) and 2006 (51.0%, which was aided by a low turnout in strongly Democratic Bridgeport) showed that Shays was becoming increasingly vulnerable as the 4th District was joining the rest of Connecticut and New England in becoming more firmly entrenched as Democratic "blue."

Like Diane Ferrell before him, Jim Himes attacked Shays for his support of the Iraq War. He accused Shays of being "an ardent supporter of the war all along and continu[ing] to be a supporter of keeping our troops there."[24] Although since 2006 Shays tried to distance himself from the Bush administration's conduct of the war, Himes pressed that "It's important to differentiate between what he says and what he does," claiming that Shays said he supported timelines for withdrawing troops yet voted against timelines in Congress.[25]

Much like the focus of the presidential election, which shifted from the war to the economy as economic conditions deteriorated in fall 2008, so did the emphasis of the Shays–Himes race. The issue, and particularly Shays's service on the House Committee on Financial Services, gave Himes an additional way to link the incumbent to the unpopular policies of the Bush administration. Himes argued that "Chris Shays doesn't understand the economy. He's been dead wrong about our economy, and he was wrong about Iraq."[26] Thus, Himes linked the Republican incumbent back to not one, but two major failures of the Bush administration (in the eyes of many voters in the district). Further, Himes hammered Shays for contributing to a "failure of oversight"[27] leading to the collapse of Wall Street and for supporting "lock, stock and barrel the economic policies of the Bush-Cheney administration."[28] The Himes campaign distributed mailers playing up the Bush–Shays connection and one of Himes's campaign commercials included a photo of Shays embracing Bush while the voice-over noted the various ways in which Shays "stood with" the President.

Himes offered his Wall Street experience and background in low-income housing as a fresh, practical perspective for addressing the nation's economic problems. Shays, however, was left to counter by trying to distance himself from Bush. In a move that clearly indicated the impact of the unpopular president in this race, he readily acknowledged that "I realize my district hates Bush."[29] Shays pointed out that a recent *Congressional Quarterly* study, which utilized the party unity scores above, had ranked him as the most moderate Republican in the House. This and other similar information was used prominently in an 88-page booklet entitled "A Record of Independent, Bipartisan and Effective Leadership" that Shays handed out and read from aloud during debates with Himes (see below).

One of the key moments in the campaign came on September 1, 2009, when Shays made what in hindsight was a strategic error by pronouncing on a New York City radio talk show that the fundamentals of the economy were still strong despite the economic collapse. Shays had already been connected to John McCain through the issue of campaign finance and as one of the McCain campaign's Connecticut cochairs. With this statement mirroring similar statements by George W. Bush and John McCain, Shays was now more closely tied to the Republican president and presidential nominee, even though his district and his state were clearly in the Obama camp.

Himes reiterated Shays's statement throughout the campaign using it as evidence that Shays had lost touch on the issues important to his constituency—one of the central themes of Himes's message to voters. On October 1, his campaign first aired an effective commercial that contained Shays's voice repeating the statement multiple times while facts and images reflecting the suffering that people had experienced during the economic crisis flashed on the screen. Himes's campaign and message started to reach voters, and by mid-October polls showed that Himes had pulled even with Shays (in a University of Connecticut poll) or perhaps even slightly ahead (in a SurveyUSA poll).

Shays did not, however, shy away from a discussion of the issues by focusing solely on his constituency service. Both candidates touted what they had done or could do for the district. The issue of constituency service, however, was never a primary theme of either candidate's campaign strategy. Nor did Shays resort to using negative ads attacking Himes, as Shays proudly proclaimed that never using such ads was a hallmark of his 34 years of service and campaigns in Congress and the Connecticut state legislature.

Instead, during the seven debates between the candidates occurring between October 14 and October 20 the discussion remained focused on substantive issues.[30] For example, Shays responded to Himes's criticism related to the economy by pointing out that he was "one of the first to voice concerns about lack of oversight of the mortgage lenders Fannie Mae and Freddie Mac, supporting legislation in 2003 to require the two companies to comply with the same reporting requirements as publicly traded companies despite fierce opposition and pressure from his party and lobbyists."[31] Shays also stood by his vote for the $700 billion bailout bill—one of five "legacy votes" that Shays felt he made during this time in the House[32]—despite constituents who contacted his office opposing the bill by a ratio of 30:1.[33] Himes, however, stayed on "the offensive in his ongoing battle to unseat"[34] the incumbent, and as a result Shays was relegated to a defensive posture on the key issues of the economy and the war.

Nevertheless and perhaps because they were his best assets in the campaign, Shays always returned to the principles that defined him politically as the reason for why voters should renew his contract. "I am independent, I am bipartisan, and I am effective," Shays proclaimed in one debate with Himes.[35] He also cited his experience of being "trained by my constituents" as one of the key differences between himself and Himes.[36] One of Shays's television campaign ads proclaimed, "The hopefulness of Obama. The straight talk of McCain. It's what Christopher Shays has always stood for. He goes where the truth takes him, never afraid to take a stand or oppose his own party. In a sea of partisanship, Shays is different. It's not what is Republican or Democrat. It's what is right for America." In other words, Shays positioned himself as, and proclaimed in the debates that he was, a "valuable and unique kind of member, who isn't partisan," and he hoped that would be enough to enable him to survive the election.[37]

Even after the debates, neither candidate emerged with a clear lead, though both maintained optimism about being victorious. One 4th District citizen may have best captured the feelings of many voters: "I wish Himes was running against someone who's less worthy than Chris Shays. Both those guys should be in Congress, in my opinion."[38] In the last week of the campaign, though, Himes received a tremendous boost when Barack Obama recorded a radio commercial endorsing Himes. Echoing the themes of both the Obama and Himes campaign that to vote for change meant voting for Democratic candidates, Obama stated:

> This is Barack Obama. I need your help in electing Jim Himes to Congress on November 4. If we want to change the way Washington does business, then we need to send the right people to Washington. Jim Himes is the son of a hard-working single mom. He left a successful career in business to build environmentally friendly affordable housing. He's someone who will expand opportunity for all Connecticut families. This is Barack Obama, asking you to support Jim Himes on November 4.

This ad proved crucial for establishing the link between Himes and Obama, and provided an important voting cue for the many first-time voters (see below) who turned out in support of the Democratic presidential candidate.

The Tsunami Hits the Ground: Voter Registration, Turnout, and the "Obama Effect"

Although Himes was in a position to beat the Republican incumbent, Shays had shown before that he could withstand a quality Democratic challenger attacking him for being too closely tied to the policies of President Bush and the Republican Party. What made 2008 different—the ingredient that was missing previously—can be found in the electoral ground game of mobilizing voters. Analyzing the where, how, and why of voter turnout shows that, in the end, Shays was unable to defend himself against the swell of support for Barack Obama in the district. As one Connecticut political blogger summarized, "The model to defeat Shays required a strong Dem (Barack) at the top of the ticket that could produce a 20-thousand plurality in the city [Bridgeport] for a well-financed congressional candidate. Throw in thousands of first-time voters in the city unaware of the name of their congressman, and you have the makings of a tsunami."[39]

The ground game starts with voter registration, and in this area the Democratic Party made great strides leading up to the 2008 election. Overall, the Democrats have an advantage in registered voters in the 4th District over the Republicans, although the plurality of voters registered themselves as "Unaffiliated" with a party. The Democratic advantage in registered partisans was 11,438 in 2004 and 15,860 in 2006, but by 2008 this advantage nearly quadrupled over the previous presidential election year to 44,142. Although registration within the Republican Party held fairly constant between the two presidential election years (actually decreasing by less than 1,000 voters), the Democrats increased their rolls by nearly 32,000 voters (a 26.5% increase). Most significantly, the large part of this increase occurred in the 12-month period leading up to the 2008 general election. During that period, the Democratic Party added over 25,000 registrants in the district. Over 60 percent of this increase was found in the three cities of Bridgeport (8,828 newly registered Democrats), Norwalk (3,399), and Stamford (3,968). As a result, the Democratic Party headed into the

2008 election with a significant partisan advantage, the likes of which had not been seen in recent years.

The next stage of the ground game is voter turnout, particularly in political strongholds. As in many localities throughout the nation, voter turnout increased in the 4th District as compared to previous years. An estimated 319,945 voters in the district cast ballots in the 2008 general election, which represents a net increase of 7,291 voters (2.3%) over the 2004 presidential election.[40] The overwhelming proportion of the increased turnout is attributable, once again, to Bridgeport (an increase of 3,527 votes), Norwalk (1,748), and Stamford (997). In both 2004 and 2006, each of these cities favored Democrat Diane Farrell by percentages ranging from 52.4 percent (Norwalk in 2006) to 70.5 percent (Bridgeport in 2004). By comparison, vote totals in five municipalities in the district decreased when compared to 2004: New Canaan (1,583), Greenwich (514), Darien (95), Trumbull (39), and Easton (25). Voters in each of these localities favored Shays over Farrell in the previous two elections, with 65 to 70 percent of voters in New Canaan casting their ballots for him. Thus, voter turnout followed a pattern much like voter registration; while Republican strongholds were stagnant and slightly declined in numbers compared to previous elections, voters in the core areas of Democratic support in the district increased their participation for the 2008 election.

On Election Day, Himes garnered 158,475 votes to Shays's 146,854 for an 11,621 total margin of victory.[41] The voting patterns in 2008 were consistent with Shays's two prior campaigns against Diane Farrell. One political analyst summarized this pattern as, "Shays' base of support has largely been in the affluent towns that make up a geographic bulk of the Fourth District. He's had to do well in there to make up for losses in Stamford, Norwalk and especially Bridgeport."[42] The problem for Shays in 2008, however, was that his losses in the three cities were larger than in years past and the other suburban towns did not assist him in making up this difference; in fact, Shays lost ground in many strongholds compared to the 2004 election.

Overall, Himes garnered 20,142 more votes than Shays's Democratic opponent in 2004, while Shays received 5,639 fewer votes compared to four years before. This variance results in a swing of 25,781 votes in Himes's favor (see Table 5.3). Himes took the Democratic stronghold of Bridgeport (over 80%), along with the other two larger cities in the district Norwalk (almost 60%) and Stamford (also almost 60%), all by large margins; these three cities also figured prominently in the 25,000-vote swing in Himes's favor compared to 2004. Over 80 percent of the lost votes for Shays, and 75 percent of his overall negative swing, can be attributed to these three cities. Even though Shays won all the other municipalities in the district, many of these suburban towns worked in Himes's favor on a comparative basis. For example, even though Shays received more than 56 percent of the vote in Greenwich, Himes had a swing of 2,359 votes in his favor compared to Shays's 2004 opponent, Diane Ferrell (with Himes getting 1,360 more votes than Farrell and Shays receiving 999 fewer votes than he did four years earlier). Even Shays's strongholds of Darien (70% voting for

Table 5.3 Vote Swings in Connecticut's 4th District, 2004–2008

	Shays	Himes	Net Swing
Cities			
Bridgeport	(2,284)	7,526	9,810
Norwalk	(1,183)	3,280	4,463
Stamford	(1,164)	4,011	5,175
Suburban Towns			
Darien	171	297	126
Easton	13	(2)	(15)
Fairfield	(129)	953	1,082
Greenwich	(999)	1,360	2,359
Monroe	(295)	690	985
New Canaan	(89)	221	310
Oxford	115	750	635
Redding	86	99	13
Ridgefield	757	(610)	(1,367)
Shelton	(783)	1,091	1,874
Trumbull	(759)	929	1,688
Weston	269	(208)	(477)
Westport	809	(474)	(1,283)
Wilton	(174)	229	403
Total	(5,639)	20,142	25,781
Margin		25,781	

Note: Negative numbers in parentheses.
Source: Compiled by author from data available through the Connecticut Secretary of State's Web site (http://www.sots.ct.gov).

Shays in 2008) and New Canaan (over 68%) produced small comparative swings favoring Himes (126 and 310 votes respectively).

The key difference in 2008 compared to previous elections, though, was the new, mostly first-time voters who made their way to the ballot box. In other words, the ground game proved to be the difference in the Fourth District for the Democratic Party in 2008. Democrats, thanks in large part to Barack Obama, got new voters to register, got core supporters to the polls, and got them to cast their ballots for Jim Himes in the congressional election. For Himes, the key was in Bridgeport. As one analyst noted, if Bridgeport were removed from the district, Shays would have won the district as easily as Himes actually defeated Shays.[43] Bridgeport saw a net gain of 8,500 registered Democrats to Republicans in the year preceding the 2008 election (and an overall net gain of over 11,000 between 2004 and 2008), and produced over 7,500 additional votes for Himes than Farrell received four years earlier.

The flood of new Democratic voters in Bridgeport, combined with similar increases in the district's other cities, Norwalk and Stamford, which combined nearly equaled the totals in Bridgeport, swung the tide in the district in favor of Himes. What these numbers also imply is that if not for the new voters, Shays may have very likely won again in 2008. Shays, therefore, was not a congressman who lost complete touch with his district. He appears to have still been very much connected to those people in the district who comprised the voting portion of the electorate as recently as two years prior. In 2008, though, the voting electorate changed just enough with the influx of new voters—new voters who had not voted for Chris Shays before and did not necessarily even know who Chris Shays was or for what he stood. Like other first time voters nationwide, they came to vote for one reason: to support Barack Obama and his message.

If the flood of new voters that hit the 4th District was the tsunami that ended Chris Shays's congressional career, Obama was the force behind the flood. Obama far and away carried Connecticut (60.5% of the vote) and the 4th District (59.7%). Shays recognized the impact that Obama was going to

Table 5.4 Split-Ticket Voting in Connecticut's 4th District, 2008

	Himes	Obama	Split Ticket Differential
Cities			
Bridgeport	80.3%	83.9%	3.6%
Norwalk	59.6%	65.9%	6.4%
Stamford	57.8%	64.4%	6.6%
Suburban Towns			
Darien	29.7%	45.4%	15.7%
Easton	40.1%	49.8%	9.7%
Fairfield	46.0%	56.9%	10.9%
Greenwich	43.8%	53.8%	10.0%
Monroe	44.1%	46.9%	2.7%
New Canaan	31.4%	46.9%	15.5%
Oxford	47.0%	43.6%	-3.4%
Redding	46.1%	58.3%	12.2%
Ridgefield	38.1%	52.4%	14.3%
Shelton	47.7%	47.0%	-0.7%
Trumbull	45.4%	49.6%	4.1%
Weston	45.0%	62.5%	17.5%
Westport	46.7%	65.3%	18.6%
Wilton	41.1%	53.7%	12.6%
Total	**52.4%**	**59.7%**	**7.3%**

Source: Compiled by author from data available through the Connecticut Secretary of State's Web site (http://www.sots.ct.gov).

have on his race, stating two weeks before the election "This [election] is a tsunami.... A tsunami means if you are not on high ground, you can lose."[44] Shays hoped that his independence and ability to work on a bipartisan basis would be the higher ground that he needed.[45] More specifically, he needed to convince Obama supporters to split their ticket and vote Republican at the congressional level. Shays had some success in this manner (see Table 5.4). With the exception of Oxford and Shelton, Shays fared better in each municipality against Himes than McCain did against Obama; and while Obama won 10 of the 17 towns in the 4th District, Himes managed to win only the three big cities

Despite this mild success in generating split-ticket voting, Shays could not stimulate enough of it where it was needed the most: Bridgeport. According to political scientist, John Orman, "In Bridgeport, they tend not to be ticket-splitters.... Shays may have been able to win other towns that went for Obama, but not Bridgeport."[46] As another analyst noted, the "Himes campaign did a nice job persuading voters to fill in the Democratic oval, not just Barack's, leading to Himes' plurality" in Bridgeport.[47]

Shays may have been willing to lose the 2008 election, but did so on his terms. Even in defeat, Shays continued to defend his principles telling supporters in his concession speech, "If you think we lost this race because we didn't go negative, you're just wrong." His wife, Betsi Shays added, "Tonight we lost an election. But we did not lose our souls." Politically, however, Shays's record of bipartisanship did not provide the high ground that the Republican hoped it would against the groundswell of support for Obama, and he and his congressional career "were overcome by a tsunami."[48]

Postscript

After winning the election, Jim Himes took office as Representative from the 4th District and, like his predecessor, serves on the Financial Services and Homeland Security committees. Shays, out of politics but not public service, was appointed to the Commission on Wartime Contracting, an independent, bipartisan commission studying wartime contracting in Iraq and Afghanistan. Prior to that appointment, Shays was mentioned as a potential director of the Peace Corps; Jim Himes even sent a letter, along with the four other Democratic members of the Connecticut congressional delegation, to President-Elect Obama promoting Shays as a possible director (Shays subsequently removed himself from consideration for this position).

The real defeat for Christopher Shays did not come on Election Day, though, but came later when he learned that he fell victim to the thing on which he built his name and reputation: fighting the corruptive force of money in politics. Shays discovered that his longtime campaign manager had allegedly embezzled nearly $200,000 from the campaign. Complicating Shays's problems was that many of the legislative constraints he helped put into place to rein in the effect of money in politics—such as rules governing the ways in which a person who is not currently running for elective office can raise funds to retire debt from previous campaigns, or restrictions permitting only sitting (but not former) members of Congress to create legal funds—limited the options available to Shays to address the problems he faced. Shays commented on the situation that, "To lose an election is difficult; what happened since then is unimaginable.... I felt like he was part of my family."[49] Throughout his 21-year congressional career, Shays often received high praise such as being "independent," a "maverick," and even a "hero." Like many heroes, though, he suffered a tragic irony in his political demise. For Chris Shays, the irony of his defeat is not the loss of his seat, but the erosion of the very ideals upon which he built his career.

Notes

1. Quoted in Cynthia Coulson. "Shays v. Himes: A Close Call for the 4th Congressional District Race," *Westport Magazine*, http://www.mofflymedia.com/Moffly-Publications/Westport-Magazine/October-2008/Shays-vs-Himes/ (accessed May 7, 2009).
2. Stephanie Ebbert. "Shays Fights to Keep 'Endangered' GOP New England Base," *Boston Globe*, October 20, 2008, B1.
3. When asked in one interview why someone should vote for him instead of his opponent, Shays reworded the question to "Why would I ask—suggest—that people renew my contract?" See Coulson. "Shays v. Himes."
4. David Rogers. "Will Connecticut's Shays be Ousted?" *Politico*, October 21, 2008, http://www.politico.com/news/stories/1008/14780.html (accessed May 16, 2009).
5. Bridgeport, Darien, Easton, Fairfield, Greenwich, Monroe, New Canaan, Norwalk, Oxford, Redding, Ridgefield, Shelton (approximately two-thirds of the town of Shelton with the remaining portion being located in a different congressional district), Stamford, Trumbull, Weston, and Wilton. The demographic data provided in the main text is compiled from the U.S. Census Bureau's 2005–2007 *American Community Survey 3-Year Estimates*, except for the following towns for which such data were not available and data from the 2000 Census were used: Easton, New Canaan, Oxford, Redding, Trumbull, Weston, and Wilton. For Census data see, http://factfinder.census.gov.
6. Approximately one-third of Bridgeport is African American and one-third is Hispanic, while Whites comprise less than half of the city's population (46.4%; U.S. census data allow respondents to self identify with more than one race, so totals may exceed 100 percent). By contrast, approximately 84 percent of the rest of the 4th District is White. The median age for the entire district including Bridgeport is 38.9 years, but Bridgeport itself has a median age of only 33.2 years. In Bridgeport, approximately 14 percent of people 25 years and over have obtained a bachelor's degree or higher, while over half the people in the rest of the district have achieved this level of education.
7. Pam Belluck, "A G.O.P. Breed Loses Its Place in New England," *New York Times*, November 27, 2006, http://www.nytimes.com/2006/11/27/us/politics/27repubs.html?pagewanted=1&ref=washington (accessed May 22, 2009).
8. "About Christopher Shays,"http://webarchives.loc.gov/collections/lcwa0002/20021212140254/http://www.house.gov/shays/bio/index.htm (accessed May 23, 2009). The Library of Congress has archived members' Web sites from the 107th, 108th, and 109th Congresses.
9. For an in-depth examination of the legislative process, and Shays's role in it, leading to the House's passage of campaign finance reform legislation in the 105th and 106th Congresses, see Diana Dwyre and Victoria A. Farrar-Myers, *Legislative*

Labyrinth: Congress and Campaign Finance Reform (Washington, DC: CQ Press, 2001). For a related analysis of the Bipartisan Campaign Reform Act from prepassage through postpassage implementation, see Victoria A. Farrar-Myers and Diana Dwyre, *Limits and Loopholes: The Quest for Money, Free Speech, and Fair Elections.*(Washington, DC: CQ Press, 2008).

10. See Associated Press, "Rep. Christopher Shays: 'I Support the War in Iraq'." September 3, 2006, http://archive.newsmax.com/archives/ic/2006/9/3/151511.shtml (accessed May 23, 2009); and Peter Urban. "Shays a True Survivor, but Will He Win Again?" *Greenwich Time*, October 12, 2008, http://www.greenwichtime.com/politics/ci_10699226 (accessed May 23, 2009).

11. The SuperShays cartoon was reprinted with permission in Diana Dwyre and Victoria A. Farrar-Myers, *Legislative Labyrinth: Congress and Campaign Finance Reform* (Washington, DC: CQ Press, 2001), 127.

12. Statement of Connecticut Democratic Party Chairwoman Nancy DiNardo, quoted in Urban. "Shays a True Survivor,"

13. Maine, New Hampshire, Vermont, Massachusetts, Rhode Island, and Connecticut.

14. David M. Halbfinger. "'Bullheaded' and a Rhodes Scholar, and Now Headed to Capitol Hill," *New York Times*, November 10, 2008, A23.

15. Ibid.

16. Altogether, Himes loaned his campaign nearly $500,000, including in-kind benefits and postelection loans.

17. Data in the above paragraph related to prior elections can be found at http://www.opensecrets.org, a campaign finance tracking Web site operated by the Center for Responsive Politics. All other data presented is available from the Federal Election Commission at http://www.fec.gov

18. All business-sector data can be found on Opensecrets.org.

19. Based on data available at OpenSecrets.org. The DCCC was in a far superior position to help Democratic candidates than its Republican counterpart. Heading into the general campaign season, the DCCC held a $54.6 million to $8.4 million fundraising advantage over the National Republican Congressional Committee. Raymond Hernandez, "G.O.P. at Risk in House Races in the Northeast," *New York Times*, August 14, 2008, A1.

20. Data regarding the Realtors' independent expenditures is available from Opensecrets.org.

21. Mark Pazniokas, "Maxine Waters Gives Jim Himes a Boost, Chris Shays an Alibi," Courant.com/CapitalWatch, October 31, 2008, http://blogs.courant.com/capitol_watch/2008/10/maxine-waters-gives-jim-himes.html (accessed June 7, 2009).

22. Teri Buhl, "Shays Backs Toxic Mortgage Bill," *New York Post*, October 26, 2008, http://promotions.nypost.com/seven/10262008/business/push_to_revive_risky_loans_135400.htm.

23. Pazniokas, "Maxine Waters Gives Jim Himes a Boost."

24. Coulson, "Shays v. Himes."

25. Ibid.

26. David Hennessey, "Himes: Shays Out of Touch on Economy, Iraq War," *Greenwich Citizen*, October 24, 2008, http://www.votesmart.org/speech_detail.php?sc_id=426519&keyword=&phrase=&contain= (accessed May 11, 2009).

27. Ibid.

28. Ken Dixon, "Shays, Himes Clash in First Two Debates," *Connecticut Post*, October 15, 2008, http://www.votesmart.org/speech_detail.php?sc_id=419733&keyword=&phrase=&contain= (accessed May 24, 2009).

29. Fran Silverman,. "In Tight House Race, Bush Record is Battleground," *New York Times*, October 12, 2008, CT1.

30. The candidates did, in fact, have seven debates in six days; on two occasions they had two in one day.
31. Silverman,. "In Tight House Race," CT1.
32. Urban, "Shays a True Survivor": Shays's other four "legacy votes" were supporting the resolution authorizing military operations in the first Gulf War in 1991; the Clinton impeachment vote; supporting the resolution authorizing conflict against Iraq in 2002; and voting against a resolution in 2007 rebuking President Bush for sending more troops to Iraq. In hindsight, Shays believed he was correct on four of the five votes, with the exception being the 2002 vote on Iraq.
33. Silverman, "In Tight House Race," CT1.
34. Hennessey, "Himes: Shays Out of Touch on Economy, Iraq War."
35. Ebbert, "Shays Fights to Keep 'Endangered' GOP New England Base."
36. Coulson, "Shays v. Himes."
37. Mark Pazniokas. "Shays, Himes on Attack in Two Debates." *Hartford Courant*, October 15, 2008, http://www.courant.com/news/politics/hc-4cddebate1015.artoct15,0,406074.story (accessed May 24, 2009).
38. Quoted in Ken Dixon, "Shays, Himes Clash in First Two Debates," *Connecticut Post*, October 15, 2008, http://www.votesmart.org/speech_detail.php?sc_id=41973 3&keyword=&phrase=&contain= (accessed May 24, 2009).
39. Quoted in Nick Keppler, "Bridgeport Killed Chris Shays: How Shays' Hometown, Swept up in Obama Fever, Laid the Fatal Blow to His 21-year Congressional Career," *Fairfield Weekly*, November 13, 2008, http://www.fairfieldweekly.com/article.cfm?aid=10503 (accessed May 11, 2009). Grimaldi operates the "Only in Bridgeport" blog.
40. The data on voter turnout in 2008 as reported by the Connecticut Secretary of State is inconsistent. According to one summary chart available through the Connecticut Secretary of State's Web site (http:// www.sots.ct.gov), 306,246 people in the 4th District were reported as having voted; however, a separate summary chart shows a total of 319,945 votes cast for presidential candidates in the district. Further, the sum of the number of voters reported in each municipality in the district equals 326,730 (this amount includes the entire town of Shelton since vote totals for 2008 were reported for the entire town instead of broken down by those totals within and outside the 4th District). Accordingly, the analysis regarding voter turnout in 2008 assumes a turnout rate equal to the number of votes cast for presidential candidates (319,945), and a total of 6,785 votes (the difference between 326,730 and 319,945) were subtracted from the vote totals for the town of Shelton to estimate the portion of votes cast in the 4th District. This estimate for Shelton (approximately two-thirds of Shelton votes being within the 4th District and one-third outside) is consistent with other reported totals that distinguish between voters in Shelton based on their congressional districts.
41. Preliminary vote totals showed Himes receiving 160,081 votes to Shays's 146,801 (e.g., Keppler. "Bridgeport Killed Chris Shays"). The vote totals used herein are available through the Connecticut Secretary of State's Web site. As discussed elsewhere in this chapter, the data reported on the Secretary of State's Web site for the 2008 election has been shown to have some inconsistencies, but is the only available source of voting returns broken down by municipality.
42. Keppler. "Bridgeport Killed Chris Shays."
43. Ibid. Excluding Bridgeport, Shays received 139,192 votes to Himes's 127,189, for a 12,003 vote margin.
44. Quoted in David Rogers. 2008. "Will Connecticut's Shays be Ousted?" *Politico*, October 21, 2008, http://www.politico.com/news/stories/1008/14780.html (accessed May 16, 2009).

45. In the *Politico* story from which the previous Shays's quotation was taken, reporter David Rogers ("Will Connecticut's Shays be Ousted?") noted that Shays has "no hesitation that he knows where that high ground is. 'I go where the truth takes me,' he says at a Fairfield debate. 'It's part of being independent and part of being bipartisan, and it's what makes me effective'."
46. Quoted in Keppler, "Bridgeport Killed Chris Shays."
47. Lonny Grimaldi, quoted in ibid.
48. All quotations in the above paragraph were taken from "Christopher Shays Concedes in 4th Congressional District." November 4, 2008, available at http://www.westportnow.com (accessed May 16, 2009).
49. Raymond Hernandez, "Ex-Congressman Says Campaign Manager Embezzled Funds," *New York Times*, May 1, 2009, A18.

6 Painting the High Plains Blue
Musgrave vs. Markey in Colorado's Fourth Congressional District

Seth E. Masket

> The radical homosexual lobby, abortionists, gun-grabbers and all the rest of the extremists finally spent enough money, spread enough lies and fooled enough voters to defeat me.
>
> —*Marilyn Musgrave*[1]

Prior to 2008, Republican Marilyn Musgrave earned a reputation as a strong closer, surging in the final days of elections that often seemed too close to call. Her 2006 reelection race against Democrat Angie Paccione was a nail-biter by any standard, with polls decidedly uncertain right before the election. Musgrave ultimately won that contest by fewer than 3 percentage points. Republicans hoped for a repeat performance in 2008. If Musgrave could survive the harshest electoral environment for Republicans in a generation, presumably she could see another reelection campaign through.

Yet it was not to be. The continued unpopularity of President Bush, combined with a meltdown of the financial sector, key demographic changes in Musgrave's congressional district, and the skills of her new challenger conspired to cost Musgrave her seat in Congress. This time, there would be no last minute rally by the incumbent.

A myriad of factors made it difficult for Marilyn Musgrave to play defense in 2008 against Betsy Markey. Elements examined in this chapter include: Musgrave's own political history, the background of her challenger, the strategies and tactics employed during the campaign, and the shifting electoral environment, both in the district and nationally. The resulting picture is one of a seat that was almost impossible for the incumbent to successfully defend given the political conditions.

The District

Colorado's 4th Congressional District is a largely rural one, spanning roughly the eastern third of the state. Noticeably, it contains none of the mountains for which Colorado is famous. Rather, the district is defined by high plains terrain, with agriculture the predominant interest. As *Congressional Quarterly* describes it, the district "looks more like Kansas than Colorado."[2] Indeed, Colorado's 4th

District is home to some of the most intensive cattle and wheat production in the country, along with a substantial meatpacking industry. The other major industry is higher education, as the district hosts both Colorado State University and the University of Northern Colorado. The district overall is 79 percent White, 17 percent Hispanic, and only 1 percent each African American and Asian.

The district is so vast that it actually borders on five other states—Wyoming, Nebraska, Kansas, Oklahoma, and New Mexico. The most densely populated part of the district lies in the cities along the I-25 corridor north of Denver; 86 percent of the votes cast in the district in 2008 came from just three of the district's 18 counties: Boulder, Larimer, and Weld. These counties are, respectively, home to the district's largest cities: Boulder, Fort Collins, and Greeley.

The district is relatively conservative, with its Democratic presidential vote share in the past few elections running 5 to 6 points behind that of the state of Colorado. Prior to 2009, it had been represented consistently in Congress by a Republican since 1974 , and its last Democratic incumbent, Wayne Aspinal, was distinguished for his opposition to the early environmental movement. As of January 2009, registered Republicans outnumbered registered Democrats in the district by about 37,000 voters, which is in contrast to trends statewide where newly registered Democrats outnumbered Republicans 4:1 in the lead-up to the presidential election (see chapter 1). However, more than 110,000 active voters (31% of all active registrants) in the district classified themselves as unaffiliated and could easily tip the balance one way or another in a general election.[3]

The district's political stripes have been shifting rapidly in recent years, driven in large part by substantial population growth in the northern counties. Between 2003 and 2007, Boulder County grew by 3.7 percent, Larimer County grew by 6.9 percent, and Weld County grew by an astounding 15.5 percent. These high-growth counties make up the more urban and suburban parts of the district. There has been little growth in the more rural areas. These trends mirror recent changes statewide, as Colorado has experienced substantial population growth in recent years, with at least a third of new migrants coming from California. The rest have arrived primarily from Arizona, Florida, Illinois, New Mexico, New York, and Texas, and have largely settled in and around the Denver metropolitan area.[4]

These shifting political currents were noted in the most recent *Cook Political Report* rankings of congressional districts. Based on its votes in 2000 and 2004, Cook had given the 4th District a rating of R+9, meaning that Republicans tend to do an average of 9 points better in this district than their national average. More recent ratings, based on votes from 2004 and 2008, reevaluated the district as R+6. Only 11 other congressional districts had a bigger leftward shift during this time period.[5]

The Incumbent: Republican Marilyn Musgrave

Marilyn Musgrave was born and raised in what is now Colorado's 4th District. She grew up poor, the daughter of an itinerant meatpacker, and she put herself through Colorado State University by waiting tables and cleaning houses. She and her husband met in Bible camp and attended school together, marrying soon after college. She worked as a school teacher for a time, and then became involved with the family's hay farm while they raised four children. Musgrave's experiences as an educator, a small businessperson, and a parent would inform her later career.

Throughout her service as an elected official, Musgrave has focused on social issues, advocating for a culturally conservative worldview. She first ran for office in a 1991 school board race, winning a seat on the Fort Morgan School Board, where she distinguished herself through her efforts to instill an abstinence-only focus in the district's sex education curriculum. She was then elected to the Colorado House of Representatives in 1992 and to the state Senate in 1998. In both chambers, she focused on a number of hot-button social issues, seeking to limit access to abortion and to allow concealed handguns in public places. Musgrave brought much attention to herself, however, through her work to prevent same-sex couples from marrying or from adopting children.[6] The state ban on same-sex marriage that she authored, which was rejected multiple times during the 1990s by Democratic Governor Roy Romer, ultimately became law with Republican Governor Bill Owens's signature in 2000.

She continued work on this controversial issue after her 2002 election to the U.S. House of Representatives. She was one of the primary House sponsors of a proposed amendment to the U.S. Constitution that would have instituted a federal ban on same-sex marriages. In a 2006 speech to the Family Research Council, Musgrave famously remarked, "As we face the issues that we are facing today, I don't think there's anything more important out there than the marriage issue." This statement invited criticism during the 2006 contest that Musgrave was single-mindedly focusing on same-sex marriage at the expense of more tangible issues important to her district's voters.[7]

To judge from interest group ratings, Musgrave maintained a very conservative voting record throughout most of her tenure in Congress (see Table 6.1).

Table 6.1 Congressional Vote Scores for Marylyn Musgrave, 2003–2008

Year	American Conservative Union	Americans for Democratic Action	Presidential Support	Party Unity
2008	87	25	67	97
2007	100	5	88	97
2006	96	0	89	98
2005	100	0	89	98
2004	96	15	85	96
2003	100	0	85	98

Source: 2003–2006 scores from various editions of CQ's *Politics in America;* 2007–2008 American Conservative Union (ACU), and Americans for Democratic Action (ADA) scores from the organization Web sites; 2007–2008 party unity and presidential support scores from CQ *Weekly Report.*

At least during her first two terms in office, the American Conservative Union (ACU) gave her ratings of close to 100 while her scores from Americans for Democratic Action remained near zero during this time. She remained a strong supporter of President Bush, voting with him between 85 and 89 percent of the time, and she nearly always voted with her party on roll call votes in the House. Her final term in office gives some evidence of moderation, however, as her ADA score rose and her ACU and presidential support scores dropped.

Interestingly, when one takes a broader look at her voting record, Musgrave appears to be somewhat less doctrinaire. Her DW-NOMINATE score[8] throughout her three terms in Congress was .663, just slightly more conservative than fellow Colorado Republican Representative Bob Beauprez of Lafayette and considerably more liberal than Representatives Joel Hefley of Colorado Springs (the home of the conservative group Focus on the Family) and Tom Tancredo of Littleton. These scores made her the 42nd most conservative member of Congress in 2003 and 2004; by comparison, Tancredo was the fourth. Even if Musgrave's overall record could be defined as moderate to conservative, it was her outspoken stances on issues relating to gays and lesbians that drew attention to her election after election.

Her tenacious focus on same-sex marriage ultimately caught the eye of Colorado's "Gang of Four," an informal group of wealthy state Democratic activists and donors who devote their considerable resources to ousting Republicans from office and fighting discriminatory initiatives.[9] The "gang's" members include Pat Stryker, the heiress to her family's medical supply company; computer entrepreneurs Tim Gill and Rutt Bridges; and businessman Jared Polis, who in 2008 got elected to Congress from Colorado's 2nd Congressional District. According to Jason Thielman, Musgrave's 2008 campaign manager, Stryker and Gill, in particular, "made it a personal vendetta [to unseat Musgrave]. They decided it was their right to determine who would represent the 4th in Congress."[10] Indeed, Stryker donated $175,000 to the Defenders of Wildlife Action Fund, which, in turn, spent roughly $1.5 million in 2008 to try to remove Musgrave from office. It is unclear to what extent Gill was involved in this effort.[11]

Musgrave has not charted the electoral path of the typical member of Congress. While she first took office with 57 percent of the two-party vote, she did not enjoy the "sophomore surge" experienced by many members during their first reelection campaigns. Indeed, her share of the vote declined each time she ran. She won a mere 53 percent of the two-party vote in her 2004 rematch with Stan Matsunaka, and barely 51 percent in her 2006 battle with Angie Paccione.

The Challengers: Betsy Markey and The Democrats

In the past, Musgrave's opponents for the 4th Congressional District seat were typically chosen for their moderate to liberal credentials. Her opponent in both 2002 and 2004 was Democrat Stan Matsunaka of Loveland, the president of the state Senate. Matsunaka was every bit as homegrown as Musgrave: his family had settled in Eastern Colorado a century earlier and he was raised in the rural areas of the 4th District. The overall Republican tilt of the district carried Musgrave to an easy victory in the 2002 open-seat race, although Matsunaka made inroads in their 2004 rematch, calling attention to some of Musgrave's more provocative statements on same-sex marriage. Musgrave's 6-point victory that year was actually the closest electoral margin the district had seen since 1974. That record was shattered two years later, when Democrat Angie Paccione, a member of the state House of Representatives, came within 3 percentage points of unseating Musgrave.

We can evaluate the partisan voting habits of Musgrave's previous opponents because they served in Colorado's state legislature and have roll call voting records. These roll calls can be aggregated to form W-NOMINATE ideal points ranging from -1 (the most liberal) to +1 (the most conservative).[12] Although these cannot be compared across different chambers or sessions, they are still helpful in interpreting the basic voting pattern of a legislator.

Matsunaka, Musgrave's opponent in 2002 and 2004, rated a -.455 during the 1999 to 2000 state Senate session. Although this makes him the third most conservative Democrat in the state Senate during that session, it was still a relatively liberal course to chart in a district that voted 58 percent to 42 percent for Bush over Gore in 2000. In the 2003 to 2004 session of the state House, Angie Paccione, Musgrave's 2006 opponent, rated an ideal point of -.534, making her the 22nd most liberal of the chamber's 31 Democrats. In short, in a fairly Republican district, Musgrave was facing off against candidates she could paint as being to the left of the district's voters.

The 2006 race was particularly challenging for Musgrave and heartbreaking for Colorado Democrats. The race was considered a tossup by many leading political observers. A brutal and expensive advertising war focusing on various charges of corruption defined the final week of that election, with Musgrave pulling away in the last few days. Despite Paccione's loss, the close nature of the election, and Musgrave's steadily eroding vote shares over the years suggested to Democrats that the right candidate with enough resources could flip the district.

In 2008, three Democratic candidates originally tossed their hats in the ring for a chance to face Musgrave. While Musgrave's previous opponents were members of the state legislature, Betsy Markey had never held public office. Markey was no stranger to politics, however, having served as U.S. Senator Ken Salazar's regional director of Colorado's north central and eastern plains since early 2005. This was a position that exposed her to many of the issues facing the voters of the 4th District. She had additional prior government experience through her service with U.S. Senator John Durkin (D-NH) and U.S. Representative Herbert Harris (D-VA) after college and her work on computer security at the U.S. State Department during Ronald Reagan's second term. She and her husband chose to leave the Washington, DC area in 1995 to raise their children in Fort Collins, where she cofounded and ran a successful software company and a coffee shop.

Many of the district's prominent Democrats were torn over whether to support Markey or the previous Democratic nominee, Angie Paccione. Certainly, Paccione had the proper credentials. She was a professor of education at Colorado State University, served as a state legislator from 2002 to 2006, and had come within 3 points of unseating Musgrave two years earlier. With her expanded name recognition and the increased vulnerability of Musgrave, Paccione looked like a strong candidate. The 2006 race, however, also brought to the surface a past bankruptcy filing by Paccione that had proven politically damaging, and many of her supporters were concerned that a 2008 rematch would just produce the same results.[13]

A third candidate, Eric Eidsness, also entered the race. He ran in 2006 under the Reform Party banner, garnering 10 percent of the district's votes. Eidsness was a lifelong Republican and a former Reagan administration appointee to the Environmental Protection Agency, but switched his party registration to Democratic for the 2008 race. A Vietnam veteran, Eidsness was eager to challenge Musgrave on the basis of her support of the Iraq War.

The nomination battle never went to a primary contest or even a congressional district assembly.[14] The three Democratic candidates essentially fought it out through a fundraising and endorsement derby. Paccione, a proficient fundraiser, raised roughly $100,000 in the third quarter of 2007, compared to Markey's $60,000 during the same period. Paccione also boasted the backing of state Senate President Peter Groff (D-Denver) and former Denver Mayor Wellington Webb. Although Denver does not lie within the 4th Congressional District, Webb remains a popular and well-known figure among Democrats throughout the state. Moreover, the more populous areas of the district are just outside Denver's city limits. While Markey ran behind Paccione in fundraising, she nonetheless grabbed the endorsements of U.S. Rep. Diana DeGette (D-Denver) and her former boss Senator Ken Salazar.[15] Several current and former Democratic state senators from the region, including Bob Bacon, Peggy Reeves, and Stan Matsunaka (Musgrave's opponent in 2002 and 2004), also backed Markey.[16]

Offering some evidence for the idea that endorsements trump money in nominations battles,[17] Paccione dropped out of the race in September of 2007 to join the business consulting firm Pathways to Leadership. Eidsness, whose lack of prominent endorsers and his multiple party affiliations in the previous few years did little to endear him to the Democratic base, dropped out a week later. This left Markey with no Democratic opponents and more than a year to introduce herself to the voters of the 4th District and build a case against the incumbent.

The General Election

From the outset, it looked to be a challenging reelection environment for Musgrave. There was only one poll, which was commissioned by the Musgrave campaign and done early in the campaign in March 2008, which showed Musgrave with a lead; the rest showed Markey with a modest but growing advantage.[18] By June of 2008, the *Cook Political Report* had shifted its classification of the contest from "Lean Republican" to "Tossup." This was partially due to shifting demographics and changes in voter registration in the state. It was also partially due to national events: President Bush and the Republican Party were proving even less popular overall than they had been two years earlier.

One of Musgrave's main tasks in reintroducing herself to the voters of the 4th District was to distance herself from President Bush. She made headlines in late 2007 by publicly criticizing U.S. progress in the Iraq War. "I'm discouraged," said Musgrave. "I do hope we will hear good things from Gen. (David) Petraeus about the troop surge and what it has done, but I am discouraged."[19] In 2008, she still supported President Bush about two-thirds of the time, but her presidential support vote scores dropped a whopping 21 points (see Table 6.1). Musgrave, however, continued to support President Bush's politically unpopular veto of the State Children's Health Insurance Program (SCHIP).[20] This is an important vote because Democrats had been planning to use it against vulnerable Republicans and had even claimed it was moving poll numbers in other races including those Michigan's 9th District as well as in Missouri (9th District) and Virginia (2nd). In fact, the Democratic Congressional Campaign Committee (DCCC) had begun touting the importance of the SCHIP issue in late 2007. DCCC Chairman Chris Van Hollen noted in a strategy memo to colleagues in November of 2007, "...vulnerable Republicans who continue to vote in lock step with George Bush against SCHIP will be held accountable by their constituents."[21]

Musgrave also sought to bolster her bipartisan credentials by building high profile alliances with Democratic lawmakers on the 2007 farm bill and drought relief programs. She worked with Colorado Democrats to block expansion of the Army's Piñon Canyon maneuver site and to designate Rocky Mountain National Park as a wilderness area.[22] Quite noticeably, Musgrave changed the tone of her fundraising appeals, describing her own personal struggles as a means of demonstrating empathy with voters. References to "radical homosexual leaders," common in her appeals in previous campaigns, were nowhere to be seen this time around.[23]

After arriving on Capitol Hill in 2003, Musgrave proved that she could be a strong fundraiser. In the 2004 and 2006 election cycles she raised more than $3 million. She also spent more than $3 million in each cycle in what turned out to be hard-fought contests.[24] As the data in Table 6.2 show, she started 2008 with $1 million cash on hand that she had raised in 2007. Normally, this would have been a tremendous asset to an incumbent, but 2008 proved to be a difficult fundraising environment for Republicans. As a result, Musgrave fell behind her fundraising marks from 2006[25] and raised less money than Markey in the last three quarters of the year. After July 1, the playing field leveled dramatically as Musgrave burned through her cash reserves. Overall, Musgrave spent just under $3 million, which was less than she spent in her successful 2004 and 2006 reelection campaigns.

Markey, meanwhile, having functionally secured the Democratic nomination in late 2007, was able to start fundraising early for the general election. She began to see some return on her fundraising efforts in the latter half of 2008,

Table 6.2 Campaign Finance Data by Reporting Period for Colorado's 4th District, 2008

Reporting Period	Musgrave			Markey		
	Receipts	Disbursements	Ending Cash	Receipts	Disbursements	Ending Cash
2007 Year End (January 1 – December 31)	$1,051,236	$437,074	$752,170	$367,870	$81,030	$286,840
2008 April Quarterly (January 1 – March 30)	$355,505	$93,668	$1,014,007	$226,641	$137,108	$376,373
2008 July Quarterly (April 1 – June 30)	$279,630	$137,738	$1,155,899	$389,771	$186,080	$580,065
2008 Pre-primary (July 1 – July 23)	$58,409	$57,168	$1,157,040	$88,993	$55,524	$613,533
2008 October Quarterly (July 24 – September 30)	$597,630	$971,068	$783,602	$725,406	$957,044	$381,895
2008 Pre-general (October 1 – October 15)	$150,022	$609,114	$324,510	$383,590	$539,687	$225,798
2008 Post-general (October 16 – November 24)	$401,077	$628,558	$97,028	$694,814	$885,662	$34,950
Total	$2,893,509	$2,934,388		$2,877,085	$2,842,135	

Note: The 2007 Year End figures represent funds raised and disbursements in the campaign cycle to date.
Source: Compiled from candidate reports to the Federal Election Commission, Form 3, Lines 23, 24, 26 and 27, various dates.

raising about $1.8 million. She was better funded than any of Musgrave's previous challengers, able to match Musgrave almost dollar for dollar in spending. Overall, she raised nearly $2.9 million.

Perhaps the bigger story, in terms of campaign expenses, was the independent expenditure campaigns waged by various outside groups. The Defenders of Wildlife Action Fund, for example, spent roughly $400,000 during July of 2008 on ads attacking Musgrave for supporting auto manufacturers over environmental needs.[26] By October, they had spent $1.16 million on ads against Musgrave.[27] Similarly, VoteVets attacked Musgrave for a vote she cast opposing combat bonus for returning soldiers. "I expected the worst in Iraq," said one of the veterans in the advertisement. "I expected better from Marilyn Musgrave."

The two congressional campaigns ended up spending almost identical sums on the race (about $2.9 million each), but outside money overwhelmingly favored Markey. This, explains Musgrave campaign manager Jason Thielman, was particularly damaging to the Musgrave campaign, as almost all these outside expenditures went toward negative advertisements. Such advertising "tears a person down without an equal and opposite force acting on that person's behalf," says Thielman.[28] "That drove up her negatives to such a point where it was easy for anyone to become an acceptable alternative." With that kind of lopsided negative campaign, says Thielman, "You could take Gandhi and turn him into a figure that scares children at night."

Meanwhile, the two major national parties spent more than $2 million on the race. The DCCC spent much of its share in the race running ads portraying Musgrave as someone who put "special interests ahead of us." As one ad claimed,

> ...She accepted $14,000 in pay raises, and voted Wall Street billions in tax breaks, but voted against a $1,500 combat bonus, against a new GI bill to help veterans pay for college, and against providing health care for our National Guard when they come home....[29]

Another ad produced an audio reenactment of her 1999 statement, "I never saw a campaign contribution I didn't like," and played it repeatedly throughout the ad.[30]

The National Republican Congressional Committee (NRCC), meanwhile, ran ads attacking Markey for basically the same things that Musgrave attacked her for: ethics violations. Markey, it turned out, had remained with her software company, Syscom Services, for nine months after accepting her job with Senator Salazar's office, and during her time with Salazar, Syscom's federal contracts increased substantially. The Musgrave campaign produced a series of advertisements alleging that Markey used her contacts in Salazar's office to steer business to her old company. A report by the General Services Administration that found no improprieties did little to dissuade this line of attack.[31]

Another of Musgrave's advertisements alleged that Markey "got rich on noncompetitive, Haliburton-style government contracts" and had directed government contracts to Syscom.[32] Markey responded by filing suit in the Larimer County district attorney's office—running false campaign advertisements is a misdemeanor under state law. That lawsuit was delayed and later dismissed.

Markey's threats of legal action did little to deter Musgrave, who escalated the attacks in the final weeks of the campaign. Notably, the Musgrave campaign released an ad showing a Markey impersonator hooked up to a lie detector. When the impersonator denies improperly using her position to channel contracts to her business, a buzzer goes off on the lie detector machine, which reads out, "False detection." At no point is the impersonator described as such. The NRCC released an advertisement that hit on this same theme and included the line, "Betsy Markey tried to hide the truth from the public, but got caught."

Bailout Blues

The September collapse of the financial sector marked a politically difficult moment for many incumbents across the country. The Bush Administration asked Congress to produce a $700 billion bailout package for various financial institutions, and worked with congressional leaders of both parties to craft legislation that could pass speedily and prevent further damage to the American economy.

Polling on the financial bailout suggested that opinions were sharply split, although virtually all respondents said that something had to be done soon. Incumbents were left in the difficult position of casting a politically unpopular vote that nearly everyone would be watching, less than two months from an election. It is no wonder, then, that the first vote on the bailout failed in the House. As analyses of the September 29 vote showed, supporters of the bill were predominately moderates and were not worried about reelection. Opponents were disproportionately ideologically extreme and were from competitive districts.[33] The votes across Colorado reflected these patterns. Rep. Mark Udall (D-El Dorado Springs), in a tight race for the U.S. Senate seat, voted no. Rep. Tom Tancredo (R-Littleton), who was retiring from the House, voted yes. Rep. Diana DeGette (D-Denver), who faced only token opposition in her safe Democratic district, also voted yes.

Musgrave, a conservative facing a tough reelection race, voted no. "Congress absolutely needs to listen to the American people," Musgrave said following the vote. "The calls into my office were overwhelmingly opposed to this bill."[34] Her exposure on this issue was reduced somewhat when her opponent, Markey, also criticized the bailout, claiming it did not include sufficient protection for taxpayers.

Although the two candidates roughly agreed on the bailout, the collapse of the nation's financial sector had a dramatic effect on the tone of the race. The economy suddenly became the overwhelming concern among voters, drowning out all other issues. This tended to work to Musgrave's disadvantage because she had built her reputation through strong stances on social issues. It also bolstered Markey, who had released an economic plan in the late spring of 2008. "We were well positioned," says Anne Capara, Markey's campaign manager; "We'd built [Markey's] business credentials [early in the campaign]."[35]

End Game

Two weeks before the election, the NRCC made a determination to cut off funding in support of Musgrave's campaign. This was a powerful signal sent by the national party, which had spent $1.8 million helping Musgrave defend her seat two years earlier and had spent nearly a million dollars in the 4th District in the first half of October 2008 alone. The decision, however, reflected various political realities. The NRCC simply lacked the funds that its Democratic counterpart, the DCCC, was spending across the country. A few weeks earlier, the NRCC decided to stop spending in open-seat races and to just focus on protecting incumbents. Then it triaged further, deciding which seats it actually had a chance of holding. To many political observers, the NRCC's pullout from the 4th District represented the national party's decision that Musgrave could not hold the district, and that the money could be better used elsewhere.[36] The NRCC was forced to take similar action in other congressional races, as well, which left incumbents to play defense by themselves in the final days of the campaign.

The final days of the campaign were spent with an odd sort of asymmetry. Musgrave used her remaining funds on a sharply negative campaign, seeking to portray Markey as corrupt. Markey conversely went more positive, apparently believing that her negative ads had done their work and that a victory was likely. In the last week her ads shifted to a biographical nature, but her ad buy was very limited.[37] Although few public polls were conducted during the campaign, the most recent polls suggested Markey had a solid lead. The final two public polls of the campaign, one by SurveyUSA in late August and one by Grove Insight (commissioned by EMILY's List) in early September, showed Markey with a 7 and a 9-point lead over Musgrave, respectively.

The Results

On Election Day, few were shocked by Markey's victory, although the size of that victory proved surprising. Markey won by double digits, taking 56 percent of the two-party vote. Although Markey only outperformed Musgrave in three of the district's 18 counties (the three largest counties: Weld, Larimer, and Boulder), she outperformed the 2006 Democratic nominee's vote share in 13 counties. Weld County marked a particularly strong victory for Markey; she won it by 5,000 votes, even though it had gone to the Republican by 7,000 votes just two years earlier and even though McCain beat Obama in the county by 10 percentage points.

Figure 6.1 provides some evidence of Markey's exceptional performance, showing how she did in each of the 4th District's counties as compared to Barack Obama's vote totals in the presidential campaign. The diagonal line marks the

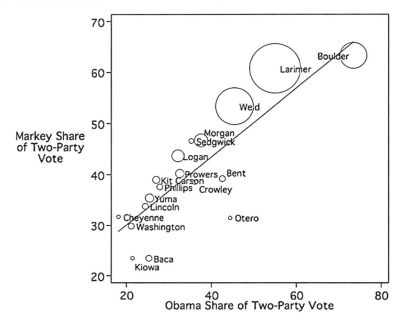

Figure 6.1 Obama and Markey performances by county in Colorado's 4th Congressional District, 2008. *Note:* Data points are weighted by the size of the 4th Congressional District electorate from each county. The diagonal line is the Obama=Markey line.

Markey–Obama line, meaning that any county above the line is one in which Markey's share of the vote was greater than Obama's. With the exception of Baca, Bent, Boulder, and Otero counties, Markey consistently outperformed Obama across the district in both moderate and conservative counties. District-wide, Markey ran 8 points ahead of Obama in what turned out to be the second biggest drubbing of an incumbent member of Congress in 2008.[38]

Markey's large victory margin appears attributable, in part, to both her prodigious fundraising and to her widespread campaigning, which improved Democratic performance even in the more rural areas of the district. According to University of Northern Colorado political scientist Steve Mazurana, "Marilyn [Musgrave] didn't seem to work very hard during the campaign, while Betsy [Markey] was in more places and talked to more people.... She went door-to-door in these rural areas and small towns, and that means a lot to people who live there."[39]

According to Markey's campaign manager, Anna Capara, part of the reason that Markey ran well ahead of Obama throughout the district was that the campaign maintained its own field organization separate from that of the Obama campaign or the state Democratic Party.[40] The 4th Congressional District, Capara notes, was not a target-rich environment for Obama or Democratic Senate candidate Mark Udall, who were seeking to win statewide, because it was predominately rural and relatively conservative. Markey, however, targeted independents and even disaffected Republicans, and her campaign hired Wendy How, an experienced field organizer with the Service Employees International Union (SEIU), to run its grassroots effort. "We relentlessly pursued people we thought would be ticket splitters," says Capara.[41]

By the beginning of the summer of 2008, says Capara, the campaign realized that "what we have to do is pretty much never talk to a Democrat ever again." They made a particular focus on small, rural towns, identifying local opinion leaders and trying to arrange for them to have 15-minute meetings with Markey. In these meetings, says Capara, "nine times out of ten, I was getting a voter."[42]

It is difficult to say how much Markey's strategy ended up mattering. Markey improved on the performance of Paccione, the Democratic nominee two years earlier, almost uniformly throughout the district. We can see evidence of this in Figure 6.2, a scatter plot of Musgrave's share of the two-party vote in the counties of the 4th Congressional District in 2006 and 2008. A diagonal line marks the 2006–2008 demarcation; if a county appears above the line, Musgrave did better in 2008 than she did two years earlier. In this plot, the county data points are weighted by the size of the 2008 electorate.

As the figure shows, Musgrave lost ground throughout the district between the two elections, although her vote share was up in a few counties. Her improvements over 2006 came exclusively in smaller counties. The three largest counties were not only the most liberal in the district, but also became less supportive

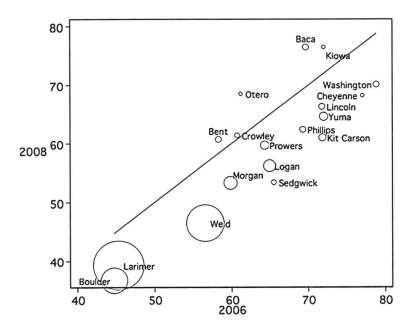

Figure 6.2 Musgrave two-party vote share by county, 2006 and 2008. *Note:* Data points are weighted by the size of the 4th Congressional District electorate from each county. The diagonal line is the 2006=2008 line.

of her between 2006 and 2008. Growth of these larger, more Democratic counties made the overall district even more hostile to Musgrave. This shift is also evidenced by the fact that George W. Bush beat John Kerry in this district 58 to 42 percent in 2004, but in 2008 John McCain only topped Barack Obama there by one percentage point. Even with this leftward shift in the district, however, Markey still made a substantial improvement over her Democratic predecessors: Musgrave ran 5 points behind the Republican presidential nominee in 2004 and 7 points behind him 2008.

The implication of this is twofold: First, Musgrave was never a great fit for the 4th District. The fact that she consistently ran behind the Republican presidential vote and that her vote share declined as her constituents got to know her better—the opposite trends from those of most members of Congress—suggest that her tenure was always in danger. Second, while the 4th remains a conservative district, it is growing steadily more moderate as outsiders flood into its more urbanized counties, which made it more difficult for her to defend her seat. All this is to say that characteristics of both the incumbent and the district contributed significantly to the outcome of the 2008 race, apart from any actions or strategic decisions by the two campaigns.

That said, the challenger's campaign was unusually disciplined and well-endowed, achieving what other experienced Democratic candidates could not do. Colorado's 4th District is surely near the top of the list of districts that Republicans will be seeking to take back in the 2010 midterm elections. Democrats are liable to face a difficult midterm election nationwide, as the president's party often does, and the district's conservative stripes will likely make this a difficult district for the Democrats to defend. It is additionally possible, should concerns over the national economy wane, that divisive social issues will reemerge that undermine Markey's 2008 winning coalition. Yet, Republican hopes for retaking the district are surely tempered by Markey's performance against a tenacious incumbent in 2008.

Notes

1. Lynn Bartels, "Musgrave's Pledge: Fight Lies with Truth," *The Denver Post*, June 2, 2009, B1.
2. Congressional Quarterly, *CQ's Politics in America* (Washington, DC: CQ Press, 2005).
3. Notably, Colorado's party primaries are closed, meaning that the third of the electorate that calls itself unaffiliated cannot participate in the selection of party nominees. This contributes to the relative extremism of the general election candidates, who must endure a contest among a fiercely ideological primary electorate.
4. Marc J. Perry, *State-to-State Migration Flows: 1995 to 2000* (Washington, DC: U.S. Census Bureau, 2003).
5. Bob Moore, *New Rating Shows Republican Advantage Shrinking in 4th Congressional District* 2009, http://www.coloradoan.com/apps/pbcs.dll/section?category=Plu ckPersona&U=07deebf354a64ac8be008d9811c3b205&plckController=PersonaBl og&plckScript=personaScript&plckElementId=personaDest&plckPersonaPage= BlogViewPost&plckPostId=Blog%3a07deebf354a64ac8be008d9811c3b205Post%3

a2e468989-54e8-49c8-a44e-a6043ff33a29&sid=sitelife.coloradoan.com (accessed April 17, 2009).

6. Chryss Cada, "A Firm Voice against Gay Marriage," *The Boston Globe*, April 11, 2004, http://www.boston.com/news/nation/articles/2004/04/11/a_firm_voice_against_gay_marriage/ (accessed June 14, 2009).

7. Greg Giroux, "Musgrave's Priorities at Issue in Increasingly Close Colo. 4 Race," *The New York Times*, September 28, 2006.

8. The DW-NOMINATE procedure was developed by Keith Poole (see note 12). It uses every roll call vote cast on the floor of the House to produce a score, ranging from -1 (most liberal) to +1 (most conservative) for every member. These dynamic scores are comparable from session to session, enabling researchers to compare members across time.

9. Robert Frank, *Richistan: A Journey through the American Wealth Boom and the Lives of the New Rich* (New York: Crown Publishers, 2007).

10. Jason Thielman, telephone interview with author, June 8, 2009.

11. Robert Moore, "Financial Role of Area Philanthropist Unclear in Group's Effort to Unseat Marilyn Musgrave," *Fort Collins Coloradoan*, November 10, 2008, A1.

12. Keith T. Poole, and Howard Rosenthal, *Congress: A Political-Economic History of Roll Call Voting* (New York: Oxford University Press, 1997).

13. Karen E. Crummy, "Dems Have Fresh Face after Paccione's Exit," *The Denver Post*, September 27, 2007, B1.

14. Colorado maintains a complex system of party nominations. Interested candidates may participate in a partisan congressional district assembly prior to the primaries. The electors at these assemblies are elected in precinct and county caucuses. If a candidate fails to receive 10 percent of the assembly vote, she is forbidden from appearing on the primary ballot. If one candidate receives at least 30 percent of the assembly vote, that candidate is automatically the party's nominee in the next general election. However, if more than one candidate passes the 30 percent threshold, those candidates' names will be placed on a primary ballot, with the one receiving the highest assembly vote share appearing on top. Candidates who receive less than 30 percent but more than 10 percent may petition to appear on the primary ballot.

15. Julia C. Martinez, "Democrats Vs. Democrats," *The Denver Post*, September 17, 2007, B7.

16. Jason Kosena, "Angie Paccione Bows out of Congressional Race," *Fort Collins Coloradoan*, September 27, 2007, A1.

17. Marty Cohen, David Karol, Hans Noel, and John Zaller, *The Party Decides: Presidential Nominations before and after Reform* (Chicago: University of Chicago Press, 2008).

18. Pollster.com, *2008 Colorado Cd-04 General Election: Musgrave (R-I) vs Markey (D)* http://www.pollster.com/polls/co/08-co-04-ge-mvm.php (accessed June 3 2009); see also, Monte Whaley, "Challenger's Poll Predicts Tough Race for Musgrave," *The Denver Post*, May 21, 2008.

19. Lynn Bartels, "Musgrave Reverses Iraq View," *Rocky Mountain News*, August 24, 2007, 29.

20. Jason Kosena, "Musgrave Holds Firm on S.C.H.I.P.," *Fort Collins Coloradoan*, October 16, 2007, A3.

21. David M. Drucker, "DCCC: SCHIP Hurts GOP," *Roll Call*, November 6, 2007, http://www.rollcall.com/issues/53_55/news/20863-1.html?CMP=OTC-RSS (accessed June 24, 2009).

22. Chris Barge, "Campaign Already Starting to Boil—Responding to Critics, Musgrave Begins Makeover," *Rocky Mountain News*, July 17, 2007, 21.

23. Robert Moore, "Musgrave Image Overhaul Continues," *Fort Collins Coloradoan*, July 13, 2008, A1.
24. http://www.opensecrets.org/races/summary.php?id=CO04&cycle=2008 (accessed on June 4, 2009).
25. Jason Kosena, "Musgrave Coffers Smaller Than '06," *Fort Collins Coloradoan*, October 13, 2007, A3.
26. Robert Moore, "Environmental Group's Anti-Musgrave Spending Tops $400,000," *Fort Collins Coloradoan*, July 29, 2008, A1–2.
27. Robert Moore, "Markey–Musgrave Race No. 3 in Outside Spending," *Fort Collins Coloradoan*, October 31, 2008.
28. Thielman, telephone interview
29. http://www.youtube.com/watch?v=Nf-sxNmQr8s
30. "Under the Dome." *The Denver Post*, 1999, A6.
31. Robert Moore, "Federal Agency: No Proof Markey Used Position to Secure Contracts," *Fort Collins Coloradoan*, September 24, 2008, A1–2.
32. Daniel Chacon, "Markey Responds to 'Desperate' Musgrave Ad by Filing Complaint," *Rocky Mountain News*, September 24, 2008, 28.
33. Dana Milbank, "A House Divided along Twisted Lines," *The Washington Post*, September 30, 2008, A3; Ian Ayres, *Why Representatives Voted against the Bailout— and a Suggestion on How to Change Their Minds*, http://freakonomics.blogs.nytimes.com/2008/10/01/why-representatives-voted-against-the-bailout-and-a-suggestion-on-how-to-change-their-minds/ (accessed October 1 2008).
34. Anne C. Mulkern, "Colo. Reps' Votes Skewed," *The Denver Post*, September 30, 2008, A8.
35. Capara, telephone interview.
36. Robert Moore, "G.O.P. Cuts Musgrave Ad Buys," *Fort Collins Coloradoan*, October 23, 2008.
37. Robert Moore, "Ads Take Different Paths," *Fort Collins Coloradoan*, October 27, 2008.
38. Robert Moore, "Group Meets Objective of Unseating Musgrave," *Fort Collins Coloradoan*, November 10, 2008, A1.
39. Jessica Fender, "4th District—Markey's Double-Digit Win Stunned Own Staff," *The Denver Post*, November 6, 2008, B2.
40. Capara, telephone interview.
41. Ibid.
42. Ibid.

7   Campaigning Against the Uncontrollable

Sununu vs. Shaheen in New Hampshire's Senate Race

Andrew E. Smith and Dante J. Scala

For John Sununu, playing offense was a cakewalk, compared to playing defense. In 2002, en route to becoming a senator at the age of 38, Sununu went on the offensive not once, but twice. The son of a former New Hampshire governor, who had also been George H. W. Bush's chief of staff, Sununu served three terms as a U.S. House member before taking on a member of his own party, Senator Bob Smith, for the Republican nomination in the 2002 U.S. Senate race. Smith had angered many Republicans in New Hampshire by making an abortive run for President in 2000, then resigning from the Republican Party before eventually returning.[1] In a September primary, Sununu defeated Smith by a margin of 54 to 45 percent, and then had to quickly pivot to face a formidable challenger: Jeanne Shaheen, a moderate Democratic three-term governor. Sununu was outspent by his opponent in a race that many saw as a possible Democratic pickup, but nevertheless won in 2002 by a 51 percent to 47 percent margin.

After running such a gauntlet to gain his seat in the Senate, one might think that Sununu could not help but have an easier time defending it, especially in a rematch against a candidate he had defeated once already. Indeed, in his reelection bid Sununu performed as well among different partisan groups in the New Hampshire electorate as he did six years earlier. Sununu slightly increased his vote share among Republicans (from 83 to 86%) and independents (from 19 to 32%), and did not lose too many votes among Democrats (falling from 11 to 7%), according to final polls from the University of New Hampshire Survey Center. Nevertheless, on election night 2008, Sununu found himself on the losing end of a 7-point loss to his longtime rival, Shaheen. In this chapter, we explore the dynamics of the 2008 rematch between these two political heavyweights and shed some light on what made playing defense so much more difficult for Sununu than offense.

The Changing Political Environment of New Hampshire

New Hampshire is a small New England state with a population of just 1.3 million, but it has political influence far greater than its size, largely due to holding the first presidential primary in the nation. Its population is almost entirely White (96% of the adult population), and generally prosperous, with the sixth highest median household income in the country and the lowest poverty rate.[2] It is the only state in the Northeast that has grown significantly since 1990, and is the only one in the region that the Census Bureau projects will grow significantly in the next 20 years. Most of New Hampshire's population is concentrated in the southeast corner of the state, which is largely part of suburban Boston. Historically, New Hampshire has voted Republican and until recently was the last holdout of GOP support in what was once solidly Republican New England. Granite State Republicans like to point out that the Republican Party was formed in Exeter, New Hampshire in 1853.[3] Migration of people into New Hampshire from other states in the Northeast, however, has slowly changed the political culture of the state, which has resulted in the state trending Democratic since the late 1980s.

Sununu's victory in 2002 was part of a Republican landslide that appeared to place the GOP firmly in charge of the Granite State for the foreseeable future. The Republicans successfully defended their Senate seat, despite a bruising primary that unseated a sitting senator. They also won back the governor's office, with millionaire businessman Craig Benson thrashing a pro-income tax Democrat; filled Sununu's vacant 1st District seat with another Republican, Jeb Bradley; and gained large majorities in both houses of the state legislature. In 2002, core Republicans made up 43 percent of the Election Day electorate while core Democrats made up only 33 percent (see Figure 7.1).[4] This 10 percentage point Republican advantage made it almost impossible for Democratic candidates across New Hampshire, unless they represented the most Democratic of districts.

Election Day 2002, however, proved to be the high-water mark of the decade for New Hampshire Republicans. In state politics, the seeds of future defeat were sown that day: the state Republican Party's executive director was one of three convicted in an Election Day plot to jam the phone lines of a local union and the Democratic Party, which were making get-out-the-vote (GOTV) calls. One of these three (not the GOP's executive director) later had their conviction overturned. As a result, the New Hampshire GOP suffered withering legal bills and a public-relations fiasco.[5] In addition, Governor Benson's administration also made several ethical missteps that were covered in the news, and the governor's determination to bring entrepreneurial business values to the state Capitol did not play well, even in his own party. New governors in New Hampshire are almost always granted a second two-year term by voters, but in 2004 Benson narrowly lost reelection to another businessman, John Lynch.

Also after the 2002 election, New Hampshire Republicans began to suffer the effects of what V. O. Key described as "secular realignment."[6] Between 2002 and 2006, New Hampshire reached a tipping point, catalyzed by new arrivals to the Granite State; the death or migration of older Republican voters; and last but not least, the unpopularity of the Bush administration, which was intense enough to make some voters switch parties. Changes in the voter rolls amply demonstrate the rapid shifts that took place between 2002 and 2008. While voter registration among all parties surged between 2002 and 2008 because of

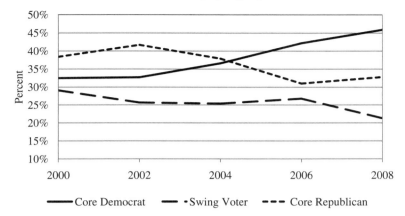

Figure 7.1 Core partisanship of New Hampshire electorate, 2000–2008. *Note:* Core partisanship is measured in the final UNH Survey Center pre-election poll of likely voters using an index based on three factors:
- Long term partisanship as measured by the 7-point University of Michigan party identification question "Generally speaking, do you usually think of yourself as a Republican, a Democrat, an Independent or what?"
- Mid-term partisanship, as measured by "Now, please think about elections you have voted in over the last five years . . . including local, state, and national elections. Would you say you have voted for more Democrats . . . more Republicans . . . or that you have voted for almost exactly the same number of each?"
- Short-term partisanship as measured by how the respondent says they will vote in each race in the upcoming election.

This index ranges from 0 to 100, where 0 is a likely voter who is a strong Republican, who says she/he has voted for only Republicans in the past 5 years, and plan to vote for all Republicans in the coming election and 100 is a likely voter who is a strong Democrat, who says she/he has voted for only Democrats in the past 5 years, and plan to vote for all Democrats in the coming election. The index is then collapsed to that scores from 0 to 33 are classified as core Republicans, 34 to 67 as Swing Voters, and 68 to 100 as Core Democrats.
Source: University of New Hampshire Survey Center, http://www.unh.edu/survey-center/news/election2008.html

population growth and increased interest in politics as a result of the war in Iraq, Democrats and undeclared voters (independents) saw their numbers rise dramatically while Republican gains were far more modest. Democratic registrations leaped by 60 percent between 2002 and 2008, undeclared voters saw a similar 52 percent growth, but Republican registrations grew by only 11 percent. Consequently, the Republican percentage of registered voters fell 7.4 percentage points from 2002 to 2008 (to 29.3%) while Democrats grew by 3.9 percent (to 29.5%), and undeclared voters grew by 3.6 percent (to 41.3%), effectively eliminating the lock that Republicans have had on New Hampshire politics since the Civil War.

There is considerable evidence that this secular realignment started across New England in the 1970s and picked up speed after 1990.[7] After the 2008 elections, only three Republican Senators hailed from New England, and in the House of Representatives, not a single Republican member remained. In New Hampshire, the Democratic candidate won four of the last five presidential elections (1992, 1996, 2004, and 2008), and six of the last seven gubernatorial elections (1996, 1998, 2000, 2004, 2006, and 2008). It was the 2006 and 2008 elections, however, that seem to have finally tipped the balance toward Democrats in New Hampshire. New England, which 100 years ago was the most Republican part of the country, is now perhaps the most Democratic.

The major driver of New Hampshire's political change comes from a change in the people who live in the state. At the end of the 20th century, the Granite State's population became more mobile, better educated, and increasingly affluent. New Hampshire is the only state in New England that has seen significant population growth since the late 1980s, growing by approximately 1 percent per year since the end of the 1989 to 1992 recession. In the southern tier of New Hampshire, lower housing costs attracted young families, which rapidly converted small towns into the far northern suburban communities of Boston. Further north, retirees settled into the state's recreational areas, while traditional Yankee Republicans either moved or passed away. These new arrivals come from across the Northeast. By 2008, due to in-migration, out-migration, and younger residents reaching voting age, approximately one-third of the electorate, 321,000 people became eligible to vote in the state for the first time, according to a study conducted at the University of New Hampshire's Carsey Institute.[8] Only 68 percent of the 2008 electorate was eligible to vote in 2000; 21 percent are people who have moved to New Hampshire since 2000, and 11 percent are people who were not 18 years old in 2000. These new voters were much more likely to consider themselves Democrats than were established voters (see Figure 7.2).

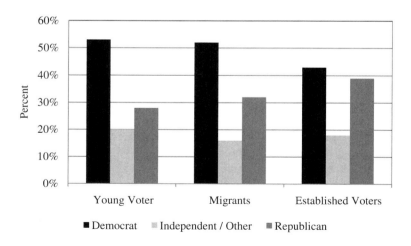

Figure 7.2 Party identification of young, migrants, and established voters, 2008. *Source:* Kenneth M. Johnson University of New Hampshire Carsey Institute, 2008

Voter registration numbers tend to underestimate the changes in partisanship among New Hampshire voters because they necessarily treat "undeclared" voters as an undifferentiated mass. A more accurate gauge of these changes is the University of New Hampshire Survey Center's gauge of the "core partisanship" of all Granite State voters, including undeclared voters (see Figure 7.1). According to this measure, after their 2002 election debacle, Democrats quickly rebounded and nearly equaled Republicans in "core partisans" during the 2004 election season. In this presidential election year, only Democrats held a contested presidential primary, won by neighboring Massachusetts Senator John Kerry. In the general election, Kerry made New Hampshire a key part of his strategy to unseat President Bush, and succeeded in flipping the state from Republican red to Democratic blue. This decision to invest resources in New Hampshire had positive long-term effects for the state Democratic Party, said Shaheen senior advisor Judy Reardon:

> In 2004, Kerry and the DNC [Democratic National Committee] invested significant resources into New Hampshire. This was the turning point in developing our GOTV effort. The Obama campaign did this as well in 2008. Our coordinated campaign was very good in our ability to contact voters. We could reach every Democrat to get them to vote as well as Independents.[9]

Bushwhacked

George W. Bush, who lost the 2000 New Hampshire Republican primary resoundingly to Arizona Senator John McCain, had difficulty in winning over New Hampshire voters. He barely won the state in 2000 and then lost to John Kerry in the 2004 general election. While his job approval ratings were sky high in the wake of the September 11 attacks, his net favorability rating (the difference between his approval and disapproval ratings) dwindled to basically zero during the 2004 campaign. After his administration's apparent mishandling of Hurricane Katrina's aftermath, Bush's job approval sank below 40 percent in New Hampshire, never to reach that figure again. Granite State Democrats turned against Bush in large numbers well before the 2004 election. Between October 2001 and October 2004, his job approval fell from 86 to 12 percent. What changed after 2004 was that New Hampshire independents followed suit, voicing discontent with Bush in percentages almost as large as the Democrats. Bush's job approval fell from 50 percent in January 2005 to less than 25 percent by the summer of 2006. In addition, Republicans also gradually but surely lost faith in Bush throughout his second term as support for the war in Iraq plummeted; but his approval rating among Republicans never fell below 50 percent.

Even though Bush did not appear on a New Hampshire ballot after 2004, throughout his second term his name arguably had ill effects on almost every Granite State politician on the ticket who shared his party affiliation. As glorious as 2002 was for the Republican Party, 2006 was disastrous. Not one, but both

Republican congressmen were victims in 2006. Six-term veteran Charlie Bass, a moderate Republican who represented the Democratic-leaning western 2nd District, seemed destined for defeat days before the election. The shock came when his counterpart, Jeb Bradley, who represented the eastern 1st District, which is more favorable to the Republicans, lost to a little-known, poorly funded antiwar Democrat, Carol Shea-Porter. With Governor Lynch winning 74 percent of the vote at the top of the ticket, Democrats swept Republicans out of office up and down the ballot, gaining majorities in both houses of the state legislature for the first time in more than a century.

Sununu's Dilemma

In the aftermath of the 2006 elections, political prognosticators immediately put John Sununu high on the list of most vulnerable incumbents. A glimpse at the incumbent's favorability ratings explains why: after the 2006 elections, Sununu rarely enjoyed the favor of a majority of New Hampshire voters (see Figure 7.3). A breakdown of his favorability rating by partisan identification indicates a pattern similar to President Bush's. While Sununu's numbers remained strong among Republicans, Democrats soured on him rapidly in the run-up to the 2008 election. Worse yet, his net favorability among independents, which stood at 40 percent in July 2005, dwindled sharply after the 2006 elections. In short, Sununu found himself caught in the same anti-Bush, anti-Republican downdraft that had trapped his GOP colleagues Bass and Bradley in 2006. As Sununu's campaign manager, Paul Collins, noted, they tried but found there was a limit to how much his candidate could do to distance himself from Bush:

> We ran a TV ad and an accompanying radio ad on how Sununu differed from Bush on some very key issues. We had to walk a narrow path because Sununu shared core Republican principles with Bush and other Republicans. It would not have been credible to say that Sununu completely differed with Bush on every policy matter. Our ads highlighted the differences as far as possible while being credible and truthful.[10]

Unlike neighboring New England Republicans, such as Olympia Snowe and Susan Collins of Maine, Sununu amassed a consistently conservative voting record during his term in the Senate. While his congressional vote scores suggest that he moderated his positions somewhat during the latter years of his Senate term (see Table 7.1), he supported the repeal of the estate tax; received a perfect 100 rating from the antitax Club for Growth; remained a supporter of the war in Iraq even as the public increasingly disapproved; and voted against federal funding for embryonic stem-cell research.[11] On the other hand, Sununu did delay reauthorization of the Patriot Act because of civil liberties concerns; voted against a constitutional prohibition of gay marriage; and was the first Republican member of Congress to call for the resignation of Attorney General Alberto Gonzalez.

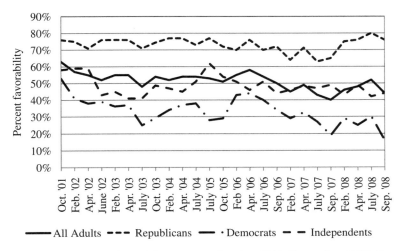

——— All Adults   ▪▪▪ Republicans   ——— · Democrats   ▬ ▬ Independents

Figure 7.3 John Sununu's favorability ratings, October 2001–September 2008. *Source:* University of New Hampshire Survey Center, http://www.unh.edu/survey-center/news/ election2008.html

The Rematch

After losing her bid for the Senate in 2002, Jeanne Shaheen departed New Hampshire politics, taking a job as director of Harvard's Institute of Politics at the Kennedy School of Government. She declined to take on New Hampshire's senior senator, Republican Judd Gregg, in his bid for reelection in 2004. Even after the strong Democratic year in 2006, Shaheen mulled over her decision for several months, as other Democrats such as Katrina Swett (wife of former House member Richard Swett (D-NH) and daughter of the late Congressman Tom Lantos (D-CA), and had run against Bass in 2002) and Steve Marchand

Table 7.1 Congressional Vote Scores for John Sununu, 2003–2008

Year	American Conservative Union	Americans for Democratic Action	Presidential Support	Party Unity
2008	75	25	79	87
2007	84	10	83	83
2006	88	20	90	91
2005	83	10	81	87
2004	100	10	96	94
2003	95	15	95	96

Source: 2003–2006 scores from various editions of CQ's *Politics in America;* 2007–2008 American Conservative Union (ACU) and Americans for Democratic Action (ADA) scores from the organization Web sites; 2007–2008 party unity and presidential support scores from CQ *Weekly Report.*

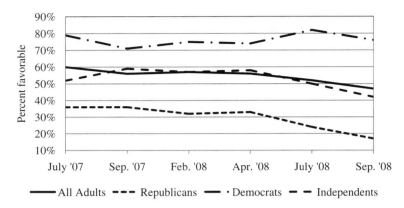

Figure 7.4 Jeanne Shaheen favorability ratings, July 2007–September 2008. *Source:* University of New Hampshire Survey Center, http://www.unh.edu/survey-center/news/election2008.html

(a former Portsmouth mayor) positioned themselves to enter the race. Shaheen eventually announced her intention to run in September 2007, 14 months before the election, and soon cleared the field of potentially significant primary challengers. Upon her return, Shaheen's initial favorability ratings were quite strong, although they dropped throughout 2008 as the campaign began (Figure 7.4). Early in the campaign, in head-to-head polls against Sununu, Shaheen led the incumbent by a double-digit margin (see Figure 7.5).

The Shaheen campaign's experience in 2002, however, kept the 2008 team always wary of good news, said Robby Mook, Shaheen's campaign manager. Mook described "two major overarching issues" for the campaign.[12] First was the

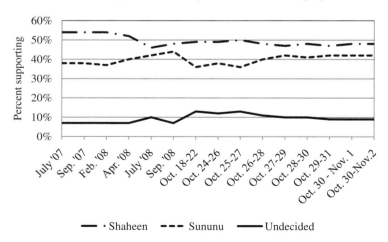

Figure 7.5 New Hampshire Senate race polling, July 2007–November 2008. *Source:* University of New Hampshire Survey Center, http://www.unh.edu/survey-center/news/election2008.html

fact that this was a rematch of a race Shaheen lost in 2002 after running ahead of her opponent in the final months of the campaign. According to Mook, it was "hard to underestimate the psychological impact" of this. Six years later, the Shaheen campaign was wary of polls that consistently showed the Democrat ahead of the incumbent. The second major issue, said Mook, concerned the implications of the 2006 elections in New Hampshire. A "tremendous tidal wave" had swept Democrats into office up and down the ticket. In a single evening, both Republican congressmen Charlie Bass and Jeb Bradley, lost their seats; and the Republicans lost control of both houses of the state legislature for the first time in more than a century. In retrospect, Mook said, one can see 2006 as a sea change in New Hampshire politics. During the 2008 election season, however, there was a "high degree of uncertainty" as to whether the 2006 results would have any effects on 2008, or whether this was the equivalent of a freak storm, the results from which could not be duplicated.

In addition, the campaign's finances were a daily concern for Shaheen, especially because Sununu had $5.1 million in the bank at the end of the second quarter of 2008. Mook said he asked himself two questions every day: "Are we raising enough money?" and "Are we running enough ads?"[13] When Mook came on board in the summer of 2008, he recommended that they use the money gap as an organizing tool in order to create a sense of urgency about the campaign; the Shaheen camp sent out e-mails highlighting the fact that their candidate was trailing the incumbent in fundraising. One reason for the concern over money was the expense of reaching New Hampshire voters. To insure that they reach voters in the populous southern tier of the state, campaigns must rely on Boston television, as well as on New Hampshire's only statewide television station, WMUR-TV. Spending money on Boston television is both expensive and inefficient, given that New Hampshire campaigns necessarily reach many Massachusetts voters who obviously have no stake in the election.

Despite Shaheen's financial concerns, the campaign decided to run an ad in the spring of 2008 in order to reintroduce the former governor to the state's voters. The campaign braced itself for an attack from Sununu, but the ad buy never came. Paul Collins, Sununu's campaign manager, explained why the campaign did not get on the air early:

> This was a topic of much discussion within the campaign. We decided that once we went up on television and radio, we would stay up. Also, until January, it was all about the [presidential] primary. Then political fatigue set in for a while and people didn't want to hear anything about politics. Shaheen went up in May, but this was to re-introduce herself to New Hampshire voters. Had we gone up earlier, it wouldn't have made any difference. We wanted to make sure in 2008 that we could match and surpass Shaheen in ad spending. That was not the case in 2002. We had enough money this year, just under $9 million.[14]

In support of this Sununu's deputy campaign manager, Jamie Burnett, added,

In retrospect, had we known what the economy was going to do in September, we might have done something different. A lot of the things we faced were out of our control—Obama and the economy. With the information we had and what we could reasonably expect in the fall, it was the right decision. In 2002, we were killed on TV by about 6 to 1. We expected 2008 to be similar and we wanted to focus our TV efforts when voters were paying attention, when it mattered in the fall.[15]

For his part, Shaheen's campaign manager thought Sununu should have gone up on the air earlier than he did. Had they done so, Mook thought the Shaheen campaign would "bleed money" and "bleed credibility."[16] If Sununu had gone up early, the Shaheen campaign would likely have felt compelled to match his ad buy. One Sununu-allied group, Americans for Job Security, did go on the radio at the time with a 60-second ad that attacked Shaheen on her record on taxes as governor,[17] but this was a far cry from the early onslaught that greeted her at the beginning of her 2002 run.

The Incumbent Is Outspent

In 2002, Shaheen outspent Sununu by $5.8 million to $3.7 million.[18] The Sununu campaign did not want to see this happen again and entered 2008 with $5.2 million in cash on hand. What is notable about this race, however, is that the challenger was not only able to keep up with the incumbent in terms of spending, but was able to surpass him, as Sununu raised and spent $8 million in comparison to Shaheen's $8.2 million (see Table 7.2).

Sununu's cash disadvantage was actually much more significant than this because of the large amount of outside money that was directed to the New Hampshire contest. The Shaheen campaign benefited because outside groups spent 1.8 times as much money on her behalf as they did on Sununu.

The biggest spender for Shaheen was the Democratic Senatorial Campaign Committee (DSCC) which spent $9,586,701; significant money was also spent by other outside groups such as the Service Workers International Union (SEIU) ($1,321,609), the League of Conservation Voters ($261,600), EMILY's List ($193,245), and the Sierra Club ($31,068). Aiding Sununu was the National Republican Senatorial Committee (NRSC), as well as a variety of probusiness,

Table 7.2 Campaign Finance Data for New Hampshire Senate Seat, 2008

	Shaheen	Sununu
Total Candidate Disbursements	$8,208,542	$8,010,010
Independent Expenditure against Opponent	$11,411,574	$6,520,122
Independent Expenditure in Support of Candidate	$949,374	$197,667
Party Coordinated Expenditures	$167,599	$170,700
Total Outside Expenditures	$12,528,547	$6,888,489
Total Expenditures for Candidate	$20,737,089	$14,898,499

Source: Federal Election Commission

anti-tax groups, including the U.S. Chamber of Commerce, American Future Fund, Club for Growth, and the Employee Freedom Action Committee.[19]

Opening Arguments

As Labor Day approached, Sununu was stuck below 45 percent in head-to-head matchups and Shaheen maintained a lead in the polls (see Figure 7.5). Mook noted that the Democrats began the air campaign with "Dig," an ad designed to frame the choice for New Hampshire voters.[20] In the ad, Shaheen states:

> There's an old saying: When you're in a hole, stop digging. George Bush put our economy in the hole. So why is John Sununu still digging in the same failed direction? We've got to stop spending billions on giveaways to big oil and drug companies. No more no-bid contracts to Iraq or runaway deficits. We need common-sense ideas like clean, alternative energy, tax breaks for the middle class. I'm Jeanne Shaheen. I approved this message because a new direction takes a new senator.

This ad succinctly summed up the Shaheen campaign's message plan for the fall, which Shaheen advisor Judy Reardon described as "Change versus more of the same." The issue on which they would be advocating for change, however, was not the one they expected. Reardon noted that "We thought that Iraq would be the major issue, but it turned out to be the economy." According to Reardon, this was the major dissimilarity between the first and second campaign: "The biggest difference between 2002 and 2008 was national security. In 2002, Shaheen was at a huge disadvantage on this issue, but this was not a voting issue in 2008."[21] Indeed, jobs and the economy were by far the most important concern for New Hampshire voters, according to a September 2008 Granite State Poll conducted by the University of New Hampshire Survey Center.

The DSCC, which invested heavily in the New Hampshire contest, followed up on this theme, emphasizing economic issues and stressing the ties between Sununu and Bush. One such ad, "Choice," debuted in September with the following voice over:

> In Washington, senators have a choice. They can fight for powerful special interests or stand up for the middle class. John Sununu has sided with George Bush to protect the special interests.
> (*Text on screen*: "Sununu Votes Against Bill on Medicare Pay
> —Concord *Monitor*, 7/10/08)

> Sununu just voted three times to protect billions of dollars in profits for the insurance companies and to cut Medicare for 200,000 seniors, veterans and disabled in New Hampshire.
> (*Text on screen: Sununu "voted to protect the powerful insurance companies"—American Medical Association, 7/1/08*)

John Sununu made his choice. Now we need to make ours.

For his part, Sununu began his argument for reelection with an ad, "Quicker." The ad highlighted the candidate's virtues, particularly his independence and youth, which was in implicit contrast with his opponent, who turned 61 in 2008.

> [Announcer]: He's younger, faster, quicker. Inexhaustible, tireless, energetic. A leader. Independent and principled. Great dad, big-hearted, funny and kind. He's the youngest member of the Senate, but *Time* says "that hasn't limited his reach." New Hampshire's in his blood.
>
> [Woman]: I think I'll stick with the future, John Sununu.

In addition, Sununu-allied groups focused on energy policy, which appeared to be a very potent issue in the summer of 2008, when gas prices topped $4 a gallon. In its ad, "Hurting," American Future Fund attempted to portray Shaheen as far too reluctant to allow more domestic oil drilling, while arguing that Sununu pursued a more balanced approach. The ad contained the following audio voice-over:

> New Hampshire families are hurting from record gas prices. But Jeanne Shaheen opposes exploring huge American oil reserves—offshore and in Alaska. The U.S. remains dependent on foreign oil, and the *Wall Street Journal* says gas could go to six bucks a gallon. John Sununu cosponsored tax credits for renewable energy. And he supports safe exploration off our coasts. Call Sununu; encourage him to pass S. 3202 for energy security.

"In the summer, hitting Shaheen about gasoline prices was a good strategy for us against Shaheen, and against Democrats in general, their not wanting to drill and opposition to nuclear energy," said Sununu deputy campaign manager Jamie Burnett. "But when the prices dropped, that issue disappeared."[22]

Other Sununu-allied groups, such as Club for Growth, also aimed at Shaheen's record on taxes as governor. The U.S. Chamber of Commerce was especially pointed, running ads that described the Democrat as a "taxing machine":

> Jeanne Shaheen's been a taxing machine. What's worse: Jeanne Shaheen's spending scheme. Shaheen proposed the largest budget in state history. And Shaheen proposed spending increases by 30 percent. The *Union Leader* called Shaheen's budget "a tax-and-spend boondoggle." Now Shaheen favors billions more in new spending. More taxes for more spending. Notice a pattern? Call Jeanne Shaheen. Tell her we can't afford another spending scheme.

The NRSC, which spent heavily in the race, ran a similar ad that hit Shaheen on taxes. The ad accused Shaheen of saddling the state with a property tax, proposing a 2.5 percent sales tax, and advocating for a state income tax.

The attacks on taxes were especially worrisome, Mook said, because they mirrored what had worked against Shaheen in the 2002 campaign. Nonetheless, because of cost concerns, the Shaheen campaign made a conscious decision not to respond to Sununu's attacks, instead concentrating on their own message.[23] In the weeks following these attacks, public polls showed no signs of imminent danger for the Democrat. Shaheen retained her lead over Sununu, and perhaps most significantly, the incumbent showed no signs of moving his standing in the polls out of the low- to mid-40s (see Figure 7.5).

September Meltdown

The collapse of world financial markets in September 2008 became a major, unexpected theme in both campaigns. It marked a turning point in the Sununu campaign's thinking about the path of the race. Deputy campaign manager Jamie Burnett said that "In September, when the banks and stocks fell," they knew 2008 would not be a year like 2002. Burnett continued: "We still thought we could win, but knew it would be close. But these things were out of our control and we focused on things we could control." This sentiment extended to the strategic nature of the race as well. According to Burnett, even if the Sununu campaign had been able to plan for this issue to take center stage, it "probably wouldn't have done anything different" in terms of a separate line of attack against Shaheen. He added, however, "I wish there was a way we could have gotten our point across that you need a real problem solver and that's what Sununu is."[24]

The Sununu campaign did attempt to turn events in their favor, portraying the senator as a far-sighted legislator in the following ad, "Common Sense," which included the following audio:

> [Announcer]: Five years ago, John Sununu wrote tough regulations for mortgage giants Fannie Mae and Freddie Mac. Democrats blocked his bill, opposing restrictions on risky investments. Six months ago, Jeanne Shaheen still saw no risk, saying, let them use "flexibility and common sense." Boy, Jeanne, that worked out well.
>
> [Woman]: We'll stick with effective: John Sununu.

The Shaheen campaign, in contrast, played connect-the-dots, describing Sununu in "Million Dollar Man" as a knee-jerk deregulator who took a million dollars in Wall Street funds for his campaign—and a Bush clone to boot:

> You know he's George Bush's man. But did you know that John Sununu is also Wall Street's million-dollar man? Sununu's taken a million dollars from

Wall Street—four times more than any other senator in New Hampshire history. What did Wall Street get from Sununu?

"Full-throated" support for "deregulation of banks and just about everything else." That's what's wrecked our economy and our life savings.

John Sununu: He's failed New Hampshire.

In addition, the DSCC lambasted Sununu for reasserting, during a debate with Shaheen, his support for privatization of Social Security in the wake of the stock market meltdown. While Mook, Shaheen's campaign manager, "couldn't believe" Sununu was still defending privatization of Social Security, he noted that the market meltdown favored every Democrat. It was "really hard" for any Republican "to dig out of there," he said.[25] "Late September brought back the anti-Bush sentiment that had been dissipating, once some financial institutions and the stock market went south," said Sununu manager Collins.[26]

Endgame

For all the charges and countercharges flying in the last weeks of the campaign, what was most notable about the Sununu–Shaheen race was how little changed in the polls (see Figure 7.5). In 2002, Sununu staged a comeback in the last days of the campaign, a turnaround that still haunted the Shaheen campaign six years later; in 2008, everyone waited for a comeback that never came to be. As Sununu manager Collins noted, the NRSC never abandoned their candidate, and the DSCC never assumed victory for Shaheen:

> We were told in early October, the NRSC knew they were going to lose the Colorado Senate seat, and other Senate races in states were moved to the unlikely-to-win column throughout the month. But they never gave up on the New Hampshire race. The NRSC spent $1.2 million and the DSCC spent $1.4 million in the final week. People who were going to be deployed in other states came to New Hampshire, but Democrats were doing the same thing—sending available resources to New Hampshire.[27]

While the national party organization remained solid, the party's grass-roots efforts fell off from 2004, said Sununu deputy campaign manager Burnett:

> Despite the impression that was created, the "72 Hour" campaign in 2002 was really very modest. It was huge in 2004 as more effort went into voter contact for the months before the final 72 hours kicked in. In 2004, we had 17–19 offices and lots of staff and volunteers. Our 2008 GOTV effort was greater than 2002 in organization, structure, and funding, but was weaker than 2004. In 2004, we had a lot of first time volunteers that did not come

back in 2008. In 2004, volunteers were highly motivated, it was hard to get and keep volunteers for the [statewide Republican] Victory effort in 2008.

Party efforts were better in 2008 than in 2002, but not as good as 2004. The national party did not inspire confidence in 2008 like we did in 2004.... Bush, McCain, the party did not inspire confidence.

Also, Democratic efforts were much better in 2008 than in 2002. We saw Obama volunteers on rural roads in Bristol, New Hampshire, in July![28]

Both Reardon and Mook said they were pleased with the Democrats' GOTV efforts in the last days of the campaign. Mook noted that the Shaheen campaign was well integrated with Barack Obama's New Hampshire operation in the last few weeks; as a result, the Democrats were able to utilize local and out-of-state volunteers effectively, knocking on thousands of doors.[29]

Shaheen's 7-point margin of victory on Election Day, however, strongly suggests that this was not a contest decided by GOTV efforts. Sununu campaign manager Collins pointed to the race at the top of the ticket, where Obama won by 9 points:

We knew it was going to be close—we were surprised at how poorly McCain was polling in New Hampshire. We thought McCain was going to lose the state, but not by the margin [54 to 45%] that he did. Obama was the wild card, Shaheen rode in on the Obama wave and we rode out on the same wave. There were 76,000 Election Day registrations, and most were coming out for Obama. This benefited Shaheen as most voted for Democrats down ticket. Polling showed there was little enthusiasm for McCain in New Hampshire by Election Day.[30]

The Shaheen camp suggested that Sununu's campaign was too overconfident to play defense effectively in such a political environment. Shaheen advisor Reardon noted that this surprised her about the opponent's campaign:

I was surprised that they did not change their approach to the campaign after things on the ground changed. They ran the same campaign that they did in 2002. They believed their own hype. We were surprised Sununu did not go up on the air with ads earlier—they repeated their 2002 strategy of running ads at the end of the campaign.[31]

Sununu's managers disagreed, arguing that they had done all they could do in such an anti-Republican year. Sununu deputy campaign manager Jamie Burnett commented that he felt the campaign did a fairly good job of distancing themselves from an unpopular president:

I think we did all we could do, but we were hamstrung a bit because we were both Republicans. We had many issues where we differed from Bush, major differences: the Patriot Act; calling for [Attorney General Alberto] Gonzales' resignation; two energy bills; immigration; the highway bill; prescription drugs; detainee treatment; wiretapping; marriage amendment. These were big philosophical differences, but were almost impossible to communicate in the political environment, especially after September.[32]

The political environment of 2008 certainly was an inverse of the 2002 election—Bush had gone from the most popular to one of the least popular presidents in American history; America had soured on the war on terror as it was being played out in Iraq; the economy had slumped; and the Dow Jones Average, which in 2002 was in the beginning of the post 9/11 bull market, had lost nearly half its value in just a year's time. Further, the Republican Party in New Hampshire had seen more than a century of political dominance come crashing down in 2006. For John Sununu, it was awfully difficult to defend his turf when the earth kept moving beneath his feet.

The cumulative impact of shifting local political demographics and the national unpopularity of the Bush administration significantly hurt Sununu's appeal among New Hampshire voters. Sununu was one of the more popular members of New Hampshire's congressional delegation after his election to the Senate in 2002, but he had seen his personal favorability ratings slump as voters became increasingly disenchanted with Bush and the Republican Party. Polls conducted by the University of New Hampshire Survey Center showed that his net favorability rating (the percentage who had a favorable opinion of him minus the percentage who had an unfavorable opinion) consistently stood over 20 percent after he was elected to the Senate, but began to slide in 2006 and continued to drop into 2007, a signal of increasing vulnerability. During that same period, Bush's approval rating in New Hampshire dropped from over 70 percent approval in 2002 to only 30 percent approval in 2007. Bush, who helped bring Sununu to victory in 2002, was dragging him down heading into his bid for reelection.

Six years earlier, Sununu had been able to parlay a bold bid for higher office into a seat in the U.S. Senate, thanks to natural Republican advantages in New Hampshire and a strong GOP year nationwide. Jeanne Shaheen, a reasonably popular, moderate, antitax Democrat who had won three terms as governor, appeared to hit her political ceiling in the Granite State in 2002. Six years later, though, it was Sununu who was hemmed in by a changing political environment, both statewide and nationwide. As a result, the Republican incumbent trailed his opponent continuously for more than a year in preelection polling. The poisonous environment for Republicans in New Hampshire forced Sununu to cast himself as an independent voice for his state, in an attempt to put some distance between himself and his party. But voters, when confronted with two candidates claiming to be agents of change, felt more confident in choosing the one from the party out of power in the White House. By 2008, the political environment for all Republicans in New Hampshire forced Sununu to play defense in a losing game. The twin anchors of George Bush and a shrinking

Republican electorate made Sununu's reelection improbable. The economic crisis in September, coupled with being significantly outspent by Shaheen and her allies, made it almost impossible.

Notes

1. John Fund, "Mr. Smith, Go Home: Why New Hampshire's Senior Senator Shouldn't Seek Re-Election," *Wall Street Journal*, April 5, 2001.
2. Alemayehu Bishaw and Jessica Semega. "Income, Earnings, and Poverty Data from the 2007 American Community Survey," U. S. Census Bureau, American Community Survey Reports (August 2008), http://www.census.gov/prod/2008pubs/acs-09.pdf
3. Hugh Gregg and Bill Gardner. *Why New Hampshire?* (Nashua, NH: Resources—NH, 2003). Residents of Jackson, Michigan; Ripon, Wisconsin; and Crawfordsville, Iowa may disagree as these towns also claim to be the birthplace of the Republican Party.
4. All polling data in this chapter come from surveys conducted by the University of New Hampshire Survey Center, http://www.unh.edu/survey-center/news/election2008.html
5. Thomas B. Edsall, "GOP Official Faces Sentence in Phone-Jamming," *Washington Post,* May 17, 2006, A10.
6. V.O. Key, "Secular Realignment and the Party System," *The Journal of Politics* 21, no. 2 (1959): 198–210.
7. Alfred J. Tuchfarber, Steven E. Bennett, Andrew E. Smith, and Eric W. Rademacher, "The Republican Tidal Wave of 1994: Testing Hypotheses about Realignment, Restructuring, and Rebellion," *P.S.: Political Science and Politics*, 28, no. 4 (December 1995): 689–96. Also see, Arthur Paulson, *Realignment and Party Revival: Understanding American Electoral Politics at the Turn of the Twenty-First Century* (Westport, CT: Praeger, 2006).
8. Kenneth M. Johnson, Dante Scala, and Andrew E. Smith, "Many New Voters Make the Granite State One to Watch in November" (Issue Brief no. 9, University of New Hampshire Carsey Institute, Fall 2008).
9. Andrew Smith's interview with Judy Reardon, May 4, 2009.
10. Smith's interview with Paul Collins, May 12, 2009.
11. Michael Barone and Richard E. Cohen. *The Almanac of American Politics 2008* (Washington, DC: National Journal Group, 2007).
12. Dante Scala's interview with Robby Mook, May 8, 2009.
13. Ibid.
14. Smith's interview with Paul Collins.
15. Smith's interview with Jamie Burnett, May 11, 2009.
16. Scala's interview with Robby Mook.
17. All political ad texts in this chapter come from *National Journal*'s "Ad Spotlight," http://www.nationaljournal.com/members/adspotlight/2008.
18. Center for Responsive Politics, OpenSecrets.org, http://www.opensecrets.org/races/summary.php?id=NHS2&cycle=2002
19. For more information on these groups' activities, see National Public Radio's "Secret Money Project," http://www.npr.org/blogs/secretmoney.
20. Scala's interview with Robby Mook.
21. Smith's interview with Judy Reardon.
22. Smith's interview with Jamie Burnett.
23. Scala's interview with Robby Mook.
24. Smith's interview with Jamie Burnett.

25. Scala's interview with Robby Mook.
26. Smith's interview with Paul Collins.
27. Ibid.
28. Smith's interview with Jamie Burnett.
29. Scala's interview with Robby Mook.
30. Smith's interview with Paul Collins.
31. Smith's interview with Judy Reardon.
32. Smith's interview with Jamie Burnett.

8 Defending the Party's Turf in the Wake of Scandal

McClintock vs. Brown in California's Fourth Congressional District

*Colton C. Campbell**

Congressional campaigns in California are frequently eclipsed by other political events, like controversial ballot measures or recall petitions. In 2008, however, the race for the 4th Congressional District in Northern California proved to be an exception. Decided by a razor-thin margin of 1,800 votes 29 days after Election Day, the open House seat was one of the country's most hotly contested congressional races. It pitted a one-time Republican and decorated Air Force veteran against a well-known GOP state legislator who represented a state Senate district in Southern California and did not live in the 4th District. The two candidates battled to succeed the retiring nine-term incumbent Representative John Doolittle (R-CA), who decided not to run for reelection because of a federal corruption investigation into his dealings with lobbyist Jack Abramoff who pleaded guilty to fraud, conspiracy, and tax evasion charges in January 2006.

Ordinarily, the 4th District would be "an easy vote generator" for Republicans,[1] but 2008 was a year of change, in which the GOP had to play defense to hold the traditionally red congressional district. At issue was whether Tom McClintock could depend on a preponderance of Republican voters to support him and continue the Republican grip on the district or whether Democrat Charlie Brown could take advantage of a volatile election cycle and flip the reliably Republican district Democratic. Democrats had an opportunity in the 4th District because, as one California House Republican said days before the general election with regard to Republican prospects, "The wind is not at our back. It is in our face."[2]

The Fourth District

The 4th District has a nomadic past. Since the end of the Second World War its boundaries have been redistricted no less than four times—most recently in 2003. Today, the elongated district is situated in the northeast corner of California, stretching from the Sacramento suburbs to the borders of Oregon and Nevada. It encompasses over 17,000 square miles and includes within its borders El Dorado, Lassen, Modoc, Nevada, Placer, Plumas, and Sierra Counties and parts of Sacramento and Butte Counties. At the district's southern edge is the vacation destination of South Lake Tahoe, with its premier ski resorts and nearby casinos. To the north is a lonesome landscape of high desert lakes and sagebrush meadows, inactive volcanoes and lava beds, and remote mountainous terrain; a site relatively unchanged from when Japanese Americans were detained there during World War II.

Nestled in the middle of the district are the foothills of the Sierra Nevada Mountains and the California Gold Country. As the rushers of 1849 once flocked to mining towns like Cool, Fiddletown, Gold Run, and Placerville (known as "Hangtown" by miners due to the vigilante hangings that took place there) in search of gold, today's prospectors are migrating to the area to find volcanic soil suitable for zinfandel grapes or to escape the state's congested cities. On a clear day, one can look down from these rolling foothills and see the urban sprawl of the Sacramento Valley rapidly developing along the I-80 corridor, where the district has experienced an influx of new arrivals—largely from the San Francisco Bay Area—drawn to the burgeoning high-tech economy and proximity to the state capital.

With a large swath of the district's land owned by the federal or state government, much of the 4th District's population huddles in and around its urban hubs close to Sacramento. Newer communities like Rocklin and Roseville (the district's population center) in Placer County are some of the fastest-growing communities in California. The town of Lincoln, for instance, grew 255 percent between 2001 and 2009.[3] Still, a third of the district's residents live in rural areas, the largest percentage in any of the state's 53 congressional districts.[4] This urban–rural dichotomy in the 4th extends to socioeconomic distinctions. Lassen and Modoc Counties in the north, for example, have substantially less wealthy and educated residents than the counties in the southern portion of the district, such as El Dorado.

Like other House districts in the northern part of California, the 4th's racial population is very homogenous—more than 80 percent are White, and the ethnic minority is predominantly Hispanic.[5] Compared to the national average, the 4th District is a fairly affluent district, with a median family income of $73,000—roughly $13,000 above the national average. Almost half of the family population (48.2%) earns more than $75,000, and only 5 percent live below the poverty line.[6] The median house is valued at $459,000, with 42 percent of homes worth more than half a million dollars.[7] A good portion of the district's prosperity derives from business ventures ranging from professional and financial services, health-oriented companies like Kaiser-Permanente, and high-tech firms such as Hewlett-Packard, Oracle, and NEC Electronics USA, which are home to most of the white collar workforce. Cattle along with agriculture and natural resources production (most notably timber and some mining) provide a significant portion of the economic base to the rural sections of the 4th District. An interesting economic characteristic is that 16 percent of the workforce (57,559) is government employed.[8] This is a byproduct of the many federal, state, and county agencies, such as forestry and transportation services and correctional facilities, as well as public schools and community colleges located within the district.

Politically, the 4th District is one of the most conservative in the state, routinely delivering the GOP a double-digit percentage-point advantage in voter registration. Until 2002, for example, Placer was statistically the state's most Republican county. Modoc County has since claimed that title, a result of the growing number of seniors living in and moving to the district's northern-most county.[9] In the 2004 presidential election, political analyst Charlie Cook rated the 4th District an average of 11 points more Republican than the nation as a whole;[10] George W. Bush won with 61 percent of the district's vote. So it is with rare exception that residents do not consistently lean toward Republican candidates. The 2006 election was a different story, however, as will be seen below.

Change in demographics resulting from recent transplants, particularly from the liberal-leaning Bay Area, has contributed to a slight shift in the political landscape of the 4th District. Since 2004 Democrats in Placer County have grown by roughly three registered voters for every two Republicans, and the party boasts a headquarters for the first time in roughly a decade.[11] The increase in district voter rolls in 2008 coincided with a statewide trend, in which more than a million new voters registered as Democrats, compared to roughly 230,000 new Republicans, a surge triggered by the interest in the Democratic presidential primary race.[12] Still, Republicans held an advantage of roughly 60,000 voters (a margin of 15%) over Democrats. More interestingly, the district has seen an increase in the number of independent voters. Between 2000 and 2008, for instance, voters declining to declare a party identification grew from just over 13 percent to more than 18 percent, thus making the district somewhat less predictable.[13] Democratic candidate Charlie Brown hoped to make capital of this surge in party registration and growth in the number of independent voters he sought to swing in his direction with the right message.

The Primary Season

Contrary to conventional wisdom, the 2008 campaign for the 4th District was a case in which the incumbent party's prospects seemed to improve when the incumbent opted out of running for reelection.[14] Representative John Doolittle (R-CA) had served the district since 1990, where he regularly won landslide elections. During his 18-year congressional career he built a potent local political machine, won a seat on the influential House Appropriations Committee, rose to a leadership position in the GOP hierarchy, and was hailed by party activists as a rising political star. Doolittle was a near perfect fit for the district: local elected officials liked him for being a mover and shaker in Congress who delivered federal funds to the district while party activists admired him for his ardent partisanship.[15] In 2004, however, Doolittle's increasing stock began to drop as he and his wife came under criminal investigation concerning their dealings with Jack Abramoff and other Washington lobbyists in connection with luxury trips, campaign contributions, and employment. Doolittle's wife ran a bookkeeping and event-planning business (Sierra-Dominion Financial Solutions) that received more than $65,000 from Abramoff and his lobbying associates.[16]

She also served as a paid fundraiser for her husband's campaigns, receiving 15 percent of what she raised,[17] an arrangement that drew voters' ire.[18]

With the Abramoff scandal prominently displayed as a campaign backdrop in 2006, Doolittle narrowly beat back his Democratic challenger, Charlie Brown, by 3 percentage points. After his close win, Doolittle took several steps to improve his public relations situation and stabilize his political footing. He relinquished his leadership post and said he would hire an outside fundraiser to replace his wife, but also agreed to pay her $137,000 that she claimed she was owed.[19] A few months later, however, GOP leadership removed Doolittle from the Appropriations Committee after the Federal Bureau of Investigations (FBI) raided his Virginia home in search of information concerning his wife's fundraising business and work for Abramoff. Mounting pressure from fellow Republicans who considered him a liability because of his associations with the Abramoff bribery and corruption scandal ultimately chased Doolittle from office and created the foundation for a competitive open-seat contest.

With Doolittle not seeking reelection, a brawling primary emerged between two experienced candidates, former U.S. Representative Doug Ose and state Senator Tom McClintock, with the former labeled a "big-spending liberal" and the latter a "greedy carpetbagger."[20] For different reasons, either would have been an excellent surrogate for the incumbent, Doolittle, but the primary between the two Republicans exposed a philosophical rift within the district between those who stood for conservative principles and those who prioritized the needs of the district—a division Doolittle had been particularly adept at neutralizing while in Congress.[21]

Doug Ose had represented the neighboring 3rd Congressional District for six years. When he was first elected in 1998, he promised to serve three terms and then retire to private life. But America was drifting, he said, of his decision to return to public life: "I want to help set a new course for our nation—to rebuild our economy, secure our borders, defend our national security and restore faith in government."[22]

Throughout the campaign Ose tried to prove that he would serve the 4th District in a fashion similar to the 3rd District, as someone who would put district needs before ideology. "I won't need a primer on what the issues in the 4th District are," he declared to a local Rotary Club.[23] As a consequence, Ose's list of endorsements read like a who's who of Republican elected officials, including former California governors Pete Wilson and George Deukmejian, an array of state and federal lawmakers (e.g., 13 of the 18 Republicans in the California House delegation), and an overwhelmingly large number of county supervisors, sheriffs, city council members, and other notables from around the district. Regional elected officials supported Ose because, as they claimed, he was better suited to secure federal funding for local projects and infrastructure. "We've got our jobs to do, and we need an elected official in Washington to help us do it," said one county supervisor.[24]

Ose also spent millions of his personal fortune in media ads disparaging McClintock as a carpetbagging Southern Californian, and for legally accepting $25,000 a year in the tax-free per-diem that California pays state legislators to maintain dual residences—one in their districts and one in Sacramento—despite living 14 miles from the Capitol.[25] In one television spot, for example, McClintock was labeled a termed-out "L.A. politician" shopping for a job. The ad's narrator playfully pushed a grocery cart across an oversized California map to illustrate how McClintock had rolled into the 4th District after testing the waters in two other congressional districts.[26]

Rooted in the conservative wing of the state Republican Party,[27] Tom McClintock entered the race well-known in California among grassroots Republicans.[28] At 52, he had virtually grown up in the state legislature, where he served for more than two decades. McClintock holds the dubious title of losing the most statewide races in modern California history. In 1994, 1998, 2002, and 2006 he won Republican primaries for various statewide offices, losing each time in the general election. He also finished third in the 2003 recall effort to replace Democratic Governor Gray Davis, campaigning as the conservative alternative to the eventual winner, Republican Arnold Schwarzenegger.

McClintock's attraction to conservatives in the 4th District was attributed to his beliefs and values. He was, as one talk radio host said, "the flag-bearer of conservatism of Republican politics in California."[29] Another political observer commented at the time: "McClintock's appeal to the right is that he is an unbending conservative who calls forth its glory days. The office he seeks or holds is far less important than the cause for which he stands, most notably his unyielding opposition to any tax increases."[30] To be expected, party activists, particularly local conservative groups and central committee members overwhelmingly backed McClintock, asserting that he stood for core party values from "guns to God," and would put "conservative principles" over excessive government spending—even at the expense of local projects.[31] These conservative credentials also won the support of national organizations such as the Gun Owners of America, the National Rifle Association, the National Right to Life Committee, the National Taxpayers Union, and the Eagle Forum. In short, McClintock was a perfect fit for a GOP primary.

Armed with endorsements from these right-of-center groups, McClintock was able to rally the GOP base by castigating Ose as a profligate spender in Congress who failed to address illegal immigration.[32] McClintock was able to compete against Ose's millions because he was also well-funded, raising over $1 million before the primary (see Table 8.1). His campaign successfully portrayed the business-oriented moderate Ose as "a Republican that votes like a liberal Democrat" out of step with the values of conservative 4th District voters.[33] "This is a battle for the heart and soul of the Republican Party," declared McClintock. "It's between one of the most constant conservatives in the legislature and one of the most liberal Republicans to serve in Congress."[34]

In the end, John Doolittle endorsed neither candidate, and McClintock handily won the Republican nomination by 14 percentage points. Neither the millions spent by Doug Ose nor his charges of carpetbagging appeared to resonate with voters in a primary that produced a light voter turnout. Instead, the

Table 8.1 Campaign Finance Data by Reporting Period for California's 4th District

Reporting Period	McClintock			Brown		
	Receipts	Disbursements	Ending Cash	Receipts	Disbursements	Ending Cash
2007 Year End (January 1 – December 31)	$0	$0	$0	$707,224	$339,496	$483,490
2008 April Quarterly (January 1 – March 31)	$315,979	$190,095	$125,884	$249,322	$142,166	$590,646
2008 Pre-primary (April 1 – May 14)	$690,021	$716,738	$99,167	$96,538	$189,258	$497,927
2008 July Quarterly (May 14 – June 30)	$590,952	$577,395	$112,724	$264,639	$87,371	$675,194
2008 October Quarterly (July 1 - September 30)	$978,568	$997,077	$94,215	$546,514	$764,874	$456,834
2008 Pre-general (October 1 – October 15)	$203,712	$244,237	$53,689	$145,644	$377,682	$224,795
2008 Post-general (October 16 – November 24)	$748,202	$616,009	$185,882	$543,387	$608,783	$159,400
Total	$3,527,434	$3,341,551	$185,882	$1,846,044	$2,170,134	$159,400

Note: The 2007 Year End figures represent funds raised and disbursements in the campaign cycle to date.
Source: Compiled from candidate reports to the Federal Election Commission, Form 3, Lines 23, 24, 26 and 27, various dates.

party's political base mobilized around McClintock's conservative credentials, which they felt better reflected the values of the 4th District, and McClintock cruised to a 15-point victory.[35]

The Democratic primary was far less contentious, with Charlie Brown decidedly winning the nomination, besting his opponent with 88 percent of the vote. A retired Air Force lieutenant colonel, Brown's military career spanned conflicts from Vietnam to Desert Storm. As a rescue helicopter pilot at the end of the Vietnam War, he participated in the evacuations of Saigon and Phnom Penh. He fought in the last conflict of that war in the infamous Mayaguez Incident— for which he earned the Distinguished Flying Cross. Cambodian forces seized the USS Mayaguez and impounded both it and its crew at the island of Koh Tang. Then-Lieutenant Charlie Brown copiloted the rescue helicopter that was part of the mission to recover the vessel and crew.

A district resident from Roseville for nearly two decades, Brown's only other foray into politics was two years earlier when he challenged then-incumbent Representative John Doolittle. Thus, voters already knew him fairly well. Running as a fiscal conservative and emphasizing personal character over party affiliation, one political observer remarked: "In another time, in another congressional district, Charlie Brown would be a Republican."[36] Brown actually had been a lifelong Republican, but he had left the party because he felt it had abandoned its conservative values and had been taken over by "extremists."[37] Brown jumped into a second bid for the 4th District with experience running a districtwide campaign and positioning himself as a moderate with a military background.

Brown's lopsided victory is due, at least in part, to his large war chest. When he declared his candidacy in 2007 he came off a strong showing after having given John Doolittle a scare in 2006, and as a result he was able to get an early start raising money. Brown's ability to attract donors showed in that he reported raising nearly $750,000 by the end of 2007. Brown, however, did not have to spend much of that during the primary to defeat his opponent which left him in good stead to start the general election.

The General Election

Neither Tom McClintock nor Charlie Brown entered the general election with a clear lead, as polls commissioned by each camp showed its candidate in front by only slim margins. The low approval ratings of outgoing President George W. Bush, growing voter frustration over an economy in turmoil, and a retiring incumbent tainted with scandal appeared to tarnish the Republican brand in the 4th District. Nonetheless, flipping the traditionally Republican district Democratic seemingly belied its conservative demographics and voting patterns.

Campaign Issues and Themes

Though Democrat Charlie Brown contended that his center-right views, especially on gun rights, deficit spending, and the war in Iraq, better fit the district than the strongly conservative positions of his Republican opponent, he campaigned largely on his biography as a career military officer.[38] To this end, similar to his strategy two years earlier, he "sought to cultivate a non-partisan appeal" by emphasizing patriotism and personal character over partisanship;[39] he often signed campaign newsletters and op-ed pieces, "Charlie Brown, Lt. Col. USAF Ret." As a way to highlight this campaign theme, he pledged to donate 5 percent of his campaign contributions to local veterans' charities offering housing, counseling, and educational opportunities to returning troops. The gesture also was intended to remind voters of the retiring incumbent, John Doolittle, who drew criticism for paying his wife a 15 percent commission on campaign money she had raised.[40] The campaign reinforced the message with patriotic-themed ads highlighting Brown's family's military service, including his wife, herself an Air Force veteran, and his son, an Air Force captain entering his fifth tour of duty in Iraq. One commercial, narrated by former Senator Max Cleland (D-GA), who lost both legs and his right arm in combat in Vietnam, said in part: "As a fellow soldier and veteran, I know it's time to restore honor and dignity to our government in Washington. Vote for Charlie Brown for Congress. It's a vote you can be proud of."[41]

With a sharp focus on the district's discontent with President Bush and the war in Iraq as well as residents' concern for veterans, Brown stumped across the district with Cleland and retired Army General Wesley Clark, calling for better treatment of returning combat veterans from Iraq and Afghanistan. To this end, at speeches and in campaign newsletters he reminded supporters about his opponent's past opposition to various military and veterans' issues while in the state Senate.

Brown also borrowed a line of political attack from McClintock's primary opponent, Doug Ose, by labeling McClintock a carpetbagger. In television and radio spots, McClintock was aggressively criticized for being registered to vote in his state Senate district roughly 400 miles to the south as opposed to the 4th District, as illustrated by the following radio ad:

> Let me get this straight. There's this guy from L.A. called Tom McClintock who's running for Congress in our district—and he says he's not going to vote for himself. Seriously, he's up here from L.A. asking us to vote for him, but he's not going to vote for himself. I know this sounds really weird—but Tom McClintock has made his decision—he's not voting for Tom McClintock. Now, L.A. Tom could vote for himself—if he would just move here. You would think if he wants to represent us, he wouldn't mind living here— it's a nice place. But wait, if he moved here, he wouldn't get that fat salary and tax-free living expenses from the state Senate. Oh, yeah, and L.A. Tom would have to give up his taxpayer-funded government car. L.A. Tom has made his decision. Let's make ours. If Tom McClintock won't vote for himself, why should we?[42]

In many respects, the campaign strategy of Brown was a page taken from the Democratic playbook used to win recent special elections in other heavily

Republican districts, such as in Illinois, Louisiana, and Mississippi: it sought to distance the candidate from the Democratic Party, thereby making it difficult for the Republican candidate to differentiate himself from his Democratic opponent and to defend the district.[43] Routinely, for instance, when asked whether he intended to vote for the Democratic presidential nominee, Barack Obama, Brown would avoid the question. Asked if he would want Obama or House Speaker Nancy Pelosi (D-CA) to campaign for him, he often called upon both parties' presidential nominees, along with Pelosi and her Republican predecessor, former House Speaker Dennis Hastert (R-IL) to come to the district and debate the issues.[44]

For his part, Republican Tom McClintock stuck largely to his strategy that worked in the primary election—focusing on broad philosophical issues such as federal spending, taxes, and immigration, as well as his high name identification, courtesy of the several times that he has run for statewide office.[45] Even in losing his 2006 bid for lieutenant governor, for example, McClintock won the 4th District. Strategically, he sought to capitalize on evangelical voters and social conservatives turning out in the district for Proposition 8, a state initiative declaring marriage to be solely between a man and a woman and overturning a California Supreme Court ruling that legalized gay marriage.[46] Campaign workers routinely made calls urging voters to support both Proposition 8 and McClintock for Congress.[47] In ads, mailers, and automated phone calls (i.e., robo calls) McClintock emphasized his core Republican values, such as opposition to taxation, illegal immigration, and gay marriage.

Believing ideology would trump representation on local issues,[48] McClintock warned supporters at nearly every turn in the race of an Obama presidency and a Pelosi Congress. "This election in the 4th District may decide whether we will return to our traditional founding freedoms or whether the nation will move to European socialism," he declared at one campaign stop.[49] In both campaign speeches and media ads, McClintock labeled Charlie Brown a liberal Democrat, who marched in lock step with Speaker Pelosi from San Francisco, in many cases mentioning Brown and Pelosi interchangeably; here he borrowed a favorite strategy used by many Democrats in linking their Republican opponents to President Bush.

Although he did not serve in the military, McClintock accused his Democratic opponent of insulting U.S. troops with his antiwar activism and failure to support the surge of troops into Iraq. His television and radio commercials effectively assailed Brown for wearing a military uniform to support a 2005 antiwar rally in which an American soldier was hung in effigy. In one 60-second radio spot featuring a woman whose son had served three tours in Iraq, Brown's appearance at the rally was maligned for helping groups like Code Pink "promote their left-wing agenda." "His campaign theme is patriotism over partisanship," argued McClintock, "when in fact he has engaged in some of the most radical activities in our region."[50] The camouflage Air Force jacket worn by Brown was not the full dress or combat uniform, as the ad suggested, but the underlying message made its point among conservative voters, portraying him as an antiwar radical who was out of touch with voters in the heavily Republican 4th District.

Money Floods the Fourth

The McClintock and Brown campaigns were waged with comparable financial measures. Table 8.1 lists the total money raised and spent by the two candidates during 2008, which provides important lessons about this contest. First, Charlie Brown began the general election campaign with a sizable fundraising advantage: at the end of June, Brown had more than five times the cash on hand that Tom McClintock did. This was due, in part, to the early successes Brown had in raising money (nearly $1 million in 2007). However, he experienced a fundraising lull in the first half of 2008; he raised only $600,000 during this period compared to McClintock's $1.5 million. Brown continued to trail McClintock in fundraising throughout the remainder of the campaign as well and ended up raising $1 million less than McClintock.

In an open-seat contest like this one, it is not unusual to see both candidates very well financed, as both Brown and McClintock were. In raising these sums, the candidates took different routes. Brown received heavy support from political action committees (PACs) ($515,465), and organized labor ($238,750). The bulk of McClintock's contributions came from single-issue groups—$575,615—and the finance and real estate sectors—$300,844. McClintock was far ahead of his opponent in contributions from individuals; 85 percent of his total contributions came from individual donations compared to Brown, who raised 76 percent of his total revenue from individuals.[51] Another important lesson is found in the data on fundraising (see Table 8.1). McClintock proved to be a prodigious fund-raiser from the start. He declared his candidacy in the first week of March, raised $1 million within eight weeks, and more than $3.5 million in all of 2008. He spent those funds, however, almost as fast as he raised them, leaving little cash on hand at the end of each reporting period. During the primary, he was obviously taking nothing for granted in his tough battle with Doug Ose. However, this continued to the general election as well; for instance, between July and October, McClintock raised nearly $1 million and spent even more, leaving him with less than $100,000 in available funds (see Table 8.1).

Without the kind of competition found in the GOP primary, Brown cruised to the Democratic nomination. He continued to raise funds during every reporting period to add to the almost $500,000 cash with which his campaign started the year, but quickly fell behind the pace set by McClintock. Unfortunately for Brown, McClintock raised more money than him in every reporting period in 2008. This allowed McClintock to spend approximately $1 million more than Brown during the primary, and about $500,000 more during the general election. Overall, McClintock raised more than $1.3 million more than Brown.

The candidates were not the only ones spending money in the 4th District. The importance of the race to both political parties was evident in the support that each candidate received from his party's Hill Committee. For the Democrats it was a chance to turn another "red" congressional district "blue," and the Republicans needed to defend this once solidly red turf which was left vacant after the incumbent got caught up in scandal.[52] As part of its national "Red to

Blue" program to turn Republican seats Democratic, the Democratic Congressional Campaign Committee (DCCC) offered Charlie Brown and other promising Democratic candidates financial, communications, and strategic support. This program had a proven success record in the 2004 and 2006 election cycles, having raised nearly $7.5 million for 27 campaigns with an average of more than $250,000 per campaign in 2004, and more than $22 million for 56 campaigns with an average of $404,000 per campaign in 2006.[53] In the final month of the 2008 cycle, sensing a plausible win, the DCCC spent more than $776,000 to boost Brown.[54] In addition to the amount of funding, the DCCC's spending for Brown is notable because he is not a prototypical Democrat as he holds moderate or even conservative views. In campaigns, however, this is not critical to the party in their decision on who to fund. Rather, all the party cares about is winning. The DCCC helped Charlie Brown not because he would be a loyal Democratic vote in the House but rather because he would cast a vote for Nancy Pelosi for Speaker of the House and add to the number of Democrats in the House.

Part of the DCCC's bankroll was a blitz of reprised districtwide television commercials, entitled "Travelin' Tom," which fit nicely with what the Brown campaign was saying, and depicted McClintock as a career politician who had failed in multiple runs for statewide office and was running in a district well north of his state Senate seat. Another charge by the DCCC, which also reinforced Brown's assertions, dealt with McClintock's votes on veterans' issues while in the state legislature. McClintock opposed a state bill to enable service members to defer financial obligations while deployed, citing violation of private contracts, as well as a bond measure to authorize $900 million to provide home loans to veterans, citing wasteful spending and federal responsibility to care for veterans.

The Republican National Congressional Committee (NRCC) responded to the DCCC with its own set of ads that cast Brown as a pawn of Speaker Pelosi, again consistent with what the McClintock was saying about Brown. One television ad in the final days of the campaign, which sought to capitalize on growing voter frustration over the economic crisis, portrayed Brown as a would-be tax-raising "yes man" for Pelosi, flashing a series of headlines: "Liberal Yes Man Charlie Brown," "Brown Supports Wall Street Bailout," "Two Trillion Dollars in New Federal Spending," and "Hundreds of Billions on Bailout and Special Interests":

> Do we really want to send another liberal Democrat like Charlie Brown to Congress? Nancy Pelosi's political machine is forcing even higher taxes on everyday Americans—over two trillion dollars in new federal spending proposals, with billions more for special interests. Big spenders like Brown and Pelosi support increasing taxes that will hurt California families. Brown even supported the Wall Street bailout—over $6,000 in new debt for each family in America.

> And don't forget Pelosi's proposal to give amnesty and Social Security benefits to illegal aliens. Just imagine what they'll propose with another liberal yes man like Charlie Brown. Compare that to Tom McClintock's record of

solid, conservative values. Tom's taken the No New Taxes Pledge, fought against amnesty for illegal aliens, and led the battle to cut the car tax, saving California families up to $600 a year. Tom McClintock—real leadership in Congress.[55]

The ad played heavily on voter discontent with congressional passage of the $700 billion economic bailout package intended to rescue the slumping credit markets, a measure McClintock opposed and Brown supported.[56] It also tried to play to McClintock's reputation as a fiscal conservative—a record underscored by another ad featuring former Republican Senator Fred Thompson (R-TN), who highlighted McClintock's budget and financial experience as strong reasons to send him to Congress. "Democrats, Republicans, and independents all agree when it comes to watching the budget and fighting for the taxpayer, Tom McClintock is the one we can trust," said Thompson. "I'll feel a lot more confident with Tom McClintock working on it, rather than some amateur."[57]

Continuing the liberal, Pelosi theme, McClintock put out a plea on his Web site for donations to hold off Brown's challenge.[58] "Nancy Pelosi's Democratic Congressional Campaign committee just spent at least $200,000 in TV ads to try to win this election for Charlie Brown," McClintock said in his fundraising appeal. "While Charlie has the 'Who's Who' of the American Left at his disposal and now the vast resources of the Pelosi machine…I have to rely on people like you who will not give up this country to the Left without a fight."[59]

Overtime in the Fourth District

In the end, the campaign strategies of both candidates effectively paid off, as neither candidate could claim victory the day after the election. From the time votes started coming in, McClintock and Brown were neck-and-neck. With McClintock leading by less than 500 votes, Brown declined to concede, declaring that thousands of provisional and absentee ballots remained to be counted. Meanwhile, McClintock cautioned supporters at his campaign headquarters in Roseville that while the 4th District would likely stop the tsunami from the left that was sweeping the nation, it would be awhile before he could confidently claim victory. Thus, as county election officials automatically began partial manual audits, each campaign predicted their candidate would eventually be declared the winner.

With still no winner declared two weeks after Election Day, both McClintock and Brown were invited to Washington, DC, to attend a week long orientation for newly elected members of Congress. Both men projected themselves as the winner of the 4th District, lobbied party leaders for committee assignments, attended various sessions to orient themselves to their new surroundings, and prepare for the 111th Congress (2009–2011). Both were also received at a celebration reception for the freshmen class of lawmakers. "Obviously, it's a little awkward," McClintock noted about their uncomfortably close arrangement.[60] Not only had the two checked into their hotel at the same time, they rode the same bus to meetings together and even selected the same congressional office.

Twenty-nine days after the election, McClintock claimed victory, confident it was impossible for Brown to overcome a deficit of more than 1,500 votes out of nearly 370,000 cast. He declared to supporters that the "liberal wave that swept over America and lapped at the edge of this district" was turned back.[61] "When the final votes were counted, it was the people of the 4th District that made the decision to stand by our traditional American principles of individual freedom and limited government," he declared.[62] McClintock also offered his Democratic opponent comfort by citing his favorite statesman. "I have always found great consolation in Winston Churchill's words. He said politics are just as interesting as war and much more exciting. When in war you can be shot dead only once, in politics it can happen 'many times.'"[63] McClintock also said that he and his wife were shopping for a house in the district. Two days later, Brown decided to concede after totals continued to show McClintock with a lead of just over 1,500 votes.

When all was said and done, McClintock tallied 185,790 votes (50.3%) to Brown's 183,990 (49.7%). Brown took Nevada, Plumas, and Sierra Counties, where 75 percent of those registered to vote did so, while McClintock won the other six counties, in which 66 percent of registered voters cast ballots. McClintock's slim margin of victory came largely from the northern part of the district, particularly Lassen and Modoc Counties. In contrast, McClintock did less well in some of the Sacramento suburbs, particularly those that have experienced a migration of new voters from the Bay Area.

Conclusion

In the race for the 4th District, Democrats hoped to exploit growing national discontent with the Republican label, an increase in the number of voters registering as Democrats, the vacating incumbent's political troubles, and an overall election theme of "change" to wrest the seat from the Republicans. "The Republican brand is being recalled," contended one Democratic state party spokesperson. "Even up there [in the 4th District]."[64] And for all intents and purposes, these hopes were answered. After it became clear John Doolittle's scandal would mean the 4th District would be an open-seat contest, Tom McClintock had to step in and defend the otherwise "safe" GOP territory against a well-funded challenger buoyed by national trends that clearly impacted the vote. This was not an easy feat. Even in this Republican district, the Republican presidential nominee, John McCain, only carried the district with 54 percent of the vote.

While Charlie Brown was well financed, one has to wonder if he did all he could with those funds. While he did well in 2007 raising money, he raised small sums early in 2008. Specifically, he only raised $100,000 in the six-week period between the start of April and mid-May. He also did not spend much immediately after the primary when the general election campaign began and he was head-to-head with Tom McClintock. Could Charlie Brown have done more?

Probably. Would this have made it more difficult for McClintock to defend this turf? We will never know.

While Tom McClintock benefited from a funding advantage, the deciding factor in the race was the fact that the philosophical issues that he championed throughout the campaign, along with his partisan credentials and strong name appeal ultimately resonated more with the conservative leanings of voters than did the center-right views of Charlie Brown. McClintock successfully deflected the charges of carpetbagging against him and, in turn, played a little offense by convincing enough supporters that his opponent's politics were more ideologically similar to those of liberal Democrats, namely Nancy Pelosi, than those held by most in the district. In short, he was able to use ideology to trump representation on local issues.

Democrats will almost certainly target California's 4th District in the 2010 electoral cycle. Indeed, the election results had barely been recorded before the DCCC issued a press statement criticizing McClintock for his vote against an economic stimulus bill and accusing him of putting partisanship before constituents. While he is not entirely invulnerable, such charges, in all probability, should not affect McClintock's chances for reelection. Rather, he will most likely represent the 4th District for some time as he accumulates the electoral advantages traditionally associated with incumbency. Recent electoral results notwithstanding, and absent any significant gerrymandering, the district's heavy Republican registration edge gives the GOP a distinct advantage in any contest in this district.

Notes

* The contents of this chapter are solely the responsibility of the author and do not reflect the views of the National War College, the Department of Defense, or any other agency of the United States Government.

1. Peter Hecht, "GOP Stronghold Has a Struggle on Its Hands in McClintock vs. Brown," *The Sacramento Bee*, November 1, 2008, http://www.sacbee.com (accessed February 27, 2009).

2. Quoted in Dan Morain, "California Elections; GOP Faces Fierce Fight for Congress; Democrats in the State Have Three Assets This Year: Money, Increased Voter Registration and Barack Obama," *Los Angeles Times*, October 27, 2008, B1.

3. State of California, Department of Finance, "E-4 Population Estimates for Cities, Counties and the State, 2001–2008, with 2000 Benchmark," May 2008, http://www.dof.ca.gov/research/demographic/reports/estimates/e-4_2001-07 (accessed March 4, 2009).

4. Michael Barone with Richard E. Cohen, *The Almanac of American Politics, 2008* (Washington, DC: National Journal Group, 2007), 173.

5. U.S. Census Bureau, "2005–2007 American Community Survey, Congressional District 4, California—Fact Sheet," http://fastfacts.census.gov/servlet/CWSADPTable?geo_id=50000US0604&ds_name=ACS_2007_3YR_G00_&qr_name=ACS_2007_3YR_G00_DP3YR4&back=%2Fservlet%2FACSCWSFacts%3F_event%3DChangeGeoContext%26geo_id%3D50000US0604%26_geoContext%3D01000US%7C04000US06%26_street%3D%26_county%3D%26_cd%3D50000US0604%26_cityTown%3D%26_state%3D04000US06%26_

zip%3D%26_lang%3Den%26_sse%3Don%26ActiveGeoDiv%3D%26_useEV%3
D%26pctxt%3Dfph%26pgsl%3D040%26_content%3D%26_keyword%3D%26_
industry%3D&_scrollToRow (accessed March 9, 2009).

6. Ibid.
7. Ibid.
8. Ibid.
9. It may be a surprise to see that senior citizens are raising the Republican advantage in this county. This is because the seniors have relatively more conservative views than the younger voters who have moved into the Sacramento suburbs from the Bay Area.
10. Charlie Cook, *The Cook Political Report*, http://www.cookpolitical.com/sites/default/files/pvichart.pdf (accessed March 6, 2009).
11. Philip Reese, "New-Voter Registrations in Sacramento Region Tilt toward Democrats," *The Sacramento Bee*, September 28, 2008; and Stuart Leavenworth, "Political Landscape of Region Shifting?" *The Sacramento Bee*, June 8, 2008, E1.
12. Mark DiCamillo, "The Continuing Growth of Mail Ballot Voting in California in 2008," *California Journal of Politics and Policy* 1 (2009): 1–6; and Phil Willon, "Democrats Hope to Wrest House Seats; With an Army of New Voters, the State Party Sees Opportunities to Make Inroads in GOP Strongholds," *Los Angeles Times*, June 5, 2008, A24; and *The Sacramento Bee*, "Democrats Improve Registration across California, Key Assembly Seats," October 31, 2008, http://www.sacbee.com/static/weblogs/capitolalertlatest/016613.html (accessed March 12, 2009).
13. Figures from State of California, Secretary of State, http://www.sos.ca.gov/elections/elections_u.htm (accessed March 11, 2009).
14. Rachel Kapochunas, "California Republican Wins Next-to-Last Nov. 4 House Race," *CQ Today Online News*, December 3, 2008, http://www.cqpolitics.com (accessed March 10, 2009).
15. Peter Hecht, "GOP Divided Over Doolittle Replacement," *The Sacramento Bee*, June 2, 2008, A1.
16. Philip Shenon, "Federal Lawmakers from Coast to Coast Are Under Investigation." *The New York Times*, July 26, 2007, 16.
17. Barone with Cohen, *Almanac of American Politics, 2008*, 173.
18. Susan Schmidt, "GOP Congressman Tied To Abramoff Will Retire; Californian Is Still Under Investigation," *The Washington Post*, January 11, 2008, A2.
19. Barone with Cohen, *Almanac of American Politics, 2008*, 174.
20. John Wildermuth, "GOP Sparks Fly in Race for Seat of Rep. Doolittle; Accusations of Carpetbagging, Liberalism in Conservative District," *San Francisco Chronicle*, May 5, 2008, B1.
21. Peter Hecht, "GOP Divided. "
22. Quoted in Jeff Munson, "Congressional Candidates Vying to Represent the South Shore," *Tahoe Daily Tribune*, May 23, 2008, http://www.tahoedailytribune.com (accessed March 23, 2009).
23. Quoted in Marcos Breton, "4th District Shows Right Stuff's Appeal," *The Sacramento Bee,* June 8, 2008, B1.
24. Quoted in Peter Hecht, "GOP Divided," A1.
25. David M. Drucker, Josh Kurtz, John McArdle, Matthew Murray, and Shira Toeplitz, "West," *Roll Call*, October 7, 2008, http://www.rollcall.com (accessed March 26, 2009).
26. http://www.dougose.com/media_tvads.asp.
27. Rachel Gordon, "Fourth Congressional District; McClintock-Brown Race Will Be Costly," *San Francisco Chronicle*, June 5, 2008, B4.
28. Drucker et al., "West."
29. http://www.tommcclintock.com/media.

30. Quoted in Tony Quinn, "Running Away From Home; Tom McClintock's Base Is in Thousand Oaks, but He Wants to Be Suburban Sacramento's Man in Congress," *Los Angeles Times*, March 16, 2008, M7.
31. Hecht, "GOP Divided," A1.
32. *Roll Call*, "California: McClintock Raps House Republicans in New Flier," May 15, 2008, ProQuest Central database (Document ID: 1479008621) (accessed March 24, 2009).
33. Quoted in Wildermuth, "GOP Sparks Fly," B1.
34. Ibid.
35. Peter Hecht, "McClintock Triumphs Over Ose in Republican House Race," *The Sacramento Bee, June 4, 2008*, A1.
36. Kel Munger, "Race for Your Life, Charlie Brown. Could ex-Republican Charlie Brown Be the One to Beat Doolittle?" *Sacramento News & Review*, May 4, 2006, http://www.newsreview.com/sacramento (accessed March 23, 2009).
37. Trina Kleist, "Air Force Vet to Face Doolittle," *Tahoe Daily Tribune*, October 19, 2005, http://www.tahoedailytribune.com (accessed March 23, 2009).
38. Drucker et al., "West."
39. Peter Hecht, "Partisanship on the Line in 4th Congress District Race," *The Sacramento Bee*, September 29, 2008, http://www.sacbee.com (accessed February 27, 2009).
40. Peter Hecht, "Brown Focuses On War Veterans to Back His Bid," *The Sacramento Bee*, May 2, 2008, A4.
41. http://www.charliebrownforcongress.org
42. Although the U.S. Constitution does not require a Member of Congress to live in his or her district, under California's Constitution, state legislators must. Script of radio spot from http://www.charliebrownforcongress.org/article.php?uid=579 (accessed March 2, 2009).
43. Tim Grieve, "In Calif., Brown Distances Self from Dems," *Politico*, September 9, 2008, http://www.politico.com (accessed February 27, 2009).
44. Ibid.
45. Drucker et al., "West"
46. Hecht, "GOP Stronghold."
47. Ibid.
48. Quinn, "Running Away from Home," M7.
49. Quoted in Hecht, "GOP Stronghold."
50. Quoted in Hecht, "Partisanship on the Line."
51. Center for Responsive Politics, "Congressional Elections," http://www.opensecrets.org/races/sectors.php?cycle=2008&id=CA04 (accessed April 21, 2009).
52. Patrick McGreevy, "4th and 11th Congressional Districts; Races draw National Attention; The Campaigns in Northern California Are Considered 'On the Line,' Prompting Party Committees To Act," *Los Angeles Times*, October 12, 2008, B3.
53. http://www.dccc.org/page/content/redtoblue (accessed March 31, 2009).
54. Peter Hecht, "Reliably GOP Region Flirts with a Left Turn," *The Sacramento Bee*, November 2, 2008, A1.
55. Script of radio spot from http://www.tommcclintock.com/media/browse/audio/?page=1 (accessed March 2, 2009).
56. Peter Hecht, "Republicans Try to Cast Brown as Pawn of Pelosi," *Sacramento Bee*, October 31, 2008, A3.
57. http://www.tommcclintock.com/media/browse/audio/?page=1 (accessed March 2, 2009).
58. Hecht, "Republicans Try," A3.
59. Quoted in ibid.

60. Quoted in Rob Hotakainen, "4th District Rivals Mingle at D.C. Orientation," *The Sacramento Bee*, November 19, 2009, http://www.sacbee.com (accessed April 6, 2009).
61. Quoted in Peter Hecht, "29 Days After Vote, Brown Concedes Loss to McClintock," *The Sacramento Bee*, December 4, 2008, http://www.sacbee.com (accessed February 27, 2009).
62. Quoted in ibid.
63. Quoted in Peter Hecht, "McClintock Declares Win in 4th Congressional District," *The Sacramento Bee*, December 2, 2008, http://www.sacbee.com (accessed February 27, 2009).
64. Quoted in Jesse McKinley and Jennifer Steinhauer, "An Open Seat in California? That's Just the Start," *The New York Times*, June 2, 2008, http://www.nytimes.com (accessed February 27, 2009).

9 Campaign Cash, Negative Ads, and Court Battles

Coleman vs. Franken vs. Barkley in Minnesota's Senate Race

Kathryn Pearson, William H. Flanigan, and Nancy H. Zingale

The battle in Minnesota between Republican incumbent Senator Norm Coleman, comedian Al Franken, and Independence Party candidate Dean Barkley made Minnesota history for its competitiveness, negativity, length, and cost. The outcome was often and appropriately referred to as a tie. After what initially appeared to be a very narrow election night victory for Coleman, he lost a recount by a 225 vote margin as well as several subsequent skirmishes in the courts. Finally, on June 30, 2009, the Minnesota Supreme Court ruled unanimously that Franken had won by 312 votes.

Putting aside the postelection legal contest, in the aftermath of the bitterly fought race, some political observers have asked why incumbent Senator Norm Coleman did not win despite his strategic and resource-intensive efforts. After all, he had the advantages of incumbency, and his Democratic challenger had no electoral experience to draw upon (but many off-color jokes for his opponent to exploit). Other observers have asked why Al Franken did not win big, running against a vulnerable incumbent in a year and state that heavily favored Democrats, evidenced by Barack Obama's 10 point victory in his battle with John McCain for Minnesota's 10 electoral votes. However the question is framed, the answer reflects the unpopularity of both major party candidates among swing voters and even some of their own partisans. The negatives associated with both Coleman and Franken shaped their campaign strategies as each sought to capitalize on the other's weaknesses, intensifying voters' dissatisfaction, and opening the door for a third-party candidate to siphon off votes. In the end, despite the polarized political environment that might have heightened the significance of voters' partisan identification, many Minnesotans were willing to split their tickets between votes for president and senator, or vote for Barkley, a third-party candidate; Franken and Coleman each received approximately 42 percent of the vote, while Barkley captured 15 percent.

Minnesota's electoral and political landscape, the roots of voters' dissatisfaction with the candidates, the costly and highly negative campaign, and the candidates' strategies, all influenced the outcome of this contest that resulted in one of the closest margins in U.S. Senate history. An analysis of these factors reveals that even in a year that favored Democrats nationally and in Minnesota, the candidates' behavior, records, and their campaign strategies significantly affected the ultimate outcome. While both candidates had serious limitations, it was the national tide that put Norm Coleman on the defensive.

Minnesota's Economic, Political, and Electoral Landscape

Minnesota is home to about 5 million people, over half residing in the metropolitan area of the Twin Cities (Minneapolis and St. Paul) and its suburbs. The population is 88 percent White; there are approximately 3 percent each of Blacks, Asians, and Hispanics and 2 percent American Indians. Agriculture remains an important economic activity in the state, in spite of increasing migration of the younger generation to urban areas. Technology, especially medical technology, is a significant element of the "new" economy. By the fall of 2008, Minnesota's unemployment rate was over 6 percent and it had the largest per capita deficit looming of any state.

Minnesota has given its electoral votes to the Democratic presidential candidate in every contest since 1976, leading to its reputation as a reliably blue state. That reputation was never totally deserved and has almost certainly required revision recently. Minnesota has sent more Republicans than Democrats to the U.S. Senate over this same period and has had a Republican governor since 1990, except for the four-year tenure of Reform Party Governor Jesse Ventura. Bill Clinton's victory in Minnesota in 1992 was aided substantially by a strong showing by Ross Perot, and George W. Bush might well have carried the state in 2000 if his campaign had put more effort into it. By 2008, Minnesota was perceived to be a state "in play," so much so that both parties considered it as a potential site for their nominating conventions, with the Republicans announcing their choice first, coincidently or by design, to preempt the Democrats.

Just as Minnesota's "blueness" has been overrated in the past, its purple hue, or swing state status, was probably exaggerated in 2008. The unpopularity of President Bush and the Iraq War was steadily increasing among Minnesotans. In 2004 and 2005 about half of the likely voters in Minnesota disapproved of the job President Bush was doing. This increased to 60 percent in 2006. By August of 2008, nearly two-thirds of Minnesotans expressed disapproval of President Bush. People who thought starting the Iraq War was a mistake grew from one-third of the population in 2004 to around half in 2008.[1] In part due to the difficult electoral conditions Republicans faced in 2006, Democrats had successes on which they were looking to build: Democrat Amy Klobuchar won an open U.S. Senate race by 20 points, an incumbent Republican member of the U.S. House from a reliably Republican district, Gil Gutknecht, was defeated, and the Democrats regained a majority in the state House of Representatives.

By 2006, polls showed some increase in Democratic party identification in the state, especially when independent "leaners" were included, as well as declines in Republican party identification. Specifically, between 2004 and 2008 Democratic identifiers among likely voters increased from around 30 percent to close to 40 percent.[2] By the fall of 2008, the economic turmoil that swept the country took its toll in Minnesota, and an Obama win was widely expected. There were also prospects of Democratic gains in the state legislature and even hopes (unrealized) of picking up one or two congressional seats from the Republicans. The U.S. Senate race, however, remained too close to call.

Minnesota typically has high voter turnout, usually leading the nation or running a close second, in both presidential and midterm elections. The state was an early adopter of same-day registration, with 15 to 20 percent of the voters typically registering to vote on Election Day.[3] Minnesota has been less pioneering with early voting. To vote absentee, a voter needs to offer one of four reasons: illness or disability; being an election judge in another precinct; being "away from the precinct" on Election Day; and religious discipline or religious holiday. The relative restrictiveness of this provision of election law became entangled in the nationwide move toward early voting along with both parties' efforts to encourage their supporters to vote early to avoid lines and machine glitches, and, not insignificantly, to lock in their votes. The dubiousness of this tactic in Minnesota only became clear during the U.S. Senate recount when a surprisingly large number of voters discovered that their absentee votes had been rejected for an assortment of violations.

Minnesota is also a firmly established party caucus state. As elsewhere, the caucus system advantages the enthusiastic and well-organized. In 2008, this meant that Barack Obama overwhelmed Hillary Clinton in the Democratic caucuses. For most of the attendees, the presidential race was the main attraction, but, importantly, the caucuses are also the first step in the delegate selection process that eventually leads to the endorsement of a candidate for the U.S. Senate. As an incumbent Senator, Norm Coleman had no viable opponent for party endorsement or in the primary[4] that officially nominated the Republican candidate in September. Al Franken, by contrast, had opponents for the endorsement and, later, in the Democratic primary, but his organizational presence in the party caucuses proved the key to his nomination.

The Incumbent: Republican Norm Coleman

As a senator, Norm Coleman had played defense for a long time. He started his career in politics as an antiwar hippie in New York City, served as a Minnesota assistant attorney general under Democrat Hubert ("Skip") Humphrey III, and was elected mayor of St. Paul as a Democrat. In 1996, however, shortly before the end of his first term as mayor, he switched to the Republican Party, recognizing that his pro-life position would never allow him to win endorsement for a higher office as a Democrat. Although he easily won election to a second term as mayor in the officially nonpartisan race, he also won the undying enmity of the Democratic Farmer-Labor (DFL) party faithful.[5] Their rancor only increased when, in 1998, he ran, as a Republican, for governor against his old boss, Skip Humphrey, both of them losing, after uninspiring campaigns, to upstart third-party candidate, Jesse Ventura.

Rather than run for a third term as mayor in 2001, Coleman declared for the U.S. Senate seat held by Senator Paul Wellstone. The Senate race in 2002 was hard-fought and extremely close, and it took a tragic turn when Wellstone's plane crashed 10 days before the election, killing him, his wife and daughter, and five others.[6] Coleman went on to beat stand-in candidate former Vice President Walter Mondale, but the circumstances increased the DFL's commitment to take back Wellstone's seat in 2008.

Throughout his political career in Minnesota, Coleman has attempted to portray himself as a moderate, an effort that has not always proven successful. He strongly supported the Bush agenda early in his term. As shown in Table 9.1, in his first year, Coleman voted for the Bush agenda 98 percent of the time. Starting in 2004, however, Coleman's support for the president began a steady decline. His presidential support score dipped to 88 percent in 2006, 68 percent in 2007, and fell to 58 percent in 2008. Coleman's party unity score declined as well, from a high of 92 percent in his first year to a low of 64 percent in 2007.

Coleman's overall record and active pursuit of the chairmanship of the National Republican Senatorial Committee (NRSC), however, made it difficult for him to move to the center as Bush's popularity waned and the 2008 election approached. Coleman remained popular with the Republican base and he generally received high marks for constituency service and for championing bipartisan causes such as the Development, Relief and Education for Alien Minors bill (DREAM Act)[7] and immigration reform. Nonetheless, as a result of his party switch more than a decade earlier and his move to the center in the Senate as the election approached, it was difficult for him to shake the image of a politician who will adopt any politically expedient position.

Coleman's approval ratings declined throughout his time in the Senate, and the campaign depressed them further, according to a series of Minnesota polls conducted for the *Star Tribune*. In January of 2004, 54 percent of voters approved

Table 9.1 Congressional Vote Scores for Norm Coleman, 2003–2008

Year	American Conservative Union	Americans for Democratic Action	Presidential Support	Party Unity
2008	48	45	58%	69%
2007	64	50	68%	64%
2006	68	25	88%	77%
2005	64	30	84%	77%
2004	84	30	92%	91%
2003	85	15	98%	92%

Source: 2003–2006 scores from various editions of *CQ's Politics in America;* 2007–2008 American Conservative Union (ACU) and Americans for Democratic Action (ADA) Web sites; 2007–2008 party unity and presidential support scores from *CQ Weekly Report.*

of how Coleman was handling his job as U.S. Senator. His approval rating sank to 47 percent in January 2005, and it would never top 50 percent again. By mid-October 2008, his approval rating had plummeted to 39 percent.[8] In a Minnesota poll conducted on October 16 and 17, both Coleman and Franken had higher unfavorable than favorable ratings (50–43 and 46–44 respectively).

The Challenger: Democrat Al Franken Gets the Nod

Al Franken, Coleman's Democratic challenger, had his own problems with the past. Franken achieved notoriety as a liberal radio talk-show host, a best-selling author of political satire, and earlier, as a stand-up comic and veteran of *Saturday Night Live.* Over the course of his career he had developed a well-documented record of off-color and sexist jokes and outrageous political harangues. Raised in a Minneapolis suburb, he moved back to the state in 2005 after a long sojourn in New York with the explicit intention of exploring a Senate run, thus opening the door to charges of carpetbagging. Franken answered this with a standard line in his stump speech, joking that of the two New York Jews in the race, he was the only one who grew up in Minnesota.

Franken had one clear advantage over his potential rivals for the Democratic nomination: he was a terrific fundraiser. Not only was he able to raise money from the show business elite for his own campaign, he also established his own leadership political action committee (PAC) in the fall of 2005, known as the Midwest Values PAC, to assist other candidates throughout the state. He also helped them raise money by appearances at fundraisers. These factors laid the groundwork for his Senate run. After only two years in Minnesota, he had ingratiated himself with DFL party activists and would-be candidates throughout the state, exactly the people who would be deciding the party's endorsement.

Franken had two serious rivals for the DFL endorsement. One was Michael Ciresi, a high-profile personal injury attorney who had made millions by suing the tobacco companies on behalf of the State of Minnesota. Several DFL officeholders and party leaders, including Congresswoman Betty McCollum, lined up in support of Ciresi. Many did so because they feared that Franken's baggage would derail his candidacy. Ciresi had run in the DFL Senate primary in 2000 and the memory of his weak showing had lingered—he had garnered only 22 percent of the vote. His 2008 campaign never gained traction and he pulled out of the race before the state endorsing convention when it became clear that he did not have the delegate votes to mount a successful challenge.

The other rival for the endorsement was Jack Nelson-Pallmeyer, an antiwar college professor from the "progressive" wing of the party. He had little money or organization, but worked hard at contacting delegates and usually bested both Franken and Ciresi in the series of public debates that led up to the endorsing convention. In spite of that, he could not overcome the first-ballot commitments that Franken had amassed and conceded defeat before the results of the initial ballot were announced so that Franken could win the nomination by acclamation. At the convention, Franken's public apology to the women of Minnesota for his past offensive sexist jokes was considered a necessary ritual that enabled the party to unite behind his candidacy.

In Minnesota DFL politics, the party endorsement is important, but not unassailable. It can be crucial if a candidate does not have personal wealth because the endorsed candidate can tap the party's financial and organizational resources. When an endorsed candidate is defeated in the September primary, it is almost always by an opponent with a great deal of money and name recognition. In this case, Franken was the one with the celebrity status and the financial resources as well as the party endorsement and he was not seriously challenged in the primary. He did have an opponent, however. Priscilla Lord Farris, the daughter of a prominent DFL family, entered the race in July. She had little electoral experience, having only served on the Sunfish Lake City Council. She won 30 percent of the vote against Franken in the primary—much of which was likely in protest of Franken, rather than in support of her candidacy. Her TV ads, quoting various DFL women officeholders saying uncomplimentary things about Franken's attitude toward women, later helped Republicans make the case against Franken when they were used in an ad run by Coleman.

The Other Challenger: Third-Party Candidate Dean Barkley

Minnesota has a history of third-party activity. In 1992, the Independence Party of Minnesota[9] was born, offering a platform that blends pragmatic and conservative fiscal policy with a libertarian social philosophy. The party is largely the handiwork of Dean Barkley who ran for U.S. Senate in 1994 and won the requisite 5 percent of the vote statewide to gain official party status. The highpoint of the party's existence was the surprise upset win by Jesse Ventura in the 1998 governor's race. Barkley served in Ventura's administration and was appointed to the U.S. Senate for the brief interlude between Senator Wellstone's death in the fall of 2002 and Coleman's entry into the Senate in January 2003. After that, Barkley's marriage fell apart and he struggled with drinking. He returned to politics in 2006, managing the unsuccessful Texas gubernatorial campaign of satirist Kinky Friedman.

Barkley entered the 2008 Senate race as the Independence Party candidate in mid-July, only after Jesse Ventura announced his decision not to do so on *Larry King Live*. Barkley raised little money and campaigned little, running only one advertisement. Nonetheless, he was a presentable and familiar figure in the candidate debates. In a race in which the two major party candidates were each perceived as having serious flaws, Barkley's candidacy served mainly as an opportunity for voters to express their reservations about Coleman and Franken.

The Candidates' Strategies

Coleman and Franken set records for the amount of money they raised and spent in the election, and, judging by the media commentary and voters' reactions, the level of negativity of the campaigns they waged. Each candidate seemed to focus on the negatives of the opponent, giving voters more reasons to vote against the other guy than for himself.

In his reelection battle, Coleman played defense by going on the offensive. In advertisements, debates, and speeches, Coleman portrayed Franken as too angry, too partisan, and too inexperienced to serve in the U.S. Senate. Coleman also reminded voters of his own independence and accomplishments, touting his ability to work across the aisle to get things done. The negative messages, however, overshadowed the positive.

Franken also went on the attack and linked Coleman to President Bush and his policies at every opportunity, keenly aware of Bush's unpopularity nationwide and in Minnesota. Indeed, it sometimes seemed that Franken was running against both Coleman and Bush. As chronicled in other chapters, this was a strategy that worked well for other Democrats in 2008 and Franken was hoping to make it work in Minnesota. Franken also tried to capitalize on Democratic support and strong Democratic candidates in Minnesota by bringing in surrogates and through the campaign's coordinated efforts with the party.

Barkley's strategy was more difficult to discern. Although he proved conversant with policy issues in debates, his sharp criticisms of both candidates served to reinforce the other candidates' attacks rather than offer a real alternative.

Stumbles and Setbacks in the News

Some notable missteps and revelations marked the Senate campaign trail, fueling the television ads and exacerbating the already negative views of the candidates. For Franken's part, throughout the campaign he had to contend with the sexist and offensive jokes from his past. In March, it was revealed that he faced fines in New York and California related to his personal corporation. Franken also failed to pay the proper tax on income earned in 17 states, and although he contended that he had simply paid the taxes to the wrong states, he was forced to pay $70,000 in back taxes and fines.

In June, *National Journal* reported that Coleman was paying only nominal rent for his Washington, DC basement apartment to landlord Jeff Larson. Democrats attacked Coleman, arguing that he was getting a below-market rate from Larson, whose telemarketing firm has done more than $1.5 million of business with the senator's campaigns since 2001.[10] Then, the week before the election, it was reported that a Coleman donor, Minneapolis businessman Nasser Kazeminy, was being sued for allegedly having directed a Texas company in which he had an interest to send $75,000 to a Minneapolis insurance firm that employs Coleman's wife, Laurie, as an independent contractor. The suit (which was dropped in September 2009) alleged that Kazeminy told executives at the Houston firm that he wanted to help the Colemans financially.

Campaign Advertising: All Negative All the Time

As the campaign went on, the economy became more and more important in the minds of voters; while polls in February 2008 showed that one-third of the electorate rated the economy as the most important problem,[11] by October, two-thirds of the electorate did so.[12] The candidates, however, did not focus solely on this issue. In fact, Minnesota's Senate race will long be remembered for its negative advertisements that discussed many other subjects. The candidates and parties alike seemed to spare no expense, and no topic was off limits. The ads featured everything from personal pleas (and mea culpas) by the candidates and their families to talking fish and bowlers denouncing the candidates. The air war also generated extensive criticism from voters, media "truth" critics, and the candidates, along with numerous press conferences denouncing the ads and even a lawsuit.

Many ads highlighted, and exaggerated, the candidates' policy differences. The candidates issued competing ads about support for seniors, with Coleman accusing Franken of not supporting Medicare prescription drugs for seniors and Franken accusing Coleman, and Bush, of jeopardizing Social Security. Like other races across the country, it seemed that every attack ad was followed by a counter attack; it came to the point that many of the ads were in dialogue with one another. To voters, though, they seemed to blur into a stream of endless attacks. In exit polls, 90 percent of voters said that one or both of the candidates attacked the other unfairly.[13]

Two of Coleman's ads featured bowlers lauding Coleman for "bringing hockey back" to St. Paul as mayor.[14] Another ad featured the bowlers criticizing Franken for not paying taxes and for his "foul-mouthed attacks on anyone he disagrees with...and writing all that juicy porn."[15] Still other ads followed up with more attacks on Franken's tax problems. The Franken campaign responded with its own bowlers criticizing Coleman for his votes for the Iraq War, the Bush tax cuts, and student loan reductions.[16]

One of Coleman's most memorable ads attacking Franken, titled "Angry Al," started with the question "Does Al Franken Have the Temperament to Serve in the U.S. Senate?" The ad then showed several clips of Al Franken yelling and swearing; at one point Franken was shown saying "I'm mean sometimes." The ad concluded with the text: "Al Franken. Reckless. Ridiculous. Wrong."[17]

The national congressional party committees contributed to the barrage of negative ads as well. Every independent expenditure made by the NRSC in Minnesota was spent in attacking Franken rather than in support of Coleman, and the majority of the Democratic Senatorial Campaign Committee's (DSCC) expenditures attacked Coleman and his record, even attacking him for attacks on Franken.

The NRSC reinforced Coleman's message in an ad titled "Unfit" showing additional clips of an angry Al Franken yelling, with a narrator describing him as prone to "violent outbursts."[18] The ad seemed effective, but it backfired when the Franken campaign responded with one of the most memorable ads of the season, an ad that made clear that the NRSC had taken the clip out of context, and reminded voters of Franken's connection to the Wellstone family. In Franken's ad, voters learned that the clip came from an event where Franken was telling a story about Paul Wellstone's enthusiastic support of his son David competing in cross-country meets. When Franken was seen screaming "you can take this guy," he was actually imitating Wellstone's cheers for his son at the end of a cross-country meet. The ad closed by saying "Ads for Norm Coleman used footage of Al telling this story about Paul Wellstone and his son and tried to make it seem like he was angry. Minnesota deserves better."[19] The DSCC added its own criticism of Coleman's attacks with an ad calling them "ridiculous," using black-and-white footage showing a ship, a train, and whimpering puppies, with a narrator saying: "Al Franken sank this ship—crashed these trains—and he hates puppies!"[20]

Other Franken ads also hit hard. One attacked Coleman's inactivity in his role as chairman of the Senate Permanent Subcommittee on Investigations. "As chairman of the most powerful investigative committee in the Senate, Norm Coleman had the perfect perch to look into no-bid contracts in Iraq. But Coleman did nothing." The Franken ad ended by saying, "Coleman did take $100,000 from defense contractors like Halliburton."[21] Another Franken ad claimed that Coleman was ranked fourth among senators in corruption and lived in a DC apartment nearly rent free. The dubious claim about Coleman's ranking led Coleman to file an unsuccessful lawsuit.[22]

The negativity—and voters' reactions to the ads—got so bad that on October 10, Coleman announced that he was going to stop airing negative ads, saying that he had "decided I was not all that interested in returning to Washington for another six years based on the judgment of the voters that I was not as bad as the other guys. I want voters to vote for me and not against the other folks."[23] A similar strategy had proven effective for Coleman six years earlier when he stopped running negative ads after Wellstone's death. In 2008, however, the damage of his steady stream of attacks on Franken was irreversible. In a *Star Tribune* poll earlier that month, 56 percent of respondents said ads aimed at Franken were "unfair personal attacks" while only 42 percent of the poll respondents had said that about ads critical of Coleman.[24] Additionally, the NRSC continued its negative ads, creating confusion among voters as to whether Coleman had actually stopped his negative ads.

Not surprisingly, the negativity extended to the ground war. One mailing in particular seemed to cross the line. Coleman, along with many Democrats, objected to a mailing sent by the NRSC. The cartoonlike mailer criticized Franken for writing "a pornographic column in Playboy" and "so-called comedy routines about raping women." On the cover, Franken was pictured opening a door and saying, "Come on in kids... Senator Franken's going to tell a few jokes...." Inside, kids are criticizing Franken, saying such things as "We shouldn't have to be ashamed of Minnesota's senator."[25]

The Saturday before the election, Coleman released an ad blaming Franken for an "11th hour attack" connected to the lawsuit alleging that a Coleman donor funneled money to Coleman's wife. In the ad, Coleman spoke directly to voters: "This time Al Franken's crossed the line.... I'm fair game for his ugly smears. My wife and family are not." Franken, in return, accused Coleman of lying about him being behind the lawsuit.[26]

Not all of the advertisements were negative, although most were. Some of Coleman's ads touted his accomplishments in the Senate and his ability to work with members of both parties. One ad featured a grateful mother thanking Coleman for his authorship of the Conquer Childhood Cancer Act to fund cancer research and help families.[27] Another ad showed a grateful family thanking Coleman for helping them to overcome international adoption difficulties.[28]

To soften Franken's angry image, Franken's wife, Franni Franken, appeared in a powerful ad discussing Al's support as she battled alcoholism. In the ad, Franni stated "When I was struggling with my recovery, Al stood right by my side.... The Al Franken I know stood by me through thick and thin, so I know he'll always come through for Minnesotans."[29]

Dean Barkley ran only one ad in an effort to connect with everyday voters and remind them of his opponents' New York connections. In it, Barkley wore a leather jacket and was surrounded by cardboard cutouts of Coleman and Franken on pedestals. Speaking directly to voters, he said: "I don't need two guys from New York to tell me why the middle class is angry...I know why. I'm one of you." He then pushed over the pedestals and walked off.[30]

Record-Setting Money

Even before the recount that would require additional funds, the Minnesota race was the most expensive in the country and no congressional candidate spent as much as either Coleman or Franken.[31] Before the election, Coleman raised $23,673,308 and spent $21,821,755. Seventeen percent of Coleman's campaign contributions came from PACs, and 65 percent came from individuals. Franken was at parity with Coleman; he raised $22,502,124 and spent $21,066,834. The source of the funds reflected the typical incumbency advantage when it comes to PAC contributions, as Franken raised only 3 percent from PACs. Barkley raised and spent only $163,358 and $162,387, respectively.[32]

The parties and outside groups invested heavily in this race, keenly aware of how competitive it was and that it had the potential to provide, or prevent, a 60th "filibuster proof" Democratic vote in the Senate. The party congressional committees made modest contributions to the candidates' campaigns and poured massive amounts into independent expenditures. Most of the independent expenditures were mainly used on negative ads to attack their candidate's opponent rather than to promote their candidate. In fact, according to Federal Election Commission reports, the NRSC spent just over $6 million in independent expenditures against Al Franken without making any independent expenditures in support of Coleman. They did spend $653,100 in party coordinated expenditures, which are funds spent by the party on behalf of and with the knowledge of the candidate, typically for television ads, direct mail literature, and other campaign services. Similarly, the Democratic Senatorial Campaign Committee (DSCC) spent over $9 million in independent expenditures against Coleman and only $59,139 to promote Franken. They also spent $73,344 in party coordinated contributions for Franken. At the state level, the Minnesota DFL spent $261,843 in party coordinated expenditures for Franken and $2,500 in independent expenditures on his behalf.[33]

In addition to the activities and ads funded by the candidates and the parties, environmental groups, antiabortion and pro-choice groups, labor unions, health-related PACs, and the National Rifle Association (NRA) all poured considerable resources into this consequential race to promote their candidate and attack the other. For example, the NRA spent $137,709 against Franken and $311,173 on behalf of Coleman.[34] The Service Employees International Union (SEIU) Committee on Political Education spent $146,219 on behalf of Franken. Pro-choice groups promoted Franken, while pro-life groups rallied behind Coleman. Planned Parenthood of Minnesota spent $295,605 in independent expenditures for Franken. Minnesota Citizens Concerned for Life spent $14,606 on behalf of Coleman; National Right to Life Political Action Committee spent $24,529; and the pro-life Susan B. Anthony List Candidate Fund spent $12,762.

Environmental groups made independent expenditures on behalf of Franken and against Coleman. The League of Conservation Voters spent $4,679 in support of Franken; Clean Water/Vote Environment spent $2,218 for Franken; and Environment America spent $134,619 for Franken and $66,667 against Coleman.

Health-related PACs spent independently for Coleman. The American Association of Neurological Surgeons spent $41,330; the American Society of Anesthesiologists spent $74,700; the National Emergency Medicine PAC spent $49,860; and the PAC of the American Association of Orthopedic Surgeons spent $199,400 on direct mail and radio advertisements.

Debates

The candidates squared off during five debates around the state beginning on October 5. All of the debates included Barkley, giving him the chance to remind voters of his presence in the race and to articulate his policy positions, particularly as they related to reducing the debt and deficit.

The debates reinforced the candidates' attacks on one another and their policy differences. In each debate, Coleman characterized Franken as too angry and partisan to serve in the Senate, while reminding voters of his own ability to "get things done." Franken sounded familiar themes linking Coleman to President Bush and harshly criticizing Republican policies, arguing at one point that Coleman had helped the outgoing president "drive the economy right into the ditch."[35]

The second debate, in mid-October, contrasted the candidates' views on the recently passed $700 billion Wall Street bailout package. Franken and Barkley voiced their strong opposition to the legislation, while Coleman, who supported it, accused them of casting stones "from the cheap seats."[36] The second debate occurred just after Coleman had announced that he would stop airing negative advertising, and he told his opponents that it would be difficult to "generate hope" by being negative. At this point, however, the debate—and campaign more generally—was already so negative that it is unlikely that Coleman's words, or the debates, generated much hope.

Party Support and the Presidential Race

Both candidates, in conjunction with the presidential campaigns, brought in party stars to generate enthusiasm and dollars. Hillary Clinton was an active advocate for Franken. She joined Franken at a rally at the University of Minnesota in late October to jumpstart a grass-roots get-out-the-vote (GOTV) campaign. In her remarks, Clinton stressed the importance of electing Franken to attain a 60-vote majority in the Senate. The Monday before the election, Hillary Clinton traveled to Duluth, joined by Franken and Representative James Oberstar (D-MN) to campaign for Obama and Franken. On October 30, Bill Clinton rallied a crowd of around 4,000 people in Minneapolis on behalf of Franken and Obama.[37]

In mid-October, Todd Palin, husband of then-Alaska Governor Sarah Palin, traveled to northern Minnesota to emphasize his support for gun rights and for Coleman, and also did so at a rally that the NRA had organized. Wayne LaPierre, head of the NRA, used the rally to announce the organization's endorsement of Coleman.[38] Rudy Giuliani also came to Minnesota and campaigned for Coleman and McCain twice. In late October, he joined Coleman on the "Hope Express" for a campaign swing through the state, referring to Coleman as "Minnesota's mayor."[39] Then, the Monday before the election, Giuliani led a rally in St. Paul for McCain and Coleman.

Perhaps more important than high profile party surrogates were the parties' coordinated campaign efforts. The Obama campaign, in conjunction with Democrats statewide, conducted unprecedented GOTV efforts in Minnesota. Although it is impossible to gauge the precise effects, there is no question that Democratic enthusiasm for Obama and the efforts of a coordinated campaign helped Franken. Even in solidly Democratic districts, such as Minnesota's 4th and 5th Congressional Districts, extensive GOTV efforts were undertaken to maximize turnout for Obama and Franken.

The Horse Race and Changing Conditions

Polling throughout the campaign revealed that each candidate had high negatives from the start; the economic downturn and Democratic surge helped Franken; and Barkley seemed to pull support from both candidates, although slightly more from Franken.

Coleman started the campaign season with a wide lead, though not high approval ratings. According to the Minnesota Poll, Coleman led Franken 51 to 41 percent in May 2008 (before Barkley entered). These leads generally persisted in polls throughout June and July; in July, McCain was not far behind Obama in Minnesota. By mid-August the Senate race had tightened. The University of

Minnesota Humphrey Institute/Minnesota Public Radio poll showed Franken at 41 percent, Coleman at 40 percent, and Barkley at 8 percent, with 11 percent undecided.[40]

All of the factors influencing the campaign, from the unprecedented spending and negativity to the national political forces contributed to making the race remained too close to call until Election Day (and beyond). The *Star Tribune* Minnesota Poll released two days before the election showed Franken leading Coleman 42 to 38 percent, within the poll's margin of error.[41] A poll released only days earlier conducted by NBC News/Mason Dixon, found that 42 percent supported Coleman while 36 percent supported Franken, also within the margin of error.[42] A Rasmussen Poll the same week showed Coleman leading Franken 43 to 39 percent, again within the margin of error. Interestingly, Obama's lead solidified as the Senate race tightened, signaling some voters were considering splitting their tickets.

The Results

Norm Coleman declared victory the morning after the election, when his unofficial lead reached 725 votes, according to the Secretary of State's tally. The Associated Press declared Coleman the winner just before 7 a.m., but two hours later it withdrew its declaration, saying that it had been premature.[43] By the end of the day, as county officials from around the state provided adjusted figures to the state, Coleman's lead had shrunk to 477 votes. An automatic recount followed (required by Minnesota law in races with margins of less than one-half of 1 percent), resulting in a 225-vote lead for Franken.

Al Franken received 1,212,431 votes (41.99% of the total), Norm Coleman received 1,212,206 votes (41.98%), and Dean Barkley received 437,505 votes (15.15%). In total 2,921,147 Minnesotans turned out to vote in person or by absentee ballot on Election Day. Over a half million of those registered to vote on Election Day itself. Of those who voted, all but about 11,000 cast a vote for president. The fall-off from the presidential race to the senate race, where some voters cast a vote for president but not senate, was about 23,000. By historical standards this is very little fall-off so there were apparently few "Obama-only" voters, likely because those dissatisfied with Franken and Coleman could register a protest vote for Barkley.

According to exit polls, partisans defected on both sides. Democrats constituted 39 percent of Minnesota's electorate; 79 percent voted for Franken, 9 percent voted for Coleman, and 13 percent voted for Barkley. Republicans comprised 36 percent of the electorate; 85 percent of whom voted for Coleman, 5 percent for Franken, and 10 percent for Barkley. Among Independents, 38 percent voted for Franken, 33 percent for Coleman, and 27 percent for Barkley.

As preelection polling indicated, a significant number of Minnesotans split their tickets. Fifty-four percent of Minnesotans voted for Obama, 74 percent of whom supported Franken, 11 percent Coleman, and 15 percent Barkley. Five percent of McCain supporters voted for Franken, 81 percent for Coleman, and

14 percent for Barkley. This is nothing new, as Minnesotans have always been willing to split their tickets. Most recently, in 2006 Democrat Amy Klobuchar won her Senate seat by 20 points while Republican Governor Tim Pawlenty was narrowly reelected.[44]

Among important electoral groups in the state, both Coleman and Franken had successes which helped create such a narrow vote margin. Despite his problems with sexist jokes, Franken had a large advantage among women, typical of Democratic candidates. Franken did 7 points better than Coleman among women (45 to 38%; 16% of women voted for Barkley). Coleman received 46 percent of men's votes, while Franken only received 39 percent. Younger voters were more likely to vote for Franken, but Coleman had a 4 to 5 point advantage with those aged 30 to 64. Coleman performed considerably better among religious Protestants and Catholics, and Franken won among the most highly educated.

Franken ran strong in the Twin Cities and the Iron Range in the north, both traditional Democratic strongholds. He won 51 percent of the vote in the Twin Cities to Coleman's 35 percent. Offsetting this, Coleman ran ahead of Franken in the outer suburbs of the Twin Cities and most of the rest of the state.

Exit polling shows that Barkley made a slightly bigger dent in Franken's support, pulling slightly more Democrats than Republicans into his camp. Among Barkley supporters, 31 percent would have voted for Franken in a two-person race, 24 percent would have voted for Coleman, and 45 percent said they would not have voted. The Barkley vote share is sufficiently small, however, that this means that Barkley took 5 percent of the total electorate from Franken and 4 percent from Coleman, so it is appropriate to conclude that both candidates were nearly equally hurt by Barkley.[45]

The Recount and Legal Battles

During the chaotic day after the election, both Coleman and Franken made statements articulating positions that they would later argue against. Coleman urged Franken to waive his right to a recount, as the prospect of changing the result was remote and a recount would be costly to taxpayers (about $86,000).[46] Franken, of course, had no intention of waiving his right to a recount, and in a press conference he asserted: "Let me be clear: Our goal is to ensure that every vote is properly counted." Ironically, over the course of the legal battles that followed it would be Coleman, not Franken, who would argue that every (absentee) vote should be counted, and Franken would argue that Coleman should concede and end his legal contest. In the weeks and months that followed, the candidates raised more than $13 million for the recount and legal contests.

Minnesota election laws significantly shaped the course of the postelection battle. In Minnesota, recounts are required in races with a winning margin of less than one-half of 1 percent, although a losing candidate may request that it not go forward. The recount provided televised drama for Minnesotans, as they watched canvassing board members determine voter intent on ballots that the machines had missed and decide what to do with ballots that included a vote for Coleman or Franken along with write-in candidates such as "The Lizard People." Franken led by 225 votes after the state canvassing board had completed the recount. Coleman challenged the results before a three judge panel. The panel was comprised of one judge appointed by a Democratic governor, one by a Republican governor, and one by an Independence Party governor. The panel ruled unanimously in favor of Franken and his lead increased to 312 votes as a result of their review. Coleman then took the battle to the Minnesota Supreme Court, which heard oral arguments on June 1.

Minnesota law also stipulates that a certificate of election is not signed until court appeals are exhausted, a provision that likely prevented Franken from being seated "without prejudice" by Democrats in the U.S. Senate in January while the legal process continued. This provision also made the stakes of the ongoing legal battle much higher. Minnesota was left with only one Senator, and the political fallout for Coleman grew higher as time passed and more and more Minnesotans thought that Coleman should concede. He finally did, on June 30, when the Minnesota Supreme Court ruled unanimously against him in a strongly-worded opinion. Coleman declined to appeal the ruling to the U.S. Supreme Court. A consideration might have been the announcement a few weeks earlier by Minnesota Republican governor, Tim Pawlenty, that he would not seek a third term, thus providing a possible opening for another Coleman run for elective office.

Conclusion

It is ironic that the Coleman–Franken battle—the contest that voters and observers alike were most anxious to end back in November—turned into the most protracted postelection Senate battle in history. Before the results were in—and disputed—the race had already made history for its cost and negativity. Even as it became clear that the close margin would trigger what could be a long recount, many quipped that at least the negative ads would stop (and they did, although the press conferences did not).

Neither Coleman nor Franken enjoyed strong support in public opinion polls as the contest began, and the campaign only exacerbated negative reactions to both of them. In the end, the candidates' strategies of filling the airwaves with negative ads seemed to convince the electorate that both candidates had major flaws. Voter dissatisfaction opened the door for Independence Party candidate Dean Barkley, who garnered 15 percent of the vote, not just among Independent identifiers, but also Democrats and Republicans who had become disaffected with their own candidates.

In this historically close contest, Norm Coleman largely played defense by going on the offensive. While defending his record, touting his independence, and reminding voters of his accomplishments in the Senate and even as mayor of St. Paul, his strategy seemed most focused on highlighting Franken's weaknesses and convincing voters that Franken was not Senate material. Franken ran against Coleman and outgoing President Bush at the same time, arguing that his values and policy positions were more in line with Minnesotans' than the incumbent Senator's. Despite Franken's baggage and the opportunity Barkley provided for voters to reject both major party candidates, after a protracted recount and legal contest Franken prevailed by the smallest of margins in a big Democratic year. This close contest in a state that voted for Barack Obama by 10 points likely means that the Republicans will target Al Franken's seat in 2014, and the political conditions and his actions as a Senator will determine how difficult it will be to defend his turf.

Notes

1. Data accessed at the Center for the Study of Politics and Governance, Hubert H. Humphrey Institute, http://www.hhh.umn.edu/centers/cspg.
2. Ibid.
3. Eric J. Ostermeier and Lawrence R. Jacobs. 2006. "Minnesota Voters Turnout," http://www.hhh.umn.edu/centers/cspg/pdf/Minnesota_Voters_Turnout.pdf.
4. Coleman's only opponent in the primary was a convicted felon living in Italy who received 9 percent of the vote.
5. Minnesota Democrats' unique name—the Democratic-Farmer-Labor Party (DFL)—results from the merger of the dominant Farmer-Labor Party and the also-ran Democratic Party in the early 1940s.
6. See William H. Flanigan, Joanne M. Miller, Jennifer L. Williams, and Nancy H. Zingale, "From Intensity to Tragedy: The Minnesota U. S. Senate Race," in *The Last Hurrah*, ed. David B. Magleby and J. Quinn Monson (Washington, DC: Brookings Institution Press, 2004), 117–136.
7. The DREAM bill would allow undocumented aliens, brought to the United States as children, to have temporary residence status while pursuing higher education or serving in the military.
8. Patricia Lopez, "The Minnesota Poll. The Senate Race," *Star Tribune*, October 21, 2008, metro edition, A1.
9. Between 1995 and 2000, the Independence Party of Minnesota was called the Reform Party of Minnesota and was affiliated with the national Reform Party.
10. Kevin Duchschere, "Coleman Defends DC Lease," *Star Tribune*, August 14, 2008, metro edition, B5.
11. Mark Zdechlik, "Poll: Franken Popular With DFLers, But Many Undecided," Minnesota Public Radio, February 1, 2008.
12. Curtis Gilbert, "MPR Poll: Senate Race Still Up for Grabs," Minnesota Public Radio, October 31, 2008.
13. http://www.cnn.com/ELECTION/2008/results/polls/#MNS01p1.
14. "One Thing," http://www.youtube.com/watch?v=P_hvPbW0jsw; "Gift," http://www.youtube.com/watch?v=5wOMUo1XOAY.
15. "Why Not?" http://www.youtube.com/watch?v=L1SpG85bGmo.
16. "A Few More Things," http://www.youtube.com/watch?v=5VHn9sQVRVM.
17. "Angry Al," http://www.youtube.com/watch?v=XJUxtfSdaX0.
18. "Unfit," http://www.youtube.com/watch?v=4N73AUnp_Wg.
19. "Disgrace," http://www.youtube.com/watch?v=Ljrh72Qy1tw&feature=related.
20. "Sank," http://www.youtube.com/watch?v=Vo4zqdD_4KI.
21. "Committee," http://www.youtube.com/watch?v=vmp3y3Sw7J0.
22. "Deserve," http://www.youtube.com/watch?v=OmaHTcdJFjI.

23. Patricia Lopez, "Coleman Withdraws His Negative Ads," *Star Tribune*, October 11, 2008, metro edition, B1.
24. Ibid.
25. Kevin Duchschere, "Coleman joins DFL Chorus against Anti-Franken Mailer," *Star Tribune*, October 28, 2008, metro edition, B2.
26. Patricia Lopez, Mike Kaszuba, and Pat Doyle, "Coleman, Franken Hip Deep in Fracas," *Star Tribune*, November 2, 2008, metro edition, A19.
27. "Wyatt's Mom," http://www.youtube.com/watch?v=cRqg3k7Ffm0.
28. "The McGarrys," http://www.youtube.com/watch?v=kbW0qne75Ig.
29. "Franni," http://www.youtube.com/watch?v=_IDjMbdgD9c.
30. "Middle Class," http://www.youtube.com/watch?v=X74KuyGzKzo.
31. http://www.opensecrets.org/overview/topraces.php. We do not include money raised after the election for the recount and legal contest in this analysis.
32. Data in this paragraph come from http://www.opensecrets.org/races/summary.php?id=MNS1&cycle=2008.
33. Data in this paragraph and those that follow have been calculated from FEC reports: http://query.nictusa.com/cgi-bin/can_give/2007_S8MN00438; http://query.nictusa.com/cgi-bin/can_give/2007_S2MN00126.
34. http://query.nictusa.com/cgi-bin/can_give/2007_S8MN00438.
35. Patricia Lopez, "Campaign 2008: Senate Debate; Now, about the Economy," *Star Tribune*, October 6, 2008, metro edition, A1.
36. Mike Kaszuba, "The Senate Race: Second Debate," *Star Tribune*, October 14, 2008, metro edition, B5.
37. Bob Von Sternberg. "Clinton Pushes for Franken, Obama," *Star Tribune*. October 31, 2008, metro edition, B4.
38. Larry Oakes, "Todd Palin Finds Kindred Souls on Iron Range," *Star Tribune*, October 17, 2008, metro edition, B7.
39. Kevin Duchschere, "Giuliani Hops On Board Coleman's Hope Express to Rally Supporters," *Star Tribune*, October 24, 2008, Metro Edition, B2.
40. Patricia Lopez, "Poll: Franken, Coleman Tied, with Barkley Seen as Spoiler," *Star Tribune*, August 23, 2008, metro edition, B1.
41. Kevin Duchschere, "The Minnesota Poll. The Senate Race. November 2, 2008," metro edition, A1.
42. Kevin Duchschere, "Campaign 2008: The Polls. Coleman Has Small Lead Over Franken among Likely Voters," October 31, 2008, metro edition, B5.
43. Kevin Duchschere, Curt Brown, and Pam Louwagie, "Minnesota Senate Race; Recount: The Brawl Drags On," November 6, 2008, A1.
44. Patricia Lopez, "Split Decisions: Voters Who Cross Party Lines on the Same Ballot Could Hold the Key to a Race's Outcome," October 28, 2008, metro edition, A1.
45. It is worth noting that Minnesota's Independence Party candidates made a strong showing in the two most competitive House races in Minnesota, with many DFLers alleging that they were spoilers, especially in Minnesota's 6th District where GOP incumbent Michele Bachmann received 46.41 percent of the vote, her DFL challenger Elwyn Tinklenberg received 43.43 percent, and Independence Party candidate Bob Anderson 10.4 percent.
46. Duchschere et al., "Minnesota Senate Race," A1.

10 All Politics Is Local...Except When It Isn't
English vs. Dahlkemper in Pennsylvania's Third Congressional District

Daniel M. Shea and Stephen K. Medvic

In an era when the vast majority of officeholders who seek reelection win (and typically do so by large margins), the rare defeat of an incumbent is a critically important phenomenon. In the 3rd Congressional District of Pennsylvania, Kathy Dahlkemper (D), a political neophyte knocked off Phil English (R), a smart, aggressive, 14-year incumbent. Part of the story is the national tide of change, sparked by the presidential campaign of Barack Obama. As a result, the Republican incumbent had no choice but to play defense. Another piece of the tale is the experience of the challenger, which provided her with a non-traditional, but crucially important source of support. Still another layer is the strategies and tactics of both candidates. No two campaigns are ever the same, and the story of the 2008 contest in Pennsylvania's 3rd District was certainly unique.

The Third Congressional District

Pennsylvania's 3rd District sits in the northwest corner of the state. The district extends from Lake Erie south to Butler and Armstrong Counties and at its southernmost point is roughly 20 miles north of Pittsburgh. Although 42 percent of the district is rural, there is also a significant industrial influence, particularly in the district's major city, Erie, which is Pennsylvania's fourth most populous city. For example, Erie boasts the General Electric Locomotive Division, which employs nearly 4,000 people, as well as numerous small manufacturing firms. The result is a district that is more blue collar (30.7%) than the rest of the state (25.2%) and one with a median income ($35,884) of roughly $4,200 less than the state as a whole.[1] In total, nearly one in five residents works in the manufacturing industry, while over a quarter work in the educational, health care, or social assistance industries; about 11 percent work in the retail industry.[2] The 3rd District is also very homogeneous: nearly 94 percent of the district is White; African Americans and Hispanics make up 3.6 percent and 1.6 percent of the district, respectively.[3]

Politically, the district leans Republican. In 2000, an estimated 51 percent of the voters in what would become the 3rd District supported George W. Bush as did 53 percent in 2004.[4] In both cases, Mr. Bush's vote totals were 5 percentage points higher in the 3rd District than were his statewide totals. In addition, the *Cook Political Report*'s Partisan Voter Index (PVI) raters the 3rd District as a R+3, meaning that Republicans do about 3 points better in the district than they do nationally. Though Erie and Mercer Counties are predominantly Democratic, the Democrats in this district are relatively conservative. The combination of conservative, blue-collar voters with rural voters explains the Republican tilt to the district, but also suggests an opportunity for Democratic candidates in the mold of Senator Robert Casey, Jr.; that is, those who are economically progressive and socially conservative. Moreover, Pennsylvania was one of the states in 2008 that saw a great surge of voters registering to vote as Democrats (see chapter 1); this certainly muted the GOP's advantage in the district. In fact, in the five counties with the largest percentage of voters in the 3rd District, by the time of the 2008 election Democrats enjoyed a 30,000-person advantage in registered voters (235,983 to 205,738) while over 50,000 were registered with another party.[5]

The Incumbent: Republican Phil English

Phil English was first elected to the House of Representatives in 1994 by a narrow victory in which he garnered just under 50 percent of the vote (the Democrat netted 47% and an Independent candidate pulled in 3%). He ran to fill the seat that had been held by Tom Ridge after Ridge decided to run for governor. It was widely reported that during the 1994 campaign English had pledged to serve only six terms in Congress, though he denied making such a pledge.

In his first reelection contest, English survived another close race, edging out Democrat Ron DiNicola 51 percent to 49 percent. DiNicola was a prominent attorney from Erie, and was able to amass a large war chest from donors in and outside the district. The American Trial Lawyers, for example, invested heavily in DiNicola's race. Beginning in 1998, however, English won four consecutive races with at least 60 percent of the vote. In the midterm election of 2006 English's vote share dropped to 54 percent against a challenger, Steven Porter, who was vastly outspent. It was a difficult year for the GOP in which fellow western Pennsylvania Republicans Melissa Hart (4th District) and Rick Santorum (U.S. Senate) lost reelection bids. Porter was new to the area, held no public position, and was essentially unheard of throughout the district. He also held positions that seemed inconsistent with the mainstream of the district. That is to say, Porter offered several "liberal" policy positions—apparently bucking the moderate temperament of most voters in Northwest Pennsylvania. Even so, the outcome of the race proved much closer than most expected. So after several years of comfortable victories, English appeared to be on relatively thin electoral ice.

During his years in the House of Representatives, Phil English's voting record was conservative, but not consistently so (see Table 10.1). His ratings from the American Conservative Union (ACU) ranged from a high of 92 (in 2002) to a low of 52 (in 2008) and averaged just over 72. His scores from the liberal Americans for Democratic Action (ADA) ranged from 0 to 65, averaging slightly more

Table 10.1 Congressional Vote Scores for Phil English, 1995–2008

Year	American Conservative Union	Americans for Democratic Action	Presidential Support	Party Unity
2008	65	52	44	82
2007	40	64	50	78
2006	15	80	95	90
2005	5	88	85	93
2004	25	68	76	88
2003	20	68	91	93
2002	0	92	87	93
2001	10	68	81	89
2000	25	56	38	83
1999	25	72	24	84
1998	35	68	35	81
1997	20	76	37	85
1996	10	74	46	79
1995	15	84	26	89

Source: 1995–2006 scores from various editions of *CQ's Politics in America*; 2007–2008 American Conservative Union (ACU) and Americans for Democratic Action (ADA) scores from the organization Web sites; 2007–2008 party unity and presidential support scores from *CQ Weekly Report*.

than 22. Through his career, English proved to be a reliable vote for his party, although he was not a rubber stamp. He voted with a majority of his party an average of 86 percent of the time and consistently voted in support of President Bush's and against President Clinton's position on legislation.

Perhaps in response to a reelection contest in 2006 that was closer than it should have been, however, English's voting record became noticeably more moderate in the 110th Congress (2007–2008). His ACU scores dropped (that is, became less conservative) to 64 and 52 in 2007 and 2008, respectively, and his ADA scores rose (or became more liberal) to 40 and 65. His party unity scores also fell from over 90 in the previous two years to 78 percent and 82 percent in 2007 and 2008, and he supported President Bush only 50 percent and 44 percent of the time in those years, respectively, after two years of 85 and 90 percent support.

With a seat on the powerful Ways and Means Committee, English could claim a significant amount of clout in the House for his constituents. He certainly worked hard to protect their interests, even if that meant occasionally disagreeing with his party. For instance, he sided with Democrats and supported an increase in the minimum wage and home heating subsidies for low-income families.

Some of English's votes were clearly influenced by the blue-collar nature of his district—he often backed positions supported by unions and working class voters. Though he voted for the Central America Free Trade Agreement (CAFTA), he did so only after certain concessions were in place and he generally considered himself a supporter of "fair trade." As such, he was willing to support tariffs on imports from China and Vietnam, a popular position in northwest Pennsylvania. As chair of the Steel Caucus in the House, he was also a staunch defender of the steel industry. This was manifested by his support for import quotas for steel and his efforts to stop Korea from "dumping" (or using predatory pricing for) steel pipe and tubing.[6]

Following the 2006 midterm elections, English hoped to enter the ranks of Republican leadership in the House. To do so, he made a bid to become chairman of the National Republican Congressional Committee (NRCC). Though that bid was unsuccessful, English was tapped to chair an NRCC task force devoted to erasing the campaign committee's $14.4 million debt.[7]

Outsider observers, such as a few local political scientists and several of the beltway handicappers such as Charlie Cook of the *Cook Political Report*, seemed reluctant to tag English as vulnerable at the outset of the 2008 campaign. He was smart, aggressive, well-positioned on key committees, well-financed, and a moderate in a moderate district. The *Cook Report*, for example, suggested the 3rd District was "solidly Republican" even after Kathy Dahlkemper swamped her primary election opponents. This was likely because traditional wisdom says that incumbents lose due to overt deficiencies and glaring missteps (to be fair, Cook's assessment slowly changed as the campaign progressed.) As noted by a prominent campaign strategist some time ago, "Deadly sins of incumbents include excessive absences, numerous junkets, and bloated office budgets, misuse of public funds, cronyism, and voting for taxes."[8] This was not Phil English; his problems did not seem obvious or significant.

The Challenger: Democrat Kathy Dahlkemper

Kathy Dahlkemper was the first woman from northwestern Pennsylvania ever elected to Congress in her own right (i.e., not filling a spot held by a deceased husband). She defeated three quality candidates, all by double digits, in a heated primary, and knocked off an attentive 14-year incumbent in the general election. One would assume that her background was a key factor in her victory, and it was, but not in the conventional sense.

Indeed, it is difficult to place Kathy Dahlkemper's background into categories common among successful challengers. For one, she had never held public office prior to running for Congress. She had never expressed any interest in public life prior to 2007, never spoken up in any public forum (e.g., letter to the editor, open city council meetings, etc.) about a public policy question, had not been a robust supporter of any other candidate or public figure. No one in her immediate or extended family could be called "political," and she was not tapped by any prominent public official to be the next rising star in local politics. Along similar lines, Dahlkemper was not an active member in local party politics. The Erie County Democratic Committee is a viable organization, boasting several dozen active members and undertaking numerous functions throughout the year, but Dahlkemper never attended party meetings and rarely took part in these events.

Further, there was no issue or set of ideological concerns that propelled her candidacy, as is often the case with challengers. In the fall of 2007, before she had entered the race, one of the authors of this chapter (Shea) was invited to have lunch with her. Dahlkemper was interested in finding out more about the rigors of a competitive congressional campaign, as well as the broad parameters of being a member of Congress. During their 90 minute conversation, Dahlkemper noted concerns about the war in Iraq, our nation's dependence on foreign oil, the loss of jobs in the region, and what she believed to be a less-than adequate health care system. No particular issue or a deep ideological agenda seemed at the heart of her potential candidacy. Instead, there seemed to be a general belief that it was time for new leadership and that she might have something to give. She was also concerned with the general direction of the community and about the "future for our children." As she explained it, several friends had made passing comments that she would make a good member of Congress, and this caught her attention. She had completed her work raising her five children, and the idea of running for Congress kept surfacing.

Dahlkemper also lacked what many *successful* challengers have—great wealth that would allow her to conduct a robust, self-financed race. She and her husband own a landscaping business, with about 10 employees during peak seasons. There was no significant pool of resources from which Dahlkemper expected to draw. Nor was she a principal figure in business circles. The Dahlkempers were known and respected in the Erie business community, but there is little evidence that they were leaders in that realm.

In short, Kathy Dahlkemper did not have a political base, resources to draw upon, a sitting elected official to help pave the way, or a deep connection to the local party organization. Additionally, her candidacy was not driven by a pressing issue or an ideological agenda.

So, what was it in her background and what resources was she able to draw upon that helped defeat an entrenched incumbent? For one, she had a much larger base than most outside observers understood. Her deep community roots sprang from an intimate tie to the Erie Diocese of the Roman Catholic Church. She and her family faithfully attended church and over the decades Dahlkemper had taken on numerous leadership roles in the church. The most important of these activities was her position as marriage encounter coordinator.

The Erie Diocese, as with most Catholic dioceses across the country, regularly holds marriage encounter weekends for parishioners. As coordinators, the Dahlkempers steadily broadened their network of *intimate* friends—not mere acquaintances, but dear friends. They were known and well-liked throughout northwest Pennsylvania. This created a steadfast base of supporters that any local elected official would covet. Unlike the followers of most politicians, Dahlkemper's base was bipartisan; many of her Catholic friends were conservative

Republicans. Thus, by the time she was gearing-up for her campaign, Dahlkemper was better known than each of her primary election opponents even though they were elected officials or leaders in the Erie legal community. We might say that her strength sprang from a *veiled base*, rather than an overt group of partisan supporters.

Also worthy of mention is the fact that Dahlkemper's name identification was buffeted from the recurrent television advertisements for Dahlkemper Jewelry Connection, a vibrant small business in Erie. The two families are related, though only distantly (as third cousins). Nevertheless, for most residents in Northwest Pennsylvania the name *Dahlkemper* was rather familiar.

A less tangible, but nonetheless critical resource for Dahlkemper was her understanding of the mood of the community. Having lived nearly all of her adult life in Erie, and having raised five children and owned a small business in the area, she had an intuitive sense of how things were going. This was quite obvious in several preprimary conversations with Shea when she articulated a growing unease with Phil English. Dahlkemper insisted that the district needed a change in leadership.

There is one other resource that may have proved quite helpful. Jim Murphy, a veteran of New York State electoral politics, once commented that the number one characteristic in successful challengers is the steadfast commitment to winning. "When you are looking for challengers to back," noted Murphy, "the depth of their conviction says as much as anything. Successful challengers have a big heart, and are not afraid to show it."[9] By all accounts, Dahlkemper was this sort of candidate. She considered her run for months, carefully charting what it would take and her own level of commitment. Once she made the decision, she worked tirelessly. She took very few days off from well before the primary until November, and on most days she put in long hours. Given the nature of her employment, Dahlkemper was able to campaign full time. She made the most of it.

The Campaign

It was clear early in the campaign season that the race between Phil English and Kathy Dahlkemper would be tight. A survey by Momentum Analysis in June suggested the race was a dead heat, with Dahlkemper at 41 percent and English at 40 percent. The polls continued to be tight through the campaign with neither candidate ever holding a lead outside of the margin of error, and the actions of the candidates reflected this dynamic.[10]

English Tries to Find His Message

Throughout the summer and into the fall, Phil English's campaign struggled to find the right message to send to voters. Through the years, English's reelection strategy had remained essentially the same. First, he would take care of the district. As member of the majority for most of his time in the House, and as a member of one of the most important committees, Ways and Means, English

Table 10.2 Campaign Finance Data for Pennsylvania's 3rd District, 2002–2008

	Disbursements		Receipts	
	English	Challenger	English	Challenger
2008	$2,615,349	$1,152,538	$2,659,966	$1,163,937
2006	$1,466,487	$63,034	$1,407,732	$81,102
2004	$1,595,195	$224,002	$1,338,016	$235,126
2002	$778,773	$19,353	$1,083,839	$20,991

Source: http://www.opensecrets.org/races/summary.php?id=PA03&cycle=2008 [accessed on June 9, 2009].

was afforded hefty earmarks. He also kept busy on legislation, sponsoring some 357 bills between 1995 and 2008, of which five were successfully enacted into law. He was skilled at advertising, which included robust use of the franking privilege and copious press releases. In 2006, for example, English sent out mailings from his congressional office totaling some $73,360.[11] He also touted his moderate voting record, and he was a skillful fundraiser on top of all this. His ability to amass a huge war chest scared off many potential opponents, often leaving the field to weaker challengers. As Table 10.2 indicates, before 2008 English had never faced a challenger in the 3rd District who raised more than a quarter of a million dollars. In each election since 2002, English was able to overwhelm his opponent with his spending.

Finally, and perhaps most importantly, English skillfully used his massive resources to create a narrative about and image of his opponents. This followed a major axiom of campaigning: define the opponent before she can define herself. A good example of English's adherence to this rule was his campaign against Stephen Porter, who ran against English in 2004 and 2006. Few expected Porter to mount a serious campaign, having few roots in the community and very modest resources, as noted above. Nevertheless, English leveled an early barrage of negative campaign ads against the retired art professor in both campaigns. Again and again, over the airways and through direct mail, English portrayed Porter as a radical, with irrational, if not dangerous, ideas about public policy. He pulled excerpts from a book written by Porter that suggested, to some, that the professor promoted "extreme" policies. Regardless of whether the attacks were founded, the barrage was devastating; Porter stood little chance. It was like watching a professional football team play against a high school squad.

In short, English's reelection strategy had always been the traditional route for most incumbents: take care of the district; be visible to voters; amass a huge war chest; and define the opposition early in the campaign so that they could never recover. Money from outside groups, a critical part of most challengers' campaigns, would sit on the sidelines. On the night that Dahlkemper won the Democratic primary, English was candid about the route to victory he would take in 2008: follow the path of prior campaigns.[12]

Things, however, took a different turn. For one, English's vote total in 2006 against Stephen Porter was surprisingly small—just 54 percent. Porter was a weak candidate with very modest resources (see Table 10.2). This, combined with a growing sense that Republicans were out of favor nationally, led to a hotly contested primary election on the Democratic side. That is to say, many Democrats smelled blood in the water and were itching for a chance to challenge English. Still, the primary was cordial and when it was over all the candidates rallied around the winner. Dahlkemper also proved somewhat adept at raising early money. While her fundraising never matched English's, by midspring she had raised more than Porter's total in 2006.

Most significantly, English's efforts to define Dahlkemper did not seem to work. His strategy of trying to label her as a "radical liberal," the approach used against Porter, did not seem to resonate because Dahlkemper was a pro-life, progun, small-business owner. Having few policy-centered lines of attack, several early negative ads in support of English, which were sponsored by the NRCC, suggested Dahlkemper had "wacky" environmental ideas.[13] One ad even featured a dogsled, suggesting that if his Democratic opponent had her way few would have gasoline to drive cars. There is little evidence that this worked. As noted by one of Dahlkemper's campaign operatives, "the polling hardly moved, and our positives remained much higher than English's throughout the course of the campaign."[14]

By late September, a SurveyUSA poll showed Dahlkemper with a 4-point lead. Other public polls still indicated a bit more volatility in the race, but it is interesting to note that Dahlkemper's own pollster had her lead at one point in July and she eventually won by just over 2 percentage points.

Thus, English's strategy of offering himself as the moderate, commonsense alternative, even if voters were not crazy about his party, stalled. By early fall it was clear that the English team understood this and a new approach was floated. During the first debate, held at Allegheny College in early October, English outlined the new strategy in his opening statement. "This district," he said, "needs a change, and I intend to be the agent of change."[15] He went on to suggest that only those who understand the complexity of the legislative process, the insand-outs of Congress, could bring meaningful change to the district. In other words, English was trying to become the change candidate; given the resonance of the "change" theme in Barack Obama's campaign, and given less than 20 percent of Americans thought the country was headed in the right direction, one can understanding the attractiveness of this new message. Only an experienced legislator can really know how to change the system, but it seemed rather odd coming from a 14-year incumbent who originally ran for Congress supporting term limits.

Near the end of the campaign, English's strategy continued to shift. It could be seen in his television advertisements, press releases, and in the final debate at the local public radio station. The message from English now was that he had delivered for the district, time and again, and the community would suffer if they lost their leader in Washington. For example, in the spring of 2008, he claimed credit for helping provide nearly $1 million in federal funds for sand restoration at Presque Isle State Park, the largest tourist attraction in the district.[16] As it became clear that Obama would likely win the presidency, English also made the pitch that Republicans should be sent back to the House in order to check radical policy changes. A final line of attack was leveled against Dahlkemper, this time attempting to paint her as wealthy and out of touch. With these various messages, the focus of the English campaign seemed muddled. Phil English and his supporters threw everything at the wall with the hope that something would stick. Likely, the inconsistency in message was due to never being able to mount a line of attack against his opponent that gave him traction with the public. As his polling numbers stalled—a DailyKos.com poll in early October had him down by 7 points—and as the attacks continued, English scrambled for any message that would take.

A Challenger in Unfamiliar Territory

As noted above, with the race close from the start, Dahlkemper did not face the same steep climb that many challengers do of having to come from far behind. Rather, with such good polling numbers she had to simply maintain her lead over English. For her part, Dahlkemper needed to remind voters that they knew her and that the image English was trying to create for her was not who she was. Early on, the Dahlkemper campaign focused on building the candidate's credentials and local ties. A series of "bio" mailings and television spots focused on her community roots and her experience as a mother and small-business owner. The message was simple: *You know Kathy Dahlkemper; she's one of us.* Dahlkemper noted, "I had connections with people from all over the district—through my life."[17]

Perhaps concerned that their opponent would slowly rise in the polls as the election drew near, or maybe as a means to offset the attacks being leveled against their candidate, near the end of the summer the Dahlkemper campaign shifted to attack ads against English. Generally, this was a two-pronged approach. First, in keeping with the theme many Democrats employed across the nation, the idea of "change" was pushed by the candidate: it was time for Phil English to step aside. Dahlkemper pounded this theme at events, press conferences, and debates. Second, a series of attack ads sponsored by the Democratic Congressional Campaign Committee (DCCC) and American Federation of State, County and Municipal Employees (AFSCME) suggested English was more concerned with protecting "special interests" and "Wall Street speculators" than with protecting the residents of northwest Pennsylvania. The message here was simple: English was out of touch; he was failing to protect average citizens. The DCCC ads "were able to take on the opposition while allowing us to stay focused on the positive message of change and vision for the district," said Tina Mengine, Dahlkemper's campaign manager. Moreover, she noted, "because we have no input into these ads nor do we know about them in advance, each ad that ran was a surprise and usually very welcome."[18] As Mengine notes, this type of activity is often viewed positively by candidates' campaigns because while the party or outside group hammers away at the opponent, the candidate can remain untainted by the charge of "negative" campaigning.

When pressed to explain the overall strategy of the Dahlkemper campaign, another staffer suggested it was "all about fight[ing] off attacks and keeping our lead." Also, "Kathy was much more popular than most of us understood. The attack ads didn't stick because they [the voters] knew her."[19]

Dahlkemper's strategy also focused on geography. As noted above, voters in the 3rd District lean Republican, but it varies greatly from one county to the next. Dahlkemper's campaign understood that if they could carry Erie County by a large margin, roughly 50 percent of the district, and hold their own in the other Democratic county, Mercer, they could pull it off. This proved to be a wise route, as she won Erie with nearly 57 percent of the vote and Mercer County with nearly 52 percent, but lost every other county.

Finally, it is likely that Dahlkemper benefited from support among women voters. The nuances of identity politics are complex and hard to fully discern when exit polling is unavailable, but it is clear that Hillary Clinton was quite popular in the 3rd District, especially among Democratic women. In the congressional primary, held the same day as the presidential primary, the margins of victory for Clinton and Dahlkemper were virtually the same throughout the district. That is, both candidates had massive wins in the rural counties—Crawford, Venango, Butler, and Mercer—and in Erie County where the race between Clinton and Obama was closer, so was the margin of victory for Dahlkemper. Did this carry over to the general election? It is hard to say, but in a year when "change" dominated the political landscape (an issue discussed in greater detail below) Dahlkemper, the first women candidate for Congress from this area, seemed to fit the bill.

Outside Groups Lend a Hand

Interestingly, even when the results of the Dahlkemper campaign's July poll showing the Democrat leading were released to the media,[20] groups that might have been willing to spend outside money continued to hedge their bets and wait on the sidelines. Typically in tight contests like this one, when an incumbent looks to be in danger, groups on both sides will start to spend money in hopes of tipping the race in one direction or another. Eventually, the party committees and some interest groups became heavily involved in the 3rd District. Of course, the candidates themselves raised and spent significant amounts of money (see Table 10.3). Faced with a serious challenge, English raised nearly $2.7 million, which was twice as much as his Democratic opponent. Though Dahlkemper's $1.3 million was an impressive fundraising haul for a challenger, her Democratic allies appear to have been concerned about the spending disparity between the candidates. Late in the summer of 2008, the DCCC added Dahlkemper to their "Red to Blue" program of targeted House races.[21] In the end, their financial commitment to Dahlkemper amounted to nearly $1.6 million in independent expenditures, a total that dwarfed spending by all other outside groups. Half that amount was spent in support of Dahlkemper while the other half was used for attacks against English.

The American Federation of State, County, and Municipal Employees (AFSCME) also spent independently in this race. In fact, AFSCME spent almost half a million dollars opposing English, which was more than any other group, save the party committees. Of course, a number of Democratic leaning interest groups endorsed Dahlkemper. Those endorsements meant not only financial contributions to her campaign, but the commitment of volunteers for canvassing and get-out-the-vote efforts. The support of organized labor is particularly valuable in this regard and Dahlkemper lined up endorsements from nearly all of the major unions including the AFL-CIO and the United Steelworkers.

As an incumbent, English was able to raise plenty of money, but his vulnerability and the DCCC's commitment to Dahlkemper worried the NRCC. As early as September 10, the NRCC paid for polling in the 3rd District, one of only two incumbent-held seats in which they were polling at that time.[22] The NRCC ad criticizing the Democratic challenger for her "wacky" ideas about energy, its first ad of the cycle, was yet another sign that English was high on the party's list of incumbents to protect.[23] The DCCC responded to this ad immediately with one that accused English of supporting the privatization of Social Security.[24]

English also received more money from Republican leadership political action committees (PACs) than all but two other Republican incumbents, an indication that his colleagues recognized the trouble he faced.[25] For its part, the NRCC spent $776,828 to help English and virtually all of that money was spent attacking Dahlkemper. Other groups that spent independently on the Republican side, including the National Rifle Association ($91,694) and the American Medical Association ($200,338), did so entirely in support of English (rather than against Dahlkemper). Despite the assistance from the party and other outside groups, English was in serious trouble by the end of October. With just about two weeks left in the campaign, *Politico* reported that the GOP was "all but writing off" English's seat.[26] Indeed, the last independent expenditure by the NRCC against Dahlkemper was made on October 24.[27]

When all was said and done, Dahlkemper's allies nearly eliminated the financial gap between her and the Republican incumbent. Democratic spending, including Dahlkemper's, amounted to $3,496,614; Republican spending totaled $3,929,721 (see Table 10.3). Clearly, the independent spending efforts in support of Dahlkemper were critical to her ability to mount a serious challenge. The

Table 10.3 Spending by Parties, Interest Groups and Candidates in Pennsylvania's 3rd District, 2008

	Party Committees[a]	Interest Groups	Candidates	Total
Dahlkemper	$1,592,099	$591,276	$1,313,239	$3,496,614
English	$858,300	$411,450	$2,659,971	$3,929,721

[a] Includes coordinated expenditures by the Pennsylvania Democratic Party (for Dahlkemper) and the Republican National Committee (for English).

Source: Center for Responsive Politics, "2008 Race: Pennsylvania District 03, Independent Expenditures," http://www.opensecrets.org/races/indexp.php?cycle=2008&id=PA03 [accessed March 18, 2009]; figures updated by a search of disclosure data for committees at the Federal Election Commission, http://www.fec.gov/finance/disclosure/disclosure_data_search.shtml [accessed March 18, 2009].

DCCC, in particular, was invaluable. As Dahlkemper acknowledged, "Having support from the party was very helpful, just in letting me compete on a level playing field."[28] Without their assistance, it is quite possible that the outcome of this race would have been different.

Lessons Learned

Incumbents lose, but not often. The conventional wisdom is that English got caught up in the national anti-Republican tide. All politics is local, except when it is not (we might say). He was an attentive, active representative, but he could not weather the storm against his party and the backlash against George W. Bush. Phil English had no choice but to play defense and that is a difficult spot for an incumbent.

There is some truth to the conventional wisdom, of course. It is likely that Dahlkemper would not have entered the race if she and others in the district did not perceive a powerful national tide. She calculated that there would be a boost for any Democratic candidate. The strategic politician model played out across the nation in the fall of 2007.[29] Indeed, "strategically sophisticated challengers carefully judge the vulnerability of their opponents...."[30] Moreover, strong potential candidates are vastly more likely to run when they see a good chance of winning;[31] this seems to have been clearly played out in this race.

In addition, outside groups might not have been able to bolster Dahlkemper's efforts if the Democratic advantage had not been as big as it was in 2008. Because there was more energy and excitement among Democrats than among Republicans, the Democratic Party and its allies were flush with money. With more money to spend than their opponents, the Democrats could compete in more races than could the GOP. So the national tide had very practical implications for the resources available on the challenger's side of this race.

Did voters, however, kick their 14-year incumbent out of office simply out of a desire for change? Many scholars have found only modest evidence to suggest a direct connection between national tides and local voting trends.[32] Did Barack Obama's message trickle down to northwest Pennsylvania and did his coattails pull Dahlkemper along? Perhaps, but one should bear in mind that Barack Obama lost the 3rd District, including every county but Erie. He did, however, perform as well or better than John Kerry in nearly every part of the district, including rural counties (see Table 10.4). Dahlkemper, on the other hand, ran ahead of Obama in some counties. In Butler County, for instance, Obama received 35.7 percent of the vote, compared to Dahlkemper's 48.1 percent.[33] So, it appears there is little evidence to suggest there were coattails in the 3rd District. Additionally, if the tide was so strong, how did some Republicans stay afloat? Again, English was a competent, moderate legislator.

Aside from Dahlkemper riding Obama's coattails, another explanation for English's defeat might be that he ran a poor campaign. Ed Brookover, the former Political Director of the National Republican Senatorial Committee and

Table 10.4 Percentage of the Vote for the Democratic Presidential Nominee by County in Pennsylvania's 3rd District, 2004 and 2008

County	Kerry (2004)	Obama (2008)
Erie	53.9%	59.3%
Crawford	41.8%	44.0%
Mercer	48.2%	49.1%
Butler	35.2%	35.7%
Armstrong	38.7%	37.0%

Note: The counties included are those in which the vast majority of residents are constituents in the 3rd District. On this basis, the results for Warren County were excluded.

Source: Pennsylvania Department of State, Elections Information, "2004 General Election," http://www.electionreturns.state.pa.us/ElectionsInformation.aspx?FunctionID=12&ElectionID=11; and Pennsylvania Department of State, Elections Information, "2008 General Election," http://www.electionreturns.state.pa.us/ElectionsInformation.aspx?FunctionID=12&ElectionID=28 [accessed June 9, 2009].

Regional Political Director of the Republican National Committee once noted, "There is nothing more pleasing, from the point of view of a strategist, than to work against an incumbent who runs the same campaign again and again."[34] There might be something to this point. English surely began his campaign against Dahlkemper the same way that he had confronted other opponents. When that did not work, however, his campaign appeared to panic and flailed from strategy to strategy until it ended up wasting a lot of money on a terribly inconsistent message, another sign of a poor campaign.

The most likely explanation of why English was not able to defend his seat contains elements of each. There was a tsunami against all GOP candidates and English was in trouble even before the Democratic primary. His team, however, probably surmised that they could survive by relying on their ability to use hefty resources to define the opponent. This would keep outside money that favored the Democrat on the sidelines as it had in the past, and push voters to see Dahlkemper as too risky. The problem was that attacks on Dahlkemper did not stick. She was too well-known and respected in the district. Over nearly two decades she had broadened her community roots into a solid foundation. *She was a political neophyte, but a known neophyte.* As months passed and Dahlkemper maintained her strength, her campaign caught the attention of the DCCC, AFSCME, and other contributors. This outside money was critical in helping to neutralize English's last-minute media blitz.

The core lesson of the race, then, is that national trends can shape local contests, but alone they cannot determine the outcome of these races. Other factors such as the quality of the candidates and the effectiveness of their campaigns also matter. For an incumbent free of scandal or controversy to lose, all of these elements must be present. In the 3rd Congressional District of Pennsylvania in 2008, they were.

Notes

1. Michael Barone and Richard E. Cohen, *The Almanac of American Politics, 2008* (Washington, DC: National Journal, 2007), 1393; 1374.

2. U.S. Census Bureau, "District 3, Pennsylvania, Selected Economic Characteristics: 2005–2007," http://fastfacts.census.gov/servlet/CWSADPTable?geo_id=50000 US4203&ds_name=ACS_2007_3YR_G00_&qr_name=ACS_2007_3YR_ G00_DP3YR3&back=%2Fservlet%2FACSCWSFacts%3F_ event%3DChangeGeoContext%26geo_id%3D50000US4203%26_geoCon text%3D01000US%7C04000US42%26_street%3D%26_county%3D%26_ cd%3D50000US4203%26_cityTown%3D%26_state%3D04000US42%26_ zip%3D%26_lang%3Den%26_sse%3Don%26ActiveGeoDiv%3D%26_useEV%3 D%26pctxt%3Dfph%26pgsl%3D040%26_content%3D%26_keyword%3D%26_ industry%3D&_scrollToRow= (accessed June 17, 2009).

3. U.S. Census Bureau, "Congressional District3, Pennsylvania—Fact Sheet" http:// fastfacts.census.gov/servlet/ACSCWSFacts?_event=ChangeGeoContext&geo_ id=50000US4203&_geoContext=01000US|04000US42&_street=&_ county=&_cd=50000US4203&_cityTown=&_state=04000US42&_zip=&_ lang=en&_sse=on&ActiveGeoDiv=&_useEV=&pctxt=fph&pgsl=040&_con tent=&_keyword=&_industry=(accessed June 17, 2009).

4. Polidata estimated the presidential vote in what would become the 3rd Congressional District of Pennsylvania following redistricting in 2001 (see Barone and Cohen, *Almanac of American Politics*, 16).

5. Commonwealth of Pennsylvania, 2008 Voter Registration Statistics—Official, http://www.dos.state.pa.us/elections/lib/elections/055_voter_registration_statistics /2008genelectionvoterregistotals.pdf (accessed June 17, 2009).

6. Barone and Cohen, *Almanac of American Politics*, 1394.

7. John Bresnahan, "House Republicans Help Make a Dent in Party's Debt," *Politico*, February 19, 2007, http://www.politico.com/news/stories/0207/2827.html (accessed March 18, 2009).

8. Ed Brookover, as quoted in Daniel M. Shea and Stephen C. Brooks, "How to Topple an Incumbent: Advice from Experts Who've Done It," *Campaigns and Elections* June (1995), 21–25.

9. Jim Murphy, as quoted in Shea and Brooks, "How to Topple an Incumbent," 23.

10. For polling results in this race, see Pollster.com, http://www.pollster.com/polls/ pa/08-pa-03-ge-evd.php (accessed June 9, 2009).

11. Jerome L. Sherman, "Rep. Murphy is the King of 'Franking,'" *Pittsburgh Post-Gazette*, May 7, 2007, http://www.post-gazette.com/pg/07127/784003-176.stm (accessed April 15, 2009).

12. Kevin Flowers, "Dahlkemper Wins Nomination," *Erie Times News*, April 23, 2008, http://kathydahlkemperforcongress.com/node/107 (accessed April 29, 2009).

13. Reid Wilson, "GOP On Air as Dems Drop the Hammer," The Scorecard, *Politico*, October 1, 2008, http://www.politico.com/blogs/scorecard/1008/GOP_On_Air_ As_Dems_Drop_The_Hammer.html (accessed March 18, 2009).

14. Michael Burton, personal interview March 17, 2009.

15. Response to a question in the first debate at Allegheny College, October 12, 2008.

16. See, http://www.legistorm.com/earmarks/details/member/221/Rep_Phil_English/ page/1/sort/amount/type/desc.html (accessed April 30, 2009).

17. Lindsay Perna, "Dahlkemper Aided by Democratic Committee in Win Over English," *News from DC*, WSEE.TV Washington Bureau, March 17, 2009, http://wsee. tv/blogs/washington/?p=58 (accessed March 18, 2009).

18. Perna, "Dahlkemper Aided by Democratic Committee in Win Over English."

19. Burton, personal interview.

20. See http://www.realclearpolitics.com/politics_nation/2008/07/english_down_one. html (accessed June 9, 2009).

21. Emily Cadei, "Six More Democratic Candidates to Get Party Help," *CQ Politics*, August 1, 2008 http://www.cqpolitics.com/wmspage.cfm?docID=news-000002932710 (accessed March 18, 2009).

22. Reid Wilson, "NRCC Polls GOP-Held Districts," The Scorecard, *Politico*, September 10, 2008, http://www.politico.com/blogs/scorecard/0908/NRCC_Polls_ GOPHeld_Districts.html (accessed March 18, 2009).

23. Ibid.

24. Aaron Blake, "Dems Raise Stakes on Social Security 'Gamble,'" *The Hill*, September 30, 2008, http://thehill.com/leading-the-news/dems-raise-stakes-on-social-security-gamble-2008-09-30.html (accessed March 18, 2009).

25. CQ Moneyline. "Close Races Draw Leadership PAC Money," *CQ Politics*, February 9, 2009, http://www.cqpolitics.com/wmspage.cfm?docID=moneyline-00000302801 6 (accessed March 18, 2009).

26. Josh Kraushaar and Reid Wilson. "GOP 'Goner' List Warns of House Rout," *Politico*, October 23, 2008, http://www.politico.com/news/stories/1008/14885.html (accessed March 18, 2009).

27. This is based on a search of independent expenditure reports for the NRCC at the Federal Election Commission Web site, http://query.nictusa.com/cgi-bin/com_ supopp/C00075820/ (accessed March 18, 2009).

28. Perna, "Dahlkemper Aided by Democratic Committee."

29. Gary C. Jacobson and Samuel Kernell, *Strategy and Choice in Congressional Elections*, 2nd ed. (New Haven, CT: Yale University Press, 1983).

30. Edie N. Goldenberg, Michael W. Traugott, and Frank R. Baumgartner, "Preemptive and Reactive Spending in U.S. House Races," *Political Behavior*, 8 (1986): 15.

31. Sandy L. Maisel, Walter J. Stone, and Cherie Masestas, "Quality Challengers to Congressional Incumbents: Can Better Candidates be Found?" In *Playing Hardball: Campaigning for the U.S. Congress*, ed. Paul S. Herrnson, (Upper Saddle River, NJ: Prentice-Hall, 2001), 12–40.

32. Gary C. Jacobson, "The Marginals Never Vanished: Incumbency and Competition in Elections to the U.S. House of Representatives," *American Journal of Political Science*, 31 (1987): 126–41; Gary C. Jacobson, *The Politics of Congressional Elections*, 3rd ed. (New York: HarperCollins, 1992).

33. Election results can be found on the Pennsylvania Secretary of State's Web page, http://www.electionreturns.state.pa.us/ElectionsInformation.aspx?FunctionID=0 (accessed April 15, 2009).

34. Ed Brookover, as quoted in Shea and Brooks, "How to Topple an Incumbent," 24.

11 Courting the Obama–Terry Voter
Terry vs. Esch in Nebraska's Second Congressional District*

Randall E. Adkins and Gregory A. Petrow

In the 2006 midterm elections, Representative Lee Terry was reelected to his fifth term by the voters of the Nebraska 2nd District, winning with 55 percent of the vote. While it is not surprising that an incumbent was reelected, 2006 was a year when the Republican brand suffered in congressional elections across the country and the Democrats won both houses of Congress for the first time since 1994. For Terry, it ended up being the third consecutive election cycle where his share of the vote declined. As a result, his 2006 opponent, Jim Esch, decided to throw his hat into the ring again in 2008. Esch ran in 2006 without the assistance of the Democratic Congressional Campaign Committee (DCCC) or other outside groups, and he believed that with their support in 2008 he might be able to ride the tide created by Barack Obama's campaign to Washington, DC. In the end, Esch came up short again. This chapter will examine how the incumbent, Lee Terry, defended his seat in a congressional district that was targeted by Democrats in Nebraska, the DCCC, and the Obama presidential campaign.

The Second District

The 2nd District lies in east-central Nebraska. It is made up of Douglas County, which encompasses Omaha, and the northeast corner of Sarpy County. The 2nd District borders the Missouri River and is the home of the city of Omaha and the surrounding suburbs. Omaha is the largest city north of Kansas City, between Minneapolis in the east and Denver in the west.

Economically, the 2nd District has changed tremendously in the past few decades. As a major port on the Missouri River and a major junction for the Union Pacific railroad, Omaha was a natural fit for what were once the world's largest stockyards and accompanying meatpacking industry. Even today, many think of the city as being predominantly blue collar, even though the city has been radically transformed into a white collar hub for the agriculture and insurance industries. Of all residents of the 2nd District, 66.8 percent work in white collar industries, 19.7 percent in blue collar industries, and 13.5 percent work in service-related industries.[1] If anything has served to change the image of the city it is the fact that billionaire investor Warren Buffett, who is the head of the investment conglomerate Berkshire Hathaway, lives in Omaha.[2]

Today, Omaha boasts of a very diverse economy. Five Fortune 500 companies are headquartered in the city, including agricultural giant ConAgra Foods, Berkshire Hathaway, Mutual of Omaha, the Peter Kiewit and Sons construction company, and the Union Pacific Railroad. Still, the district's largest employer is Offutt Air Force Base, which is located in Sarpy County and employs over 10,000 military personnel and civilians. Offutt is the headquarters of the U.S. Strategic Command.[3] Omaha is also the home of First National Bank, which is one of the largest banks in the United States and one of the largest hubs for credit card processing operations. Further, Omaha is widely considered to be the nation's leading telemarketing and customer service call center, handling more than 20 million calls per day.

In general, residents of the district enjoy both a very high standard of living and a relatively low cost of living. Douglas County is one of the few counties in the state of Nebraska where the median household income, $50,941, exceeds that of the state ($47,072) and the country ($50,233). Sarpy County actually leads the state with a median household income of $63,776.[4] That is not true, however, for all residents of the district.

While racially the 2nd District looks a lot like the rest of the United States (83.3% White, 11.7% Black, and 9.4% Hispanic),[5] more than one in three African Americans live below the poverty line, and Omaha has the fifth highest poverty rate among African Americans of the largest 100 cities.[6] Like most other major urban areas, racial relations have never been particularly good. As the city's industrial base grew in early 20th century, European immigrants and African Americans migrating from the South came to Omaha. The European immigrants settled in what is today known as South Omaha, where the stockyards and the meatpacking industry were located, and the African Americans moved into North Omaha.

In the latter half of the 20th century the suburbs of West Omaha grew exponentially as the children of those European immigrants moved West (in many cases to escape the racial unrest that the city saw in the 1960s). Another aspect of West Omaha's growth was the children of farmers in western Nebraska who moved to the city to find employment. In the past two decades, the South Omaha neighborhood has become home to a growing number of Latinos that have either migrated or immigrated.

Politically, the 2nd District has been considered a reliable Republican district for some time. It has voted for every Republican presidential candidate since Harry Truman upset Thomas Dewey in 1948, and since 1950 the congressional seat has only been won by two Democrats, John Cavanaugh (95–96th Congresses) and Peter Hoagland (101–103rd Congresses). In the 2000 presidential election, George W. Bush won the 2nd District handily, commanding 57 percent of the vote to Al Gore's 39 percent. In the 2004 race, Bush pushed his lead over John Kerry in the 2nd District to 61 to 38 percent.[7]

In spite of the Republican dominance of the 2nd District's congressional and presidential races, Democrats were gaining ground in 2008 due, in part, to the decision of Barack Obama to actively campaign to win the state's first-ever Democratic presidential caucuses in February and to compete for the single electoral vote of the 2nd District (Nebraska allocates electoral college votes on a district-by-district rather than a winner-take-all basis). In 2008, 40.3 percent of voters in the 2nd District were registered Republican and 38.7 percent were registered Democrats. The remaining 20 percent were registered nonpartisan or independent. In Douglas County, where 80 percent of the district's population lives, 40.3 percent were registered Democrats and 39.1 percent were registered Republicans, but in the portion of Sarpy County where the other 20 percent live, Republican registrants outnumbered Democrats 45.7 to 31.0 percent.[8]

The major north–south thoroughfare in the 2nd District, 72nd Street, is the dividing line between traditional Democratic neighborhoods and the Republican suburbs.[9] Like other areas of the country, that is changing. Democratic voter registration surged in Douglas County compared to 2004. Democrats added about 2,300 registered voters to their totals. The number of nonpartisan registrants grew even more (by almost 4,000), but the number of Republicans dropped by about 9,500.10 The 2008 election cycle was the first time that Democrats enjoyed a voter registration advantage in Douglas County since the 1994 midterm election.

The Incumbent: Republican Lee Terry

Lee Terry is a product of Nebraska, attending the University of Nebraska for his undergraduate studies and Creighton University, which is in Omaha, for his law degree. His interest in politics can be traced back to his father Lee Terry, Sr.'s unsuccessful attempt to win the 2nd District seat in 1976. After practicing law in Omaha for a few years, the younger Terry decided to run for City Council in 1991. He won and served there until his election to Congress in 1998. When Jon Christensen decided to run for governor in 1997 rather than reelection to Congress, Terry quickly announced his intent to seek the 2nd District seat. The Republican primary was competitive. Terry fended off challenges from political veteran Steve Kupka and businessman Brad Kuiper, and emerged with 40 percent of the vote compared to Kupka's 30 percent and Kuiper's 26 percent, in spite of being out-spent. In November he easily defeated his underfinanced Democratic opponent, Michael Scott, by 32 percentage points.[11] In 2000, 2002, and 2004, Terry won reelection easily, garnering roughly two-thirds of the vote. This was unusual for new members of Congress who typically face very difficult challenges early in their careers and then go on to win handily in later years. In 2006, however, Terry faced a tough challenge against political newcomer, Jim Esch. Without assistance from outside groups Esch captured 45 percent of the vote, which led to his decision to seek a rematch in 2008.

In general, Terry considers himself a conservative, but a pragmatist. On social issues such as abortion, stem-cell research, and same-sex marriage he sides with conservatives. On economic issues such as regulation and taxation, he also consistently sides with conservatives. As a member of the powerful Energy and Commerce Committee, Terry has developed expertise in the areas of telecommunications policy and alternative fuel sources. More specifically, heading into the 2008 election cycle he argued regularly for increasing federal funding for the development of alternative fuels such as ethanol and hydrogen fuel cells in order to decrease U.S. dependence on foreign oil. Of course, these issues are very important to both the 2nd District and to Nebraska. As mentioned above, Omaha is considered the telemarketing capital of the United States, and an increase in the demand for ethanol would certainly benefit farmers in Nebraska, where the largest crop is corn.

Terry has a pretty conservative voting record. His voting scores from the American Conservative Union (ACU) and Americans for Democratic Action (ADA) are listed in Table 11.1. On the issues that the ACU and ADA consider to be the important ideological bellwethers over the past decade, Terry took the conservative position on average more than 90 percent of the time. Table 11.1 also lists his party unity and presidential support scores. To date, Terry has voted with the Republicans at least 90 percent of the time. His support of President Bush's policy positions, however, is more complex. While the Republicans were in the majority in the House from 2001 to 2006, Terry's support of the president was never lower than 84 percent and as high as 97 percent. In 2007 and 2008, however, his support of President Bush's position dropped to 76 and 68 percent, respectively. This is not surprising. Not only was the president (and his policies) unpopular, but Terry faced his stiffest challenge in 2006. Like other incumbent

Table 11.1 Congressional Vote Scores for Lee Terry, 1999–2008

Year	American Conservative Union	Americans for Democratic Action	Presidential Support	Party Unity
2008	92	15	90	68
2007	88	10	93	76
2006	92	0	97	97
2005	92	0	94	85
2004	92	0	93	88
2003	76	5	96	89
2002	88	5	92	84
2001	96	0	95	91
2000	96	5	96	25
1999	96	10	92	21

Source: 1999–2006 scores from various editions of CQ's Politics in America; 2007–2008 American Conservative Union (ACU) and Americans for Democratic Action (ADA) scores from the organization Web sites; 2007–2008 party unity and presidential support scores from CQ Weekly Report.

Republicans, he needed to distance himself from the Bush administration. Esch was planning a rematch.

The Challenger: Democrat Jim Esch

Jim Esch was also a product of Omaha, attending Creighton University for both his undergraduate degree and law school. After graduating from law school in 2000, Esch worked for a local public relations firm and later for the Greater Omaha Chamber of Commerce and the Greater Omaha Economic Development Partnership, as well as serving on the board of directors of several charitable organizations in the city. In 2006, Esch chose to challenge Terry, the four-term incumbent from the 2nd District, even though he was only 31. He surprised everyone by finishing only 10 points behind Terry on election night (Terry's 2002 and 2004 opponents were better-funded, but lost to Terry in landslides).

Esch closed in on Terry in 2006 by running a very different kind of campaign than that of the previous Democratic challengers. First, Esch chose not to take money from political action committees (PACs) and made an issue of it during the campaign. Of course, the issue itself was more important to Esch than the little money he could raise from PACs, given that PACs donate significantly more money to incumbents than they do to challengers. In the 2nd District, for example, 47 percent of Terry's contributions in 2005 and 2006 were from PACs.[12] Second, what money he spent focused on building name recognition and brand identity. Rather than using traditional campaign consultants, Esch hired an advertising firm to develop a rather modern looking logo. Then, months before the Democratic primary, he plastered that logo on billboards all over the district, and even more importantly he purchased advertising on practically every bus stop bench in the city of Omaha. Third, given that his cash was more limited than Terry's (in the end Esch self-financed $145,706 of his campaign), Esch aired television ads only late in the campaign. When he did, his ads were very simple, biographical ads that featured Esch talking to the camera. While this may appear to be a liability to his campaign, it was in reality a blessing in disguise. Since Esch's campaign appeared to be poorly funded, and in some respects amateurish by modern campaign standards, Lee Terry's campaign never took Esch seriously. As a result, Terry virtually ignored Esch, never running ads that either attacked Esch or compared their records. Finally, Esch invested what money he had in hiring staff to work the grass roots, relying on a young and energetic group of staff and volunteers to walk the more Democratic neighborhoods east of 72nd Street and make phone calls.

As a conservative Democrat, Esch was also different ideologically from previous Democrats seeking to represent the 2nd District. While not all Catholics hold the traditionally conservative positions espoused by the Catholic Church on hot-button social issues, Esch does. This means that Esch was positioned to be an acceptable alternative to the conservative Catholic voters in the 2nd District that place a high priority on these issues. Given the percentage of the overall population of the 2nd District that is Catholic (23.7% in Omaha[13] and

27.7% in Douglas County),[14] this means that Esch could hope to neutralize Terry's advantage with many social conservatives who found previous Democratic challengers simply unpalatable. Across the country, other pro-life Democratic congressional challengers were making their positions on these issues known to voters too.[15]

The Campaign

Jim Esch came closer than anyone expected in November of 2006, losing by 16,971 votes. The question in 2008 was whether he could close that gap. Initially, veteran election observer Charlie Cook, publisher of the *Cook Political Report*, called the 2nd District "likely Republican" as late as June 2.[16] This means that the district was not considered competitive, but the possibility existed that it could become competitive. While the race did not tighten up overnight, there were a number of factors that together forced Lee Terry to make the most vigorous defense of his congressional career.

After the close contest in 2006, Terry called up his campaign manager from his very successful 2004 election, Dave Boomer, and asked him to return. Boomer, a native of Nebraska and veteran of numerous close campaigns, devised a new strategy for winning the 2nd District in 2008. He suggested that Terry try something he had not done before: bring in 10 young, energetic students to work in the field for the campaign over the course of the summer. According to Boomer, the campaign "focused like a laser beam on getting out to talk to people."[17] They targeted voters in precincts where Terry garnered between 45 to 55 percent of the vote in 2006, by walking neighborhoods to knock on doors, leaving handwritten thank you notes, and making phone calls. Some Republicans familiar with the 2nd District questioned Terry's campaign tactics, arguing that his ground game should focus on precincts with a higher proportion of GOP voters.[18] Boomer disagreed with that premise stating, "If you don't have your base locked up after 10 years, you're in trouble."[19]

The earliest polls of the race were taken over the summer. One internal poll commissioned by the Esch campaign generated some enthusiasm for the challenger when it was leaked to the public in August. The survey was originally reported as a phantom poll in the *Lincoln Journal Star* (a phantom poll is one that is referenced by a journalist without providing the details). In this case, the newspaper reported that Esch trailed Terry by only one percentage point.[20] The survey, which was conducted by Anzalone Liszt, actually found Terry leading Esch, 48 to 37 percent.[21] The error was corrected when the full results of the poll were reported later in the week in other news sources, but the damage was done. Democrats that wanted the 2nd District race to be competitive now saw it as within their reach, even though it was not as close as they thought. Democrats also saw the presidential race within the district as being within their grasp. At the time, Barack Obama only trailed John McCain by 4 percentage points.[22]

Over the summer, as Obama closed in on receiving the nomination at the Democratic National Convention, his campaign decided that the race in the

2nd District was sufficiently close, and that they had enough money, to compete for the single Electoral College vote in the 2nd District. On Wednesday, September 10, the Obama campaign opened up their first campaign office in Omaha, just west of 72nd Street.[23] Over 900 people attended the event, and many of them signed up to volunteer.[24] It was unfortunate for Lee Terry that the McCain–Palin campaign still had not opened an office at the time the Obama campaign opened a third office in early October. According to Hal Daub, the Chairman of the McCain–Palin campaign in Nebraska, "We don't have all the money the other side has."[25]

Obama opening an office in the 2nd District was a real benefit to the Democrats. Everyone expected that the Obama campaign would invest funds in promoting voter registration and voter turnout that would affect the fortune of Democrats down the ticket. To counter this, Lee Terry fired back that he was ready to fight by organizing "Obama–Terry" voters across the district. When asked who the Obama–Terry voters were, he responded that they were "people who want the right kind of change." Esch, however, countered that he wanted to meet the group too because he could not "imagine what they look like."[26]

Although it was difficult for either campaign to articulate an illustration of the Obama–Terry voter, Terry's campaign made a concerted effort to reach out to Democrats and independents they thought might fit the mold. First, Terry walked door-to-door with the students his campaign hired whenever he could, and he was keen on finding potential Obama–Terry voters. "We knew it was going to be difficult replacing a new Obama voter with a new Republican voter," Terry said. "So, we knocked on doors where there was an Obama sign in the yard, but if there was a sign for my opponent we just kept walking."[27] Second, they developed a direct mail piece using the photo of a typical voter, Melanie. The piece read,

> Obama–Terry Voter, anyone? I'll admit it: I'm voting for Obama *and* Lee Terry. Why? Because I want our officials to work hard, be honest, exhibit strong ethics and be accessible. That's Lee Terry. Ever talked with Lee? I have. You ask him questions, you get straight answers. I like that. Please join me in voting for Lee Terry.[28]

Therefore, the Terry campaign did not assume that a new voter registered by Obama's campaign would vote a straight Democratic ticket. According to campaign manager Dave Boomer, "if you're voting for Obama, you can still vote for Terry."[29] This meant that during the fall campaign Terry had to be careful not to criticize Senator Obama or align himself too closely with Senator McCain.

With the Olympics and then the party conventions dominating the news for the next six weeks, there was no movement in the polls. In the first week of October a survey conducted by Research 2000 showed essentially the same results as those in August.[30] Terry still held a double-digit lead over Esch, 49 to 39 percent, and McCain bested Obama 53 to 40 percent.

As Terry swam against the national tide, Esch and the Democrats raised and spent about $1.7 million to try to win the 2nd District seat from him. It turned out that Esch was a much more formidable fundraiser than he was in 2006. Overall, Esch raised $843,545 (see Table 11.2). This was more than double what he raised in the 2006 cycle, but less than what Nancy Thompson raised in her campaign against Terry in 2004. Esch knew he needed cash in order to defeat Terry in the rematch. So, reversing his decision from 2006, he decided to accept PAC contributions. Esch ended up raising 23 percent, or $195,269, from PACs. In order to level the playing field, the DCCC also stepped up to the plate in 2008 to help Esch, which it had not done in 2006. They spent $745,801 on independent expenditures, primarily on television advertising, split evenly in support of Esch and in opposition to Terry. The Nebraska Democratic State Central Committee spent an additional $111,850 on independent expenditures supporting Esch.[31]

On the other hand, Lee Terry was always an impressive fundraiser. As the data in Table 11.2 show, Terry typically raised more than double that of his Democratic challenger in each of his previous congressional campaigns. In the past three election cycles, Terry's campaign established fundraising goals of $1.1 million or more, and set $1.3 million as the goal for 2008. They actually exceeded that goal, raising $1,746,226. Of that total, 46 percent or $805,074, were contributions from PACs.[32] Once Barack Obama decided to campaign in the 2nd District and the congressional race tightened, Terry actually found it easier to raise money.[33]

While finances were never an issue for Terry before 2008, the two months before Election Day brought challenges his campaign had never faced before. First, on September 11, Chris Van Hollen, the Chairman of the DCCC, announced the addition of the 2nd District to the DCCC's Red to Blue program.[34] Within two weeks the DCCC spent over $400,000 in the district in support of Esch. In response to this action Terry's campaign manager, Dave Boomer, said, "They're gambling they can take him out with three weeks of slash-and-burn attack ads, and we're going to continue to talk about his 10 years of solid experience."[35]

Table 11.2 Campaign Finance Data for Nebraska's 2nd District, 1998–2008

Year	Disbursements		Receipts		Vote	
	Terry	*Challenger*	*Terry*	*Challenger*	*Terry*	*Challenger*
2008	$1,838,836	$826,986	$1,746,226	$843,545	51.9	48.1
2006	$998,578	$419,785	$1,116,825	$412,329	54.7	45.3
2004	$1,454,559	$869,399	$1,335,016	$880,047	61.1	36.2
2002	$974,788	$495,675	$1,090,500	$504,649	63.3	33.0
2000	$844,465	$345,347	$887,946	$358,029	65.8	31.1
1998	$868,153	$94,939	$875,074	$96,876	65.5	34.2

Source: http://www.opensecrets.org/races/summary.php?id=NE02&cycle=2008 [accessed on June 4, 2009].

Soon thereafter, however, the National Republican Congressional Committee (NRCC) announced their intent to spend almost $500,000 defending Terry.[36] Overall, the NRCC spent $518,966 on independent expenditures, almost all of which was spent attacking Jim Esch. The Republican Party of Nebraska spent an additional $56,710, again mostly in opposition to Esch.[37]

Second, even Lee Terry's well-funded campaign was susceptible to the failures in the financial industry. Less than two weeks before the election, the Terry campaign was forced to borrow $100,000 when it was unable to access money invested in the Reserve Fund, the oldest money market fund in the nation. After Lehman Brothers failed, the Reserve Fund froze the assets of its investors with money in one of the funds hit by losses.[38] Of course, given the timing of the loan, Democrats were quick to attack Terry for taking it.

Due to the nature of the rematch, the candidates were already well-known in the 2nd District. Esch won an important endorsement from the AFL-CIO, but as the challenger it was more of a priority for him to encourage voters to carefully reexamine Lee Terry's record in Congress, decide whether he was on the right side of the issues, and whether his performance was up to par. Terry won the endorsements of the U.S. Chamber of Commerce, the National Federation of Independent Business, and the National Right to Life Committee.[39] Each of these endorsements was a serious blow to Jim Esch who had run a pro-business, pro-life campaign. As the incumbent, however, it was up to Terry to remind voters of his accomplishments and to demonstrate that his challenger really was not an acceptable alternative. Even as the first television advertisements hit the airwaves in the late summer, the sparring started. Considering how competitive the race was, no attack could go unanswered. When the DCCC and the NRCC got involved it grew even worse.

A number of the advertisements produced by Esch's campaign focused on issues, but rather than clearly comparing their issue positions Esch went after Terry. Of course, this type of attack required Terry to respond. In an ad entitled, "Chaos," Esch attacked Terry on the privatization of Social Security. Given the economic meltdown on Wall Street that occurred after Labor Day, many retirees were both worried about their investments and skeptical of whether Social Security funds should be invested in the markets.[40] Terry quickly responded with an ad entitled, "The Facts," where he relied upon the *Congressional Record* to demonstrate that he did not support the plan to privatize part of Social Security, and then attacked Esch for supporting an increase in Social Security payroll taxes.[41] In a second attempt to go after Terry on the issues, Esch ran an ad attacking Terry for voting against extending health care coverage and cutting health care benefits for veterans.[42] Terry quickly responded with an ad that called Esch a liar and touted his endorsement by the Veterans of Foreign Wars.[43]

While Esch stung Terry in the air war over policy, he went after Terry's performance in Congress during the debates. In front of the Omaha Press Club on October 17, Esch questioned why Terry had not been tapped by the party for a leadership position, as well as why he took campaign contributions from PACs. Terry first responded that his interest was in policy and not power, and second that Esch was taking the same campaign contributions for which he was criticizing Terry. Of course, neither of the arguments made by Esch were unique to Terry or the 2nd District. In fact, the same criticisms are often made by challengers of almost all incumbents.[44]

In the last week of the campaign Esch also tried to tap into the anxiety of voters who felt the country was off on the wrong track with an ad entitled, "Wrong direction." In this ad, Esch reiterated his criticism of Terry for the issues that he brought up in his previous advertisements: investing Social Security benefits in the stock market, giving tax breaks to oil companies making record profits, and health care benefits for veterans. The ad even ends with an apparent endorsement of Esch by Terry recorded during a campaign appearance where Terry says, "My opponent is correct that we need new leadership in Congress" (Terry was actually referring to the Democratic control of the House).[45]

Even without movement in the polls, the DCCC purchased their first $200,000 of airtime at the end of September after adding Esch to their Red to Blue program. The move by the DCCC was expected, but the Terry campaign intimated no change in campaign strategy.[46] Since the stock market was in meltdown at the time, the DCCC also decided to hammer Terry on the economy and reinforce Esch's ads that criticized Terry for his support of the president's plan to privatize parts of Social Security. The DCCC released another ad in mid-October entitled, "Wrong on the issues. Wrong direction." The goal was to tap into the anxiety the public felt, that the country was off on the "wrong track" and voters could not "roll the dice" and reelect Terry.[47] A week later, the DCCC let loose another ad attacking Terry entitled, "Whose side is he on?" This ad again attacks Terry on the issue of privatizing Social Security and for accepting campaign contributions from individuals and PACs in the financial services industry.[48] The DCCC did not let up the attack. In a final ad entitled, "Big Government: He's Part of the Problem," they blamed Terry for most of the calamities that the federal government faced including the federal budget deficit, the bank bailout, and tax breaks to corporations (particularly oil and drug companies).[49] While the Democrats were running ads like this against Republican incumbents throughout the country, the 2nd District was different from many others. Even though President Bush's approval ratings were in the low-20s nationally, they were almost 40 percent in the 2nd District.[50]

Taking Esch's challenge more seriously in 2008, Terry chose to draw the sharpest contrasts with Esch on energy and tax policy.[51] Given the high cost of gasoline over the summer, the price of fuel was on everyone's mind. So, his first ad, "Energy," touted his stance on different aspects of energy policy.[52] Esch too was better funded than in 2006, so he wasted little time in answering Terry in an ad entitled, "Nothing." The ad attacked Terry for inaction by Congress (as gas prices rose and oil companies drew record profits) and for his connections with lobbyists on Capitol Hill (for taking campaign contributions from oil companies).[53] Of course, the latter criticism was not a surprise given that Terry sits on the powerful Committee on Energy and Commerce and has historically taken between 34 and 52 percent of his campaign contributions from PACs.[54]

Once the gloves were off, Terry decided to hit his opponent hard. At the end of September, Terry took aim at Esch with a contrast ad entitled, "Economy," that focused on the issue of taxes.[55] He continued this theme in a similar ad at the end of October that took on a darker tone, arguing that Esch would raise taxes if elected, while at the same time continuing to draw a subsidy of $102,707 from the government for a farm he owns near Denver.[56] By the end of October, Terry ran arguably his harshest ad of the campaign season entitled, "Checks," where he again contrasts Esch's position on taxes with his willingness to accept farm subsidies. In this ad, however, Esch is depicted very negatively as a "trust fund baby."[57] At one point in the ad Esch is portrayed standing leisurely on a hotel balcony while the narrator reads the following words as they scroll across the screen, "Worked only 30 days in last 3 years. No clue about middle class families."[58]

In order to hold onto socially conservative voters, Terry worked hard to demonstrate the differences between he and Esch on the issue of abortion. Esch opened the door for Terry to do so during an interview with *City Weekly* magazine where he referred to opponents of abortion as "a little more extremist." Terry later responded by saying, "I don't agree with that. I think it shows his true colors on that issue." This was reminiscent of an exchange between the candidates in the 2006 campaign after Esch revealed in a radio interview that he was supportive of in vitro fertilization, and subsequently for stem cell research on embryos that are left over after successful fertilization. This caused Nebraskans United for Life to withdraw their endorsement of Esch (they originally issued a joint endorsement of both candidates). In the final days of the campaign Terry used targeted direct mail to highlight differences between himself and Esch on the abortion issue.[59]

In the final week of the campaign Terry backed off strongly worded attacks, allowing others to speak for him by using testimonials and endorsements. In the first, a number of different individuals, including an African-American woman voting for Obama, Richard Carter (Jim Esch's opponent in the Democratic primary who endorsed Lee Terry in July),[60] and Republican Governor Dave Heineman, all spoke in favor of reelecting Terry. In a final ad, Terry touted his endorsement from the *Omaha World-Herald*.[61]

While Lee Terry refrained from attacking Jim Esch in order to avoid a backlash, the NRCC stepped up their attack on Esch. They chose to focus on Esch's lack of experience and criticized him for poor judgment. In their first ad entitled, "Bad Judgment," they attacked Esch for his position on the economy and Social Security and then slammed him for a drunken driving conviction seven years earlier. In the ad the narrator says, "Jim Esch's bad judgment. It's not only chronic, it's dangerous." [62] Terry stated publicly that the NRCC was wrong to mention the drunken driving conviction, but stopped short of asking the NRCC to withdraw the ad.[63] The NRCC used the drunken driving issue again along with Esch's views on tax policy in an ad released the week before the election that claimed, "Jim Esch doesn't care about us."[64] In many respects, advertisements like this were essential to Terry's victory. He needed to cast doubt on

Esch's previous business and political experience because Esch and the DCCC were attacking Terry for his lack of accomplishments in Washington.[65]

The final poll released to the public was taken in mid-October, about two weeks prior to the election, and showed the race tightening. The survey, again conducted by Anzalone Liszt, also revealed a number of very interesting findings when contrasted with the results of the earlier surveys. First, since the first week of October Esch closed the gap from 10 percentage points to one, 47 to 46 percent. Second, since July Terry's favorability ratings dipped about 6 percentage points to 54 percent, but Esch's favorability ratings shot up from 35 percent to 51 percent. For each candidate, however, there was a similar increase in their unfavorability ratings (+6 for Terry and +17 for Esch). Finally, Terry's approval ratings also dropped slightly, from 60 to 53 percent.[66]

While none of these were good news for Terry, what is surprising is that his numbers did not drop even further given the volume of attacks aimed at him by the Esch campaign and the DCCC, and his vote on the $700 billion financial bailout package known as the Troubled Asset Relief Program (TARP). Politically, Terry knew that continuing to oppose TARP would put him over the top and seal his victory by appeasing fiscal conservatives in the 2nd District. In behind the scenes meetings in Washington, however, both the Democratic and Republican leadership were very worried that it was time to engage the doomsday scenario to save the economy. Terry voted against the TARP legislation the first time on September 29 because he felt it lacked sufficient accountability, but he voted for the bill when it was presented to Congress again on October 3 because he believed the state of affairs was very grave. Surprisingly, neither Esch nor the DCCC seriously targeted this specific issue during the last three weeks of the campaign.

Given the presence of the Obama campaign in the district and the amount of money they were spending, it is not surprising that those who either voted early or requested absentee ballots tended to be both Democrats and new voters, or infrequent voters. More than 56,000 voters either voted early or requested an absentee ballot, 49 percent of which were Democrats and 35 percent were Republicans. Assuming that those voters voted along party lines, Obama and Esch should have started the day on November 4 winning by a margin of almost 8,000 votes.[67] Esch said of the race as it grew close near the end, "I think it's going to be a neck-and-neck race. To me, this is going to come down to turnout."[68]

The Results

In the end, Lee Terry successfully defended his seat, winning 51.9 to 48.1 percent. He won the 2nd District by 10,572 votes, or 6,399 less than his 2006 victory. Jim Esch did very well in many parts of the district, but not well enough in others (see Table 11.3). Overall, the race in Douglas County turned out to be extremely competitive. Each candidate received 50 percent of the vote, but Terry emerged with 779 more votes than Esch out of over 123,000 votes cast.

Table 11.3 Election Results for Nebraska's 2nd District, 2008

Percentage of 2nd District	Lee Terry	Jim Esch	Barack Obama	John McCain
2nd District overall (100%)	142,473 (51.9%)	131,901 (48.1%)	138,809 (49.9%)	135,439 (48.8%)
Douglas County only (81.4%)	112,055 (50.1%)	111,276 (49.8%)	116,810 (51.7%)	106,291 (47.1%)
Sarpy County only (18.6%)	30,418 (59.4%)	20,625 (40.3%)	21,999 (42.4%)	29,148 (56.2%)
City of Omaha only (47.5%)	64,641 (48.8%)	65,668 (50.6%)	68,967 (52.2%)	60,754 (46%)
East of 72nd Street (21.1%)	21,468 (36.4%)	36,296 (63.2%)	38,141 (65.1%)	19,199 (32.8%)
West of 72nd Street (26.4%)	43,173 (59.9%)	29,372 (39.5%)	30,826 (41.9%)	41,555 (56.5%)
Douglas County outside the City of Omaha (14.4)	25,334 (63.7%)	14,257 (35.9%)	15,565 (38.7%)	24,146 (60%)
Douglas County early vote (19.5%)	22,080 (41.2%)	31,351 (58.6%)	32,278 (59.4%)	21,391 (39.3%)

Source: Nebraska Secretary of State; http://www.sos.ne.gov/elec/pdf/2008%20General%20Canvass%20Book.pdf [accessed June 15, 2009], http://www.votedouglascounty.com/election-results.asp [accessed June 15, 2009], http://www.sarpy.com/election/election_results.htm [accessed June 15, 2009].

On the other hand, Terry ran well ahead of Esch in Sarpy County, winning 59.4 percent of the vote.

Within the more populous Douglas County, Lee Terry defended his seat by performing well where Republicans typically perform well and fending off challenges from Esch in traditional Democratic precincts. The two candidates ran fairly even within the city limits of Omaha, with Esch narrowly defeating Terry, 50.6 to 48.8 percent. As expected, Esch ran very well in East Omaha, emerging with a whopping 63.2 percent of the vote. This area includes the predominantly African-American North Omaha, the predominantly Hispanic South Omaha, the Downtown area, and Midtown area, which extends as far west as 72nd Street. This part of the district made up 21.1 percent of the vote on Election Day. The question was how far ahead Terry would run in the suburbs west of 72nd Street and in the portion of Douglas County that lies outside of Omaha (primarily west of the city limits), which are each predominantly White. Terry won 59.9 percent of the vote in West Omaha, which was 26.4 percent of the vote in the 2nd District. Terry also won 63.7 percent of the vote in the portion of Douglas County that lies outside of the city, which was 14.4 percent of vote in the 2nd District. Finally, Esch won the early vote within Douglas County pretty convincingly with 58.6 percent of the vote. The early vote in Douglas County represented 19.5 percent of the congressional vote within the county, but when the early vote was added to the election night returns it was not enough for Esch to carry the election.

For Esch, this was closer than he came in 2006, when Terry defeated him with 54.9 percent of the vote, or 16,971 votes.[69] Esch did so by closing the gap in both Douglas and Sarpy Counties. Esch's percentage of the vote in Douglas County grew from 47.2 to 49.8 percent (a total of 41,000 more votes this time) and in Sarpy County it grew from 37.2 to 40.3 percent (more than 9,000 additional votes). Even though turnout was up, due to the presence of Barack Obama's campaign in the district, Terry still won a majority of the vote in both counties.[70]

While Lee Terry narrowly won reelection, Senator Barack Obama won the presidential vote in the district and, therefore, the electoral vote representing the district. Obama ran ahead of Esch across the district and, like Esch, won the vote in the city of Omaha and took in almost two-thirds of the vote east of 72nd Street. In spite of his strong showing, Obama still ran 2 percentage points behind Terry in the district overall.

At first glance the data in Table 11.3 suggest there is a great degree of party-line voting in the 2nd District, and this is likely true. It also appears that a significant number of Barack Obama voters defected to either vote for Terry (Terry ran 7,034 votes ahead of John McCain) or failed to even mark a candidate for Congress on their ballot (there were 6,089 undervotes). In examining the underlying dynamics of how Terry managed to defend his seat against Esch, it is more important to examine the partisan landscape of the district along with the force of the tide introduced by the presidential election.

The following paragraphs will analyze precinct-level returns in order to explore the underlying dynamics that explain the vote. It is important, however, to recognize that inferences attributed to the behavior of individuals based on aggregate-level data can be dangerous. At times, such ecological inferences can be misleading, and so any conclusions about how individuals behaved should be viewed with appropriate caution.

Partisans do not always vote for their party's candidate, although they often do. This was true in the 2nd District, but more so for Republicans than for Democrats. The correlation between the percent of Republicans in a precinct and the vote margin between Lee Terry and Jim Esch in the precinct (measured as a percent of vote) produced a result of .96. Similarly, the correlation between the percent of Democrats in a precinct and the vote margin was -.96. In other words, highly Republican precincts were highly likely to vote for Terry and highly Democratic precincts were just as likely to vote for Esch. Within Douglas County the results are nearly identical to those for the entire district (.96 and -.96, respectively). In Sarpy County, however, the percent of Republicans registered to vote in the precinct was correlated with the Terry margin at .88, while the percent of Democrats registered to vote in the precinct was correlated with the Terry margin at -.82. Although the difference in the magnitude of these relationships is small, it suggests that Republican precincts in Sarpy County were a bit more loyal to Terry than Democrats were to Esch.

In comparison, the returns from the presidential election in the 2nd District produced very similar results. The correlation between the percentage of registered Democrats in a precinct and Senator Obama's margin over Senator McCain was .94. For Republicans the correlation was -.96. In other words, more partisans in a precinct were strongly associated with more votes for the in-party presidential candidate. This held true in both Douglas and Sarpy Counties. In Douglas County the percentage of Democrats within a precinct (.95) and the percentage of Republicans in a precinct (-.96) were both highly correlated with Obama's margin over McCain. In the Sarpy County precincts that are part of the 2nd District, the percentage of Democrats in a precinct correlated with Obama's margin over McCain (.80), but the percentage of Republicans in a precinct correlated slightly higher with Obama's margin over McCain (-.90). In other words, even though the magnitude of the difference is minimal, the data suggest that more Democratic precincts in Sarpy County were slightly less likely to vote for the Democratic presidential and congressional candidates than the more Republican precincts were to vote for the Republican candidates.

While Republicans in Nebraska enjoy a voter registration advantage over Democrats (48 to 34%), independent or "nonpartisan" voters also represent a sizable portion of the state (17%).[71] Generally speaking, 2nd District voters registered as either nonpartisan or in other parties favored Barack Obama and Jim Esch. Overall, the percentage of voters in a precinct registered as nonpartisan or with third parties was correlated with the presidential vote margin at .11 and the congressional vote margin at -.08, suggesting that these voters tended to favor Obama and Esch. Within Douglas County, the percentage of voters in a precinct registered as nonpartisan or with third parties was correlated with the presidential vote margin at .14 and the congressional vote margin at -.12, suggesting that these voters tended to favor Obama and Esch. These voters make up 20.5 percent of the overall voters registered in Douglas County.[72] The results in Sarpy County are more consistent with that of the district overall and more exaggerated. The percentage of nonpartisan and third party voters in a precinct was correlated with the presidential vote margin at .49 and with the congressional vote margin at -.41, suggesting that these voters were fairly likely to favor Obama and Esch.[73] In Sarpy County this group of voters makes up 23.3 percent of the registered voters overall.

Obviously, the answers to how Lee Terry successfully defended his seat lay outside the explanations that partisanship offer. Terry's defense of his seat was not successful because a significant number of Democrats in the 2nd District turned their backs on Esch. The district is relatively evenly split between the two major parties, and the data suggest that the major party voters were almost equally likely to vote their party loyalties. Nor was Terry's defense of his seat successful because third party voters preferred him. Here the data suggest that nonpartisan and third party voters overall tended to vote for the Democratic candidates.

Even though partisanship appears to do little to explain how Terry defeated Esch, other alternatives are still worth exploring. First, voter turnout is often important to determining the outcome of elections, and in 2008 it appears that it was critical to Lee Terry's defense of his seat in Congress. In the 2nd District overall, turnout was approximately 72 percent of registered voters. Across the 2nd District, voter turnout was correlated with Lee Terry's margin of victory over Jim Esch (.50). This means that the greater the percent of voters that turned out in a precinct, the better Lee Terry did. The corresponding correlation for Obama's margin over McCain and voter turnout is -.50, which means that Obama tended to do better in precincts where turnout was lower. At first glance these findings appear to contradict the conventional wisdom that as turnout increases so do the prospects of Democrats. While that is still true, one must keep in mind that precincts with a greater number of Republicans also tend to be higher in socioeconomic status, relative to Democratic precincts. Thus, given that the measures were taken at the precinct-level, these correlations should not be surprising. This does not mean that Obama was unsuccessful at mobilizing voters. In fact, it's actually easier to influence the outcome of an election by mobilizing voters when turnout is low.

The second alternative to understanding how Lee Terry defended his seat in Congress may be found in the number of drop-off voters, those voters that cast a vote for president but not for Congress. In the 2nd District overall, the drop-off in the congressional vote in each precinct (as a percent of the total vote) was positively correlated with Terry's vote margin over Esch (.24). In Douglas County the correlation was .18 and in Sarpy County the correlation was .43. In other words, the greater the percent of the vote in a precinct that dropped off after casting their presidential vote, the higher Lee Terry's margin of victory in the precinct. Apparently, many voters turned out to vote for president and left their vote for Congress (or even further down the ballot) blank.

Finally, evidence suggests that Terry's field operation may have been critical to winning the election in 2008. As previously mentioned, his campaign targeted 118 precincts where he received between 45 and 55 percent of the vote in 2006 (of 422 total).[74] In 2006, Terry won these precincts on average with 50.5 percent of the vote. Surprisingly, his share of the vote in these precincts actually increased to 51.3 percent on election night in 2008. Of those precincts in West Omaha he won on average 52.2 percent of the vote, but in East Omaha he garnered a respectable 47.2 percent of the vote on average. Even though it is difficult to assess the magnitude of this benefit given that Terry targeted all of the swing precincts (leaving no basis for comparison), the evidence still very clearly suggests that his effort at reaching voters individually contributed to his reelection margin over Esch.

Conclusions

After a very successful 2006 election, Democrats were hoping to build on their congressional majorities in 2008. With Barack Obama's decision to compete for one Electoral College vote in Nebraska's 2nd District, it appeared as if the Democrats could pick off a seat they had not won since 1992. While the DCCC and the NRCC entered the fray late in the game in order to level the playing field between the two candidates, Lee Terry still had to contend with the Obama factor. The last Democratic presidential candidate to have a field operation in the 2nd District during a general election was Lyndon Johnson in 1964. Terry faced this challenge by adopting an unconventional strategy on the ground and punching back hard over the air.

In the past Terry typically emerged on election night with very comfortable margins of victory. This was not the case in 2008. Evidence suggests that there are a number of explanations for why Terry won. First, voters in Sarpy County were a bit more loyal to the Republican candidate. Otherwise, voters in both parties were equally loyal across an evenly divided district. Second, there was a sizable drop-off between the presidential and congressional vote and as the number of drop-offs in a precinct increased, Terry's margin of victory over Esch increased. Third, Terry ran better in precincts where turnout was greater. Fourth, Terry's outreach effort in the swing districts from the 2006 election really paid off. While Esch improved over 2006 within both Douglas and Sarpy counties, Terry improved within the precincts where he received 45-55 percent of the vote in 2006. Finally, while it is impossible to calculate the exact number, in order for Terry to best Esch (by 10,572 votes) and McCain (by 7,034 votes) there were certainly a sizable number of Obama-Terry voters. [75]

Given that his margin of victory has declined every year since 2002, the Democrats will certainly target Lee Terry again in 2010 and possibly thereafter. In order for the Democrats to win, however, they are going to need a quality candidate that is well-funded and is willing to go on the offensive. If Lee Terry could emerge the winner in a year like 2008, then that challenger will find an incumbent who is pretty good at playing defense.

Notes

* The authors wish to express their appreciation to Jennifer Fulcher for her assistance.

1. http://www.cqpolitics.com/wmspage.cfm?docID=profile-000000000307 (accessed June 1, 2009).

2. L. Kroft, "Special Report: The World's Billionaires," *Forbes Magazine,* March 5, 2008.

3. http://www.cqpolitics.com/wmspage.cfm?docID=district-ne-02 (accessed June 1, 2009).

4. http://www.ers.usda.gov/Data/Unemployment/RDList2.asp?ST=NE (accessed June 1, 2009).

5. Based on 2007 U.S. Census data. Note that the percent of Hispanics should not be added to the percentages from other races as those who identify themselves as Hispanic may be of any race, http://quickfacts.census.gov/qfd/states/31/31055.html (accessed June 6, 2009).

6. C. David Kotok, "Big Plans in Store for North Omaha," *Omaha World-Herald,* October 3, 2007, http://www.omaha.com/index.php?u_page=2798&u_sid=10148991 (accessed June 2, 2009).

7. http://www.cqpolitics.com/wmspage.cfm?docID=profile-000000000307 (accessed June 1, 2009).

8. http://www.sos.ne.gov/elec/pdf/10-28-08_Final_VR_Report.pdf; http://www.sarpy.com/election/election_results.htm (accessed June 15, 2009).
9. Michael Kelly, "Election May Turn on What's In a Name," *Omaha World-Herald*, May 10, 2009, B1.
10. Tom Shaw, "Republican Voter Rolls Down in Nebraska," *Omaha World-Herald*, October 29, 2008, 1A.
11. Michael Barone. 2005. *Almanac of American Politics* (Washington, DC: National Journal), 1019–22.
12. http://www.opensecrets.org/races/summary.php?id=NE02&cycle=2006 (accessed June 6, 2009).
13. http://www.thearda.com/QuickLists/QuickList_70.asp (accessed June 6, 2009).
14. http://www.thearda.com/QuickLists/QuickList_3.asp (accessed June 6, 2009).
15. Raymond Hernandez, "Democrats Carrying Anti-Abortion Banner Put More Congressional Races in Play," *New York Times*, October 26, 2008, A26.
16. http://www.cookpolitical.com/charts/house/competitive.php (accessed June 15, 2009).
17. Cindy Gonzalez and Tom Shaw. "New Terry Strategy Paid Off With 2nd District Voters," *Omaha World-Herald*, November 6, 2008, A 7.
18. David M. Drucker, "Republicans' Tales of Woe Grow," *Roll Call*. Monday, October 14, 2008, http://www.rollcall.com/issues/54_47/news/29262-1.html (accessed August 12, 2009).
19. Personal interview with David Boomer, April 26, 2009.
20. http://www.journalstar.com/articles/2008/08/18/news/local/doc48a8bb2d86f88468480501.txt%22 (accessed June 15, 2009).
21. The survey was conducted July 27–August 2 with a sample size of 600 and a margin of error +/-4 percent, http://swingstateproject.com/showDiary.do;jsessionid=A5CB263FC514F7E74D96B2A3B60B016B?diaryId=2818; http://www.realclearpolitics.com/politics_nation/2008/08/ne_terry_9.html (accessed June 15, 2009).
22. The survey was conducted July 27–August 2 with a sample size of 600 and a margin of error +/-4 percent. http://swingstateproject.com/showDiary.do;jsessionid=A5CB263FC514F7E74D96B2A3B60B016B?diaryId=2818; http://www.realclearpolitics.com/politics_nation/2008/08/ne_terry_9.html (accessed June 15, 2009).
23. http://www.nebraskademocrats.org/blog/1665/wednesday-obama-campaign-office-opening-in-omaha (accessed June 15, 2009).
24. Paul Delehanty, "This is Omaha," *The Daily Kos*, http://www.dailykos.com/storyonly/2008/9/10/22712/8380/582/594365.
25. "Both Presidential Campaigns Hope to Sway Second District Voters," http://www.kptm.com/Global/story.asp?S=9156226&nav=menu606_2 (accessed June 15, 2009).
26. "Obama Targeting Omaha," http://www.action3news.com/Global/story.asp?S=8391714 (accessed June 15, 2009).
27. Personal interview with Rep. Lee Terry, February 19, 2009.
28. http://www.swingstateproject.com/showDiary.do?diaryId=3397 (accessed June 15, 2009).
29. Paul Goodsell, "In Nebraska Older, Rural Residents Favored McCain," *Omaha World-Herald*, November 6, 2008, A1.
30. The survey was conducted on October 6–8 with a sample size of 400 and a margin of error of +/-5 percent, http://www.dailykos.com/story/2008/10/10/83251/646/368/626098 (accessed June 15, 2009).
31. http://www.opensecrets.org/races/summary.php?id=ne02&cycle=2008 (accessed June 15, 2009).
32. Ibid.
33. Personal interview with Lee Terry, February 19, 2009.

34. http://www.politico.com/blogs/scorecard/0908/Van_Hollen_touts_minority_out-reach.html?showall (accessed June 15, 2009).
35. Robynn Tysver, "Terry's Campaign Plans to Combat TV Ads by Emphasizing 'Solid Experience'," *Omaha World-Herald*, October 10, 2008, B3.
36. Robynn Tysver, "GOP Calls, Raises Democrats in 2nd District," *Omaha World-Herald*, October 23, 2008, B3.
37. http://www.opensecrets.org/races/summary.php?id=ne02&cycle=2008 (accessed June 15, 2009).
38. Joseph Morton, "Terry Works Around Money Fund Snag: With a Campaign Account Frozen, the Campaign Resorts to a Bank Loan," October 31, 2008, B2.
39. Kate Ackley, "Competitive Terry Rematch Draws Both Parties' Interest," *Roll Call*, October 23, 2008.
40. http://www.youtube.com/watch?v=0WFM4l42hlk&feature=related (accessed June 15, 2009); Robynn Tysver, "Candidates Lack Control: Parties Take House Race to New Depths," *Omaha World-Herald*, October 27, 2008, A1.
41. http://www.youtube.com/watch?v=ft6qnpv357o (accessed June 15, 2009).
42. http://www.youtube.com/watch?v=9ySzSq8HFoY (accessed June 15, 2009).
43. http://www.youtube.com/watch?v=LwBuibTo-qY&NR=1 (accessed June 15, 2009).
44. Robynn Tysver, "Terry, Esch Spar on Role of leadership. The Incumbent Defends His Record Against Charges that He Should Be Held Accountable For Failures of Congress," *Omaha World-Herald*, October 17, 2008, 1B.
45. http://www.youtube.com/watch?v=vOhibM9x4qk&NR=1 (accessed June 15, 2009).
46. "DCCC Offers Boost to Esch Campaign: Party Money Could Offer Edge in Race against Lee Terry," October 8, 2008, http://www.ketv.com/news/17667587/detail.html (accessed June 15, 2009).
47. http://www.youtube.com/watch?v=vJuYqrtY5q0&feature=related (accessed June 15, 2009).
48. http://www.youtube.com/watch?v=3gqfqjwPQ2E&NR=1 (accessed June 15, 2009).
49. http://www.youtube.com/watch?v=YKlxLUpEs3k&feature=channel (accessed June 15, 2009).
50. http://swingstateproject.com/showDiary.do?diaryId=3503 (accessed June 15, 2009).
51. http://www.cqpolitics.com/wmspage.cfm?docID=district-ne-02 (accessed June 1, 2009).
52. http://www.youtube.com/watch?v=15UBF2GnIm0 (accessed June 15, 2009).
53. http://www.youtube.com/watch?v=52K622AsYyg&feature=related (accessed June 15, 2009).
54. http://www.opensecrets.org/races/election.php?state=NE (accessed June 15, 2009).
55. http://www.youtube.com/watch?v=b7GaPLvG4gs&feature=related (accessed June 15, 2009).
56. http://www.youtube.com/watch?v=uyI6IiWcP1k&feature=related (accessed June 15, 2009).
57. Anna Jo Bratton, "Terry: Bailout Vote Was Right, Even if He Loses," Associated Press State and Local Wire, October 16, 2008.
58. http://www.youtube.com/watch?v=q3zm1QVWjQE&NR=1 (accessed June 15, 2009).
59. "Abortion Comment Heats Up Esch-Terry Race: Terry Demands Apology after Magazine Interview," http://www.ketv.com/politics/17116248/detail.html (accessed June 15, 2009); Cindy Gonzalez, "Anti-Abortion Group Revokes Esch Endorsement," *Omaha World-Herald*. October 28, 2006, 8B.
60. "Democrat Carter joins Republican Terry's campaign," *Lincoln Journal-Star,* http://www.journalstar.com/articles/2008/07/17/news/nebraska/doc487f7b600566b642044645.txt?orss=1 (accessed June 15, 2009).

61. http://www.youtube.com/watch?v=Q08zH3C1aCo (accessed June 15, 2009).
62. http://www.youtube.com/watch?v=ZS4--wRFEZk&feature=related (accessed June 15, 2009).
63. Anna Jo Bratton, "GOP Ad Brings Up Nebraska Hopeful's Drunken Driving," The Associated Press State and Local Wire. Wednesday, October 22, 2008.
64. http://www.youtube.com/watch?v=weqej-ZuThw&feature=related (accessed June 15, 2009).
65. Cindy Gonzalez and Tom Shaw, "New Terry Strategy Paid Off with 2nd District Voters," *Omaha World-Herald*, November 6, 2008, A 7.
66. http://swingstateproject.com/showDiary.do?diaryId=3503 (accessed June 15, 2009).
67. Paul. Goodsell, "Democrats Count on Early Edge Initial Voters Give Party a Boost in Douglas County Tallies," *Omaha World-Herald*, Sunday, November 2, A1.
68. Kate Ackley, "Competitive Terry Rematch Draws Both Parties' Interest," *Roll Call*, October 23, 2008, http://www.rollcall.com/issues/54_50/politics/29490-1.html (accessed August 12, 2009).
69. http://www.cqpolitics.com/wmspage.cfm?docID=profile-000000000307 (accessed June 1, 2009).
70. Unfortunately, comparison of the 2006 and 2008 vote at the precinct level in different parts of Douglas County is impossible due to the reorganization of precincts in 2007.
71. Shaw, Tom. Democrats add 30,000 to state voting roster In Douglas County, they pass GOP number Registered voters. *Omaha World-Herald*. Friday, October 24, 2008, 1A.
72. http://www.sos.ne.gov/elec/pdf/10-28-08_Final_VR_Report.pdf (accessed June 15, 2009).
73. The correlations for the two counties are both larger than the correlation for the entire district. This may seem counterintuitive at first, but a scatter plot reveals that the Sarpy County data points are clustered in the upper right quadrant of the scatter plot. When the two counties are run separately, removing Sarpy County from Douglas increases the magnitude of the negative Douglas County correlation.
74. Personal interview with David Boomer, April 26, 2009.
75. http://www.sos.ne.gov/elec/pdf/2008%20General%20Canvass%20Book.pdf (accessed June 15, 2009).

12 Back to Blue? Shifting Tides in the Tar Heel State

Dole vs. Hagan in North Carolina's Senate Race*

Jody C Baumgartner, Peter L. Francia, Brad Lockerbie, and Jonathan S. Morris

At the start of the 2008 election cycle, not many observers or analysts would have predicted that Senator Elizabeth Dole would be forced to play defense in her reelection bid. Indeed, in their January 2008 analysis of U.S. Senate races, the nonpartisan *Cook Political Report* rated Dole's seat "solid Republican." The dynamics in North Carolina began to change, however, and Dole found herself on the long list of Republicans who had the potential to lose. By May the race had shifted to the "likely Republican" category; by the end of summer was classified as "lean Republican;" and in the middle of the fall campaign, it was judged as a "toss-up."

Several factors allowed this apparently "safe" Republican seat to be captured by Democrats in 2008. While we discuss a number of these factors that help to explain Hagan's victory, we suggest that a changing partisan electoral environment resulting from the immigration of non-Southerners to the state not only favored this outcome, but may auger well for the Democratic Party in the future. In other words, a state that had shifted red during the past several decades may be turning blue again. In the end, Dole was unable to defend her seat and was defeated by Kay Hagan.

In order to address why Dole was unsuccessful in her reelection effort, we first examine the setting for the race, particularly North Carolina's recent electoral history, the mood of the state, and its shifting demographic landscape. Next, we examine and contrast the candidates. Then, we look at the campaign in some detail, including a discussion of the popularity of Democratic presidential candidate Barack Obama in North Carolina, a competitive Democratic primary that drew out a large number of newly registered Democrats, the important issues of the campaign, strategies and tactics of the candidates, and a brief look at campaign finance. Finally, we briefly examine how the vote broke down for the two candidates.

The Setting in the Tar Heel State

Conventional wisdom suggests that North Carolina, like most Southern states in the past 40 years, is a state that consistently votes for Republican candidates, and both the popular press and scholarly research reflect this.[1] The tide in North

Carolina presidential politics began shifting toward the GOP as early as 1952, when Dwight Eisenhower captured a respectable 46 percent of the vote. In 1956, he increased his vote share in the state to 49.3 percent, and in 1960, Nixon garnered 47.9 percent of the vote.[2] Since 1968, Republicans have dominated in the state at the presidential level; the only Democratic presidential candidate to win in North Carolina was Georgia native Jimmy Carter in 1976. Based upon this recent history, the idea that North Carolina was "in play" for Barack Obama in 2008 attracted a good deal of media attention. Below the surface of presidential politics, however, the Tar Heel state is not reliably Republican. Unlike some other Southern states, North Carolina has a fairly competitive two-party system.[3]

Like much of the South, North Carolina was a solid Democratic state before about 1950. Then, starting at the presidential level, this began to change. As noted above, Republican candidates for president (with the exception of Barry Goldwater) were competitive in North Carolina in the 1950s and 1960s. Since 1976, Republican presidential candidates consistently garnered greater than 50 percent of the vote, and from 1984 through 2004, a greater percentage of the popular vote in North Carolina than their national average. Although there were a few election cycles in which their support declined, North Carolina Republicans have steadily increased their share of seats in the U.S. House of Representatives since 1960; their support peaked in 1994 and it has declined somewhat since then (see Figure 12.1).

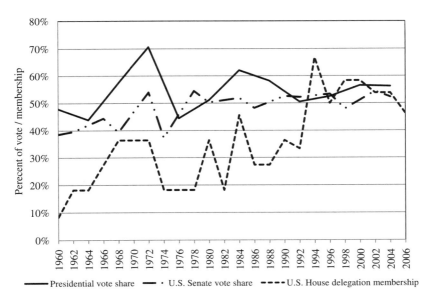

Figure 12.1 Republican strength in North Carolina federal elections 1960–2006. *Source:* Charles Prysby, "The Reshaping of the Political Party System in North Carolina," in The New Politics of North Carolina, ed., Christopher A. Cooper and H. Gibbs Knotts (Chapel Hill, NC: University of North Carolina (2008); David Leip, "Dave Leip's Atlas of U.S. Elections," http://uselectionatlas.org/.

Elections to the 120 member state House and the 50 member state Senate followed a similar pattern. In the state House, Republican strength waned somewhat throughout the past decade, and they lost their majority in 2006 (see Figure 12.2). In the state Senate, although Republicans have seen gains, Democrats have remained firmly in control. Republican success at the gubernatorial level has been limited as well. They won only three of the 12 elections for governor since 1960 (James Holshouser, Jr., in 1972, and James Martin in 1984 and 1988). At no point during this period, however, did the Republican vote share fall below 43 percent.[4] Figures 12.1 and 12.2 illustrate that North Carolina cannot be simply characterized as a "red" state, and that two-party competition is alive and well in the Tar Heel state.

Partisan trends in elections to the U.S. Senate in North Carolina are harder to identify. Elections for Elizabeth Dole's Senate seat, occupied by Jesse Helms from 1973 to 2003, have consistently been very competitive. For example, in spite of being fairly popular in North Carolina, Helms, never won more than 55 percent of the vote at any point in his career. The other Senate seat in North Carolina has been even more competitive and saw even narrower margins of victory as well as a good bit of partisan turnover. In fact, since 1974, the seat has changed parties in every election cycle.

Looking beyond electoral history, there were other factors that suggested Dole's defense of her seat may have been problematic. In particular, the mood of the nation as well as the state seemed to conspire against her. First, President Bush's approval ratings dropped steadily in North Carolina throughout his second term. As much as a year before the 2008 election, only 10 percent of North Carolinians strongly approved of President Bush while 40 percent

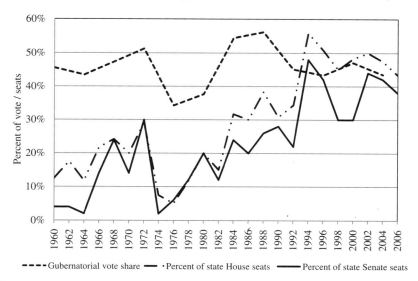

Figure 12.2 Republican strength in North Carolina state elections, 1960–2006. *Source:* Prysby, "The Reshaping of the Political Party System in North Carolina."

strongly disapproved.[5] Second, the economy was in freefall in the fall of 2008, which always bodes ill for the party in power. Worse, however, the economic crisis hit North Carolina particularly hard, and did so in two major ways. First, while the manufacturing base located in Eastern and Northern North Carolina had been bleeding jobs for decades, job loss was further accelerated by the 2008 crisis. Indeed, during the year preceding the election, unemployment in North Carolina rose from 4.7 percent to 7.7 percent. Second, the crisis within the financial industry hit North Carolina hard. Charlotte is the financial hub of the Southeast, home to two major banks, Wachovia and Bank of America. Fairly or otherwise, President Bush and the Republican Party absorbed the majority of the blame for these crises, which made the task of Republican incumbents seeking reelection even more difficult.

The GOP's efforts to defend their control of Dole's seat may have also been hampered by demographic trends within the state. In particular, North Carolina appears to be in the midst of a demographic realignment. The population of the state has consistently grown in the past 15 years, with net growth never falling below 100,000 persons annually, and exceeding the national average. Since 2003, however, the number of people coming into the state has increased every year; in both 2006 and 2007 nearly 200,000 new people moved to the Tar Heel state.

Of course, by itself, population growth does not signify a partisan shift. But recent survey data suggest a distinct trend among those migrating to North Carolina. Relying on data from 2005, one analyst found that native born North Carolinians tended to be more conservative than residents born outside the state.[6] He also concluded that this trend was more pronounced in North Carolina than in the rest of the South.

More recent data further demonstrate a strengthening of the progressive base in the state. An Elon University Poll taken in March of 2009 found that 23 percent of those who have lived in the state 10 years or less classify themselves as "liberal" or "very liberal." This is in clear contrast to those who have lived in the state 30 years or more: only 7 percent of this group identify themselves as liberal or very liberal. Furthermore, those moving into North Carolina who do not classify themselves as liberal are still more likely to register to vote as Democratic or unaffiliated rather than Republican. In fact, the percentage of unaffiliated voters in the state increased by 18 percent between 2000 and 2008.[7]

Migration to North Carolina appears to be most pronounced in major metropolitan areas of the state, which have traditionally leaned further to the left than the rest of the state. The net effect of this migration is that the size of the Democratic electorate has increased.

> The sizable migration of non-southerners into the state beginning in the 1980s has at least partially offset the growing conservatism of native North Carolinians. Less conservative newcomers have relocated to the metropolitan areas in the Piedmont section of the state, along with counties popular with retirees.[8]

More recent data indicate this trend may have accelerated in recent years. For example, Mecklenburg County, which contains the city of Charlotte, has grown by 25 percent since the turn of the century, and Wake County, which contains the Raleigh–Durham area, grew by 33 percent over the same time period.[9] The increasing population (and newcomers' greater likelihood of voting Democratic) was another factor in the long list already in place that would make it difficult for Elizabeth Dole to defend her seat in 2008.

The Candidates

A native of North Carolina, Elizabeth Dole spent much of her career in Washington holding executive branch positions under five presidents. Some of these were fairly high profile, including Deputy Assistant in the U.S. Office of Consumer Affairs under President Nixon (1969–73), membership on the Federal Trade Commission under Presidents Nixon and Ford (1973–79), Secretary of Transportation under President Reagan (1983–87), and Secretary of Labor under President George H.W. Bush (1989–90). Later, she left government to become president of the American Red Cross (1991–2000). In 1999, she began an unsuccessful bid for the Republican presidential nomination. In spite of a fairly strong showing in the Iowa straw poll in August of that year, she withdrew from the race in October, citing a lack of funding.

Upon Senator Jesse Helms's retirement in 2001, and at the urging of national and state party leaders, Dole reestablished residence in North Carolina in order to make a run for his seat. With the endorsement of Helms, Dole won the nomination with 80 percent of the vote and faced off in the fall against former President Bill Clinton's chief of staff, Erskine Bowles. Her campaign was fairly aggressive in a race that saw close to $30 million spent. While Dole had to contend with charges that she was not a true North Carolinian (i.e., a carpetbagger), her national reputation as influential within the national political scene and her national connections appeared to benefit her campaign, especially with regard to her ability to raise funds. Indeed, the race was by far the most expensive of the 2002 election cycle (the next closest was the Missouri senate race, which saw approximately $21 million raised and spent).[10] Furthermore, her marriage to 1996 GOP presidential nominee (and former Senate Minority Leader), Bob Dole, helped her name recognition against the lesser-known Bowles. Dole won the race with 54 percent of the vote (Bowles received 45%).

Dole established a solidly conservative voting record as a member of the U.S. Senate from the time she arrived. For example, she sided with the positions of the American Conservative Union (ACU) better than 90 percent of the time from 2004 to 2007; her voting record scores from the liberal Americans for Democratic Action (ADA) were similarly conservative during this time period, as her ratings were typically under 20. In addition, she was a reliable vote with her fellow Republicans in the Senate and for President Bush, with high party unity and presidential support scores through 2007 (see Table 12.1). In specific policy areas, Dole supported making President Bush's 2001 tax cuts permanent, the invasion

Table 12.1 Congressional Vote Scores for Elizabeth Dole, 2003–2008

Year	American Conservative Union	Americans for Democratic Action	Presidential Support	Party Unity
2008	54	40	58	72
2007	92	15	85	93
2006	96	5	90	94
2005	96	5	93	93
2004	92	25	92	94
2003	80	15	98	96

Source: 2003–2006 scores from various editions of CQ's *Politics in America*; 2007–2008 American Conservative Union (ACU) and Americans for Democratic Action (ADA) scores from the organization Web sites; 2007–2008 party unity and presidential support scores from CQ *Weekly Report*.

of Iraq in 2003, and a "do-it-all" approach to energy (including offshore drilling), while opposing same-sex marriage and abortion rights. Dole also helped secure federal money to fund several North Carolina projects that included programs to assist local law enforcement in identifying and processing illegal immigrants with criminal records, antigang initiatives, and road construction.[11]

In 2008, however, Elizabeth Dole's actions in the Senate changed dramatically, clearly showing she knew she was in danger of being defined as someone out of touch with her constituents and too close to President Bush and congressional Republicans. After five solid years of a strong conservative voting record, Dole only rated a 54 from the ACU and her rating from the ADA ballooned to 40. Moreover, Dole broke with her party on several key votes and had a party unity score 20 points lower than the year before. Her support for President Bush fell even further in the election year as she supported the president's position on the floor of the Senate less than 60 percent of the time. This was a stark change of direction compared to her previous voting patterns; Dole was clearly trying to temper her voting record so she could appear to be more moderate when she faced the voters in November.

Despite Dole's work as an incumbent Senator, she obviously faced some potential problems heading into her reelection campaign. Her support for President Bush was a benefit in the years immediately following her 2002 election, when Bush was exceedingly popular in North Carolina, but became a major drawback in 2008 when his approval ratings reached historical lows. In addition, Dole presided over the National Republican Senatorial Committee (NRSC) in 2006 when Republicans lost six Senate seats and control of the U.S. Senate. Not only did the Republicans' disappointing performance earn Dole criticism for the defeats,[12] but her high-profile role as a national leader in the Republican Party also contributed to a growing perception among North Carolina residents that she was out of touch with their concerns. As one voter explained to a reporter during the campaign, "Dole hasn't lived among us that much. She doesn't know what's going on in North Carolina."[13]

Kay Hagan ultimately took advantage of these electoral circumstances as the Democratic Party's nominee in the 2008 general election. In the year leading up to the election, however, Hagan was not viewed as a likely challenger to Dole. As potential Democratic challengers, including Governor Mike Easley and former Governor Jim Hunt decided not to run, Hagan emerged as the favorite. She secured the nomination for the seat in May of 2008 when she defeated her main opponent, Jim Neal, by a 32 percentage-point margin (60 to 18%) in the Democratic primary.

Hagan is also a native of the Tar Heel State, although her family moved to Lakeland, Florida when she was young. Like Dole, Hagan became active in politics at a young age. As a youth she worked on the campaigns of her uncle, former Florida Governor and U.S. Senator Lawton Chiles Jr., and interned at the Capitol as well. After marrying her husband Chip, she moved to Greensboro, North Carolina, where she practiced law and was later vice president for NationsBank (now Bank of America). Hagan remained active in community and state Democratic politics throughout this period, eventually serving as local chair for Democratic Governor Jim Hunt's 1992 and 1996 reelection bids.

In 1998, Governor Jim Hunt persuaded Hagan to run for the state Senate in the 32nd District, which includes most of the city of Greensboro. With the help of her uncle Lawton, who walked the district with her, she won the seat and was reelected to four more terms. During her time in Raleigh, she served as chair of the Appropriations Committee and the Pensions, Retirement and Aging Committee. While known as a "probusiness Democrat," she was far from conservative, supporting pay increases for teachers, a moratorium on executions, and opposing a constitutional amendment banning same-sex marriage.[14]

The Campaign

Despite early polls showing Dole in the lead, there was some indication of trouble to come. Although she enjoyed a large lead in early polling (she had a 13-point lead in an April 2008 Rasmussen poll), it was short lived.[15] During the whole month of May Dole's lead was down to the low single digits. Interestingly, during June and July, her lead crept back up to what might have been considered a comfortable margin (between 10 and 14 points). While she had a lead, however, Dole never garnered more than 55 percent in any of the polls; this could have been another sign of trouble. By late August, Hagan was leading in some polls; thereafter she led in every poll conducted except a handful. Clearly the dynamics of the race had changed through the campaign. One thing that might have given the Dole campaign some hope, even as it saw its early lead evaporate, was that Hagan never polled above 50 percent. With this maybe Dole could find a way to keep her seat.

As to how the race developed, following her win over Neal, Hagan wasted little time in attacking Dole, accusing her of spending too much time in Washington and not enough time in North Carolina. At one campaign stop, Hagan joked that Dole had been absent from North Carolina for so long that, "I don't think she'd qualify for in-state tuition."[16] Hagan positioned herself as a moderate Democrat on major issues such as taxes. For example, she supported tax cuts for the middle class, but criticized Dole for supporting "tax cuts for the wealthy."[17] She carefully developed a "responsible withdrawal" position on the Iraq War to avoid upsetting either promilitary or antiwar voters. With the price of gasoline topping $4 a gallon as the election approached, Hagan also connected her support for renewable "green" energy technologies with jobs, telling an audience: "Energy cost is the first thing that people mention to me every day.... We need to become the state that says 'Alternative energy sources (are) important to us.' We need to be helping people with manufacturing solar panels and windmill parts, creating those jobs in North Carolina. Once we do that, those jobs aren't going to be outsourced."[18]

Hagan was also the beneficiary of a far more significant factor: the unprecedented size and energy of Barack Obama's campaign organization in North Carolina. Obama won the North Carolina primary against Hillary Clinton in May of 2008 by building a sizable grassroots operation throughout the state. For example, Obama had field organizers in all 100 North Carolina counties, as well as more than 400 paid staff members in North Carolina compared to just 35 for the McCain organization.[19] Grassroots efforts by the Obama organization and other allied groups helped to expand voter registration of African Americans and young voters (18–29 years old) and they were effective in getting these voters to the polls, especially to participate in early voting.[20] As Figure 12.3 demonstrates, the association between Barack Obama's public approval and Kay Hagan's tightened significantly following the primary season. In the last month

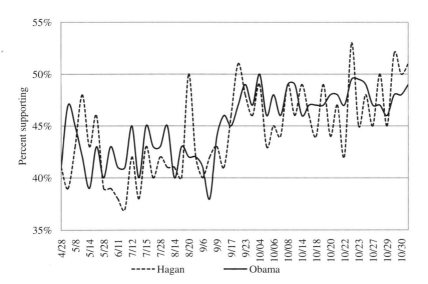

Figure 12.3 Approval of Barack Obama and Kay Hagan, April 2008–October 2008.
Source: RealClearPolitics.com

of the general election campaign, this association became even closer (r = .45 in October, p<.05 [N = 22]).

In addition to Obama's popularity and organization in North Carolina, Hagan also benefited from the competitiveness of the Democratic presidential primary in North Carolina six months earlier. While some Democrats were concerned that the close contest between Obama and Hillary Clinton would drive a wedge through the party and discourage some Clinton supporters from turning out in the general election, in hindsight it is clear that North Carolina Democrats were energized by the state's unexpectedly important role in the primary. Newly registered Democrats outnumbered newly registered Republicans by a margin of six to one.[21] This clearly served as an advantage to all Democrats on the ticket in the general election.

Candidate and Outside Group Messages

Much of the campaign in North Carolina was fought along many of the typical battle lines in American elections. Elizabeth Dole relied on a few issues traditionally owned by her party and tried to remind her constituents of what she had done for North Carolina while in office. In addition, outside groups came into the state to augment the messages of the candidates. There was even a bit of controversy in the Tar Heel state as the campaign came to a close.

Throughout the campaign, television advertisements became the dominant weapon for allies of the Dole and Hagan campaigns, with estimates indicating that some $34 million was spent for and against each candidate.[22] One of Dole's primary backers was the outside group, Freedom's Watch, which bought ads in October that were highly critical of Hagan. In one ad ("Runaway") the group accused Hagan of supporting increases in state taxes and fees. The announcer in the ad stated: "Kay Hagan voted for over 50 higher taxes and fees on income, birth, medical care, cars, food, even death."[23]

Allies of Hagan were active as well. In August, MoveOn.org spent nearly $500,000 on commercials that attacked Dole for "being in the pocket of Big Oil."[24] A month later in September, the League of Conservation Voters (LCV), added Dole to its "Dirty Dozen" list for her poor legislative record on environmental issues. Labor groups, such as Citizens for Strength and Security (CSS), also targeted Dole. The LCV and CSS combined spent more than $1 million on ads against the incumbent.[25] Organized labor's active involvement in the election led to charges from the Dole camp that Hagan was "in the tank for big labor" and that Hagan's efforts to "sneak into office as a Trojan horse for her big labor backers" were a "slap in the face to voters."[26] The Employee Free Choice Act (EFCA), which would make it easier for workers to unionize, became a focal point for much of Dole's opposition to organized labor. Hagan claimed to be looking "favorably" at the bill.[27]

Still, the most memorable and controversial advertisements did not come from the interest group community, but rather from the candidates and the party committees. Initially, though, the ads were relatively benign. In June, Dole put out a series of ads touting her legislative work and constituent service for the people of North Carolina. The ads discussed Dole's "clout" and effectiveness in handling the tobacco buyouts and in mitigating the effects of the 2005 Base Realignment and Closure Act by keeping all military bases in the state from closing.[28] Another set of ads extolled Dole's role in assisting local law enforcement with illegal immigration.[29] These early ads attempted to portray Dole as an effective senator as well as distance her from charges of being a Washington insider.

Later that summer, the Democratic Senatorial Campaign Committee (DSCC) countered Dole's message with one of the more memorable commercials of the election. The ad relied on a double entendre, seeming at first to be about Dole's age (she was 72 at the time of the election), but was in actuality about disappointment in her lack of effectiveness as a senator and her close association with President Bush. The ad began with two elderly men sitting in rocking chairs on the front porch of a country store where they engaged in the following exchange:

> [Senior 1]: "I'm telling you, Liddy Dole is 93."
>
> [Senior 2]: "Ninety-three?"
>
> [Senior 1]: "Yup, she ranks 93rd in effectiveness."
>
> [Senior 2]: "After 40 years in Washington?"
>
> [Senior 1]: "After 40 years in Washington, Dole is 93rd in effectiveness, right near the bottom."
>
> [Senior 2]: "I've read she's 92."
>
> [Senior 1]: "Didn't I just tell you she's 93?"
>
> [Senior 2]: "No, 92 percent of the time she votes with Bush."
>
> [Senior 1]: "What's happened to the Liddy Dole I knew?"
>
> As both men rock in their chairs, "Senior 2" ends the ad with the line: "She's just not a go-getter like you and me."

The ad drew attention in the *Washington Post* when polls began to show Hagan leading Dole after the commercials had blanketed the state.[30] The DSCC continued with its "rocking chair" theme, and in another ad, the two seniors criticized Dole for outsourcing jobs to China. The commercial ends with same tag line, "What's happened to the Liddy Dole I knew?" The DSCC also followed a line of attack raised earlier by Moveon.org that criticized Dole for her associations with oil companies. The ad told viewers, "She [Dole] voted for billions in tax breaks for big oil, against funding for alternative energy like wind and solar...[and] even tried to eliminate mileage standards. On gas prices, she's part of the problem."[31]

The Dole campaign returned fire with a series of its own ads attacking Hagan. In one notable commercial, a yelping dog exclaims, "Fibber Kay Hagan."

The "fib," according to the ad, involved Hagan falsely minimizing her husband's financial interests in oil stocks.[32] These ads were supplemented with additional ones from the National Republican Senatorial Committee (NRSC). A popular line of attack against Hagan was on the issue of taxes. In one ad, a narrator told viewers: "Taking a closer look at Kay Hagan? She's been in the state legislature for a decade. Hagan helped double the state debt, gave us the highest tax burden in the Southeast, higher income taxes, sales taxes, too. Now Kay Hagan wants to go to Washington?"[33]

Another NRSC ad focused on national politics and implored viewers to consider the prospects of liberal politicians controlling all of Washington. As Democrats looked to be doing well in several other Senate races, the prospects that they could reach the magic 60-vote (or "filibuster-proof") threshold became greater. The NRSC hoped to use this possibility to help Dole retain her seat. The announcer in the commercial asks: "Who's the Senate race really about? Hagan or Dole? Neither one. It's about liberals in Washington. They want complete control of government...the left wants 60 votes in the Senate"[34]

Interestingly, critics of the ad pointed out that the NRSC—by suggesting that the Democrats would have complete control of government with 60 votes in the Senate—was tacitly conceding the Electoral College votes of North Carolina, if not the presidential election itself to Barack Obama. John McCain, the Republican presidential nominee, followed with his own ads, pleading for support from North Carolina voters to block the possibility of 60 Democratic votes in the Senate—a similar example of what some saw as a concession of a Dole defeat. DSCC spokesman, Matthew Miller, compared the situation to a "circular firing squad."[35]

Still, without question, the most controversial advertisement came in the election's final week when the Dole campaign ran its now infamous "Godless" spot. In the ad, the Dole campaign questioned Hagan's ties to the group, Godless Americans Political Action Committee. Most controversially, the ad ends with what critics saw as an effort by the Dole campaign to paint Hagan as an atheist. The commercial closes with an image of Hagan and a voice that sounded similar to Hagan's, but was not, that says, "There is no God." The full text went as follows:

[Announcer]: "A leader of the Godless Americans PAC recently held a secret fundraiser in Kay Hagan's honor."

The ad transitions to a clip of Godless Americans' PAC Executive Director, Ellen Johnson.

[Johnson]: "There is no God to rely on."

A second clip of Johnson appears.

[Johnson]: "There was no Jesus."

The ad moves to a clip of Bill O'Reilly of Fox News who questions Godless Americans' PAC director, David Silverman.

[O'Reilly]: "But taking 'under God' out of the Pledge of Allegiance—you're down with that?"

[Silverman]: "We're down with that."

[O'Reilly]: "'In God We Trust'—are you going to whip that off the money?"

[Silverman]: "Yeah, we would."

[Announcer]: "Godless Americans and Kay Hagan. She hid from cameras. Took godless money. What did Hagan promise in return?"

The ad then shows an image of Hagan as an unidentified female voice exclaims, "There is no God!"

The media, both local and national, were quick to report on the truthfulness of the ad and Hagan's incidental association with the group. The association appears to have been tied to a fundraiser hosted by Wendy Kaminer and Woody Kaplan, members of the Secular Coalition of America and organized by Democratic Senator John Kerry and a group of some 35 people who were campaigning to support a Democratic majority in the U.S. Senate. When questioned about the event by the press, Kaplan claimed that the fundraiser for Hagan had nothing to do with Godless Americans PAC or its cause.[36] According to Kaplan, "This event happened to be at my house. I don't know if any of those people are religious or not, whether they're Muslims, Christians, Jews, or whoever. I have no idea, I never asked them when I went to their houses, and I bet you no candidate did either."[37]

Hagan, a Sunday school teacher and elder at First Presbyterian Church in Greensboro, responded that "Elizabeth Dole is attacking my strong Christian faith" and that Dole should be "ashamed."[38] The Hagan campaign filed a defamation lawsuit, alleging "personal slander."[39] The Dole campaign, however, defended the ad. Dan McLagan, a Dole spokesperson, replied to the Hagan campaign's countercharges that, "The facts remain: Kay Hagan attended a fundraiser in her honor hosted by the founder of the Godless Americans. Kay Hagan accepted their money."[40]

The controversy that ensued may have ultimately backfired on Dole. In press accounts, several voters expressed their displeasure with the advertisement. At a Greensboro shopping center, one voter was quoted as telling Hagan: "Dole did you a favor. I was a Dole fan before this. I just think this a below-the-belt, dirty, nasty way to try to campaign."[41] Another voter from Charlotte called the commercial "reprehensible" and added that "it's the lowest common denominator; it's hate speech."[42] The Hagan campaign further claimed to have received a flood of telephone calls from undecided voters who voiced their support for Hagan because of the advertisement.[43]

The godless ad remained a controversial subject right through the end of the campaign. In and of itself it was not responsible for Dole's eventual defeat. It did, however, fit into a larger theme that Hagan was able to craft—that Elizabeth Dole was out of touch with North Carolinians and outside of the ideological mainstream of America. The backlash against the godless advertisement illustrated the popular perception that Dole was attempting to use political maneuvering in order to cover up for her shortcomings as a Senator. Of course, Hagan was equally responsible for the negative tone of the campaign over the airwaves, but was quite effective in keeping Dole on the defensive throughout the campaign.

A Costly Campaign

In terms of money, the race was the third most expensive in the country with a total of $28 million spent ($43 million was spent in Minnesota and $32 million in Kentucky). The distribution of funds, however, underscores the idea that Dole was on the defensive. She spent more than twice the amount that Hagan spent to fund her campaign ($19.5 million versus $8.5 million). Dole raised her funds primarily from individual donations ($13.4 million, or 69%); political action committees (PACs) contributed another $2.6 million (14%), approximately $2 million of which came from various business groups. Dole herself contributed $2.5 million (13% of her total) in the form of self-financed loans.[44] In addition, NRSC spent more on Dole's behalf ($2.8 million) than it did for any other candidate.[45]

A full 86 percent of Hagan's funding came from individual donors, while PAC donations comprised 10 percent of her total receipts. Hagan's PAC donations came primarily from labor groups (38%) and ideological/single issue PACs (49%), but she also received significant contributions from EMILY's List ($269,658), MoveOn.org ($25,504), and lawyers ($379,000).[46] By late October, the DSCC had spent more than twice the amount of money ($6.6 million) than its Republican counterpart on the race, and some estimates suggest that in total, the DSCC may have spent as much as $8.1 million on the television ad war to support Hagan.[47]

In the end Dole's efforts were not enough to stave off defeat. Hagan's victory was a relatively decisive one—53 percent to 44 percent. Exit polls suggest that her support came from women, young voters, African Americans, those with minimal and high amounts of education, as well as individuals who were on the lower end of the socioeconomic scale. Dole had a clear advantage with White evangelical/born-again voters, and was slightly more likely to carry Obama voters (93%) than she was to carry McCain voters (86%).[48]

As Table 12.2 shows, rural voters represented the most sizable chunk of the electorate followed by urban voters and suburban voters. While Dole had a slight edge with suburban and rural voters, Hagan won more than two-thirds of urban voters. Not surprisingly, Hagan carried the eastern part of the state, including the Raleigh–Durham metropolitan area, with almost two-thirds of the vote. The city of Charlotte split 50 to 47 percent in favor of Hagan, and Dole won a majority of the Greensboro metropolitan area and the western part of the state. In the end, the vote in the east simply overwhelmed the west, and the city won out over the country.

Table 12.2 Selected Exit Poll Results from the 2008 North Carolina Senate Race

	Percentage of the Electorate	Hagan vote percent of category	Dole vote percent of category
Location			
Urban	30	68	30
Suburban	28	45	54
Rural	43	44	51
Region			
Raleigh-Durham area	20	63	36
East	17	57	38
Greensboro area	29	44	51
Charlotte area	22	50	47
West	11	43	55
Vote for President			
Obama	49	93	3
McCain	51	11	86

Note: Hagan and Dole row totals may not add up to 100% as the result of non-responses.
Source: http://www.cnn.com/ELECTION/2008/results/polls/#val=NCS01p2.

In Dole's concession speech, she acknowledged the ugly tone that both campaigns had taken. Even in defeat, however, Dole defended her campaign and service one last time, "I will never regret fighting as hard as I could for the privilege of continuing to serve you."[49]

Conclusion

Of course hindsight is 20-20, but looking back it should have been much less of a surprise that Dole was unsuccessful in the defense of her seat against the challenger Hagan in 2008. This is in spite of the fact that reelection rates for incumbent senators have well exceeded 80 percent in the past few decades.[50] North Carolina has a vibrant two-party system which should have suggested that no Republican candidate could easily count on being returned to office. This was particularly the case in 2008, when national tides clearly favored Democrats. Beyond this, the Democratic Party machine and a superbly organized and energized Obama campaign created a favorable environment for, and lent support to, Hagan's effort in the state.

That said, it might be the case that the most decisive factor in Hagan's victory was a shifting partisan environment in North Carolina resulting from the influx of more progressively oriented individuals to the state in the past decade, particularly into the more populous areas of the state. For example, in the 2008 Senate race, Hagan far outperformed Dole in these counties. In Mecklenburg County where the city of Charlotte is located, Hagan won 62 to 35 percent, and Hagan won Wake County, where the city of Raleigh is situated, 56 to 41 percent.

This trend shows little sign of waning. If the ideological orientation of North Carolinians continues to move to the left, the national voting trends of the state will begin to reflect the past tendency to vote more Democratic in state and local elections. Of course, this will be a much different Democratic constituency than that of yesteryear—leaning more to the left than the right. Certainly, recent population growth benefited Hagan and Barack Obama in 2008, and there is little reason to expect that it will do anything except hurt Republican senatorial candidates in the future. Indeed, polling from early 2009 indicates that first-term incumbent Republican Senator Richard Burr will likely face a tough uphill battle in defense of his seat in the 2010 midterm election.[51] If the electorate does indeed continue to move leftward, North Carolina's national image as a "red state" will fade to blue.

Notes

* We would like to thank Hunter Bacot and the Elon University Polling Center for their assistance with providing data.
1. For popular press accounts see: Christina Bellantoni, "The Color Purple, One of Change," *The Washington Times*, October 26, 2008, A1; Larry Eichel, "Both Sides Targeting Red States," *The Philadelphia Inquirer*, October 26, 2008, A1; David Jackson, "'Die-hards' Want to Set Eyes On McCain," *USA Today*, October 20, 2008, A9; Kathy Kiely and David Jackson, "McCain Wages Fight 'Behind His Own Front Lines'," *USA Today*, October 29, 2008, A5; Anne E. Kornblut and Dan Balz, "U.S. Fiscal Crisis Seems to Have Altered Political Map," *Washington Post*, October 5, 2008, A10; Peter Nicholas and Bob Drogin, "Campaign '08: Race For the White House," *Los Angeles Times*, October 22, 2008, A16; and Lisa Wangsness, "Even In Deep-Red States, GOP Feels the Heat," *The Boston Globe*, October 24, 2008, A1. For scholarly accounts see Susan A. MacManus, "Kerry in the Red States: Fighting an Uphill Battle from the Start," in *Divided States of America*, ed., Larry J. Sabato (New York: Pearson Longman, 2006), 131–164; Daron R. Shaw, *The Race to 270: The Electoral College and the Campaign Strategies of 2000 and 2004* (Chicago: University of Chicago, 2006); Stephen J. Wayne, *The Road to the White House: The Politics of Presidential Elections*, 8th ed. (Boston MA: Thompson, 2008).
2. David Leip, "Dave Leip's Atlas of U.S. Elections," http://uselectionatlas.org/.
3. Charles Prysby, "The Reshaping of the Political Party System in North Carolina," in *The New Politics of North Carolina*, ed., Christopher A. Cooper and H. Gibbs Knotts (Chapel Hill: University of North Carolina (2008), 61–84.
4. Ibid.
5. Elon University Poll, "Elon Poll Finds a Lack of Confidence in Bush, Congress," Survey report released November 16, 2007.
6. Timothy Vercellotti, "How Southern is the Old North State? Public Opinion in North Carolina," in *The New Politics of North Carolina*, ed. Christopher A. Cooper and H. Gibbs Knotts (Chapel Hill: University of North Carolina, 2008), 38–60.
7. Charles Prysby, "The 2008 Elections in North Carolina: Change or Continuity?" (paper delivered at the annual meeting of the North Carolina Political Science Association, Greensboro, NC, February 27, 2009).
8. Vercellotti, "How Southern is the Old North State?" 42.
9. Prysby, "The 2008 Elections in North Carolina."

10. See http://www.opensecrets.org/bigpicture/topraces.php?cycle=2002.
11. Andrew Barksdale, "Who Knew the Senate Race Would Be So Close?" *The Fayette Observer,* September 14, 2008, http://www.ncbusinessvotes.com/northcarolina?action=viewNewsArticle&documentId=2c9e4f691c5f72ba011c60a606dd021e&issueId= (accessed August 12, 2009); Barbara Barrett, "Dole, Hagan Pledge to Disclose Their Earmark Requests," *The News & Observer,* October 30, 2008, http://www.newsobserver.com/politics/story/1274483.html (accessed August 12, 2009).
12. Barbara Barrett, "Fundraiser Dole Not Likely to be Blamed for GOP Losses," Scripps News, November 21, 2006, http://www.scrippsnews.net/node/16256.
13. Associated Press, "In a Shift, Dole Faces Uphill Battle in Re-Election," *Newsday,* October 18, 2008, http://www.newsday.com/news/politics/ny-usdole185888827oct18,0,5725809.
14. Jim Morril, "Kay Hagan's Giving Elizabeth Dole a Fight She Never Expected," *Charlotte Observer,* October 5, 2008, http://www.mcclatchydc.com/100/story/53485.html; Martin Kady, "Hagan Wins North Carolina Senate Seat," Yahoo! News, http://news.yahoo.com/s/politico/20081105/pl_politico/15273.
15. Polling data in this paragraph are taken from RealClearPolitics, http://www.realclearpolitics.com/epolls/2008/senate/nc/north_carolina_senate-910.html#polls (accessed June 28, 2009).
16. Keren Rivas, "Hagan Talks Jobs in Campaign Stop: Democrat Swings Through County in Bid to Unseat Dole," *Times-News,* October 24, 2008.
17. Ibid.
18. Mark Binker, "Dole, Hagan Debate Energy," *News & Record,* August 10, 2008, http://www.news-record.com/content/2008/08/09/article/dole_hagan_debate_energy (accessed August 12, 2009).
19. Peter L. Francia, Steven H. Greene, and Eric S. Heberlig, "The 2008 Election in North Carolina: The Return of the National Democratic Party" (paper presented at the Annual Conference of the North Carolina Political Science Association, University of North Carolina at Greensboro, February 27, 2009).
20. Ibid.
21. Alec MacGillis and Alice Crites, "Registration Gains Favor Democrats," *Washington Post,* October 6, 2009, A1.
22. Kaiser, "In Senate Battlegrounds, Fusillades of TV Ads."
23. See http://www.youtube.com/watch?v=N1hmrYb46O8.
24. Barksdale, "Who Knew the Senate Race Would Be So Close?"
25. Jim Morrill, "N.C. Campaigns Rake in More Than $20 Million from Outsiders," *The Charlotte Observer,* October 24, 2008.
26. Matthew Murray, "North Carolina: New DSCC Ad Doles Out Attack on Energy," *Roll Call,* September 9, 2008.
27. Binker, "Dole, Hagan Debate Energy."
28. Murray, "North Carolina."
29. Gordon Anderson, "Lee County Sheriff Appears in Campaign Ad for Sen. Dole," *Sanford Herald,* June 4, 2008.
30. Kaiser, "In Senate Battlegrounds, Fusillades of TV Ads."
31. Murray, "North Carolina."
32. Barksdale, "Who Knew the Senate Race Would Be So Close?"
33. Murray, "North Carolina."
34. Ken Dilanian, "GOP Takes New Approach in Ads for Senate Contests," *USA Today,* October 31, 2008, 4A.
35. Ibid.
36. Lisa Zagaroli, "Dole's 'Godless' Ad Riles Hagan," *The News & Observer,* October 30, 2008, http://www.newsobserver.com/641/story/1274507.html (accessed August 12, 2009).

37. Ibid.
38. Ibid.
39. Binker, "Dole, Hagan Debate Energy."
40. Ibid.
41. Lisa Zagaroli and Rob Christensen, "Dole, Hagan Finishing Pitch to Voters, *The News and Observer*, November 2, 2008, http://www.newsobserver.com/politics/story/1278603.html (accessed August 12, 2009).
42. Zagaroli, "Dole's 'Godless' Ad Riles Hagan."
43. Michael N. Graff, "Fiery Senate Battle Plays Out in Hard-Hitting TV Ads," *The Fayette Observer*, November 2, 2008, http://zope.fayobserver.com/article?id=309263 (accessed August 12, 2009).
44. Center for Responsive Politics, at http://www.crp.org.
45. David B. Magleby (ed.), *The Change Election: Money, Mobilization, and Persuasion in the 2008 Federal Elections*. Provo, UT: Center for the Study of Elections and Democracy, Brigham Young University.
46. Center for Responsive Politics, at http://www.crp.org.
47. Morrill, "N.C. Campaigns Rake in More Than $20 Million from Outsiders."
48. http://www.cnn.com/ELECTION/2008/results/polls/#val=NCS01p2.
49. Ryan Teague Beckwith, "More from Dole's Concession Speech," *News & Observer*, November 4, 2008, http://<projects.newsobserver.com/under_the_dome/more_from_doles_concession_speech.
50. Gary C. Jacobson, *The Politics of Congressional Elections*, 6th ed. (New York: Pearson Longman, 2004).
51. Public Policy Polling, "Burr Continues Weak Poll Standing." Survey report issued March 19, 2009, http://www.publicpolicypolling.com/surveys.asp?@spdT=ECF791E062CD404AAB75.

13 One Election Is Not Enough

Chambliss vs. Martin in the Peach State's Senate Race

Charles S. Bullock, III

The 2008 election cycle was filled with surprises. A year before the November election, few anticipated that the 44th President of the United States would be the son of a Kenyan and a Kansan, or that the Republican vice-presidential nominee would be Alaska's female governor. Record numbers of voters opted to cast ballots prior to Election Day, which helped produce a record number of votes for president. While perhaps not in the league with some of these other unexpected results, the relative competitiveness of the Georgia Senate election was also unanticipated until the closing weeks of the campaign. This chapter will detail the reasons for the narrowing of the gap which forced the incumbent, Republican Saxby Chambliss, into a runoff against his little-known Democratic challenger Jim Martin.

The New Georgia

Until the 1990s, Georgia showed little inclination to vote Republican except in presidential elections. After becoming the last Southern state to vote for a Republican for president in 1964, Georgia voted Democratic only three times and twice it was for its former governor Jimmy Carter. Indeed, over the last generation, only in 1992 did presidential candidates contest the state. That year the outcome in Georgia was closer than anywhere else in the nation as Bill Clinton defeated George Bush by about 13,000 votes thanks to Ross Perot who siphoned off thousands of what would have been Republican votes.

In state-level contests prior to the 1990s, Georgia Republicans fit V.O. Key's description of the GOP in the South: "It scarcely deserves the name of party. It wavers somewhat between an esoteric cult on the order of a lodge and conspiracy for plunder in accord with the excepted customs of our politics."[1] Going into the 1992 election, none of Georgia's statewide officials were Republicans and the GOP held only one of the state's 10 seats in Congress. In the state General Assembly, approximately 80 percent of the members belonged to the Democratic Party. Indeed, prior to 1992, the only major nonpresidential Republican success registered in Georgia had come in 1980 when Senator Herman Talmadge, weighted down by scandal, lost in an upset to Mac Mattingly. Mattingly, like the other Southern Republican senators initially elected in 1980, did not succeed in winning a second term.[2]

Between 1992 and 2004, the GOP first became competitive in Georgia and later became the dominant party in the Peach State. The transformation began with the election of Paul Coverdell to the Senate under circumstances somewhat similar to the 2008 contest. That is, Coverdell, who trailed in the general election by 35,000 votes, won his seat in the course of a runoff necessitated when no candidate polled a majority in the November election. By 1995, Republicans took over Georgia's congressional delegation holding 8 of its 11 seats. In 2002, Sonny Perdue pulled off the year's "most stunning upset"[3] and ended 50 consecutive gubernatorial victories by Democrats. Republicans made gains in state legislative elections and in 2003 had a narrow majority in the state Senate. Two years later, following the imposition of a court-drawn redistricting plan, they took over the state House. Republican successes continued so that as of 2007, of 15 partisan offices chosen statewide, Republicans held 12. They continued to fill most of the seats in the congressional delegation including both senators and had approximately 60 percent of the membership in each chamber of the state legislature.

While Republicans made gains fairly consistently in the 1990s, they did especially well in 2002. Not only did they secure a majority in the upper house of the legislature and elect their first governor since Reconstruction, they reclaimed one of the U.S. Senate seats when Saxby Chambliss defeated Max Cleland in a plurality victory of approximately 30,000 votes.[4]

Georgia's political change has been accompanied by demographic changes. During the 1990s Georgia grew faster than any other state east of the Mississippi and gained two additional congressional seats through reapportionment. Georgia even recently surpassed New Jersey to become the nation's ninth largest state and, as the decade ended it was rapidly closing in on Michigan. All projections show Georgia securing its 14th House seat after the 2010 census.

Jobs provided the impetus for this growth. For instance, Atlanta is the home of Coca Cola, CNN, the Centers for Disease Control, Home Depot, and Delta Air Lines; United Parcel Service and Rubbermaid relocated their headquarters to the Atlanta area; and Lockheed operates a major assembly plant just north of the city limits. The managers of these enterprises, some of whom relocated from other parts of the country and augmented by younger generations of White Southerners who lacked their ancestors' ties to the Democratic Party, have contributed to the GOP dominance in many suburbs in Atlanta and also other metro areas.

At the center of the Atlanta region, the city itself and two older suburban counties, DeKalb to the east and Clayton to the south where Hartsfield-Jackson Atlanta International Airport, the world's busiest, is located, are majority Black. These two counties along with Fulton, which contains most of Atlanta, provided the only Democratic majorities in the area until 2008 when Barack Obama carried three additional counties. The Democratic hole has expanded into the GOP donut as a diverse set of minorities move further out from the older urban core.

The Incumbent: Republican Saxby Chambliss

Incumbents usually win reelection and everyone expected Max Cleland to secure a second term in 2002. Saxby Chambliss, however, made national headlines in 2002 by upsetting Cleland. Retrospectively, it appears that Democrats sowed the seeds of their own destruction prior to this election. In an aggressive redistricting plan designed to unseat Republicans in Congress and the state legislature, Democrats who controlled the process paired incumbent Republicans. In redrawing the congressional map, they extended the 1st District from the coast halfway across the state and then sent a finger inching into Colquitt County in order to include Chambliss's home in the same district with Rep. Jack Kingston. In another miscalculation, they significantly altered the state Senate district of Sonny Perdue. Both Chambliss and Perdue, rather than competing in the less favorable districts Democrats had drawn for them, opted to seek statewide office, and in the end both of these Republicans terminated the careers of Democratic incumbents thought to be invulnerable.

In 2002, Chambliss launched the kind of campaign frequently run by Southern Republicans. That is, the Republican charges that the Democratic opponent has a record that is too liberal for the constituency. Cleland developed a record that gave credence to the Chambliss charges with the coup de grace to his reelection aspirations coming when he voted against President Bush's homeland security plan because it did not provide for unionization of workers in the new department.

Once in office, Chambliss developed a strong conservative voting record during his first term, continually earning high ratings from conservative groups. As his career progressed, however, he irritated his conservative base with some of his positions. Chambliss initially supported President George Bush's immigration policy that was dubbed an "amnesty bill" by those in the right wing of the GOP. Support of this bill earned him boos at the 2007 state GOP convention.[5] Conservatives also criticized him for coauthoring the pork-laden $300 billion Farm Bill in 2007. Moreover, Chambliss was the Republican leader of the "Gang of 10," a group of senators working to craft a bipartisan energy bill.

While some conservatives chastised Chambliss for what they saw as liberal heresies, a review of his voting record as a senator reveals him to be squarely positioned toward the right end of the continuum. Table 13.1 contains vote scores from the Americans for Democratic Action (ADA), the American Conservative Union (ACU), and reports the extent to which Chambliss voted with the GOP on issues that divided the two major parties and his support for President Bush. Since moving to the Senate, Chambliss has voted very conservatively, scoring 90 percent or higher with the ACU and 10 percent or lower with the ADA until 2008. In addition, he consistently backed President Bush's agenda (except in 2008) and always stood with his fellow partisans more than 90 percent of the time. In short, notwithstanding carping from some Georgia Republicans, Chambliss was one of the chamber's most conservative members.

Table 13.1 Congressional Vote Scores for Saxby Chambliss, 2003–2008

Year	American Conservative Union	Americans for Democratic Action	Presidential Support	Party Unity
2008	76	25	95	72
2007	92	10	96	83
2006	96	0	94	93
2005	96	5	95	91
2004	90	5	99	100
2003	90	5	97	97

Source: 2003–2006 scores from various editions of CQ's *Politics in America*; 2007–2008 American Conservative Union (ACU) and Americans for Democratic Action (ADA) scores from the organization Web sites; 2007–2008 party unity and presidential support scores from CQ *Weekly Report*.

Chambliss also drew criticism for weak constituency service.[6] Critics contended that instead of developing close ties with voters, he spent too much time on the golf course soliciting large contributions from wealthy Republicans.[7] Building strong ties with constituents and being able to deliver for them is one of the most important aspects of the incumbency advantage; those close relationships are important at reelection time.[8]

It was in September 2008, however, that Saxby Chambliss's vulnerability became visible after he voted on an issue very salient with the public. Chambliss irritated his base, and others, when he supported the $700 billion Troubled Asset Relief Program (TARP) that was to be disbursed by the Secretary of the Treasury with relatively few strings attached. This massive bailout for Wall Street found little favor in Georgia. Initially, all seven Republicans in the state's congressional delegation opposed it as did four of the Democrats. On final passage, after some modifications, the initiative gained two more Democratic votes but continued to be spurned by all Georgia Republicans in the House. Chambliss, however, along with his colleague Johnny Isakson joined in supporting the bipartisan effort in the Senate. This vote caused some conservatives to question his commitment to their ideals. It also reminded conservatives of other objections they had to the Chambliss record and created problems at a time when Chambliss most needed his base.

Democrats Jousting to Challenge Chambliss

At the end of 2007, long-time Southern politics observer Hastings Wyman wrote that Chambliss "looks like a solid re-election bet for 2008."[9] In turn, the field of Democrats was not stellar, illustrating the point made in the first chapter that politicians are strategic in their decisions of whether and when to run. At the outset, four Democrats announced their intention to challenge the incumbent with retiring DeKalb County Chief Executive Officer Vernon Jones the only one with electoral experience. Very early polling showed Chambliss beating each of the prospective opponents by at least a 2:1 margin. Chambliss did what incumbents do and amassed a sizable war chest of $4.5 million by the end of 2007. Only one of the announced Democrats had more than $20,000 and Jones led the field with $269,000.

While Jones was twice elected to lead Georgia's third most populous county, he had baggage.[10] The hopes of some Democrats both in Georgia and at the national level for an experienced alternative to Jones came in the guise of Jim Martin, the party's 2006 candidate for lieutenant governor. While Martin had managed only 42.3 percent of the vote in that contest, he fared better than any other nonincumbent Democrat competing statewide and ran 4 percentage points ahead of the Democratic candidate for governor. Martin had a long career in state politics having served in the state House for 18 years before being appointed to head the state Department of Human Resources.

Despite not declaring his candidacy until March 19, Martin demonstrated greater fundraising ability than the Democrats already in the race. After less than two weeks as a candidate, Martin reported over $300,000 cash on hand at the end of the first quarter of 2008, compared with Jones' quarter of a million. Chambliss remained far ahead with $3.6 million on hand (see Table 13.2).

The Democratic primary on July 15 proved indecisive as Jones led Martin 40 to 34 percent. Like the general election that came later, the Democratic primary was decided in a runoff. On August 5, Jones failed to improve on his showing and Martin took the Democratic nomination by a 60 to 40 margin.

Candidate Activity in the General Election

The possible matchups for the general election that pollsters surveyed during the first half of 2008 continued to show the incumbent with a commanding lead. A poll taken in late June by Strategic Vision, a Republican polling firm, gave Chambliss a lead of 2:1. A Rasmussen Poll three weeks later had the contest closer but Chambliss remained ahead by 11 points. The first poll that hinted at the incumbent's vulnerability came from a Democratic firm, the Mellman Group, which in early August showed Chambliss up by only 6 points. Shortly thereafter Rasmussen found a similar spread. Right after the Republican National Convention, however, both a Republican polling operation as well as SurveyUSA had Chambliss up by at least 17 points.[11]

It was at that point that Chambliss's support of the Wall Street bailout became an issue and the incumbent's lead shrank dramatically. According to the Chambliss campaign consultant, Tom Perdue, "Up until the recovery bill, I think Martin's name identification was at 24 percent, and he had done literally nothing in the campaign. To say the recovery bill was controversial is an understatement. I have never seen the numbers and forcefulness of the calls, even to the campaign office."[12] In contrast to early polling, no post-bailout polls showed the incumbent with a double-digit lead. The polls conducted immediately after the bailout vote put the Chambliss lead within the margin of error and also

Table 13.2 Campaign Financial Data by Reporting Period for Georgia's Senate Seat, 2008

Reporting Period	Chambliss			Martin		
	Receipts	Disbursements	Ending Cash	Receipts	Disbursements	Ending Cash
2007 Year End (January 1 – December 31)	$8,202,059	$3,547,638	$4,459,794	$0	$0	$0
2008 April Quarterly (January 1 – March 31)	$668,829	$1,491,231	$3,637,392	$346,675	$13,543	$333,132
2008 Pre-primary (April 1 – June 25)	$1,808,117	$1,390,335	$4,055,174	$431,321	$434,499	$329,954
2008 July Quarterly (June 26 – June 30)	$27,210	$0	$4,082,384	$70,698	$224,767	$175,885
2008 Pre-runoff (primary) (July 1 – July 16)	NA	NA	NA	$226,514	$346,161	$56,237
2008 October Quarterly (July 17 – September 31)	$1,127,463	$4,022,279	$$1,187,567	$1,317,383	$1,281,280	$92,340
2008 Pre-general (October 1 – October 15)	$292,221	$643,780	$836,009	$637,129	$164,872	$564,597
2008 Pre-runoff (October 16 – November 12)	$1,925,602	$1,296,669	$1,464,942	$2,400,262	$2,347,517	$617,342
2008 Post-runoff (November 13 – December 22)	$4,316,356	$5,427,551	$353,746	$2,060,220	$2,695,889	-$18,306
Total	$18,367,857	$17,819,483		$7,490,202	$7,508,528	

Note: The 2007 Year End figures represent funds raised and disbursements in the campaign cycle to date. Because Saxby Chambliss did not compete in a primary runoff, he did not have to file a pre-primary report. After the July quarterly report was filed, he did not have to file again until the October quarterly which covers the July 1 – September 30 time frame.

Source: Compiled from candidate reports to the Federal Election Commission, Form 3, Lines 23, 24, 26 and 27, various dates.

found him with less than 50 percent support. Even a poll by a Republican pollster gave the incumbent only a 3-point advantage. Nine of 17 polls conducted during the last month of the campaign and reported on the Real Clear Politics Web site showed the race within 3 percentage points and only one had Chambliss with a majority. Clearly Chambliss was in trouble. While Chambliss lost support, not all the defectors went to Martin. In fact, Martin stalled at approximately 44 percent of the vote. All but four of the polls had his vote share between 43 and 45 percent and none ever showed him with more than 46 percent.

Another factor that helped Martin was the timing and style of television advertising. During the summer, Chambliss bought television time to run positive ads but largely ignored his opponent. Although, as shown in Table 13.2, Chambliss had more than $4 million on hand at the end of June, compared with Martin's $176,000, Chambliss did not use his financial advantage to define Martin negatively. Strategically, this is important because a poll conducted in the third week of September, at about the time that Martin launched his television advertising, found that 46 percent of likely voters had no opinion of the Democratic nominee.[13] Chambliss missed his opportunity to define his opponent before his opponent had the chance to define himself.

For two and half weeks, through the first week of October, Martin dominated the ad wars. Thereafter, both campaigns advertised heavily on television. Martin's early dominance of the airways allowed him to introduce himself in a positive light as he stressed his service in Vietnam, his service in the General Assembly, and as the director of the Department of Human Resources. As a consequence of his television buys, Martin became widely known and there was a dramatic increase in his positives.

Martin also went on the attack. One Martin ad linked the Chambliss vote for the $700 billion bailout to earlier votes by the Senator which, Martin claimed, relaxed federal regulation of Wall Street activities. Martin tied the Chambliss votes in favor of Wall Street deregulation to campaign contributions the Senator had received from those sources.[14] This ad picked up on a criticism noted earlier that Chambliss solicited funds from fat-cat, golfing-buddy contributors and had little concern for the middle and working class having become a pawn of moneyed interests. "Isn't it time that someone stood up for the middle class?" Martin repeatedly asked in television ads.

In contrast with Martin's effective ads, those released by Chambliss drew widespread criticism from fellow Republicans. An article by Georgia's premier political reporter quoted Republican insiders asking of the Chambliss television effort, "Where are your ads?" and "Your ads suck."[15] Another Republican insider observed that a frequent topic for GOP activists was, "What the (expletive deleted) is going on with Saxby? It looks like he's running a bad state House race. The ads are deplorable, there's no real strategy. Everybody from his donors in the state to the leadership in Washington was just appalled." With the campaign faltering, criticism focused on the seasoned Georgia operative in charge of the effort.

As the campaign grew competitive, Chambliss finally got around to trying to define his opponent and he dusted off a claim from his 2002 race against Cleland charging Martin with being too liberal for Georgia. Specifically, Chambliss's ads alleged that Martin had voted for the largest tax increase in Georgia history while serving in the General Assembly. Another claim was that Martin had voted to increase the allowance allotted to state legislators. Yet a third attack highlighted Martin's dismissal as the director of the Department of Human Resources (DHR) by Governor Perdue after two children being overseen by DHR died while in foster care. The implication of this ad was that Martin was not sufficiently diligent when leading the agency. Martin objected strongly noting his long interest in promoting the welfare of children and explaining that Chambliss's tax allegation involved increasing the state sales tax from 3 to 4 percent.

As the campaign came to a close, Martin made the $700 billion bailout of financial institutions a major theme in his ads. Chambliss spokesperson Michelle Grasso acknowledged that the mail received in the Senator's office overwhelmingly opposed the bailout.[16] Trying to take advantage of the public's opposition to the bailout, Martin characterized the Senator's vote in the following terms: "It's classic Saxby economics—$700 billion for Wall Street, while Georgia families get stuck with the bill. That's just wrong."[17] Chambliss responded that in light of the crisis, "You have to worry about the country first."

Outside Factors Play a Role

A number of players outside of the two campaigns impacted the Chambliss–Martin contest including the presidential candidates, party committees, and independent groups. At the same time that Martin was closing the gap in the Senate race, Barack Obama was cutting into John McCain's lead in Georgia. The surge for Obama came even though neither he nor any of his top surrogates campaigned in Georgia (at one point he even redeployed paid staff to other states). The Obama effort rested on an impressive grassroots organization with approximately three dozen campaign offices along with more than 100 trained volunteers and literally thousands of others who got involved with the campaign. Obama activists registered voters throughout the year, having begun these activities in anticipation of Georgia's February 5 presidential primary. After Obama scored his largest victory in any state, winning 66 percent of the primary vote, the campaign continued signing up new voters. As elsewhere, the Obama campaign developed an extensive list of e-mail contacts and used these along with phone banking to encourage likely supporters to go to the polls in November.

In contrast, the McCain campaign provided Chambliss with nothing comparable to the help that Obama gave Martin. Indeed McCain's Georgia effort was not even headquartered in the state, but instead operated out of Tallahassee, Florida. While the Republican Party in a number of counties worked diligently to identify likely supporters and encourage them to vote, the effort overall paled in comparison with Democratic activities. The disparity was so great that Eric

Tanenblatt, who had been Sonny Perdue's first chief of staff, said admiringly of the Obama effort, "They've used technology better than any campaign I've ever seen. They have taken networking to that next level to social mobilization."[18]

Additionally, the Democratic Senatorial Campaign Committee (DSCC) spent at least $500,000 to run an anti-flat tax ad similar to ones directed at other Georgia Republicans. The DSCC ad stated that the flat tax would add 23 percent to the cost of all purchases and calculated the flat tax on several items. The ad directed viewers to a Web site where they could enter the cost of an item and see how much the flat tax would add. While national Democrats saw this ad as effective, Martin preferred not to stir up opposition from fair tax support-ers some of whom Chambliss might have alienated by voting for the bailout. When asked about the antifair tax ad in the course of a televised debate, Martin responded, "It's not my ad. I wish it wasn't running but it's factually correct."[19]

With almost a week to go before the November election, the *Atlanta Jour-nal-Constitution* reported the expenditure of $9.4 million on television in the Atlanta market for the Senate race. In the last two weeks of October more than $5 million went for television ads with much of it coming from the DSCC and the National Republican Senatorial Committee (NRSC).[20] One of the NRSC's ads was on message with the Chambliss attacks and painted Martin as a liberal by claiming the Democrat was soft on crime. Martin, however, responded to this allegation by noting that the kidnapping of his 8-year old daughter had made his family crime victims.[21] The young girl escaped unharmed but this experience prompted Martin to introduce anticrime bills while in the legislature. Martin never came close to matching the incumbents' fundraising (as shown in Table 13.2), but as the race tightened, the DSCC leveled the playing field by investing almost twice as much as the NRSC.

Deep Divisions in Election Day Results

The polls prior to the election proved accurate as Chambliss led Martin by 3 percentage points, 49.8 to 46.6 percent, once the votes were tallied. The Sena-tor, however, failed to achieve a majority of the vote as a result of just over 128,000 votes cast for the Libertarian candidate Allen Buckley.

Race and party correlated strongly in Georgia on Election Day and influ-enced the outcome of this contest. African Americans are the core constituency of the Democratic Party. They made up 30.1 percent of all voters on Election Day and the exit polls show 91 percent of the black vote going to Martin, who had his largest vote shares in majority-Black counties. Indeed, Martin carried all but two counties in which Blacks constituted more than 40 percent of the reg-istrants and took approximately 80 percent of the vote in the two most heavily Black counties in the state. A regression analysis of county level data shows that for a 10 percent increase in the Black percentage among registrants, Martin's vote share increased by 6.22 percentage points.

Martin still could not match Barack Obama's appeal. Obama won the sup-port of 98 percent of Georgia Blacks who cast a ballot. Moreover, although the

Senate contest appeared immediately below the presidential contest on the touch screen voting machines used throughout Georgia, one in 15 African Americans expressed no preference for senator. Exit polls showed Blacks casting 30 percent of the vote in Georgia for president, but only 28 percent of the vote for senator.[22] Regression analysis shows that for each 10 percent increase in the African Americans in a county, Martin ran one percentage point behind Obama. Had African Americans voted as frequently for senator as for president and had those Blacks who did not vote in the Senate contest been as supportive of Martin as Blacks who expressed a preference, Martin would have had a narrow plurality but still not a majority. A runoff would still have been necessary.

Obama ran ahead of Martin in all of the state's more heavily urbanized counties, both those that had city cores as well as many suburban counties. In the county with the biggest difference Obama ran 4.6 percentage points ahead of Martin. On the other hand, in 120 smaller counties, Martin's vote share exceeded Obama's with the greatest disparity reaching 14.5 percentage points. That Martin did better than Obama in smaller and rural counties, which have not experienced dramatic in-migration that other areas have, may suggest a degree of lingering racism.

According to exit polls, Chambliss won the White vote by a 70 to 25 percent margin. Martin's share of the White vote was 2 percent better than Obama's, as well as John Kerry's in 2004, and it was in line with that received by the Democratic gubernatorial candidate in 2006. The core constituency for the GOP in Georgia comes from White evangelicals or born-again Christians. This group accounted for 38 percent of the participants in the Senate contest and they preferred Chambliss over Martin by 81 to 15 percent. Chambliss carried 116 of Georgia's 159 counties and did especially well in several suburban counties north and east of Atlanta. In Forsyth, one of the nation's fastest growing counties, he took 75 percent of the vote.

While each party's loyalists overwhelmingly supported their nominee, independents lined up in Chambliss's corner 54 to 38 percent. Not surprisingly, 84 percent of the liberals preferred the Democrat, but accounted for only one in seven voters. The 40 percent of the electorate that identified itself as conservative cast 77 percent of their votes for the Republican and moderates preferred Martin to Chambliss by 56 to 41 percent. Among voters younger than 30 years, Chambliss edged out Martin 47 to 44 percent. If the future looks bleak for Republicans nationwide, the situation in Georgia is far more positive for the GOP in that the youth vote split very much like that of their elders.[23]

One Election was not Enough to Pick a Winner

In any state other than Georgia, Chambliss's 3 percent advantage would have returned the Republican to Washington for a second term in the Senate. Georgia law, however, requires that a candidate win a majority of the vote. Since Chambliss came up 9,200 votes short of a majority, he was forced to meet Martin head-to-head in a runoff on December 2. With all other elections now resolved except for recounts or litigation, Georgia became the center of the electoral universe. Both parties focused their attentions exclusively on the Peach State.

As political activists across the nation concentrated on Georgia, liberals remembered that they had a special reason to dislike Chambliss. The focus of their ire was the 2002 Chambliss–Cleland contest and specifically the Chambliss ad that featured the Democratic senator along with pictures of Osama Bin Laden and Saddam Hussein.[24] Since Cleland had lost both legs and one arm to a Vietcong land mine, Democrats felt that linking him with two enemies of the United States unfairly questioned his patriotism.[25]

While general elections rarely go to runoffs, numerous primary battles extend to a second round. Analyses of nomination contests show that the vote leaders from the first primary election go on to win nominations approximately 70 percent of the time; however, a narrow lead and being an incumbent are both factors that reduce the likelihood of the frontrunner winning in the second round.[26] On the other hand, Republicans won each of three statewide general election runoffs held in Georgia since 1992. In short, lessons from previous runoffs indicate that Saxby Chambliss had reason to be both confident and worried headed into the December 2 vote.

Historically, Georgia primary runoffs often attracted more voters than the initial primary.[27] Once the Democratic nomination ceased to be an almost certain guarantee of a general election victory (i.e., when Republicans became competitive in Georgia), however, the drawing power of runoffs declined. In the election sequence most analogous to the Chambliss–Martin runoff, a 1992 Senate runoff pitting Paul Coverdell against Wyche Fowler, participation fell by almost 45 percent from the general election to the subsequent runoff. Since it could be expected that far fewer voters would turn out for the runoff, both the Chambliss and Martin campaigns had as their principal objective encouraging individuals who had voted for them on November 4 to return to the polls on December 2. In other words, mobilizing each party's base became the goal.

Each candidate invited leaders of his party to come to Georgia and make endorsements. Because a number of leading Democrats are far to the left of Georgia's political mainstream, Chambliss had a longer A-list of Republicans who could lend a helping hand. A visit or even an endorsement from Speaker of the House Nancy Pelosi (CA) or Senate Majority Leader Harry Reid (NV) would reinforce the Republican claim that Martin was a liberal and therefore out of step with the policy preferences of most Georgians. John McCain, Mike Huckabee (who narrowly won the Republican presidential primary in Georgia), Mitt Romney, and Rudy Giuliani all responded to the Chambliss S.O.S., and lent their help by attending rallies and taping automated phone calls (i.e., robo calls). The superstar of the 2008 election cycle for Republicans was vice presidential nominee Sarah Palin, and Chambliss very much wanted her blessing. Just before December 2, Palin appeared with the candidate at four campaign stops with the finale in the Atlanta suburbs, and drew thousands of cheering supporters.

Martin desperately wanted to counter Palin by bringing in the president-elect, and rumors circulated during most of the runoff that Obama would visit the state. Ultimately, perhaps wanting to avoid what many believe to have been a mistake by Bill Clinton when he came to Georgia to help the ill-fated Fowler runoff campaign in 1992, the president-elect stayed away.

Former President Bill Clinton and former Vice President Al Gore were the biggest names to endorse Martin. On the final day of the campaign while Palin inspired the Republican faithful, Martin appeared with Ludacris, Young Jeezy, and other rap artists. The Clinton visit also featured a rally at historically Black Clarke Atlanta University. Clearly Martin sought to mobilize African Americans, but his appearance with rappers did little to appeal to middle aged and older Whites, another important electoral constituency.

Even though Obama lost Georgia, Martin tried to make his commitment to the new president's agenda *the* issue of the runoff. Martin said in his first press conference launching the runoff, "This isn't going to be a difficult race for anybody to figure out. I'm going to do everything I can to help Barack Obama get off to a fast start. Saxby Chambliss has promised to do everything he can to stop Barack Obama from succeeding."[28] One Martin television ad showed a clip from a debate in which the incumbent indicated he would oppose Obama's economic stimulus plan.

Chambliss also linked Martin to Obama during the runoff as a continuation of the Republican strategy of pinning the liberal label on Martin. The Republican warned that Martin would be a "yes man" for the liberal agenda that would come from the Obama White House. Moreover, some of the television advertising run by pro-Chambliss independent groups ratcheted up the rhetoric. While for years attacks on Democrats have characterized them as liberal, some of the ads in the runoff chastised Martin as being too radical.

The Chambliss campaign aired the most effective ad during the runoff. As in the 2002 challenge to Cleland, the key ad in the runoff preyed on voter's fears. Known as the "Firewall" ad, Chambliss cautioned that his election could be decisive in denying Democrats a filibuster-proof Senate. With recounts continuing in the Minnesota Senate contest (see chapter 9), Chambliss pointed to his effort to become the Senate's 41st Republican. This issue had some traction in Georgia, as a Rasmussen poll showed that 52 percent of respondents indicated less likelihood of supporting Martin if they believed that he would be the 60th Democrat.[29] More importantly, 9 percent of those who earlier in the survey had expressed a preference for Martin said they would be less likely to vote for him if they thought he would give the Democrats a filibuster-proof Senate. In an expected shift, some conservatives who supported the Libertarian candidate in the general election got behind Chambliss when their first choice was no longer on the ballot. Their questions about Chambliss's commitment to conservative values paled in comparison to their fear of what the Obama Administration might push through Congress if there was not at least the possibility of a check through a GOP filibuster.[30]

With Martin heavily dependent upon strong Black turnout, the peek at participation offered by figures on early voting released daily by the secretary of state had to be discouraging for the Democrat. By the time early voting wrapped up on November 26, Blacks had cast 21.8 percent of the ballots. Not only was that figure substantially below the Black proportion of registered voters, 30 percent, it was far below the level of interest demonstrated by African Americans in the lead up to the November 4 election. Early voting prior to the general election saw Blacks cast 35.1 percent of the ballots. Emory University political scientist Merle Black explained declining Black turnout as follows, "For a lot of African-American voters, the real election was last month. The importance of electing the first African-American president in history generated enormous enthusiasm, everything else was anticlimactic."[31]

Early voters during the runoff phase were much more likely to use absentee ballots than did early voters in the days before the November election. Prior to the December vote, 26.8 percent of the ballots came from those mailing in absentee ballots in contrast with only 11.1 percent of the early voters prior to the November election. As they had for the past decade, the Georgia Republican Party mailed out election literature that included the form for a recipient to request an absentee ballot. That practice continued as the state party mailing included a facsimile of Governor Perdue's signature. The message from the governor admonished voters that, "Our votes are necessary to help ensure the most radical schemes of the liberal agenda are not imposed on us, and to protect and provide for Georgia's future energy needs." Although some Republicans sent these requests back without signing them, making them invalid, many completed the requests as required. In one of the state's most heavily Republican counties, however, eight workers in the election supervisor's office devoted their full attention to sending back absentee requests that had not been signed, as required by state law.[32] Only about 20 percent of the unsigned requests got resubmitted in time for their votes to count.

Part of the reason that Republicans did better at getting their supporters to vote early in the runoff compared to the general election may be the heightened effort to mobilize GOP supporters. Michael Beach who directed the GOP's National Victory Center reports that Republicans made a major effort to get voters out for the runoff.[33] More than a score of Republican operatives and 300 activists came to Georgia for the runoff to promote turnout in the final days of the campaign.[34] The chair of the Republican National Committee, Mike Duncan, spent the last days before the runoff overseeing the get-out-the-vote effort.[35] No comparable effort was made prior to the general election, in part because the Chambliss campaign rejected NRSC plans to send in workers.[36] One thing that hurt the Chambliss campaign was the inability to build on the remains of the McCain campaign which had no operation in Georgia. To fill this void, Chambliss opened 10 field offices to coordinate runoff efforts.[37]

While Barack Obama did not visit Georgia, he did not divorce himself from Martin. In a radio ad Obama called for Martin's election so that he can "help me change Washington"; and Obama and his wife both recorded "robo-calls" that many Georgia voters received. In contrast to the situation faced by Chambliss, 25 of Obama's 33 campaign offices in Georgia remained open and the staff in these offices worked for Martin. In addition to Obama staff already in Georgia, approximately 100 field workers from around the nation who wanted to continue in campaign mode came to Georgia to help.[38]

Chambliss budgeted $4.5 million for the runoff, roughly a quarter of the $18.4 million total he raised, but according to one of his consultants actually raised an additional $5.5 million during the four weeks.[39] Again, Martin could not keep pace although he raised $2 million more to contest the runoff. A number of partisan and interest groups augmented the candidate's expenditures. Freedom's Watch spent more than $500,000 charging that Martin would increase taxes, support government-run health care programs, and support new environmental regulations. The Employee Freedom Action Committee attacked Martin claiming that he would support the proposal to eliminate secret ballots on issues of unionization (i.e., the "card check" legislation). The U.S. Chamber of Commerce did a mailing comparing the two candidates on taxes, job creation, increased drilling for oil and healthcare. The NRSC and the National Republican Trust PAC together bought more than $2 million in television ads.[40]

On the other side, there was much less outside activity on Martin's behalf. Americans for Job Security ponied up slightly less than $1 million to promote Martin's candidacy. The DSCC also spent heavily.[41]

When the ballots were tallied, Chambliss won the runoff in a landslide, 57.4 to 42.6 percent. The largest factor in this result was that turnout was only slightly more than half what it had been in November. While that is a dramatic decrease from November's 3.9 million voters, the total of 2.1 million voters who went to the polls is similar to the turnout generated in the 2002 and 2006 midterm general elections. The Chambliss runoff vote equaled almost two-thirds of his general election support. In contrast, Martin managed to attract slightly more than half as many votes in the runoff as he had four weeks earlier. Consequently, while Chambliss led Martin by only 110,000 votes in November, in the runoff, despite a substantial decrease in participation, Chambliss expanded his lead to more than 300,000 votes. As Bill Clinton warned in his speech promoting Martin's candidacy, "The person who wins [the U.S. Senate race] will be the one whose supporters want it the most."[42]

Chambliss improved his showing across the board. In a dozen counties he received more than 80 percent of the vote, a level of support not achieved in any county in the general election. In 58 counties Chambliss's vote share exceeded 70 percent and he won majorities in 131 counties compared with 116 in which he got a majority in the general election.

Martin continued to win all counties in which most registrants were Black, but lost eight counties in which Black registration exceeded 40 percent. These results provide further evidence that the Black electorate did not turn out in large numbers for the runoff. The excitement generated by the Obama campaign dissipated substantially during the month since the election. Martin's efforts to align himself with Obama did not inspire a large number of Georgia's African Americans.

Conclusion

Saxby Chambliss's story line in 2008 resembles a melodrama. At the outset, the senator is carefree; reelection is assured. Then he encounters a series of mishaps culminating in the bailout vote which alienate some in his conservative base and reveal unexpected weaknesses. After a narrow escape from disaster, Chambliss returns to his happy life in the Senate with a landslide victory in the runoff.

Chambliss's difficulties stemmed in part from choices he made that were magnified by forces outside his control. Had he and his congressional staff assigned higher priority to constituency service and downplayed the senator's frequent golf outings, he might have accumulated a reservoir of good will that would have reduced the fallout from a few unpopular votes in an overwhelmingly conservative record. Had Chambliss unleashed the kinds of attack ads he ultimately ran much earlier, he might have so damaged Martin that the challengers' charges would have gotten less traction. As is true of most incumbents, Chambliss's decline from commanding frontrunner to runoff participant cannot be attributed to inadequate resources. His final campaign finance report (see Table 13.2) showed him spending $17.8 million to Martin's $7.5 million. Wiser spending decisions earlier could have saved the campaign the added expense of the runoff.

While Monday morning quarterbacks point to a number of ways that Chambliss and his handlers could have played better defense, the senator had no control over one of the most critical elements. Barack Obama's ground-breaking campaign mobilized far more African Americans than had ever participated in a Georgia election. Especially active were Black women who turned out at higher rates than White women or White men. While Martin, like any Democrat, would draw overwhelming shares of the Black vote, no one anticipated that almost 1.2 million African-Americans in Georgia would turn out. When the Obama campaign pulled staff out of Georgia in early September it looked like Democrats were doing as they had in 2000 and 2004 and ceding the state to the GOP, but the long lines of Blacks queuing up to vote prior to Election Day and tightening polls made Georgia a battleground in October and that gave Democratic campaign workers a second wind.

The turnout of Blacks on November 4 in part led to the close U.S. Senate contest; it also explains the lopsided result on December 2. Indeed, the foremost contributor to the drop in Democratic performance from November to December was the drop in the number of Black voters. In November, probably for the first time in history, Georgia Blacks participated at rates slightly above their share of the registrants. While we lack official or even exit poll estimates of Black runoff participation, the tabulations from the early vote suggest that much of the enthusiasm that surrounded Obama's candidacy dissipated a month later.

Midterm elections almost invariably attract fewer participants than do presidential elections. If Black voters do not turn out massively in 2010, Democrats will have another trying time cutting into GOP advantage.

Longer term, Democratic prospects look better. They regularly poll 90 percent or more of the Black vote. Obviously, however, in a state where African Americans constitute less than a third of the electorate, successful Democrats need substantial support in other quarters to win. Two growing components of the electorate, Latinos and Asian Americans, have favored Democrats although less enthusiastically than Blacks have done. Over the last decade or so, most Whites have voted for Republicans. By 2008, Whites constituted less than 63 percent of Georgia's registered voters and 64 percent of the turnout. The math is straightforward: when about 78 percent of the votes came from Whites in 1996, Republicans could win with 65 percent of the White vote and very little else. In November 2008 when Whites made up 64 percent of the participants, Republicans who relied exclusively on Whites would need 78 percent of the White vote if they attracted nothing from other groups. As the electorate becomes less White, Republicans must get larger and larger shares of the White vote or come up with appeals that attract other parts of the electorate.

The narrowing of the partisan vote gap in November 2008 is largely attributable to Barack Obama's charisma, a will-o-the-wisp that was gone by December. Georgia Democrats can wait patiently for the stately pace of demography to give them victories or come up with appeals that chip away at the GOP's base of support.

Notes

1. V. O. Key, Jr., *Southern Politics in State and Nation* (New York: Knopf, 1949), 277.
2. The other members of the GOP's short-lived 1980 cohort were Paula Hawkins (FL), John East (NC), and Jeremiah Denton (AL).
3. Larry J. Sabato, ed., *Midterm Madness: The Elections of 2002* (Lanham, MD: Rowman and Littlefield, 2003), 14.
4. After Coverdell came from behind to defeat Wyche Fowler in the 1992 Senate runoff, Democrats dropped the threshold for general election victories from a majority to 45 percent and that explains why Cleland was able to win election in 1996 with a plurality. When the Republicans took control of the legislature, they reimposed the majority vote requirement.
5. While Chambliss initially supported immigration reform, he quickly backed away in the face of withering criticism from back home.
6. Dick Pettys, "What Went Wrong for Chambliss that Race Now Is So Close," *InsiderAdvantage Georgia*, October 30, 2008, http://www.insideradvantagegeorgia.com/restricted/2008/October%202008/10-30-08/What_Went_Wrong103019642.php (accessed August 12, 2009).
7. Alan Judd, "Chambliss: South Georgian Pays Attention to Constituent Interests, Builds Clout with GOP Colleagues," *Atlanta Journal-Constitution*, (November 23, 2008, A1, A12.
8. Richard F. Fenno, Jr., *Home Style* (Boston: Little, Brown, 1978).
9. Hastings Wyman, "Georgia: Chambliss Strong as Onions," *Southern Political Report* 715 (December 31, 2007), 1.

10. Jim Galloway, "DeKalb's Jones Launches Quest for Senate," *Atlanta Journal-Constitution,* July 21, 2007, http://www.ajc.com/metro/content/shared-blogs/ajc/politicalinsider/entries//2007/07/ (accessed August 12, 2009); Cynthia Tucker, "Vernon Jones a Real Liability for Democrats," *Atlanta Journal-Constitution,* August 3, 2008, http://www.ajc.com/homefinder/content/opinion/tucker/stories/2008/08/01/tucked_0803.html?cxntlid=inform_sr (accessed August 12, 2009)

11. Polling data in this section can be found at http://www.realclearpolitics.com/epolls/2008/senate/ga/georgia_senate-302.html

12. Pettys, "What Went Wrong for Chambliss."

13. "Numbers Tumble for Georgia Political Leaders," *InsiderAdvantage Georgia,* September 25, 2008.

14. Richard Hallman, "Foes Focus on Financial Woes Link," *Atlanta Journal-Constitution,* October 23, 2008, D5.

15. Pettys, "What Went Wrong for Chambliss," is the source of quotes in this paragraph.

16. Jim Tharpe and Ben Smith, "Bailout Furor Could Shake Up Some Georgia Races," *Atlanta Journal-Constitution,* October 5, 2008, C3.

17. Ibid.

18. Jim Galloway, "Campaign Turned Strategy on Its Head," *Atlanta Journal-Constitution,* November 3, 2008, B7.

19. Associated Press, "Martin Backs Away from Ads Slamming Chambliss," *Athens Banner-Herald,* October 19, 2008, A9.

20. Nancy Albritton, "Senate Showdown Spurs Big Spending," *Atlanta Journal-Constitution,* October 29, 2008, C4.

21. Jim Tharpe, "Miller Says Chambliss Is Only Man Left to Halt 'Far-Left Agenda,'" *Atlanta Journal-Constitution,* November 27, 2008, E12.

22. The postelection audit conducted by the secretary of state's office showed Blacks accounting for 30 percent of Georgia's voters, right in line with the exit poll estimates for president.

23. Nationally Obama won two-thirds of the youth vote.

24. The ad can be viewed at http://www.youtube.com/watch?v=tKFYpd0q9nE.

25. See for example Leslie Savan, GOP Plays a Mean Saxby," posted at http://www.thenation.com/blogs/state_of_change/385276/print.

26. Charles S. Bullock, III and Loch K. Johnson, *Runoff Elections in the United States* (Chapel Hill: University of North Carolina Press, 1992); Cortez A. M. Ewing, *Primary Elections in the South: A Study of Uniparty Politics* (Norman: University of Oklahoma Press, 1953).

27. Bullock and Johnson, *Runoff Elections,* chapter 2.

28. Dick Pettys, "Chambliss, Martin Get Set for Runoff," *InsiderAdvantage,* November 6, 2008.

29. "Rasmussen Reports, "Election2008: Georgia Senate," http://www.rasmussenreports.com/public_content/politics/elections/2002/2008_senate.

30. Shannon McCaffrey, "Former Critics Rallying to Chambliss in Runoff," *Athens Banner-Herald,* November 16, 2008, A6.

31. Bobbie Brown and Carl Hulse, "Republican Wins Runoff for Senator in Georgia," *New York Times,* December 3, 2008,

32. Gary Smith, election supervisor of Forsyth County, personal interview, December 9, 2008, and e-mail, June 1, 2009.

33. Michael Beach, personal interview, December 9, 2008.

34. Dick Pettys, "RNC Chair in Georgia for Chambliss," *InsiderAdvantage Georgia,* November 25, 2008.

35. Jim Tharpe, "Big Push to Campaign End," *Atlanta Journal-Constitution* (December 1, 2008), B1, B5.

36. Pettys, "What Went Wrong for Chambliss." In an e-mail communication, June 1, 2009, Pettys reports that his sources attribute the decision against using outside GOP help in the general election to hubris on the part of the consultant. The consultant denies this and says that no help was offered.

37. Jim Tharpe, "Senate Runoff Fast and Furious," *Atlanta Journal-Constitution*, November 11, 2008, A1, A9.

38. Aaron Gould Sheinin and Jim Tharpe, "Obama Lends Staff to Help Martin," *Atlanta Journal-Constitution*, November 12, 2008, C1.

39. Jim Tharpe, "Senate Runoff Brings Big Spending," *Atlanta Journal-Constitution*, November 16, 2008, C3; e-mail from Tom Perdue to Charlie Harman, Senator Chambliss's chief of staff, June 2, 2009.

40. Robbie Brown, "Presidential Race Is Still Alive in Georgia Runoff," *New York Times*, December 2, 2008, http://www.nytimes.com/2008/12/02/us/politics/02georgia.html (accessed August 12, 2009) http://www.nytimes.com/2008/12/02/us/politics/02georgia.html (accessed August 12, 2009) ,.

41. Aaron Gould Sheinin, "Outside Cash Pumps Up Runoff," *Atlanta Journal-Constitution*, November 22, 2008, A1, A8.

42. Thomas Wheatley, "Fear and Loathing in Chambliss-Martin Runoff," *Creative Loafing*, November 26, 2008,

14 The Goal Line Stand

David A. Dulio and Randall E. Adkins

Before and during the 2008 congressional elections, analysts and prognosticators predicted big losses for Republicans in the U.S. House of Representatives and U.S. Senate. For the most part, they were correct. Of the 11 most competitive[1] Senate contests (five of which are discussed in this volume), as identified by the nonpartisan *Cook Political Report*, only one was a seat currently held by a Democrat, which meant that all of the competition in Senate contests was going to be on Republican turf. Democrats won eight of the 11 races, and took seven seats from the GOP. In House contests, the *Cook Report* identified 58 highly competitive races, and again the vast majority (42) were held by Republicans (all of the House races in this book were on the "toss-up" list, signaling these were the most competitive). In these races, Democrats won 30 seats. Certainly Democrats had a good year. As we explained in chapter 1, however, with all the dynamics working against Republicans in 2008, why did Democrats not win more seats? More specifically, how did several of the most vulnerable GOP incumbents survive? This is more pointed in the House where Republicans defended half of the "toss-up" races, kept all but one of the "lean Republican" seats, took two of the "toss up" races being defended by Democrats, and even took one of the few "lean Democratic" seats.

In short, many Republicans were able to play effective defense in 2008 and the question becomes: how did they manage to win these elections? The case studies contained in the previous chapters were designed to help us answer this question and to give us some ideas about how incumbents generally defend their turf in difficult times. These lessons extend beyond 2008 and will be informative for future election cycles in 2010, 2012, and beyond. This is because at some point in the future many other candidates, both Democrats and Republicans, will find themselves in a position where they have to defend their seat when the political currents of the moment are running strongly against them.

In chapter 1, we outlined a number of the important macrolevel or national dynamics that were working against Republicans. These included factors focused on the GOP: the poor perception of the Republican brand, the low approval ratings of President George W. Bush, and the troubled economy. It also included factors that focused on Democrats: large surges in voter registration for the party and the excitement about Barack Obama's presidential campaign. These set the table for the difficult year Republicans faced, but they did not seal the outcome of individual congressional races.

The American system of campaigns is very campaign-centered. Each candidate is responsible for running his or her own race and for strategic and tactical decisions, which, for the most part, drive outcomes.[2] These candidate- and race-specific dynamics are what we turn to in this final chapter to help explain why some Republicans won in difficult times when many of their fellow partisans were defeated. First, we examine dynamics that were present in specific districts and states that worked against the GOP and then discuss those strategies and tactics that did and did not work in 2008.

Additional Dynamics Working Against the GOP

In addition to the tides flowing against the GOP that we outlined in chapter 1, there were several district- or statewide factors present that made playing defense more difficult for these endangered incumbents. These were forces that Democrats were also able to use to their advantage.

New-Look Electorates

One of these factors, which was present in many of the races analyzed in this volume, is the changing nature of the constituencies in particular districts or states. Candidates, in some cases long-term incumbents, found themselves trying to get reelected in a district or state where the electorate looked different from the one they faced in previous election cycles during the past two decades (or even different from what they faced in 2006). Sometimes this was due to more Democratic voters coming to the polls as a result of increased turnout or the surge in voter registration discussed earlier.

The latter was certainly the case in Connecticut's 4th District. In the 12 months prior to the 2008 elections, Democrats were able to add over 25,000 new registrants to the voting rolls, 60 percent of which were in the three key cities of Bridgeport, Norwalk, and Stamford. This changed the look of Chris Shays's district. In 2008, the influx of new voters—that is, those who had not voted before—changed the district just enough to make it that much more difficult for Shays to play defense.

Colorado also saw a large number of new Democratic registrations after the 2006 election and leading up to 2008. The state was one of the most discussed in terms of Democratic gains. In the 4th District, however, Republicans managed to maintain a 37,000-vote advantage in voter registrations. The changes here were due to a number of new residents from several other states who had moved to the suburban and urban (i.e., Democratic) areas of the district in comparison to the more Republican and rural areas. This created a shift in the political nature of the district as it became more Democratic and gave Betsy Markey an opening to beat an incumbent who had garnered fewer and fewer votes during each of the last few election cycles. Similarly, the demographics of California's 4th District also changed quite a bit. This is attributable to redistricting as well as an in-migration of new residents to the district from the liberal San Francisco Bay area.

Shifts in other districts and states were driven by other demographics. In Michigan's 9th District, changes to Oakland County saw more African Americans, blue collar workers, and members of other traditionally Democratic groups move into the district. The effect was similar to what happened to Shays in Connecticut, but this shift began nearly a decade ago and reached a point in 2008 where it could make a difference on Election Day when combined with other forces that were in play during this historic election cycle. The shift in Shays's district was more a function of field work by the challenger's campaign and the Democratic Party. Thus, who knows if those first-time voters that turned out in 2008 will do so in future cycles? In Michigan the shift was more fundamental to the political and socioeconomic aspects of the district.

Shifts of this nature made a difference on a larger scale in states like Georgia, North Carolina, and New Hampshire, where, an influx of new residents from different states started to change the outlook of the parties' electoral prospects. Democrats did better in Georgia in 2008 than they had in quite some time at both the congressional and presidential levels; whether these gains can be sustained is the real question. In North Carolina and New Hampshire there are signs that Republicans will soon be or will continue to be in trouble in those states. North Carolina has seen dramatic growth among non-Southerners who do not have the same ties to the GOP that established residents of the state do. In New Hampshire, there has not been as much growth, but while some have left the state others have moved in. In both states, the empirical evidence shows recent arrivals are more likely to be Democrats than Republicans with the net effect a gain for Democrats and more difficult campaigns for Republicans.

Whether these trends are a part of a larger realignment in American politics is nearly impossible to determine at this point; we will have to see the results from several elections to draw that conclusion. What is clear, however, is that as demographic and partisan groups shift out of or into different populations, those running campaigns will have to give this issue due consideration.

Race in Congressional Elections

The presence and importance of race in the 2008 presidential election is clear—Barack Obama became our first African-American president. In some cases, the impact of this factor was also felt at the congressional level. Obama was breaking the racial barrier at the presidential level and promoting higher turnout that helped Democrats across the country; however, in both Georgia and Kentucky Republicans retained their seats. In Kentucky, some analysts argued that if Hillary Clinton had been at the top of the ticket rather than Barack Obama, she might have helped Bruce Lunsford win by either drawing more Democrats to the polls or encouraging more voters to vote a straight ticket.

In Georgia the influence of race was more specifically about who turned out to vote. With a huge African-American turnout on November 4, Barack Obama put Georgia "in play" in the presidential race for the first time in many years. This turnout also helped Jim Martin get very close to Saxby Chambliss, forcing a runoff a month later. In the runoff a much smaller Black turnout sealed the fate of Martin as he was only able to garner about half the votes in December that he won in November. Had African Americans turned out like they did in November, the runoff results would have been much closer.

The Mother's Milk of Politics

In chapter 1, we outlined the large advantage the Democratic Party had in terms of financial resources. In sum, the Democratic Congressional Campaign Committee (DCCC) spent nearly $60 million more than the National Republican Congressional Committee (NRCC), and the Democratic Senatorial Congressional Committee (DSCC) spent almost $70 million more than the National Republican Senatorial Committee (NRSC). These funding differences also spread down into individual races, and for the most part, Democratic candidates had more help from their party than Republicans did. Every chapter in this book illustrated the advantage the Democratic challenger enjoyed. In today's campaigns the most important spending by the parties comes in the form of independent expenditures. This money is spent by the party without the candidate's knowledge or input. The real key to independent expenditures is that the parties can spend in an unlimited manner, which they cannot do in providing either a direct contribution or coordinated expenditures. Party committees typically use independent expenditures to try and persuade potential voters to vote for their candidate and many times this is in the form of television ads. In most races followed for this book, the Democratic Hill committees helped their candidates more than the Republican party committees helped their candidates with this kind of spending.

Candidates like Joe Knollenberg in Michigan's 9th District were probably counting on help from the party during the last weeks of the election. When that help did not come it was going to be hard for these candidates to win. In Knollenberg's case the NRCC had planned to spend roughly $600,000 in the 9th District either supporting Knollenberg or attacking Gary Peters. The party decided late in the game to pull their funding and that money never found its way to the airwaves in Detroit. The NRCC made a similar move in Colorado's 4th District. After spending a great deal of money ($1.8 million) to help Marilyn Musgrave, they decided to pull the money they had planned to spend. On the other hand, as they were pulling resources from other races, the NRCC stepped in and spent more than $500,000 to assist Lee Terry in Nebraska's 2nd District. Clearly, the NRCC had to make difficult choices as to whom they could lend help. Not only was the NRCC at a financial disadvantage in 2008, but they found that as the campaign went on they had more and more seats to defend, which meant that the cash they did have did not go as far.

The importance of funding at the presidential level was also felt at the congressional level. The disparity between the resources of John McCain and Barack Obama are well documented: in total Obama spent roughly $730 million compared to John McCain's roughly $340 million. Obama's advantage came from his opting out of the public funding system during the general election that every major party candidate, including John McCain, has participated in since its inception in the early 1970s. Candidates that accept the public funding are not permitted to raise or spend additional funds beyond the money they receive from the federal government; candidates outside of the system can raise as much as they like. This allowed Obama to raise remarkably more money than McCain. In many ways, Obama was able to overwhelm his opponent with resources. For instance, by the middle of October, Obama was spending about four times as much on television compared to what McCain was spending,[3] and in some states the disparity was even greater.

Obama's cash advantage over McCain also spilled over into congressional races. With Obama at such an advantage, he could spend money on voter registration and voter turnout efforts that helped other Democrats. For instance, in Georgia, Obama aggressively worked the state with about three dozen field offices, a lot for a state that has voted Republican reliably since the 1960s. Jim Martin was able to utilize this infrastructure during the runoff in that state; comparatively, Saxby Chambliss did not have that benefit because the McCain campaign did not even have the state headquarters in Georgia, but rather in Tallahassee, Florida. In North Carolina, another state thought to be reliably Republican, the Obama campaign helped Kay Hagan by having field organizers in all 100 of the state's counties, with more than 400 paid staff members on the ground; this was compared to just 35 for the McCain organization.

Similar help was felt in states like New Hampshire, where there was a very strong coordinated campaign between Obama and Jean Shaheen. The same could not be said for the GOP, however as with the Sununu campaign noting a falloff in effort from the presidential race in 2008 from 2004. The same was true in Minnesota. Barack Obama even had enough cash to set up three field offices in Omaha to campaign for the single Electoral College vote of Nebraska's 2nd District, which had not voted Republican since Thomas Dewey lost to Harry Truman in 1948!

The vast difference in resources may have been felt most in Michigan. In the first week of October, the McCain campaign announced that it was pulling all its resources from the state and transferring them to other battlegrounds. The effect of this was strong; according to Joe Knollenberg, "It's like telling the world, 'the hell with it....'" While the resources that could have helped Knollenberg were gone, the Obama campaign stayed active in Michigan. Not only did they keep much of their staff in the state, but they stayed on the air with television ads, thus keeping up the excitement in the Democratic base. This was a luxury only a candidate who raised $750 million could afford.

Defensive Strategies at the Goal Line

Although several of the most endangered GOP candidates managed to win on Election Day, there was no specific tactic that those campaigns collectively employed. Even GOP candidates who were running in favorable districts where the political tendencies of the constituency were generally very consistent with the Republican's ideology did not always win. Yes, Mark Kirk (Illinois 10th), Tom McClintock (California 4th), and Mitch McConnell (Kentucky Senate) won in areas like this, but others including Phil English (Pennsylvania 3rd), Joe Knollenberg (Michigan 9th), and Marilyn Musgrave (Colorado 4th) did not. Not surprisingly, the candidates relied on different, varied, and idiosyncratic strategies in their campaigns. When methods common to several races were uncovered, they did not always deliver the same result. In other words, while some strategies worked in some campaigns for some candidates, they failed in other districts or states.

Moving to the Middle

In the races analyzed in this volume, there were a few strategies nearly all Republicans employed during 2008, again with varying results. First, sensing a difficult election ahead, and sometimes because of a tougher-than-expected 2006 contest, every candidate in this volume altered his or her behavior during the 110th Congress by becoming (or at least appearing to be) more moderate on some important issues. This is reflected in the scores these vulnerable candidates received from groups like the American Conservative Union (ACU) and Americans for Democratic Action (ADA) (see Table 14.1). Eight of the 11 incumbents (Tom McClintock, remember, was running in an open seat in California's 4th District) received lower ratings from the ACU in 2008 than they did in 2007. Most were moderate shifts of between 8 and 16 points, but Elizabeth Dole's rating decreased by 38 points! Other large shifts are not reflected in the table because they took place before 2007. For instance, Saxby Chambliss went from an ACU score of 96 in 2006 to 76 in 2008, and Phil English went from a score of 80 in 2006 to 52 in 2008. Two incumbents, Mark Kirk and Chris Shays, actually saw their ACU scores increase during this time period, however they already scored quite low to begin with and were already bona fide moderates (Shays had an ACU score of 60 or higher only twice in his time in Congress).

More dramatic shifts are seen in the candidates' ADA scores. Every candidate but one, Norm Coleman in Minnesota, received higher scores from the ADA in 2008 than they did in 2007, and most were between 15 and 25 point shifts (both House and Senate Republicans, taken in groups, shifted only 6 points on average in the same time frame). Coleman, however, already had a relatively high rating from the ADA because he had begun to take votes friendly to their agenda earlier in his career—his ADA score went from 25 to 50 between 2006 and 2007. Even Chris Shays, who already received high scores from the group, increased his score from 55 to 75. In chapter 2, Joe Knollenberg described his approach to decisions in the 110th Congress,

> I began to look at some things a little differently.... [T]here were some things that we could vote for that we had traditionally been voting against,

Table 14.1 Comparison of GOP Candidates' Congressional Vote Scores, 2007 and 2008

Candidate	American Conservative Union			Americans for Democratic Action			Presidential Support			Party Unity		
	2007	2008	Difference	2007	2008	Difference	2007	2008	Difference	2007	2008	Difference
Knollenberg	84	72	-8	20	40	+20	74	60	-14	87	90	+3
McConnell	92	80	-12	10	20	+10	86	76	-10	95	97	+2
Kirk	40	48	+8	40	55	+15	41	53	+12	70	73	+3
Shays	20	32	+12	55	75	+20	33	34	+1	67	68	+1
Musgrave	100	87	-13	5	25	+20	88	67	-21	97	97	0
Sununu	84	75	-9	15	25	+10	83	79	-4	83	87	+4
English	64	52	-12	40	65	+25	50	44	-6	78	82	+4
Coleman	64	48	-16	50	45	-5	68	58	-10	64	69	+5
Dole	92	54	-38	15	40	+25	85	58	-27	93	72	-21
Terry	88	92	+4	10	15	+5	76	68	-4	93	90	-3
Chambliss	92	76	-16	10	25	+15	83	72	-9	96	95	-1

Source: Prior chapters where available; *Congressional Quarterly* (capolitics.com); Americans for Democratic Action (http://www.adaction.org/) and American Conservative Union (http://www.acuratings.org/).

or maybe not giving a whole lot of support…. I did vote for the minimum wage…[and] I voted against big oil in '07….

Another clear sign that Republicans were doing something different while in Congress was their support of the Republican president. Many of these endangered candidates began to support President Bush less and less (see Table 14.1). So far as campaign strategy goes, this was imperative. George Bush was radioactive in 2008. The president had dismal approval ratings and no Republican wanted to be tied to him or his policies. Plus, breaking with the president allowed many of these candidates to also tout their "independent" credentials. This was common among Republicans in Congress. On average, Senate Republicans supported President Bush only 70 percent of the time, and in the House the average Republican supported him only 64 percent of the time. In each case this was down 8 percent from the year before and marked the lowest support for a president's party since 1990.[4] Every Republican followed in this book supported the president less often in 2008 than 2007, with the exception of Mark Kirk and Chris Shays. Kirk stopped supporting Bush faithfully in 2007 as his 2006 support score was 80. Shays was never an easy vote for the White House to get, but in 2002 (post-September 11) he voted with the president 80 percent of the time and then started to defect more readily.

Interestingly, Republicans overall were more likely to vote with their party in 2008 than they were in 2007. On average, House Republicans voted with their party 87 percent of the time and Senate Republicans did so 83 percent of the time, an increase of 2 percent in each chamber. Most of the party unity scores of the vulnerable incumbents studied in this volume, with the exception of Elizabeth Dole, were steady or increased a bit in 2008; although some incumbents had already stopped solidly voting with their party by 2006.

Of course, this strategy of moderating did not always pay off. For some, Mitch McConnell, Saxby Chambliss (Georgia Senate), and Lee Terry (Nebraska 2nd), moving closer to the position of the average Republican in the chamber may have helped them retain their seat. For others it made no difference. The strategy did not appear to pay any dividends for Marilyn Musgrave and Elizabeth Dole—the two candidates who moderated the most of the candidates in this volume—because they lost anyway. These candidates, however, had established strong conservative voting records that were difficult to run away from, especially when they were hit on important issues by their opponents. In some respects, their records were clear and a few different votes in the last year or two were not enough to change their image with voters.

Others, however, like Chris Shays and Phil English, are more interesting. Neither of these candidates was considered to be an extremist by any fair-minded observer. In fact, Shays had a more liberal voting record in Congress than many Democrats (which irritated his own partisans to no end). In this race, Jim Himes and his allies did a masterful job of tying Shays to President Bush and national Republicans even though Shays had very low presidential support scores and party unity scores. In the end, both Shays and English moved further away from their party and still came up short on Election Day.

Focusing on the Folks at Home

Another common theme among the races chronicled in this book was the focus on the candidate's home district or state. Making the campaign about local issues rather than national tides was what every Republican hoped to do during 2008. As others have explained, this is a smart strategy. For those that managed to focus the race on these issues, some found success while others did not. Mitch McConnell made his race almost entirely about how he could deliver for the Commonwealth of Kentucky. He was able to convince voters that they would be better off with him serving in the U.S. Senate than if Bruce Lunsford were there. McConnell said plainly during the campaign, "The guy running against me, if he was successful, would be a rookie. Do you want to send Kentucky to the back bench with little or no influence?"

Mark Kirk was also able to play defense by focusing on his constituents. He was able to cater to the interests of the people in the Illinois 10th District; in addition to a moderate voting record that meshed with the attitudes of the district, Kirk championed issues that were important to the constituency, such as environmental protections for Lake Michigan as well as lower capital gains taxes. Moreover, Kirk used the perks of his office—the franking privilege, attention from local media for delivering for the district, and others—to help during the campaign season.

Others, like Phil English and Joe Knollenberg, were not so successful. Each of these candidates tried to make his district and what he had done for his constituents the focus of his campaign. Knollenberg, facing an electorate that did not identify him with anything in particular heading into 2008, maneuvered himself to be the Big 3's congressman, which he thought would connect with this auto-dependent district. Unfortunately for Knollenberg, this message gained no traction whatsoever. This may have been due, at least in part, to the fact that as a Republican Knollenberg was not going to get the support of union workers or other groups that typically vote Democratic even though he was trumpeting issues—like opposing steel tariffs and hikes in Corporate Average Fuel Economy (CAFE) standards—that would be beneficial to the entire industry. Phil English experienced something similar in his battle for Pennsylvania's 3rd District. English tried to make the case to voters that only someone with experience in Congress could bring the change his district wanted. In other words, he would be able to deliver for the district, as he had in the past, because of his experience.

A National-Level Appeal

In races for the U.S. Senate, many of the candidates made a common appeal when a victory appeared to be even more out of reach near Election Day. As

Democrats became more and more confident that they would pick up seats in states like Virginia, Oregon, Colorado, and New Mexico, and it appeared that they could reach the 60-vote mark in the Senate for the 111th Congress, some Republicans began to argue that they should be elected simply to keep Democrats from having that 60th Senator.

Races in North Carolina, Georgia, and Minnesota all found either the candidates or the NRSC making this case. In North Carolina, the NRSC went a step further saying that a 60th vote in the Senate would mean complete control of government by Democrats, an argument that seemed to concede the presidential election to Barack Obama. Only in Georgia, however, did this seem to make a difference, where 52 percent of Georgians said in a poll that it would make them less likely to support Jim Martin if he would be the 60th Senate Democrat; even 9 percent of those poll respondents who initially said they would vote for Martin indicated they would change their vote for this reason alone. The issue had little or no traction in North Carolina or Minnesota, where the case was made by the NRSC more than the candidates themselves.

Calling the Right Defensive Strategy

Barack Obama's well-funded, well-organized campaign was an asset to virtually all of the Democrats discussed in this volume. Likewise, it was an obstacle that many Republican incumbents had to overcome. In two cases, the incumbent members of Congress chose to specifically align themselves with Obama in the hope of convincing a portion of the Democratic voters in their district to vote a split ticket. It worked in one case and not in the other. For the conservative Lee Terry of Nebraska's 2nd District, it was simply a pragmatic decision to reach out through targeted direct mail to "Obama–Terry" voters. Depending on how you look at it, this decision may be the one that saved Terry's congressional career. Chris Shays, on the other hand, chose to do it in a very high-profile television advertisement that emphasized Obama's hopefulness and McCain's straight talk in a bipartisan appeal. The Shays advertisement must have piqued the interest of Obama who recorded a radio endorsement of Himes that was released in the final days of the campaign.

Congressional Campaigns Matter

In the political science literature, there is a debate about whether campaigns really matter and to what degree they matter.[5] The cases in this volume clearly show that congressional campaigns do matter, and they matter quite a bit. Yes, Republicans faced major roadblocks in 2008, specifically those macrolevel factors mentioned throughout the volume, but as we have also noted, some Republicans fought back against the national trends and defended their turf in a year of change. Although forces outside the campaign's control affected their choice of strategies, tactics, and decisions, the activities of candidates, their advisors and consultants, parties and interest groups, and other actors determined the results of elections. For example, in two of the races analyzed for this book, candidates had a difficult time finding a message that resonated and was salient with voters. Both Phil English and Joe Knollenberg revised their message several times during the campaign hoping to find something that would connect with the electorate. Both of these Republicans lost. Others identified a consistent message that resonated well with voters in their state or district. It did not matter what that message was; what mattered is that it was centered on issues that voters thought were important. In the Illinois 10th District, Mark Kirk discovered that it was a combination of issues like environmental protections for Lake Michigan and taxes. For Tom McClintock in California's 4th District the issues were federal spending and immigration. For Mitch McConnell, the issue was how much bacon he could bring home.

In addition, candidates must never take anything for granted. Even in such a bad Republican year it seems as if some did. For example, Saxby Chambliss drew heavy criticism from fellow Republicans for running a bad race during the heat of the campaign. It took several pleas to turn things around and it almost cost him the seat. Chambliss may have been lulled into false confidence when Jim Martin appeared as the strongest candidate among four other less-than-stellar Democratic candidates. In New Hampshire, some of those involved in Jean Shaheen's campaign argued that those in John Sununu's campaign "believed their own hype" and got ahead of themselves. Here, this overconfidence appears to have played a big part in Sununu's defeat.

In North Carolina, Elizabeth Dole's campaign aired a television ad late in the campaign that created a good deal of controversy. Her "Godless" spot appeared to question Kay Hagan's faith. The spot was designed to make voters question the challenger, but it did not have the desired impact. In fact, it backfired and probably turned a number of voters against Dole. While this was not the reason Dole lost, if they had it to do over again, the Dole campaign team may not have run the ad.

Candidates also matter. A candidate's fit with his or her constituency can have a major impact on a campaign. If that candidate is a good fit for the district, the path to electoral victory can be much smoother. This was the case of Tom McClintock in California's 4th District as well as candidates like Saxby Chambliss in Georgia and Mark Kirk in the Illinois 10th District. Still, fit does not always guarantee a victory. For instance, Chris Shays was a great fit for the 4th District in Connecticut yet he did not win. In his case, there were other things working against him. His firmly established, moderate credentials, which are what made him a good fit, could have worked against him in that his actions and record made everyone mad. He irritated Republicans by voting with Democrats on key issues (remember his ADA score was 75) and he irritated Democrats with his staunch support for President Bush on key issues like the Iraq war. On the other end of the spectrum are candidates like Marilyn Musgrave who are too extreme for their districts. Even in a relatively conservative area, Musgrave did not fit well with the district in 2008 after the changes to the district took hold.

Looking Ahead

We can learn a great deal about congressional elections by looking back, and the case studies in this book have helped us do that. We can also learn by looking ahead. In this case, we can use what we know about what happened in 2008 to think about what might happen in 2010 and 2012. Certainly the political landscape will be different, but many incumbents will certainly be playing defense.

In the coming election cycles, the presidency of George W. Bush will *not* be part of the political context, and this will impact campaigns from the strategic decisions made by prospective candidates to the themes and messages candidates use in their appeals to voters. Democrats had a huge advantage over their Republican rivals because they could campaign against Bush as well as the incumbent they were challenging on the ballot. With Bush out of the picture, Republican's fortunes already look better.

An additional factor that will be important as we move into 2010 and then 2012 is Bush's successor, Barack Obama. It would be difficult for Obama to become the lightening rod that Bush was, but he will still be a factor for several reasons. First, midterm elections, which 2010 will be, are typically referenda on the incumbent president and his policies. When November 2, 2010, arrives many of Obama's policies will be in full effect and the elections will give the public a chance to judge them. It is likely that chief among these will be the $787 billion economic stimulus bill passed early in the president's term. Other contenders will be bank and auto bailouts, as well the highly controversial health care reform legislation and a bill that would curb carbon emissions and health care reform. How the public judges these programs will decide whether and how Democrats defend *their* turf. *National Journal's* Amy Walter wrote: "Some congressional Democrats…will be tempted to vote against the president to avoid being pulled down in 2010. But with their party in control of Congress and the White House, it's going to be really hard for any Democrat to run as a 'lone wolf,' especially if that member is a freshman without an established identity back home."[6]

In addition, a 2010 referendum on the Obama administration will certainly include broader policy areas like the economy and foreign policy. Should the economy recover, Democrats will likely do well; if we are still mired in recession or the recovery is slow, they will not. According to Walter, "…the next election will be a referendum on the economy. Period."[7] The same is true of foreign affairs. Should the president successfully deal with international issues his party will be in a better position. Included here would be the U.S.'s involvement in Iraq and Afghanistan and potential hotspots such as Iran and North Korea. Should President Obama successfully navigate these conflicts, including following through on his campaign promises of bringing the troops home from Iraq, his party will be on a good footing heading into 2010.

Second, if prior midterm elections are any clue as to how President Obama's party will do in 2010, history is not on the Democrats' side. In every midterm since Franklin Delano Roosevelt's first term, with the exception of three, the president's party has lost seats in the House during that election, and in some instances the losses have been dramatic (see Figure 14.1). The president's party made modest gains in the House in 1934 (FDR), 1998 (Clinton), and 2002 (Bush); a few other years saw even smaller gains in the Senate. In every other year, however, there were losses in the House—including 45 seats in 1946 (Harry Truman), 48 seats in both 1958 and 1974 (Eisenhower and Ford, respectively), 52 in 1994 (Clinton), 55 in 1942 (FDR), and a whopping 71 in 1938 (FDR)—and Senate. It is possible that the Democrats could pick up seats, but history tells us this is unlikely. The most instructive lesson for Barack Obama may actually come from George W. Bush. In 2002, Bush made good use of his high public approval ratings to raise funds and campaign on behalf of Republican congressional candidates across the country. Many attributed the president's vigorous campaign schedule as one of the principal reasons Republicans gained seats in Congress when history predicts they would have lost seats.[8] Obama appears to be taking that lesson to heart by adopting the role of "fund-raiser-in-chief" on behalf of the Democratic Party early in his administration.[9]

Third, President Obama may impact the 2010 elections by something he does not do. This will be a midterm year so the president will not be on the ballot. This could have major ramifications for his party, especially given the successes he helped generate in 2008. As several of the cases in this volume have shown, the "Obama effect" in 2008 was difficult to miss in the form of dramatic increases in Democratic voter registrations and a healthy increase in turnout. The impact of Obama on the ballot, however, is not something that Democrats will be able to take advantage of in 2010.

The runoff in Georgia chronicled here may offer a bit of a hint as to what we can expect in 2010. Voter turnout is generally around 10 points lower during midterms than in presidential years. In these nonpresidential years, the lack of a

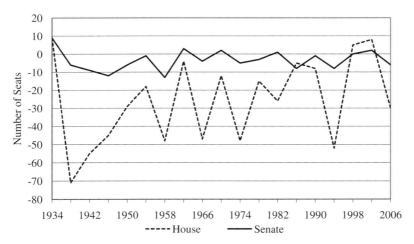

Figure 14.1 Midterm gains and losses by the Presidents' party, 1934–2006. *Source:* Gerhard Peters, "The American Presidency Project" http://www.presidency.ucsb.edu/data/mid-term_elections.php [accessed June 29, 2009].

presidential race means generally lower interest in elections and therefore lower turnout. This lower participation is something that Democrats will have to contend with, but it will likely be heightened with their party's leader not on the ballot. In Georgia, 3.9 million voters turned out on November 4, many of them brought out by the excitement about Obama's candidacy. Only one month later, on December 2, only 2.1 million went to the polls for the Chambliss–Martin Senate contest, which is similar to the turnout in the two most recent midterm elections. If voter turnout is down dramatically in 2010, some Democrats may have a hard time defending their seats.

The gains Democrats made in 2008 (and 2006 for that matter) have been impressive and they have occurred across the nation. Some of those gains, however, were in traditionally Republican districts. A quick look at the *Cook Political Report's* Partisan Voter Index ratings, which tell us how much better Democrats or Republicans do in a congressional district compared to nationally, shows that Democrats made gains in traditionally GOP areas. In the most recent edition of the *Cook Report's* analysis of House races, Democrats hold 19 seats with a PVI that favors Republicans and in 12 of those races, the PVI is R+5 or higher.[10] In only four districts do Republicans hold seats where the PVI favors Democrats (two are D+5 are higher). Moreover, after 2008, Democrats hold 49 seats in districts that McCain won, while Republicans hold 34 seats in districts where Obama won.[11] While the GOP has more seats to defend in the Senate (19 compared to 18 for the Democrats), there are vulnerable members on each side, with some high-profile targets for the GOP including Majority Leader Harry Reid (D-NV) and Chris Dodd (D-CT). What is more, should the political context shift to where Democrats are on their heels there could be a large swing in the House.

In 2012 there will be both similarities and differences with 2008. The political context incumbents will face is almost impossible to predict, but suffice it to say that it will be different from what GOP incumbents faced in 2008. We are unable, at this point, to say which party it may favor and how that will impact incumbents playing defense. While that is uncertain, what is not is Barack Obama's place on the ballot above Democrats running for the House and the Senate. Will they take advantage of similar benefits of his candidacy in the next presidential year? Will Democrats be as excited in 2012? Will African Americans turn out in similar numbers? Will Republicans be as deflated as they were in 2008? All of these questions will be answered in the next presidential election cycle. While we can only guess what the answers to those questions are, we do know that in every election cycle to come there will be incumbents who find themselves trying to hold their seat by playing defense.

Notes

1. The *Cook Political Report* rates races in varying degrees of competitiveness from "likely" Democratic and Republican to "lean" Democratic and Republican with the most competitive being "toss-ups"; those not appearing on the list are consid-

ered safe. We identify the most competitive as those in the lean Democratic, lean Republican, and toss-up categories.

2. This is opposed to party-centered systems present in many European democracies where parties are the most important electoral actor and where campaigning is centralized in party headquarters. In these systems, parties take the lead and drive many aspects of campaigning to the point where in some countries candidates' names do not even appear on the ballot, only the party names do.

3. Jim Rutenberg, "Nearing Record, Obama's Ad Effort Swamps McCain," *New York Times*, October 17, 2008, http://www.nytimes.com/2008/10/18/us/politics/18ads. html?_r=5&hp&oref=slogin (accessed June 23, 2009).

4. Richard Rubin, "2008 Vote Studies: Presidential Support—An Unpopular Lame Duck Prevails," CQ *Weekly*, December 15, 2008, http://www.cqpolitics.com/ wmspage.cfm?docID=weeklyreport-000002997729 (accessed June 29, 2009).

5. Thomas M. Holbrook, *Do Campaigns Matter?* (Thousand Oaks, CA: Sage, 1996) makes a convincing case that campaigns do matter. Others, however, argue that macrolevel factors trump microlevel factors and hold the key to electoral victory.

6. Amy Walter, "For Dems In 2010, Tomorrow May Not Come," *National Journal*, June 16, 2009, http://www.nationaljournal.com/njonline/print_friendly. php?ID=ol_20090616_4902 (accessed June 26, 2009).

7. Ibid.

8. Dan Balz, "Campaigner in Chief Has Limited Reach: An Unpopular President Avoids Many Key Races," *Washington Post*, November 1, 2006, A1.

9. John R. Emshwiller and Brody Mullins, "Obama Aims to Trim Party's Money Gap with GOP," *Wall Street Journal*, May 16, 2009, http://online.wsj.com/article/ SB124243502639525867.html (accessed June 29, 2009).

10. *The Cook Report* only calculates a PVI for House races. See, "2010 Competitive House Race Chart," http://cookpolitical.com/charts/house/competitive_2009-06-18_23-46-19.php (accessed June 26, 2009).

11. Charlie Cook, "A Split Decision in 2010 Races?" *National Journal*, June 6, 2009, http:// www.nationaljournal.com/njonline/print_friendly.php?ID=cr=20090606_3396 (accessed June 24, 2009).

About the Contributors

Jody C Baumgartner is assistant professor of political science at East Carolina University. He has written or edited five books including, *Conventional Wisdom and American Elections: Exploding Myths, Exploring Misconceptions, Laughing Matters: Humor and American Politics in the Media Age*, and *The American Vice Presidency Reconsidered* as well as several other articles. Baumgartner teaches courses in American and Comparative politics.

Charles S. Bullock, III is the Richard B. Russell Chair in Political Science and Josiah Meigs Distinguished Teaching Professor at the University of Georgia. Bullock is author, coauthor, or coeditor of 23 books and more than 150 articles. He has published in major political science, public administration and education journals. *Runoff Elections* in the United States, a comprehensive analysis of runoff elections, which Bullock coauthored with Loch Johnson, won the V. O. Key Award as the best book on Southern politics published in 1992. His most recent books are *The Triumph of Voting Rights in the South* (with Ronald Keith Gaddie), *The New Politics of the Old South*, 4th edition (with Mark Rozell), and *Georgia Politics in a State of Change* (with Ronald Keith Gaddie).

Colton C. Campbell is associate professor of national security strategy at the National War College. Prior to joining the War College, he was a legislative aide to Representative Mike Thompson (CA-01). Before that, he was an analyst at the Congressional Research Service, an Associate Professor of Political Science at Florida International University, and an American Political Science Association Congressional Fellow, where he served as a policy adviser to Senator Bob Graham of Florida. He is the author, coauthor, and coeditor of several books on Congress and congressional campaigns, most recently the *Guide to Political Campaigns in America* (with Paul S. Herrnson, Stephen K. Medvic, and Marni Ezra) and *Impeaching Clinton: Partisan Strife on Capitol Hill* (with Nicol C. Rae). He has also published many chapters and articles on the legislative process.

Victoria A. Farrar-Myers is professor of political science at the University of Texas at Arlington. Her research on the presidency, presidential–congressional relations, and campaign finance reform has been published in such journals as

Political Research Quarterly and *Congress & the Presidency* as well as in numerous edited volumes. She also authored or co-authored books including, *Legislative Labyrinth: Congress and Campaign Finance Reform*, *Scripted for Change: The Institutionalization of the American Presidency*, and *Limits and Loopholes: The Quest for Money, Free Speech, and Fair Elections*. She has received such honors as the American Political Science Association Congressional Fellowship where she served as a legislative assistant to U.S. Representative Christopher Shays (R-CT), a research grant from the Dirksen Congressional Center, and several teaching awards.

Jasmine Farrier is associate professor of political science at the University of Louisville, where she teaches courses on U.S. political institutions and elections. She has authored *Passing the Buck: Congress, the Budget, and Deficits* and *Congressional Ambivalence: The Political Burdens of Constitutional Authority*. Farrier was also a fellow with the Miller Center of Public Affairs at the University of Virginia from 2000 to 2001.

William H. Flanigan is professor emeritus of political science at the University of Minnesota. He is the coauthor of *Political Behavior of the American Electorate*, 11th ed. (with Nancy H. Zingale), *Partisan Realignment: Voters, Parties, and Government in American History* (with Jerome M. Clubb and Nancy H. Zingale), and co-editor of *The History of American Electoral Behavior* (with Joel H. Silbey and Allan G. Bogue). Flanigan's research interests are American public opinion and voting behavior.

Peter L. Francia is associate professor of political science at East Carolina University. He is the coauthor of *Conventional Wisdom and American Elections: Exploding Myths, Exploring Misconceptions* (with Jody C Baumgartner), *The Financiers of Congressional Elections: Investors, Ideologues, and Intimates* (with Paul S. Herrnson, John C. Green, Lynda W. Powell, and Clyde Wilcox), and the author of *The Future of Organized Labor in American Politics* as well as dozens of articles and book chapters. Francia has also been a frequent analyst for several media outlets, including CNN, National Public Radio, and the *Wall Street Journal*.

John S. Klemanski is professor of political science at Oakland University. He has authored books that include *The Mechanics of State Legislative Campaigns*, and *Power and City Governance: Comparative Perspectives on Urban Development*. Klemanski teaches courses on political campaigns, media and politics, American politics, and urban politics.

Brad Lockerbie is professor and chair of the political science department at East Carolina University. He is the author of *Do Voters Look to the Future? Economics and Elections*, and articles appearing in journals including *American Journal of Political Science*, *Public Opinion Quarterly*, *British Journal of Political Science*, *Public Choice*, and *Legislative Studies Quarterly*. Lockerbie's teaching and research specialties are elections and public opinion.

Seth E. Masket is assistant professor of political science at the University of Denver. His book *No Middle Ground* (University of Michigan Press, 2009) examines the local sources of modern party polarization. His research has been published in the *American Journal of Political Science*, the *Journal of Politics*, the *British Journal of Political Science*, *State Politics and Policy Quarterly*, the *Quarterly Journal of Political Science*, *Public Opinion Quarterly*, and *American Politics Review*. In 2008, Masket was recognized with the Emerging Scholar Award presented by the Political Organizations and Parties section of the American Political Science Association.

Stephen K. Medvic is associate professor of government at Franklin and Marshall College. His research and teaching interests include campaigns and elections, political parties, the media and politics, public opinion, and ideology. Medvic has coedited *Guide to Political Campaigns in America* (with Paul S. Herrnson, Colton C. Campbell, and Marni Ezra) and *Shades of Gray: Perspectives on Campaign Ethics* (with Candice J. Nelson and David A. Dulio) and is the author of *Political Consultants in the U.S. Congressional Elections* and a textbook entitled *Campaigns and Elections: Players and Processes*. Medvic has provided political analysis for numerous media outlets including PBS's *NewsHour with Jim Lehrer*, NBC *Nightly News*, CNN, *The Washington Post*, *Philadelphia Inquirer*, Salon.com, and Fox News Online.

Jonathan S. Morris is assistant professor of political science at East Carolina University. Morris conducts research in the fields of political communication, public opinion, and the U.S. Congress. He has authored *Laughing Matters: Humor and American Politics in the Media Age*, as well as over a dozen articles in referred journals. Morris worked for U.S. Representative Sherrod Brown as an American Political Science Association Congressional Fellow.

Kathryn Pearson is assistant professor of political science at the University of Minnesota. Pearson specializes in American politics; her research focuses on the U.S. Congress, congressional elections, political parties, women and politics, and public opinion. Her research has been published in *The Journal of Politics*, *Perspectives on Politics*, and *Legislative Studies Quarterly*. She is working on a book based on her dissertation, *Party Discipline in the Contemporary Congress: Rewarding Loyalty in Theory and in Practice*, which won the APSA Legislative Studies Section's Carl Albert Award for the best doctoral dissertation in the area of legislative studies in 2005. From 2002 to 2003, she was a Research Fellow at the Brookings Institution, and from 1993 to 1998, she worked on Capitol Hill as a Legislative Assistant for two members of Congress.

Gregory A. Petrow is assistant professor of political science at the University of Nebraska at Omaha. Petrow conducts research in the impact of group identity on political participation, the role of political values and self-interest in affecting policy preferences, and the influence of political tolerance on evaluations of political candidates from nontraditional groups. He has published articles in *Presidential Studies Quarterly, Congress & the Presidency,* and the *Journal of Homosexuality.* Petrow teaches courses in political behavior, methodology, and American government.

Dante J. Scala is associate professor and chair of the department of political science at the University of New Hampshire. Scala has authored *Stormy Weather: The New Hampshire Primary and Presidential Politics.* He often discusses politics in nonacademic settings, and during the last 10 years, has done hundreds of interviews with local, national, and international media on a wide range of issues. Scala has been interviewed by journalists from ABC, CBS, CNN, Fox News, MSNBC, C-Span, and National Public Radio. His newspaper interviews include *The New York Times; Washington Post; Philadelphia Inquirer; Boston Globe; Chicago Tribune; Los Angeles Times; Le Monde;* and the Associated Press.

Daniel M. Shea is professor of political science and director of the Center for Political Participation at Allegheny College. He has authored, coauthored, or edited more than a dozen books including *Campaign Craft* (with Michael John Burton), *The Fountain of Youth* (with John C. Green), *Campaign Mode* (with Michael John Burton), *Living Democracy* (with Joanne Connor Green and Christopher Smith), *Transforming Democracy,* and *New Party Politics* (with John Kenneth White). Shea has also published numerous scholarly book chapters and articles. His teaching specialties include campaign management, the legislative process, politics of the media, and political behavior.

Andrew E. Smith is associate professor of political science and director of the Survey Center at the University of New Hampshire where he oversees the Granite State Poll, a quarterly survey of public opinion and public policy in New Hampshire.

Wayne P. Steger is professor of political science at DePaul University. He has published *Campaigns and Political Marketing* (with Sean Q. Kelly and J. Mark Wrighton), as well as over 30 articles, book chapters, and essays on campaigns, elections, and the American presidency. His research has appeared in journals including *Political Research Quarterly, American Politics Research, Presidential Studies Quarterly,* and *Congress & the Presidency.* His current research focuses on presidential nominations and party politics. Steger is also former associate editor of *The Journal of Political Marketing.*

Nancy H. Zingale is professor emerita of political science at the University of St. Thomas in St. Paul, Minnesota. She is coauthor of *Political Behavior of the American Electorate,* now in its eleventh edition (with William Flanigan), and *Partisan Realignment: Voters, Parties, and Government in American History* (with Jerome Clubb and William Flanigan).

About the Editors

Randall E. Adkins is professor of political science at the University of Nebraska at Omaha. He teaches courses on the presidency, Congress, political parties, and campaigns and elections. Adkins is the editor of *The Evolution of Political Parties, Campaigns, and Elections*, and is the author of numerous articles and chapters in edited volumes on the presidency and campaigns and elections. His research is published in *American Politics Quarterly, American Politics Research, American Review of Politics, Journal of Political Marketing, Political Research Quarterly, Presidential Studies Quarterly*, and *Publius: The Journal of Federalism*. He is also a former American Political Science Association Congressional Fellow where he worked for the Hon. David E. Price (NC-4).

David A. Dulio is associate professor of political science at Oakland University in Rochester, MI, where he teaches courses on campaigns and elections, Congress, political parties and interest groups. Dulio has authored or edited six books including, *For Better or Worse? How Political Consultants are Changing Elections in the United States, Vital Signs: Perspectives on the Health of American Campaigning* (with Candice J. Nelson), and *Shades of Gray: Perspectives on Campaign Ethics* (edited with Candice J. Nelson and Stephen K. Medvic). Dulio's work has appeared in *Party Politics, Political Research Quarterly, American Review of Politics* and other outlets. Dulio is also a former American Political Science Association Congressional Fellow where he worked in the U.S. House of Representatives Republican Conference headed by Rep. J. C. Watts, Jr. (OK-4).